THE GRAMMAR
OF CASTE

THE GRAMMAR OF CASTE

Economic Discrimination in Contemporary India

Ashwini Deshpande

OXFORD
UNIVERSITY PRESS

OXFORD
UNIVERSITY PRESS

Oxford University Press is a department of the University of Oxford.
It furthers the University's objective of excellence in research, scholarship,
and education by publishing worldwide. Oxford is a registered trademark of
Oxford University Press in the UK and in certain other countries.

Published in India by
Oxford University Press
2/11 Ground Floor, Ansari Road, Daryaganj, New Delhi 110 002, India

First published 2011
Oxford India Paperbacks 2017

ISBN-13: 978-0-19-947198-0
ISBN-10: 0-19-947198-3

Typeset in Lapidary 333 BT 11.5/13.3
by Eleven Arts, Keshav Puram, Delhi 110 035
Printed in India by Repro Knowledgecast Limited, Thane

In Aai's memory, for Baba...
And now for Sudhanva and Ketaki, in Baba's memory

Contents

Contents

Introduction to the Paperback Edition

Fifteenth August 2016 marked India's 70th anniversary of independence from British colonial rule. As the Prime Minister unfurled the national flag from the ramparts of the Red Fort and laid out his vision of development in his annual address to the nation, an unprecedented gathering was underway in Una, Gujarat, about 1,300 kilometres from the national capital. Thousands of Dalits, who had embarked upon a *Dalit Asmita Yatra* (Dalit Pride March) ten days earlier from Ahmedabad, congregated in Una to declare their independence. Not from colonial Britain, but from the traditional stigmatizing and dehumanizing occupations of manual scavenging, and lifting and skinning dead cattle. Occupations that branded them the lowliest of the low within the caste system, stamping them with a stigma that did not seem to become weaker with post-independence growth and development. They pledged never again to lift human excreta and dispose of cattle carcasses. It is noteworthy that this gathering took place in Gujarat, the poster child for the presumed ability of economic growth to lift all sections out of poverty and put everyone on the path of socio-economic advancement, regardless of their social identity. The congregation demonstrated that something was not quite right with this development-lifts-all rhetoric.

The choice of Una for this momentous event was especially apt, as earlier in the year in July, this was where a cow vigilante group had chained seven Dalit youths to a van and publicly thrashed them for skinning a dead cow. This atrocity, which was proudly filmed and circulated by the perpetrators, went viral through online sharing on various social media platforms, leading to a wave of anger and protest, finally culminating in the historic march. In sharp contrast to the official gathering consisting of dignitaries and school children, this Independence Day celebration was bursting at the seams with voluntary participation of the marginalized. They too saluted the national flag, but the flag was unfurled by Radhika Vemula, the courageous mother of Rohit Vemula, the Dalit research scholar at the University of Hyderabad who had committed suicide earlier in January, pushed over the edge as a result of disciplinary action taken against him and others for their activities as members of the Ambedkar Students' Association.

Five years ago, writing the Preface to the hardcover edition, I started on a defensive note, justifying the appearance of yet another book on caste when so much scholarship on the subject had been in the public domain for decades. Today, caste contradictions and tensions have come to the foreground so sharply that attempting to summarize even the key economic contours of the contemporary caste system through just one book seems woefully inadequate. Oxford University Press's decision to bring out a paperback volume of *Grammar of Caste* (*Grammar* hereafter) produces mixed feelings in me. As an author, the continued interest in *Grammar* and my later *Affirmative Action in India* (of the Oxford India Short Introduction series) is immensely gratifying. However, if the reason for the relevance of the book is the underlying reality of tenaciousness of caste, the ability of the system to reinvent itself to suit the contemporary reality, such that Bhimrao Ambedkar's vision of 'annihilation of caste'[1] seems like a mirage, growing more distant each time we feel we are within touching distance of it, that is certainly not a cause for joy. Yet, as Independence Day this year reminds us, each time caste reasserts its presence, it lends fillip to the anti-caste movement, and it is this dialectic, if anything, that has the potential to annihilate caste.

[1] See www.ambedkarintellectuals.in/attachment/2.annihilation-of-caste[1].doc (accessed on 13 November 2016).

As caste contradictions have sharpened over the last five years, it is harder for observers to deny the continued hold of the caste system. In *Grammar*, my purpose was to make an economic intervention in the debate over whether social identity, particularly caste, shaped economic outcomes. Both due to events on the ground that occurred between the appearance of the hardcover edition and this paperback, as well as due to advances in scholarly research, including the wider burgeoning field of Identity Economics and Stratification Economics, it is now indisputable that caste *does* define economic outcomes in India. We now know a great deal about the economic ramifications of caste, but there are new aspects unfolding continuously. In the last five years, my own understanding of the caste system has deepened due to the appearance of new research by a multitude of scholars, as well as due to the fact that my own research has branched off in new directions. Summarizing all the new evidence would require a new book altogether, maybe a sequel to *Grammar*. My attempt in this introduction is much more modest—it is to provide a brief glimpse into some of what I have been able to discover over the last five years. The basic point, namely, the need for an evidence-based approach to the study of caste inequalities and discrimination, has already been made in *Grammar* and continues to remain as valid as when it was made earlier.

MOVING CLOSER OR FURTHER APART?

In *Grammar* I investigated if caste matters in the sphere of economic outcomes. Today, the more interesting question is whether there has been a large enough flux in the caste system to upturn, or at least flatten, the traditional hierarchies. Since the publication of *Grammar*, I have been exploring this aspect more deeply by trying to plot changes in key economic dimensions of caste inequality over time. The ascendancy of members of Other Backward Classes (OBCs) in the political arena has been heralded as India's 'silent revolution' (Jaffrelot 2003). This political ascendancy has also been viewed as representing a large enough flux in the traditional hierarchies of the caste system, such that we now have a plethora of 'assertive caste identities [that] articulate alternative hierarchies' leading to a scenario where 'there is hardly any unanimity on ranking between jatis' (Gupta 2004: x). Indeed, there is no doubt that the so-called lower castes have become an important force in

Indian politics at all levels—local, state, and national. The question is: To what extent has this political shift translated into shrinking the economic distance between caste hierarchies?

In order to answer this, it is necessary, but not sufficient, to do a static stocktaking, that is, look at caste gaps in various indicators at a given point in time, as Chapter 3 does. Recognizing this, a part of my recent work has consisted of investigating changes in caste disparities over time in order to determine if caste gaps are closing or not (Deshpande and Ramachandran 2016). The ideal way to assess changes over time would be to look at a panel, that is, longitudinal data, which collects data on a set of respondents over time. The only nationally representative panel dataset in India is the India Human Development Survey (IHDS), which released the second wave only in the latter half of 2015.

In order to circumvent the lack of panel data covering a longer duration, Rajesh Ramachandran and I created ten-year age cohorts within National Sample Survey (NSS) data, using data from the 1999–2000 (55th) round and 2011–12 (68th) round of the Employment–Unemployment Survey (EUS) of the NSS. Our assessment, which is more nuanced than the other major comparable study (Hnatkovska et al. 2012), is based both on documenting changes over the decade, as well as on a comparison of five age cohorts across the three social groups—Scheduled Castes and Tribes (SC–ST),[2] OBC, and 'Others' (everyone else).[3] Hnatkovska et al. (2012) compare SC–STs to the 'Non-SC–ST', where the latter combines both the upper castes and the OBCs in one group, whereas we are able to distinguish between the OBCs and upper castes in tracing the evolution of caste (dis)advantage. This distinction is important as the story of convergence/divergence between caste groups changes depending on the level of aggregation. Second, whereas Hnatkovska et al. (2012) concentrate on relative gaps between caste groups in basic indicators, we present the evidence on both absolute as well as relative gaps. The importance of the latter

[2] We are well aware of the difference between SCs and STs, and in other contexts, of the need to study them separately. The only reason to club the two categories is that their economic outcomes are very similar; also, this essay is concerned with tracing changes vis-à-vis the OBC category, thus clubbing them into a composite category is not unreasonable.

[3] See Chapter 2 for explanations about these data categories.

is obvious. We believe, however, that absolute gaps convey important information that is distinct: the importance of absolute gaps is most obvious in the context of educational attainment (one of the key indicators of caste [dis]advantage), as each additional year of education confers distinct economic advantage, that is, it increases labour market returns for individuals, in addition to the fact that it matters how much we know (via education) in an absolute sense. Thus, even if relative caste gaps in educational attainment fall, but absolute gaps do not, wage or occupational gaps will not decrease, ceteris paribus.

We are able to build a comprehensive trajectory of change for each of the caste groups since independence, since the oldest cohort in our analysis consists of individuals born between 1947 and 1956, and the youngest cohort of those born between 1987 and 1996.[4] Thus, we are able to track outcomes for successive generations of individuals who reached adulthood in half a century between Indian independence (in 1947) and 1996, and examine changes in multiple indicators using a difference-in-differences (D-I-D) approach comparing gaps between caste groups over time.

If gaps in a given indicator (say, years of education or occupational attainment) between younger cohorts across caste groups ('Others'– OBCs and 'Others'–SC–ST) are smaller than those between older cohorts, we would conclude that there is convergence between caste groups, that is, caste disparities in that indicator are reducing, and caste groups are moving closer over time or over successive generations. The scenario would be one of divergence, or caste groups moving further apart if the opposite were true.

What do we find? At the household level, we find that the gap in average monthly per capita expenditure (MPCE)—whether absolute or relative—often used as a proxy for income, has increased over time

---

[4] We look at individuals between 16 and 65 years and construct the following cohorts using age relative to 2012:

	Age	Birth Year
Cohort 1	65–56	1947–1956
Cohort 2	55–46	1957–1966
Cohort 3	45–36	1967–1976
Cohort 4	35–26	1977–1986
Cohort 5	25–16	1987–1996

between caste groups. Thus, caste groups have moved further apart over time in terms of this key average.

At the individual level, we find evidence of convergence between OBCs and 'Others' in educational attainment till secondary level, whether measured by relative or absolute gaps, over successive cohorts. For higher secondary education and graduates and above, we find that the absolute gaps between 'Others' on the one hand, and OBCs and SC–STs on the other hand, have increased, despite convergence in terms of relative gaps.

Intergenerational Transmission of Education

Education, especially higher education, is seen as a key to achieve socio-economic upward mobility, and the degree to which children's achievements do not depend upon their parents' if they have 'what it takes' (that is, education, skills, and talent backed by hard work) can be seen as a gauge of how fair and meritocratic societies are. We have already noted that substantial gaps exist in higher educational attainment across caste groups and a comparison of absolute gaps indicates divergence between caste groups over time. A related question is to what extent is higher educational attainment correlated with parental education. This would help us assess the role of education in social mobility: Is it enabling intergenerational mobility, that is, weakening the hold of parental education on the child's education, or is it an instrument of intergenerational persistence? How does this picture differ by caste?

In order to estimate this, we match the years of education of every male household head to the years of education of the male child.[5] The regression results show a decline of 17 percentage points in the intergenerational persistence of education, that is, a reduction in the effect of father's education on son's education, over the two NSS rounds. Comparing intergenerational persistence across caste groups, we find that relative to the OBCs, the effect of father's education

---

[5] We identify father–son pairs based on the household identifier and 'relationship to head of household' variable in the data. Thus, we can only identify father–son pairs residing in the same household. Since daughters typically marry early and move to the marital home, NSS data does not have a mechanism to match daughters with either fathers or mothers, unless they are resident in the same household. Most resident daughters are minors, and many are still studying, so their ultimate educational category is not known at the point the survey is conducted.

on son's education is lower for the 'Others', which implies that the education level of sons of OBC fathers is more dependent on their fathers' education, compared to upper castes. Comparing OBCs and SC–STs, we see greater intergenerational persistence for the SC–ST in 1999–2000, but the two groups exhibit statistically similar rates in 2011–12.

White Collar Jobs and Labour Market Discrimination

In the realm of occupation, younger cohorts of OBCs seem to be closing the gap with 'Others' in access to prestigious white-collar jobs, both in the public sector and outside it. We find that male average wages of 'Others' are higher than those for OBCs and SC–STs for both years, and the mean wage gap has gone up over the period. Looking at the wage gap across the entire wage distribution, we find that this increase in the mean wage gap is primarily accounted for by an increase in the wage gap for the top 30 per cent of wage earners. Decomposing the average wage gap between 'Others' and OBCs, as well as between 'Others' and SC–STs, we find that the unexplained part of the wage gap, commonly seen as a proxy for labour market discrimination, has gone up over the decade. While the 'Others'–SC–ST absolute gap in mean wages is higher than the 'Others'–OBC gap in both years, the unexplained part of the wage gap is higher for OBCs. In 2011–12, as much as 44 per cent of the wage gap between 'Others' and OBCs, and 32 per cent of the wage gap between 'Others' and SC–STs is unexplained and could be attributed to labour market discrimination.

Overall, the evidence across age cohorts or generations indicates that that contours of caste disadvantage *are* changing in terms of some dimensions of the relative distance between OBCs and 'Others', that is, upper castes, but there is no indication of a reversal of the broad historical caste hierarchies, with the upper castes on top, OBCs in the middle, and Dalits–Adivasis at the bottom.

DALITS IN BUSINESS

Given compelling evidence of labour market discrimination, there is a view that members of marginalized groups should turn to self-employment. Indeed, there are several examples where ownership of small business has been an important factor in the economic success and mobility of immigrant groups such as the Chinese, Koreans, Jews, and Italians in the United States[6] and ethnic minorities in England and Wales (Clark and Drinkwater 2000). The implicit assumptions underlying these claims have been that, one, a sufficiently large part of the self-employment activity would be entrepreneurial rather than survivalist; and two, discriminatory tendencies that characterize the labour market would somehow be missing from other markets, such as land, credit, or consumer markets, critical to the success of entrepreneurial activities.

The suggestion that marginalized groups should focus on setting up their own businesses has several strands, one of which argues that members of these groups should create jobs, especially for members of their own community. This argument has prompted, in India, the advocacy of 'Dalit Capitalism'—inspired by 'Black Capitalism' in the United States—the first step of which has been the formation of the Dalit Indian Chamber of Commerce and Industry (DICCI), mirroring the old, established industry association Federation of Indian Chambers of Commerce and Industry (FICCI).

The Dalit Indian Chamber of Commerce and Industry was founded on 14 April 2005 on the birth anniversary of Dr B. R. Ambedkar, acknowledged by the DICCI as their 'messiah and the intellectual father'. Interestingly, while Ambedkar was responsible for making compensatory discrimination for Dalits mandatory through constitutionally guaranteed quotas in government jobs, the DICCI group rejects job reservation as a means to Dalit emancipation as they feel quotas have added yet another (negative) stereotype to the Dalits, seen as they are as 'the State's *Jamais*' (sons-in-law of the state). Instead of depending on the state to provide Dalits decent jobs, the DICCI has adopted as its mission statement 'be job givers, not job seekers', exhorting members of the Dalit community in India to become entrepreneurs.[7] On Republic Day in 2013, two Dalit billionaires, Kalpana Saroj and Milind Kamble, featured among the Padma awardees, the nation's highest civilian honours. The award was less a celebration of material wealth and more of human triumph over adversity, as these two awardees had risen from a life of crushing poverty and marginalization, and against all odds achieved unprecedented success.

---

[6] See Fairlie (2006) and the references therein.

[7] See http://www.dicci.org/about.html, accessed on 31 October 2012.

The DICCI believes that a proliferation of such success stories will help Dalits rise to the top of the social pyramid, and will pave the way for the end of the caste system. However, the long history of engagement with the question of annihilation of caste should make clear how vexed this question is, with no easy answers. In any case, the evidence, summarized below, indicates that the climb to the top of the social pyramid through business ownership is likely to be extremely long and arduous, without even going into the fact that capitalism would come with its own set of internal contradictions between owners and workers.

I have been investigating the contours of self-employment in order to gain a better understanding of whether self-employment does indeed reveal a different picture of caste disparities and discrimination compared to labour markets. In Deshpande and Sharma (2013), we argue that in order to understand the spread of 'Dalit Capitalism' it is not enough to focus on the top end of Dalit businesses (the billionaires), but instead, to investigate the extent and spread of Dalit participation in small businesses, which more accurately reflects the material conditions of millions of Dalits who are not in wage employment. The small group of highly successful Dalit industrialists represents a minuscule fraction, not only of the overall Dalit population, but also of Dalit businesses. While the success of Dalit businesses against all odds must be applauded, the reality is that an overwhelming proportion of Dalit businesses are small, household enterprises that are often owner operated.

Caste in the Small-business Sector

We use unit-level data from the registered manufacturing segment of the Third and Fourth rounds of the Indian Micro, Small, and Medium Enterprises (MSME) census data for 2001–2 and 2006–7 respectively, to understand the changes in involvement and dynamics of Dalits, Adivasis, and women in this sector. We find clear caste and gender disparities in ownership of registered manufacturing MSMEs, where SCs and STs are under-represented compared to their population shares, OBCs are roughly equal to their population share, and 'Others', especially Hindu upper castes, are over-represented.[8] Caste disparities have marginally increased over 2001–2 and 2006–7, whereas gender

---

[8] The fourth round of the MSME census breaks down 'Others' into 'Hindu upper castes' and 'rest of Others'.

disparities have marginally decreased. Proportions of SC, ST, OBC, and female ownership are higher in rural compared to urban areas.

How is Production Differentiated by Caste?

The top five activities, which collectively account for roughly 62 per cent of all registered manufacturing MSMEs, are food products and beverages, apparel, fabricated metal products, furniture, and textiles. This overall picture changes somewhat when we differentiate by caste of the owner. Activities dealing with leather tanning and dressing of leather, manufacture of luggage and footwear—stigmatizing jobs traditionally associated with one of the Dalit castes—are the most important activity for SC manufacturing and do not appear in the top five activities of any other caste group. However, over the period, the proportion of SC-owned enterprises engaged in leather has shown a decline. Also, leather forms a larger share of urban SC-owned units, compared to rural. From the Una incident described earlier, it is clear that involvement in leather work continues to be deeply stigmatizing.

The stigma of untouchability has traditionally kept Dalits out of food-related industries (Navsarjan Trust 2010; Shah et al. 2006). We find that the proportion of Dalit firms in food products and beverages is significantly lower than the national average, and that of all other caste groups. However, over the period, this proportion has increased, both in rural and urban areas, and again, proportions are smaller in urban areas compared to rural. To the extent that Dalit participation in leather and exclusion from food are indicators of traditional caste practices, we find some evidence of loosening of these ties, but find that these practices more strongly entrenched in urban compared to rural areas, which is an enigma.

Employment

The typical MSME enterprise had 6.4 employees in 2006–7, with a higher average in urban enterprises. The MSME census does not specifically ask what proportion of employees are family labour versus hired wage employees, but it would be reasonable to infer that the probability of use of family labour would be higher, the lower the number of average employees.

The average number of employees is also an indication of the scale of the enterprise. We can see that this number has gone up for all manufacturing enterprises regardless of the caste and gender of the owner, but shows differences by caste and gender of owner/manager. The SC-, ST-, and OBC-owned enterprises tend to be smaller than the 'Others'-owned ones, with the Hindu upper-caste enterprises employing the highest average number of employees (8.59) in 2006–7.

Owner-operated Enterprises: Survival Activities?

Whether a self-employed individual is an entrepreneur or simply involved in survival activities is a matter of inference based on attributes of the business. Owner-operated units, which by definition have one employee, can be reasonably seen as representing survival activities, possibly distress driven. The proportion of such units has increased over the period to stand at 22.6 per cent in 2006–7. Not surprisingly, the proportion of such units in rural areas is greater, but the increase in urban proportions has been sharper compared to rural.

Proportion of owner-operated manufacturing enterprises is highest among Dalits: 40 per cent in 2006–7, an increase from 38 per cent in 2001–2, indicating that a large part of Dalit manufacturing is small-scale and survival driven. Proportions of owner-operated units in ST- and OBC-owned businesses are significantly lower than that among SCs. However, the biggest contrast is between these three groups and the 'Others', whose proportions of owner-operated enterprises have remained practically unchanged over the period, whereas the other three groups have registered significant increases. The proportion of owner-operated enterprises among the Hindu upper castes at 11.5 per cent is the lowest among all caste groups, indicating that these businesses are more entrepreneurial than survival driven.

Are Businesses Creating Jobs for Dalits?

What about the caste break-up of the employees? Over the period, the proportion of employees who are SC, ST, and OBC have gone down, with a corresponding increase in the proportion of 'Others'.[9] The employee share of SC, ST, and OBCs is greater in rural enterprises than in urban, with the share of 'Others' being exactly the opposite. The gender break-up reveals that manufacturing MSME employees are

---

[9] The MSME census does not ask for the religion of employees, so we cannot identify the Hindu upper castes among the employees.

overwhelmingly male, with less than one-fifth of the employees being female; female proportions being higher in rural than urban areas, with the rural–urban gap having narrowed over the period.

Looking at the distribution of employees by caste of owner, we find that between 2001–2 and 2006–7, the share of SC employees in SC-owned enterprises *declined* from 85 to 61 per cent (for STs, the corresponding figures in ST-owned enterprises are 70 to 60 per cent). There is a similar decline for percentage of OBC employees in OBC-owned firms, but an *increase* in 'Other' employees in 'Others'-owned firms. In 2006–7, in OBC- and 'Others'-owned enterprises, between 74 and 77 per cent of employees belong to the owner's caste group.

It could be argued that these numbers simply reflect the use of family labour and not homophily, or affinity for one's own type. While we cannot distinguish between the two with exact certainty, we can provide pointers. In 2006–7, the median number of employees in the manufacturing MSME sector was 3. Now, smaller enterprises are more likely to use family labour, so we can look at employee shares separately for units above and below the median number of employees. For firms with more than 3 employees (presumably with greater use of hired labour), 65 per cent of employees in OBC firms are OBCs and 70 per cent of employees in 'Others' firms are 'Other' (similar to upper caste firms), whereas only 39 and 49.7 per cent of employees in SC and ST firms are SC and ST respectively. Thus, the majority of employees in the *larger* SC–ST firms are *not* SC–ST. This outcome could potentially be explained by the skill differential between SC–ST and 'Other' employees, but data do not allow us to separate employer preferences that are due to caste affinity from those that are due to the potential skill of the employees. Also, it should be noted that what we observe are outcomes as a result of the hiring process. Whether these outcomes are due to homophily or simply reflect the relative availability of employees from different caste groups is difficult for us to ascertain, since labour demand and supply cannot be separated.

Recall the DICCI mission statement: 'Be job givers, not job seekers'. Empirically, how does the ability of Dalit enterprises to create jobs compare with that of other caste groups? At the national level, of the total workforce in registered manufacturing MSMEs, only 4 per cent is employed in SC-owned firms, 2.2 per cent in ST-owned firms, 27.7 per cent in OBC-owned firms, and 66 per cent in firms owned by 'Others' (of which, 41.5 per cent is employed in Hindu upper-caste owned firms). Over time, the share of OBC and 'Other' employees in SC–ST-owned enterprises has risen significantly, whereas the share of SC–ST employees in OBC- and 'Others'-owned enterprises has shrunk. Both due to the smaller size of SC–ST firms and the strong possibility that OBCs and 'Others' practice homophily, evidence suggests that the beneficiaries of jobs created in the registered manufacturing sector will be disproportionately OBCs and 'Others'. Thus, based on the evidence so far, the potential of Dalit businesses to create jobs for Dalits seems to be limited. However, in firms above the median number of employees, the highest proportion of SC and ST employees is in firms owned by SCs and STs respectively, and is significantly greater than the corresponding proportions in firms owned by other caste groups. Thus, the likelihood of SC and ST employees getting hired is far greater in SC–ST-owned firms, indicating that the DICCI has a point: a rise in Dalit–Adivasi entrepreneurship is critical to improving employment outcomes for members of these groups, but given the small share of Dalit–Adivasi ownership, their potential, at the moment, as job givers is limited.

Entrepreneurship or Survival?

Our estimates reveal that in comparison to 'Others'-owned firms, SC-, ST-, and OBC-owned firms register significantly lower growth, after controlling for size and other characteristics. Given that high-productivity entrepreneurial firms are likely to grow fast, while firms that are in low-productivity survival activities register lower growth, based on evidence in this paper, and on other evidence on the informality and low-productivity nature of SC–ST economic activity (NCEUS 2008), we can say with greater certainty that SC- and ST-owned businesses are more likely to be survivalist than entrepreneurial.

There exists independent evidence that Dalit firms face discriminatory barriers to expanding their businesses and this could be a possible mechanism to explain our growth results. In a case study of Dalit businesses in north-west India, Jodhka (2010) finds that most Dalit businesses are small in size, run mostly as self-proprietorships in the informal sector (these would be classified as own-account enterprises in our data set). Some Dalits in his study felt that they had been victims of prejudice. Locally dominant communities, who have traditionally controlled the business scene, do not like Dalits getting into business: 'they hate us' or they 'do not like us being in the business' were some of the common responses from Jodhka's Dalit businessman respondents (Jodhka 2010: 46). Some other reported being regarded as outsiders or 'odd actors' (Jodhka 2010: 46). Many felt handicapped because of not being part of traditional business communities. Large proportions of his Dalit respondents felt that caste affected their business negatively, both because of discrimination from traditional business communities, as well as from consumers. 'Identification with my caste name tends to discourage my clients. Even when they do not have caste prejudice, they feel we may not be able to deliver because we are traditionally not the ones who have been in business or possess enough resources to run a good business' (Jodhka 2010: 47). This is similar to evidence from other countries too. For instance, it has been noted that the large observed differences in self-employment rates across racial groups (Asians, blacks, Hispanics, and whites) in the US is partly due to consumer discrimination (Borjas and Bronars 1989).

In India, certain castes and communities have traditionally been business communities, and entrepreneurs from these communities start with clear natural advantages, in that they possess insider knowledge, know-how, and strong business networks passed down through generations (Damodaran 2008). In this context, an important channel of social mobility would be the extent to which marginalized groups, whose traditional occupations have not been business based, have been able to break into established networks and set themselves up as entrepreneurs. While this data set does not provide detailed and specific *jati* information, the evidence suggests that entrepreneurship as a significant vehicle for social mobility among Dalits is yet to become a reality in India.

In an op-ed piece, Chandra Bhan Prasad and Milind Kamble (2013) argue, 'Capital is the surest means to fight caste. In dalits' hands, capital becomes an anti-caste weapon ... dalit capitalism is the answer to that regime of discrimination.' The best site to test the validity of this proposition is the private manufacturing sector. Our analysis of changes in the private manufacturing sector in the era of market-led and globalized development finds that caste continues to shape virtually all aspects of production and that so far, capital has not countered the deep-rooted inequities produced by caste.

The Indian state is often berated for *creating* casteism through reservations, the implicit argument being that economic and social outcomes would not be mediated by caste if the state did not intervene to change the caste mix of institutions. Until April 2012, there was no systematic policy of affirmative action in the sphere of small business activity, and therefore, the picture described earlier could not possibly be caused by state intervention. On the contrary, this picture clearly indicates the need for concerted policy interventions to correct historical caste-based inequalities. The 'supplier diversity' initiative of the Madhya Pradesh government in 2002 was one such beginning, but the focus there was on government procurement from SC–ST suppliers. The 'Public Procurement Policy for MSEs' of 2012 mandates that central government ministries, departments, and public-sector undertakings should procure a minimum of 20 per cent of their annual value of goods or services from MSEs (Micro and Small Enterprises) and that within this, 20 per cent should be earmarked for SC–ST-owned MSEs—that is, a total of 4 per cent of the total MSE purchases. Lest we think of this as too radical, note that the Malaysian affirmative action programme directly seeks to redress wealth disparities between the Malays and the Chinese by reserving 30 per cent of all business ownership for ethnic Malays. The policy of the Indian government is considerably weaker. While we debate the efficiency and efficacy of this policy, we have to be mindful that altering the no-intervention status quo in the private sector would not introduce disparities, but correct them.

Discrimination in the Small-business Sector

The evidence of systematic and persistent caste differences outlined above does not prove discrimination along caste lines in the business sector; all the gaps could, in principle, be accounted for by the fact that businesses owned by Dalits and Adivasis have characteristics that might be systematically inferior compared to those of non-SC–ST-owned businesses. For instance, SC–ST owners could be less educated, poorer, lack strong business networks, and so forth, and accounting for these characteristics might explain the entire gap in business earnings. Of course, the fact that SC–STs enter the field of self-employment with inferior characteristics indicates the presence of 'pre-market' discrimination.

In Deshpande and Sharma (2016), we examine whether differences in earnings between SC–ST- and non-SC–ST-owned household non-farm businesses could be entirely explained by differences in characteristics, or whether there is a residual unexplained gap in earnings, which is indicative of discrimination. Using the India Human Development Survey (IHDS) data for 2004–5, we estimate mean earnings for SC–ST and non-SC–ST businesses, and go beyond the mean to understand 'what happens where' in the earnings distribution. We decompose the average earnings gap as well as the gap at each percentile of the earnings distribution in order to examine whether and how the extent of discrimination changes along the earnings distribution.

We find clear differences in observable characteristics between SC–ST and non-SC–ST businesses. The latter are more urban, record larger number of total man-hours, owners are more educated, less poor, possess a greater number of assets, have better networks, and are more likely to have a business in a fixed workplace. These disparities get reflected in both indicators of business performance in the data—gross receipts and net income—such that SC–STs on average perform significantly poorly compared to non-SC–STs.

The decompositions of average earnings reveal that depending on the specification of explanatory variables, as much as 55 per cent of the net income gap could be attributed to the 'unexplained' or the discriminatory component.

We also find that gaps are higher at lower deciles than higher ones, and the decompositions also reveal that the unexplained component is higher at the lower deciles than higher, suggesting that lower earning SC–ST-owned businesses face greater discrimination, as compared to those at the higher end.

The Sticky Floor

Our analysis shows the presence of greater discrimination at the lower end of the earnings distribution. The actual magnitudes vary according to the specification used, for instance, one specification shows that the unexplained or discriminatory component declines from 46 per cent at the 10th percentile to 42 per cent at the 90th percentile. This indicates that those at low-earning activities might face greater constraints, but those constraints ease as businesses earnings increase. For labour markets, a possible explanation for the 'sticky floor' (in contrast to the 'glass ceiling' effect, which refers to increasing wage gaps as one moves from lower to higher quantiles) is statistical discrimination.[10] For self-employment, reasons behind the sticky floor need to be explored further.[11]

CASTE AND CHARITABLE GIVING

Mukund Kamalakar, a successful entrepreneur, who now owns a flourishing solar equipment firm, was originally Mukund Kamble, from a Dalit caste. He changed his surname when he was in college, from the caste-revealing Kamble to the Brahminical Kamalakar. 'The attitudinal change in the people and groups that I interacted with then on was remarkable. Access into the competitive world was so much easier.' (Karunakaran 2009: 24)

Evidence both from the labour market as well as from self-employment is clear and compelling—caste, especially Dalit status—still matters in shaping outcomes. Insights from social psychology are particularly useful in understanding patterns of (dis)advantage, and I have been drawing upon several of those in my recent papers. One of my recent studies (Deshpande and Spears 2016) marries the experimental technique used by labour economists—'correspondence studies' of discrimination[12] that randomly assign names associated with social groups to fictional persons in order to test for an effect of group membership—with the social psychological concept of 'identifiable victim effect' (Jenni and Loewenstein 1997): 'People are much more

---

[10] See Chapter 2 for an explanation of statistical discrimination.

[11] A possible suggestion, which we tested and found to be invalid, is that the firms at higher percentiles of the income distribution might be larger (in terms of number of employees). In that case, if the source of discrimination is consumer discrimination, then information about the caste of owner might not be common knowledge and the business might be evaluated on characteristics. However, our estimates reveal that the average number of employees, first, varies very little across deciles of net income; and second, the limited the limited variation is similar to the earnings gap, that is, businesses in the first decile have the highest average number of employees (1.7). This declines steadily up to the fifth decile (1.3) to rise to 1.4 in the 10th decile. Variation is similar to the earnings gap, that is, businesses in the first decile have the highest average number of employees (1.7). This declines steadily up to the fifth decile (1.3) to rise to 1.4 in the 10th decile.

[12] See Chapter 5 for an explanation of correspondence studies.

willing to aid identified individuals than unidentified or statistical victims' (Slovic 2007: 88).

It has been argued that such helping behaviour is explained by the interaction of sympathy and deliberation, where sympathy is 'caring but immature and irrational' and subject to a range of influences (Loewenstein and Small 2007: 112). Thus, people give more to the identified victim because they feel sympathy for her plight, but the statistical victim evokes no such emotion. However, emotional reactions to others are not always sympathetic. This suggests an interaction between identifiability and social hierarchy: the reaction to identifiable victims is motivated by sympathy, but members of low-ranking groups in need often do not evoke sympathy, and might even prompt disgust or aversion.

To study how caste and religious identities in contemporary India interact with the identifiable victim effect—does identifiability encourage donations to low-ranking out-groups—we conducted three randomized experiments with educated, computer-using Indian participants. In order to learn about caste attitudes in modern Indian society, we targeted a special set of participants: participants in our study used English-language websites, but in the 2005 India Human Development Survey, less than 1 per cent of Indian households owned a computer; of course, personal ownership of a computer is not necessary for internet access. In the same survey, only 7 per cent of 8–11-year-old children chose to take a reading test in English, rather than another language. This confirms that participants in our study were drawn from the relatively better-off sections of Indian society.

Our three studies were the following: one, a survey experiment with detailed information about participants; two, a natural setting experiment with 56,000 purchased advertisements, studying economic behaviour in a real market for charitable giving; and three, an internet choice experiment in which participants allocated real money. We indicated group membership of identified recipients subtly, using names that connote caste or religion; in a separate 'first-stage' experiment, we verified that respondents were able to identify group membership correctly based on the names we were using, that is, Dalit names were correctly identified as Dalit, and so on.

In all three studies, we found an identifiable victim effect for generic Indian and high-caste recipients, which is absent or reversed for low-caste recipients. This means for generic Indian and high-caste names, our respondents were more willing to donate to identified victims than to statistical ones. However, for low-caste recipients, this was absent or even reversed, that is, respondents were more willing to donate to generic Dalit charities, than to identified Dalit names. We find that participants in all three studies respond similarly to statistical high- and low-caste recipients but demonstrate the least generous responses to identifiable low-caste named recipients.

Our participants' donations are motivated not merely by poverty or wealth but also by labels of social identity, as we found that despite an identifiable victim effect for generic Indian recipients, participants were the least generous in all three studies to a named low-caste family. Yet, in each case participants were as willing to donate to statistical low-caste victims as to statistical high-caste victims. A psychological account of this outcome is beyond the scope of this essay. However, one consistent explanation seems to fit our findings: that responses to statistical victims are governed by deliberation, while responses to identifiable victims depend on emotion (Loewenstein and Small 2007). Also, Fiske et al. (2002) argue that low-ranking out-groups can generate aversive emotion rather than sympathy, which could explain the behaviour of the participants of our study.

Our study establishes that social identity matters in charitable giving, just as it matters in labour, credit, or consumer markets. However, does identity matter because donors have a taste for discrimination,[13] which manifests itself through disgust towards or hatred of the stigmatized groups, or through a statistical discrimination channel in which caste identity is seen as a proxy for ability or effort (and therefore deservedness), such that needy upper castes are seen as worthy or deserving of charitable giving? Economists typically address such questions by assessing whether observable characteristics correlated with race can plausibly and statistically account for discrimination—for example, if the evidence showed that employers were equally willing to hire black and white employees known to have the same levels of education, then lower hiring rates of blacks might be interpreted to reflect lack of access to education rather than discrimination per se.

---

[13] See Chapter 2 for an explanation of the taste for discrimination.

However, in our case this method cannot apply: our unidentifiable victims are experimental fictions.

Finally, our results contribute to a literature debating the continuing relevance of caste in modern India that *Grammar* attempted to establish. We find that the caste identity of the identified victim matters. Earlier in this essay (section titled 'Moving Closer or Further Apart?'), we have examined evidence on caste-based inequality in order to see if it is decreasing or increasing; additionally, there are claims that the well-being of Dalits has improved over time.[14] The results of this paper suggest that caste prejudice still exists even among Internet-using, English-speaking, young, educated Indians. Other recent randomized studies have made related observations: Hanna and Linden (2012) show that teachers in India give lower grades to the same exams when randomly assigned low-caste student names; Lamba and Spears (2013) document that rural villages randomly assigned a low-caste village leader are less likely to subsequently be recognized with a sanitation prize. Although strategies to resolve caste discrimination are well beyond the scope of this essay, our results and others make clear that finding such strategies continues to be of policy importance.

GLOBALIZATION, LIBERALIZATION, AND GROUP DISPARITIES

There is a belief that as the Indian economy liberalizes, becomes more market-oriented, and increases its integration with the global economy, intergroup disparities (such as those between broad caste groups or between men and women) are likely to reduce because of several reasons. First, labour market discrimination on account of social identity is expected to decline;[15] and second, because the creation of new and new types of jobs is likely to provide an impetus to members of marginalized groups to acquire new skills to break out of traditional, caste-based, dead-end, oppressive, and stigmatizing occupations (Omvedt 2012). The argument that discrimination is likely to reduce is based on the belief that market orientation would give primacy

---

[14] Kapur et al. (2010), discussed in the next section.

[15] Black and Brainerd (2004) make this argument in the context of trade liberalization, that while it may lead to increased wage inequality, it reduces the ability of the employers to discriminate, thus benefiting women.

to profit maximization, and more generally, to efficient allocation of resources—a process in which the social identity of agents ought to be irrelevant (Wilfred 2007). Foreign agents are especially less likely to be concerned with local hierarchies and the accompanying prejudices. Additionally, theory suggests that gender (or caste) wage gaps should narrow with globalization because greater integration with the global economy could promote competition and lower discrimination between social identities (Artecona and Cunningham 2002).[16]

Contrary to this set of arguments is the view that traditionally marginalized groups might be at a disadvantage even in this new scenario given that they are under-represented at levels of education needed to take advantage of these emerging opportunities. Also, multinational companies (MNCs) do not work in a vacuum—their hiring decisions are taken by local employees who are as aware of local social cleavages and are driven by the same prejudices as the hiring managers of domestic firms. Foreign agents are not likely to disturb domestic norms and practices unless it is absolutely essential since their bottom line is profits. Indeed, research into the mechanics of the hiring process in urban formal labour markets, reported in Chapter 6, indicates that lip service to merit notwithstanding, managers show a deep awareness of the overlapping and complex categories of caste, class, religion, and gender, and of the strong stereotypical beliefs that merit is distributed along axes defined by these social identities. This is as true for private domestic firms as it is for MNCs. Chapter 3 in the book ends on a speculative note about the likely impact of globalization and liberalization on inter-group disparities.

In a recent study (Deshpande forthcoming), I investigated one aspect of issue, namely, association between FDI, and caste and gender wage gaps. For this purpose, I used a unique dataset that I created from a variety of sources. I got data for 14,627 cases of Foreign Direct Investment (FDI) projects that were approved from 1995 to July 2010 from the Department of Industrial Policy and Promotion, Ministry of Commerce, Government of India. These data allow us to identify the

[16] Specifically, for women, increase in trade is supposed to drive up relative demand for female labour because its supply tends to be more elastic than male labour supply; this effect will be enhanced if women are disproportionately represented in export-oriented sectors.

location of the project at the district level. I matched these with NSS data at the district level from three large employment–unemployment surveys: the 55th round (1999–2000), the 61st round (2004–5), and the 66th round (2009–10). Since the main concern of this exercise was to examine the association of FDI with group disparities, the empirical strategy consists of matching outcomes, calculated from the three rounds of NSS data, to cumulative approvals in the preceding four years.

The results indicate that the basic outcome variables, namely, caste wage gap and gender wage gap, are positively correlated with FDI approvals (as FDI increase, caste and gender wage gaps increase). Admittedly, the magnitudes are small, and this analysis is not causal as there would be a number of other factors that would affect the wage gap that have not been controlled since data at the district levels is not easily available. However, we do control for variables for which data are available, namely relative educational levels, proportions in regular wage and salaried employment, and sector of economic activity, in addition to state and time period controls and district fixed effects. Thus, these results provide evidence suggesting that increases in FDI approvals are *not* correlated with a decline in wage gaps.

Foreign Direct Investment is only one aspect of globalization and liberalization that would affect caste disparities. The broader argument for the emancipatory effect of globalization has several contours. In particular, it hinges on the fact that globalization will make the market salient as well as unleash competition between Indian and foreign firms, impacting Dalits positively in many dimensions. Multinational corporations and FDI would be an implicit and important, but not the only, part of this process. Chandra Bhan Prasad, one of the most vocal supporters of globalization and the market economy for its capacity to empower Dalits, argues that one of the ways in which globalization empowers Dalits is by 'universalising access to aspirations'. He is referring here to the process of certain consumer goods being plentifully and cheaply available (for example, colour TVs, mobile phones, refrigerators, air conditioners, and so on) and within reach of the Dalits—goods that are supposed to be considered 'material markers of pride'. He suggests that this has broken the exclusivity of the 'predominantly Upper Caste Consumer Club', a process aided also by the rise of Dalit entrepreneurs.[17]

[17] See http://www.chandrabhanprasad.com/frmGlobalization.aspx, accessed in February 2011.

Omvedt (2005) argues that globalization is an inevitable reality for India and it has many positive aspects. Thus, instead of taking the blind anti-globalization position demonstrated, according to her, by the Left political parties and ecologists in India, she suggests that we need to think about a comprehensive and nuanced response of Dalits and Adivasis to these changing realities. Chandra Bhan echoes this sentiment by asking Dalits to view globalization as an opportunity rather than as a threat.[18]

Based on a survey of all Dalit households in two blocks of two districts in Uttar Pradesh, Kapur et al. (2010: 39) suggest that the shift from a state-led to a market-led path of development has changed patterns of interaction between castes, leading to a 'rapid erosion in discriminatory practices that stigmatized Dalits'. They also find large shifts in the pattern of economic life, both within and away from the village. They find this change manifesting itself in terms of a change in occupational patterns with Dalits moving away from traditional occupations and the nature of contracts between Dalits and upper castes such that practices such as bonded labour that tied Dalits to generations of servitude appear to have become obsolete. However, it is not clear to what extent these outcomes are a result of the regular process of development and not especially attributable to a *shift* from state-led to a market-led path. In other words, the role of market-oriented liberalization in bringing these changes about needs to be proven, not assumed.

QUOTAS AND BEYOND

The tragic suicide of Rohit Vemula brought to the fore the issue of marginalization that Dalit students face after being admitted through affirmative action. In other words, a procedural or mechanical understanding of affirmative action can increase access either to education or jobs, an important goal in itself. However, in order to make affirmative action a meaningful and substantive policy with strong transformative potential, we need to create structures in place that ensure acceptance, assimilation, and inclusion—steps that come after access. We need to address stigmatization of affirmative action

---

[18] See http://www.chandrabhanprasad.com/frmGlobalization.aspx, accessed on 13 November 2016.

beneficiaries, a necessary step for which is developing an understanding of the nature of stigma. In Deshpande (2016), I investigate precisely this issue through an attitude survey, and find that despite the presence of stigma, affirmative action beneficiaries do not internalize the negative evaluation that their peers place upon them.

Affirmative action (AA) beneficiaries view access to preferred positions through AA as a life-altering event, and would not forego that opportunity on account of possible stigma inside higher educational institutions, to which they probably would not be admitted without AA. The presence of greater number of qualified individuals owing to AA provides role models to other members of the community, and weakens the stigmatizing association between group membership and incompetence. More importantly, AA recipients face stigmatization or battle with a stigmatized ethnic identity already regardless of whether they actually use AA. This underlying context of stigmatization is precisely the context that justifies AA in the first place.

The results of this paper (Deshpande 2016) have implications for practice. To begin with, publicizing achievements of AA beneficiaries and highlighting success stories instead of focusing on dropouts could, over time, weaken the stigma of incompetence. Also, institutions should take steps to increase self-confidence of beneficiaries with a view to eliminate self-driven processes that propel the academic performance burden.

More importantly and urgently, establishing a climate of mutual respect where bullying, derogatory remarks, and instances of open ostracism are discouraged and met with clear disapproval would be the key policy lessons for higher educational institutions. Establishment of norms about what kind of behaviour is tolerated might be difficult and contentious, but not impossible. Indeed, within the domain of gender and sexual harassment, following the Sexual Harassment of Women at the Workplace (Prevention, Prohibition and Redressal) Act of 2013, it is now mandatory for all educational institutions and workplaces to constitute a sexual harassment committee at the institutional level, which not only publicizes norms of acceptable behaviour and offers a legitimate institutional mechanism for redressing grievances and complaints but also promotes gender sensitization at the institutional level (Ministry of Women and Child Development 2015). Indeed, following Rohit Vemula's suicide, the University Grants Commission, under the Ministry of Human Resource Development of the Government of India, has sent a circular [D.O.F. No. 1-7/2011(SCT), dated 1 March 2016] to all higher educational institutions to initiate steps to prevent caste-based discrimination inside their institutions.

The anti-discriminatory legal provisions in India are patchy. The Scheduled Castes and the Scheduled Tribes (Prevention of Atrocities) Act 1989, a modified version of the first anti-untouchability Act,[19] amended in December 2015 to include new categories of actions to be treated as offences, including barring entry into an educational institution on account of caste, mainly targets caste-based hate crimes. Offences under this Act are treated as a criminal liability, which means that the burden of proof required is much larger than that for a civil liability, as, indeed, is the punishment, if guilt can be established. However, the conviction rate under this Act is low (the three years from 2012 to 2015 have seen a conviction rate of 30 per cent). This low rate, in addition to indicating possibly inherent pro-elite and pro-upper caste biases in the system, reflects a critical difficulty in the use of this law: the aggrieved party has to be able to prove that the crime was committed because of their caste status and not because of any other motive. This is often impossible unless the offence was accompanied by open slurs that establish caste as the key reason for the perpetration of the crime. Also, conviction is only possible if a complaint has been filed under this Act. Descriptive accounts suggest that even the filing of a complaint—the first step towards redressal and justice—is extremely daunting, especially for those already humiliated by atrocities. Upper-caste policemen are unwilling to file cases against fellow caste members because of the severity of possible punishment. Those who actually manage to file a complaint face even greater hurdles afterwards in terms of inordinate judicial delays, threats, and harassments, as the decks are stacked against them at all levels (Verma 2016: 32–3).

Although this Act is extremely important, as it has the potential to deter violent hate crimes, there is need for a broader anti-discriminatory legal provision. At the time of writing, there are discussions for a Delhi

[19] Article 17 of the Indian constitution abolished 'untouchability' and forbade its practice in any form. To enforce this, in 1955, the Indian parliament passed the Untouchablility (Offences) Act. In 1976, this was made more stringent and renamed as the Protection of Civil Rights Act. This was made even more stringent in 1989, taking shape as the current Prevention of Atrocities Act (Verma 2016: 26).

Equality Bill 2016, which, if operationalized, would seek to create a civil liability for acts of discrimination along various dimensions, including but going beyond caste.

Focusing specifically on educational institutions, evidence suggests that the more challenging issue might be 'micro-aggressions' (Lukes and Bangs 2014). Micro-aggressions refer to everyday verbal, non-verbal, and environmental slights, snubs, or insults, intentional or unintentional, which communicate hostile, derogatory, or negative messages to target persons based solely on their marginalized group membership.

These are difficult to tackle legally, as micro-aggressions often constitute acts that are, strictly speaking, not illegal. Also, as academic institutions are meant to uphold and accommodate discord, dissent, and a diversity of views, it is difficult and indeed undesirable to muffle freedom of expression, even of those unpleasant views that might be derogatory towards marginalized groups. This constitutes a huge challenge in terms of creating an atmosphere inside academic institutions that is based on mutual respect and does not stigmatize individuals on account of their group membership.

TO BE CONTINUED

These issues are complex and contain many interwoven strands that are not necessarily easy to disentangle. *Grammar* made a strong case for an evidence-based, multifaceted, and multidisciplinary approach towards the study of caste inequality and discrimination. As the underlying material reality is reshaping itself, a *new grammar of caste* is getting established. Studies that aim to understand these evolving realities need to use new and innovative methods, and listen to voices beyond strict disciplinary boundaries. Such an approach would produce the necessary richness and depth in scholarly research that can provide inputs into policy. In this essay, I have attempted to summarize the key findings of my main research in the five years since the first publication of *Grammar*—research that has raised more questions than it has answered, and which also propelled me beyond economics. However, several of these issues have a strong economic dimension, thus calling for more economic research, not less—a quest that is far from over.

I started this essay with a reference to the Una gathering, a powerful expression of anger at the Dalit–upper caste conflict. As

Dalits are mobilizing, we have also witnessed other kinds of caste-based movements over the last two years—vociferous demands by landowning, dominant castes such as Patels, Jats, Marathas, and Kapus to be classified as OBCs in order to be eligible for quotas. Are their demands justified? This question can only be settled empirically,[20] and available evidence suggests that perhaps they are not. We should note that the spectre of privatization is already threatening to erode the scope of affirmative action, applicable as it is only to government jobs. If dominant castes got access to quotas, there is a fear that the already shrinking entitlement for Dalits would be further eroded.

Unless we fathom and grasp the new grammar of caste, we could miss the true significance of the resurgence of Dalit aspirations. To explain it in simple electoral terms—a gain for this or that political party, or as an expression of a particular political tendency—would be to miss the wood for the trees. We need to understand and engage with the new grammar of caste to appreciate the significance of long-term changes in the caste system, as well as to understand the resistance to those changes.

[20] Deshpande and Ramachandran (2016) examine this precise issue.

Tables and Figures

TABLES

FIGURES

Preface

This book has been in the making for a while. Since it is appearing at a time when writings on caste are suddenly becoming plentiful, it is necessary to justify the existence of yet another book on the subject, especially when Oxford University Press has recently published an excellent collection of essays called *Blocked by Caste*, to which I too have contributed. While it is true that the literature on caste is vast, the bulk of it comes from sociology, political science, and history. There is still a dearth of economic analysis of caste disparity and discrimination. This book seeks to fill that gap and, in doing so, makes a number of useful interventions.

It addresses the larger community of all social scientists, economists included, because it integrates discussions on caste from other disciplines with those from within economics. Also, economics of discrimination is not a very mainstream sub-discipline *within* economics, so some of the material in this book is likely to be unfamiliar to economists as well. However, the discussion is deliberately non-technical so that it makes for easy reading; all the technical details can be followed up by those interested in doing so. The book reviews a wide range of the major theories of discrimination and caste from Indian theoreticians of caste such as Phule, Ambedkar, and Periyar to economic theorists' models of discrimination, such as those contributed by Kenneth Arrow, Gary Becker, and George Akerlof. It brings together evidence on different dimensions of caste disparities based on two large national-level data sets in order to comment on the degree of change in the caste system over the last two decades. A lot of the evidence is based on my own research over the past decade, but I have also summarized most of the other available significant research. I have constructed a multifaceted 'Caste Development Index' (CDI) that allows a broader assessment of standard of living of caste groups than what a narrow focus on income or consumption would allow. One can use this index to compare a caste group across states or time, and the gap between CDI values across caste groups can serve as a measure of disparity. I discuss the degree of continuity and change in caste disparities, and find that data point more towards continuation of traditional hierarchies rather than towards their dissolution, with upper castes at the top, Scheduled Castes–Scheduled Tribes at the bottom, and Other Backward Classes (OBCs) somewhere in between, with significant inter-state variation.

At first glance, this might seem like a restatement of traditional wisdom or a reinvention of the wheel. However, the dominant schools of thought today forcefully question the continuation of traditional hierarchies from a variety of perspectives. One perspective, predominantly from within sociology, argues that caste is dead or that hierarchy is replaced by competing equalities. Another perspective, predominantly from within a section of Dalit advocates, has suggested that liberalization and globalization of the Indian economy have unleashed forces that have upset, often obliterated, traditional caste distinctions.[1] Thus, the evidence presented in this book, which is based on economic analysis, runs contrary to these views and does not reiterate traditional wisdom. The idea is to use the evidence presented in this book to acknowledge the gravity of the persistence of caste disparities, and to also recognize that contrary to wishful thinking, liberalization and a greater market orientation of the economy is not going to eliminate disparities on its own.

Measuring disparity is relatively straightforward; estimating discrimination is not. This is another area where economists have made important contributions. This book presents to the readers the latest

---

[1] The latest contribution to this corpus is Kapur et al. (2010).

set of methods that allow researchers to gauge discrimination and shows how some of these methods have been used in the Indian context and what that quest has yielded. What is very revealing is that lip-service to merit notwithstanding, contemporary, formal, urban sector labour markets show a deep awareness of caste, religious, gender, and class cleavages, and that discrimination is very much a modern sector phenomenon, perpetuated in the present. So it is neither a thing of the past nor confined only to the rural areas.

Finally, the book ends by discussing policy responses to disparities and discrimination with a review of the existing quota policy. I present the very latest research that shows, contrary again to popular belief, that affirmative action does not have adverse effects in employment and education. Given the multifaceted nature of deprivation, I argue that increasing quotas mechanically cannot be a solution to caste discrimination. Access to higher education and formal sector employment (which quotas address) is important and should be continued, but the lives of the majority of rural Dalits are untouched by this. It is important, therefore, to look beyond quotas. Increased access to productive assets, such as land, via land reforms, and to alternative sources of livelihoods, via generation of rural non-farm employment, is imperative. Also, in urban areas, we have to look beyond quotas and increase diversity in public spaces. Caste discrimination is clear and persistent, and needs targeted interventions.

Acknowledgements

To start on a trite note, there is a journey underlying every book. I do not intend to test your patience by recounting the vicissitudes of this particular journey, but would like to outline the broad course, essentially to acknowledge the invaluable role of several individuals without whom this journey would not have been completed.

When I completed my PhD on the intricacies of the international financial system, I had never imagined that I would turn to issues such as caste. Like all Indians, I had some views on the matter without knowing much about it; given my self image as someone committed to democracy and equality, I rejected caste boundaries in all aspects of my personal life. Four years after working on international debt–related issues, William Darity Jr. invited me for a two-year post-doctoral fellowship at the University of North Carolina at Chapel Hill in 1998. He asked me if I was willing to examine, from an economist's point of view, the contemporary nature of caste disparities in India. To cut a long story short, I agreed, and that was how this quest began. He has been a co-author, a friend, and a steadfastly loyal supporter of my work.

After I came back to India, Kaushik Basu planted in my head the idea of consolidating my research findings into a book. Optimistically, I started working on it and immediately wrote a proposal with a timeline. In drawing up the timeline, I had erroneously assumed that Kaushik had passed on some of his efficiency to me during the time that he was my PhD advisor. I realized very soon that he had not, and in the time he has finished several books, I finally managed to complete this one.

I introduced a course called 'Economics of Discrimination' for Masters' students at the Delhi School of Economics in 2000 and have been teaching it ever since. It was wonderful to design a course that emerged out of my research, and from then on the teaching and the research fed on each other and grew in sync. I tested many of the ideas contained in these pages first on successive generations of my students and I thank all of them for being eager recipients and perceptive critics. Whenever the class size was manageable, I took the students on field trips to villages in Khurja district in western Uttar Pradesh as a part of the course. I thank Rajesh Paswan and our hosts in the different villages for selflessly supporting our trips logistically and for being gracious hosts year after year. My students, each year, before the field trip, would suspect me of exaggerating the importance of caste in my lectures; and each year, on the way back to Delhi, they would berate me for underestimating the vicious hold of caste.

The material contained in this book has emerged out of several of my papers. My co-authors, most notably Thomas Weisskopf and Katherine Newman, significantly enriched my understanding of disparity and discrimination, and demonstrated how collaborative work can be both productive and pleasurable. Some of the material has emerged out of broad group collaborations, which included Sukhadeo Thorat, Paul Attewell, Surinder Jodhka, S. Madheswaran, Nitya Rao, Amitabh Kundu, and Sugata Marjit. The manuscript improved greatly as a result of comments from Thomas Weisskopf, Himanshu, Parikshit Ghosh, and Bhaskar Dutta on specific chapters and from two anonymous referees of Oxford University Press on the entire manuscript. The shortcomings that remain, of course, reflect my own weaknesses.

Satish Saberwal was extremely supportive of my idea of converting my research into a book and asked me to send him some of my papers when I first told him about my plan. After several reminders, I finally did, and with his characteristic efficiency and organization, he read them carefully and sent me very detailed comments, even before the first word of the manuscript had been typed. This book would have been completed in less than half the time, if only I had heeded his sage advice to be focused and single-minded.

The research that forms the basis of this book was presented at several conferences and seminars in India and abroad, and benefited hugely from comments and criticism of the various audiences as well as from the comments of several anonymous journal referees. Bidisha Barooah, Kamaal Khan, and Smriti Sharma provided excellent research assistance for specific research projects.

The liberal and collegial working environment of the economics department at the Delhi School of Economics allowed me to pursue my own research agenda without any hindrances. My colleagues at the department provided the right mix of intellectual stimulation and social companionship that was vital for this endeavour to continue. I would especially like to thank K.L. Krishna and J.V. Meenakshi who responded to my endless stream of questions, on the intricacies of econometrics, with unfailing patience and urgency. The staff at the Centre for Development Economics, located in my department, was extremely responsive and I would especially like to thank Surjeet Singh, Sanjeev Sharma, and Rajesh Papnai for all their help.

Then there are individuals whose influence and contribution might have been indirect but are as vital as the direct influences, if not more. Sometimes, one realizes their worth only in retrospect. My paternal grandparents—Ashatai and Purushottam Narahar Deshpande—were remarkable individuals. Freedom fighters, true socialists, dedicated to a just social order, they were pioneers in initiating social reform from below in our village of Rahimatpur in Satara district of Maharashtra, where I spent my first 25 summers and several others thereafter. My grandmother started the first public library in the village in our house in 1947, where it resided until 2009, and actively motivated the women, especially Dalit women, to set aside some time each day for reading. My grandfather was a very popular and respected medical doctor, catering not only to Rahimatpur but also to several villages in the vicinity. They risked the wrath of their friends by breaking the boundaries and barriers of the established religious and caste codes in their everyday lives, but the enormous crowds of mourners after their deaths bore testimony to the popular support and respect they received. When I was growing up, I could sense that they were unusual, but had very little idea why; it is in only in the last few years that I have come to realize and appreciate the enormity of what they started and managed to accomplish in their lifetimes. My lasting regret is that I will never be able to convey to them what an enormous debt I owe them for quietly imparting a lesson in how to question boundaries and reject them, quite apart from making Rahimatpur an inseparable part of my identity.

My parents, Kalindi and Govind Deshpande, provided another set of unusual and remarkable inputs by being who they are. My mother's relentless activism in the women's movement, her unbounded optimism and zest for life, her enthusiasm to constantly explore new avenues and her multifaceted and courageous persona have tremendously influenced not just me but everyone who ever came in contact with her. The only battle she lost turned out to be her last; I can only draw sustenance from the fact that I was at least able to share the joy of having completed a rough first draft of the full manuscript with her, and can vividly picture her excitement and pride, whether or not she agreed with all my arguments, had she been around to read this.

My father, popularly known as GPD, is a Renaissance man in the truest sense of the word. It is not possible for me to capture the wide range of his interests and expertise in a few words, and I am acutely aware that my work cannot match the depth, sharpness, and wit that characterize his prolific academic and literary output. However, I continue to learn a great deal from his formidable intellectual prowess and his keen understanding, among other things, of the caste system and the Indian social order, from the ancient to the contemporary, and his superb mastery over ancient Hindu philosophy.

Sudhanva Deshpande read the entire manuscript carefully and critically, and helped me chisel it through a combination of his meticulous editorial skills, his intelligent insights, and his interest in, and knowledge of, the caste system and the intricacies of punctuation.

Ketaki was curious, supportive, and accommodating all along and participated in this long journey with her characteristic good humour, patience, maturity, and poise. The good times in the company of Antara and Jeff, Sanchari and Raf, all my friends and extended family, have provided the requisite warmth that forms the invisible backdrop to this book. Aruna Dutta provided the indispensable envelope of love and concern.

It is never sufficient to have a plan—each project needs a catalyst in order to see the light of day. The catalyst for this book has been Bhaskar Dutta. This book would not have been completed if it were not for his insistence, encouragement, and support. He helped in the completion of this book in ways too numerous to be recounted. The differences in our 'ways of seeing' compelled me to sharpen my arguments and substantiate assertions carefully. The peace and solitude at the cottage in Coventry provided the much-needed and welcome break from the maddening pace of Delhi, and it was during the summers spent there that the manuscript proceeded forward in quantum jumps.

I dedicate this book, with love and gratitude, to my father, in my mother's memory.

Ashwini Deshpande
April 2011
New Delhi

Abbreviations

AA	affirmative action
CDI	Caste Development Index
DI	Diversity Index
GCDI	Gender–Caste Development Index
GDP	gross domestic product
HDI	Human Development Index
IT	information technology
LFPR	labour force participation rate
MCR	Mandal Commission Report
MPCE	monthly per capita expenditure
NCBC	National Commission for Backward Classes
NFHS	National Family and Health Survey
NSDP	net state domestic product
NSS	National Sample Survey
NSSO	National Sample Survey Organisation
OBC	Other Backward Class
SC	Scheduled Caste
SDP	state domestic product
SLI	standard of living index
ST	Scheduled Tribe
UNDP	United Nations Development Programme

1   The Economics of Caste

A decade ago, when I started working on economic aspects of caste inequality, the primary response of my colleagues, both economists and sociologists, was that of incredulity. At the time, insights into the economic features of the Indian caste system, in its changing manifestations from the ancient, through the colonial to the contemporary, came primarily from the vast pool of research undertaken by sociologists, historians, political scientists—all other social scientists but the economists. Thus, the reaction of my sociologist friends was: What can an economic investigation possibly uncover that we do not already know? The other side of the coin was the reaction from my economist colleagues: Why caste? Is that not something sociologists do?

I found this relative neglect by economists puzzling; one would have expected the discipline to seize upon the unique economic features of the system as tools for theoretical modelling or as the subject matter for empirical work to examine the continuing relevance or otherwise of the occupational structure dictated by the caste system. Faced with analysing persistent underdevelopment in India, the primary focus of empirical economic research then was on the causes of overall inequality and poverty, and their remedies. Inter-group disparity had just started coming to the fore in shaping the contours of research on inequality. My belief was that an understanding of group disparities was essential if one wanted to gain a deeper and nuanced insight into the complex patterns of stratification.

The state of economic discourse among researchers on India has changed drastically from then to the present. Among economists writing on inequality, poverty, and a host of other development issues, caste is now very clearly centre stage, while analysts of Indian politics and society continue to debate caste as before: its relevance, dynamism, new manifestations, and so forth. This is mirrored in (and perhaps partially caused by) the serious attention that caste inequality now receives in the agendas of the multilateral funding agencies. With this shift, the Indian economic discourse now parallels the engagements of the American economic academe that has been engaged much longer with researching questions around racial identity and economic outcomes, inter-group disparities, and discrimination. Needless to add, this shift in academic attention is long overdue and very welcome, quite in addition to providing a personal vindication.

To restate an obvious point, inter-group disparity in India is multifaceted: religion, language, sub-nationality, region, further complicated by interactions with class and gender, are all very important descriptors of inter-group disparity. One implication of the multifaceted nature of group identities is the following, especially important when comparing caste inequality to group divisions in other societies. Unlike several other countries, for instance the US, it is not very meaningful to talk in terms of a single majority or a dominant group that is in conflict with one or several minority groups in understanding the *totality* of group divisions in the country. Thus, within, say, Hinduism, caste is an important group identifier.[1] Viewed this way, no single caste is 'the majority', and a large group of castes low in the hierarchy would be considered subaltern. However, based on the religious schisms, Hindus (including the so-called 'low' castes) as a whole are the numerical majority and the dominant group, in contrast to the Muslims or Christians or other religious minorities. In addition, linguistic groups, regional groups, women within each of the groups— all add layers of complexity to the phenomenon of inter-group disparity, which makes straightforward generalizations confounding.

[1] While I use Hinduism for illustrative purposes, it is important to note that caste is a feature of all major religions in India, indeed in South Asia. This is discussed more clearly in Chapter 2.

Prima facie, there is no objective yardstick on which the relative importance of these schisms can be evaluated; indeed, conflicts based on any of these descriptors can be, and have been, equally heinous and bloody. I focus on caste because of the enduring relevance of caste categories in contemporary India, and due to the presence of caste-based affirmative action policies enshrined in the Constitution of the country. In the eyes of the rest of the world, caste is a defining feature of India: omnipresent and defiant to change. One can focus on caste either to endorse this view or to investigate it—this book does the latter. As elsewhere in the world, in addition to prejudice and the consequent social discrimination, affirmative action is based on an *economic* rationale. While this provides a prima facie case for viewing caste as an ingredient of stratification, it does not reveal the contours of contemporary nature of caste inequality.

WHAT CONTRIBUTION CAN ECONOMISTS MAKE?

The non economic literature on the caste system is so vast that it may legitimately be asked if an economic inquiry can make any additional worthwhile contribution. However, this (non-economic) literature frequently makes *economic* assertions that have important implications defining the contemporary nature of caste inequality. The validity of these propositions, especially the extent to which they can be generalized, is not always apparent on the basis of the evidence presented. Thus, the need for an all-India economic investigation is strong.[2] To consider one example, Mayer (1996: 49) talks about the 'general disengagement of occupation from its association with a particular caste, and with any ranking which might stem from this'. An article from the *New York Times*[3] argues, albeit for south India, that 'the breakdown of the caste hierarchy has broken the traditional links between caste and profession, and released enormous entrepreneurial energies in the South'. How does one evaluate these propositions? It is true that over time, occupational structure itself has undergone a profound change,

[2] Indeed, there is a section of sociologists who make a similar argument. See, for example, Satish Deshpande (2003).

[3] 'Entrepreneurs Rise in Ashes of India's Caste System', available at http://www.nytimes.com/2010/09/11/world/asia/11caste.html?_r=3&pagewanted=1&partner=r, accessed on 20 September 2010.

while caste divisions have been *relatively* static. In addition, the post-independence Constitution guarantees each Indian the freedom of choice of occupations. Thus, without fear of contradiction, one can uphold this statement for several castes, for example, members of the erstwhile warrior castes will not necessarily choose the military as a career in the present. Conversely, the military is no longer the preserve of certain castes, to the exclusion of others. It is also true that any kind of skill acquisition (for example, admission to a management or a computer course, or to a dental school) is not contingent upon one's caste status. Indeed, none of the modern occupations are determined by birth, and most are not caste-based.

Having said this, there is another level at which this statement needs to be approached in order to gain an insight into the exact nature of change in the caste–occupation nexus. For instance, what has happened to ancient occupations that have survived changes in economic structure, for instance, the priests in temples, scavengers, traditional moneylenders, and several of the agricultural jobs? Are these jobs still performed by castes to which they were traditionally allocated? Or, is the reshuffling of the deck total, that is, is the modern occupational structure randomly distributed across castes? It is likely that here we may find more continuity than change. It is here that an economic investigation can make a decisive intervention—does the story reported by the *New York Times* represent the rule or the exception?

Also, what happens to those who are released from traditional jobs, either because those occupations themselves are vanishing or because of the quest for better jobs? Is it true that lower castes tend to get absorbed into lower paying and less prestigious modern occupations and higher castes get concentrated at the upper end of the modern spectrum? Indeed, if this is happening, then we would be witnessing the result of, what can be termed, accumulation of advantage or privilege over the years (or its reverse, disadvantage or denial of privilege). For instance, Mencher (1974: 472) finds that '[among the] present day Chamars, [al]though known as leather workers, only a small proportion of caste members do this work, [and their] ... major function [is] ... to serve as a source of agricultural labor'. This also raises the question of why the link breaks for some castes—is it the 'pull' of economic opportunities or the 'push' of economic deprivation that compels caste members to seek alternative occupations? This issue is additionally complicated by the gender angle. Chapter 4, on the gender–caste overlap, discusses how the responsibility of preserving traditional occupations often falls on the women while the men seek alternative employment. Or, is it the case that members of stigmatized, disadvantaged castes end up becoming successful entrepreneurs? Studies of social mobility in India, including on south India, such as Nafziger (1975), Munshi and Rosenzweig (2006, 2009), Deshpande and Palshikar (2008), and Jodhka (2010), reviewed later in the book, find that social and economic mobility for lower castes is extremely low.

It is possible then, that the link between caste and occupation can be broken and yet the overlap of caste and class can be very strong.[4] If this is true, then the contemporary situation could be regarded as a permutation of an earlier caste structure where the link between caste and occupation may be strong for some castes, weak for others, but the association between caste and status or, more correctly, between caste and privilege persists, albeit in a different form. It can even be argued that the cumulative advantage of the upper castes has been so strong that they no longer need an institutional structure of hereditary 'reservations' (I refer to the monopoly over jobs determined by birth into a privileged family) in order to perpetuate their privilege. This is one more instance where a rigorous economic investigation into the caste composition of the occupational structure can help derive an objective, larger picture of the nature and degree of change.

Does this suggest that caste today simply captures class? This is a perennial question, confounded by the fact that the overlap between the two is very strong. However, the belief in this book is that the two are distinct, despite the very large overlap, as the discussion on discrimination illustrates (Chapter 6). Dr B.R. Ambedkar, an outstanding theoretician of caste, an icon of the Dalit movement,

---

[4] The issue of the overlap between caste and class is complex and is not being discussed here in detail. For instance, while untouchable castes have often turned to 'jobs which could be done without coming into close physical contact with caste Hindus' (Mencher 1974: 473) and thus form a large proportion of landless labour, not all landless labourers are untouchables (as Mencher discusses). There are issues about the growing proletarianization and the role of economic policy that are fascinating, but are beyond the scope of this exercise.

the chairman of the drafting committee of the Indian Constitution, and independent India's first law minister, outlines the caste–class distinction very succinctly:

The relationship between the ideas of caste and class has been a matter of lively controversy. Some say that caste is analogous to class and there is no difference between the two. Others hold that the idea of castes is fundamentally opposed to that of class ... Although caste is different from and opposed to the notion of class yet the caste-system—as distinguished from caste—recognizes a class system which is somewhat different from the graded status referred to above. Just as Hindus are divided into so many castes, castes are divided into different classes of castes. The Hindu is caste conscious. He is also class conscious. Whether he is caste conscious or class conscious depends on the caste with which he comes in conflict. If the caste with which he comes in conflict is a caste within the class to which he belongs he is caste conscious. If the caste is outside the class to which he belongs he is class conscious. Anyone who needs any evidence on this point may study the Non-Brahmin Movement in the Madras and the Bombay Presidency. Such a study will leave no doubt that to a Hindu caste periphery is as real as class periphery and caste consciousness is as real as class consciousness (Rodrigues 2002: 104).

One area where the predominant role of caste is clearly seen is that of marriage alliances. But here, within caste, preferences are nuanced by class. As Ambedkar has written, class awareness is both distinct from caste awareness as also inter-related, depending on the context. In this book, I have sought to illustrate how economic outcomes are shaped by caste, even after all other attributes, including class, have been accounted for.

Of course, as the voluminous research on caste demonstrates, as an institution it has several other facets that merely an economic investigation, which mainly focuses on standard of living indicators, occupational structure, and market outcomes, will not be able to capture. It has been viewed very differently by different observers: either as a system of reciprocity (the *jajmani* system) or as a system that formalizes exploitation and inequality.[5] Then, of course, there is the larger question of the meaning of caste, a detailed analysis of which is outside the area of expertise of this author. There is a belief that the British efforts to categorize Indians into fixed identities of religion and caste ended up essentializing these categories into static, timeless,

---

[5] See Chapter 2 for extracts from thinkers such as Jotirao Phule and B.R. Ambedkar on the exploitative nature of the caste system.

and rigid boxes, instead of the fluid and dynamic categories that they were on the ground. This exercise prevented an understanding of the important ways through which castes changed: through fission as well as fusion. The popular notion, especially among non-Indians, of a static 3000-year-old immutable dinosaur called 'caste', ostensibly immune to any change, is a legacy of the colonial conception of caste.

A variant of this view argues that caste is actually a colonial 'invention', that the British forced their subjects, who would naturally identify themselves in very diverse ways, to adhere to a common categorization of caste. Dirks (2003: 5) argues that:

[C]aste (as we know it today) is a modern phenomenon, that it is, specifically, the product of a historical encounter between India and Western colonial rule .... It was under the British that 'caste' became a single term capable of expressing, organizing, and above all 'systematizing' India's diverse forms of social identity, community and organization .... In short, colonialism made caste what it is today.

The arguments about the role of the British state apparatus in shaping caste identities into a fixed format are compelling; however, the writings of D.D. Kosambi, Jotirao Phule (discussed in Chapter 2), and most of all, Ambedkar, very firmly establish the reality of the caste system pre-dating the British, admittedly more fluid and less rigid than what the British imagined it to be. Also, the relationship between colonial rule and the caste system has many dimensions, some of which have been discussed in Chapters 2 and 3: the British quest to view it as a system of racial divisions; the 'liberating' role of colonial rule in that it provided the untouchables access to English language education, and so forth.[6] So, overall, the impact of the British rule on the caste system is complex and multi-dimensional, and this book touches on some aspects of this complicated relationship.

(IR)RELEVANCE OF CASTE?

There is, in fact, an obituary of caste written by none other than one of the titans of Indian sociology and one of the most significant

[6] The role of English as a liberating force continues to be raised even today. See, for example, Chandra Bhan's campaign to portray English as the new Dalit goddess, available at http://blogs.wsj.com/indiarealtime/2010/04/30/a-dalit-temple-to-goddess-english/tab/article/, accessed on 8 May 2010.

contributors to the study of caste, M.N. Srinivas (2003). He argues that the subsistence economy of rural India, dependent on the *jati*-based division of labour, is the 'essence of caste'. As this is rapidly breaking down, it 'augurs the end of a social order which has continued for 2000 years or more'. He thus suggests that 'production will become freed from jati-based division of labour, economic relations will become autonomous and grain payments will be replaced by cash. Indian rural society will move, or is moving, from status to contract.' The extent of each of these changes is empirically verifiable, and prima facie this statement seems to be a fairly accurate description of the system of production. However, in what exact ways this has altered the workings of the caste system needs to be studied.

The reality, as any serious observer of India can tell, is that caste has changed tremendously over time. So much so that many, especially those with exposure only to the metropolitan cities, believe that for all practical purposes it is virtually dead. It could be argued, for instance, that the fewer overt instances of untouchability in urban areas than in the more traditional rural settings demonstrate that caste is increasingly irrelevant. However, that should be the least of the outcomes expected in a society in which untouchability has been formally abolished for six decades. What is astonishing is the extent of untouchability that continues to be practised in the country, even in urban settings, despite its abolition after Independence, the bulk of which is unreported and goes unpublished. Caste-based matrimonial alliances continue to be more the rule than the exception, even among otherwise westernized, modern, apparently caste-blind youth. The agitations against caste-based reservations in education and employment that are predominantly urban-based, display a very high level of caste consciousness and use overtly casteist slogans and acts of protest, thus putting a question mark on the supposed 'castelessness' of urban India.

In rural India, despite the breakdown of the traditional subsistence economy, caste seems to be making its strong presence felt in many different dimensions. Shah et al. (2006: 15) document untouchability in rural India, based on the results of an extensive survey carried out over 2001–2 in 565 villages across 11 states. They find that untouchability is not only present all over rural India, but it has 'survived by adapting to new socio-economic realities and taking on new and insidious forms'.

The extra-judicial power that caste panchayats exercise, particularly in the domain of inter-caste romantic/matrimonial alliances, is additional proof of the lasting relevance of caste. It also gives considerable ground for pessimism, if abolition of caste is at all a goal. In the battle between the presumed caste codes, as defined by their self-appointed guardians, and modern legislation, the latter might never win, although at the time of writing, there seems to be some movement towards trimming the tentacles of the notorious and dreaded *khap* panchayats in Haryana that routinely award death sentence to all those who flout the caste norms for marriage. Politics, of course, is inextricably intertwined with issues around caste identities and there is no reason to believe that the two will be dissociated any time soon.

Thus, evidence points more to the enduring relevance of caste categories, rather than to its increasing irrelevance. It would, therefore, not be an exaggeration to argue that caste remains a powerful and potent force in Indian society, decisively shaping the contours of social and political development. Here again, Srinivas (2003: 459) takes the view that while the caste system is dying, individual castes are flourishing. He discusses the post-independence mobilization of people on the basis of ethnicity and caste, and how this has resulted in the 'horizontal stretch' of caste. Thus, he suggests, what are called castes today are more accurately clusters of (agnate) sub-castes that have come together for 'better access to such scarce resources as political power, economic opportunities, government jobs and professional education'. While this would be true for a group of castes, there is another way to assess the degree of change in the caste system. As Chapter 2 discusses, caste has been viewed as a system that formalizes exploitation, rather than as a benign division of labour or as a system of reciprocity. It can be argued that the real key to the degree of change in the caste system is the degree of change in the conditions of those who are its worst sufferers—the (ex-) untouchables. As long as the three dimensions of untouchability—exclusion, humiliation, and exploitation—continue to persist, we cannot declare the caste system to be dead.

The claim in this book is *not* that an economic investigation alone can capture these myriad expressions of caste, but simply that it can provide crucial insights into the material aspects of disparity and into the degree of change, say, in the caste–occupation nexus, and assist in outlining the contours of discrimination in the modern Indian economy. Thus, even though this volume focuses on a subset of issues related to caste, specifically those related to caste and the economy, the belief is that this could make potentially useful interventions in policy debates, such as that over affirmative action.

SCOPE OF THE BOOK

This volume is based primarily on my own academic inquiry over the last decade into the nature of contemporary caste inequalities in India. The volume takes a macro, all-India view, with full recognition of the regional and sub-regional variations. I am entirely aware of the pitfalls of a macro picture: important nuances might get swept under the broad brushstrokes. However, outlining the larger picture has its own strengths, the most important being that it provides an overall perspective within which one can analyse any specific case: whether it confirms the broad picture or questions it.

The individual chapters, in addition to taking stock of the state of literature on specific topics, summarize and rephrase several of my papers that appeared in various economics journals. Since each of the papers tells only a part of the story, in weaving them together as a narrative, a lot of other material got added that is not previously published. The idea was that the findings of a large body of research, hitherto scattered in specialized subject journals, available only to a select audience of a few economists, be made accessible to a wider audience, adding to the corpus of inter-disciplinary research on caste identities and discrimination. Since the target audience of the volume includes, but is wider than, only economists, there are no technical details: readers interested in greater detail can easily access the original papers. Given the caveat stated earlier, that an economic investigation cannot fully capture all the facets of caste inequality, it is important to emphasize that the findings contained in this volume have to be read in conjunction with very important findings emerging from a host of other studies, especially the rich insights from smaller fieldwork-based accounts. Equally importantly, this volume fills an important lacuna in discussions of caste in other disciplines, and thus the hope is that it will contribute to an enrichment of inter-disciplinary discussions on caste, by providing some critical pieces of the jigsaw puzzle.

Chapter 2 summarizes and critically discusses the few economic theories that specifically investigate how social identity can impact economic outcomes and why we might encounter discrimination in market settings. This is not a trivial question at all, as both in the classical/neo-classical world as well as in several other heterodox traditions (for example, the Marxian), the social identity of the economic agent should not matter. In mainstream neo-classical theories, profit maximizing firms have no reason to distinguish between black and white or male and female (or upper-caste and lower-caste) workers. Most theoretical writings in economics have replaced 'he' with 'she' in referring to economic agents. That satisfies the constraints of political correctness; however, the point is that the results of the model do not change as 'he' becomes a 'she'. In other words, the social identity of the agent is not critical to the results of the model. Analogously, in a typical Marxist analysis, class would be the primary analytical category and social identities like caste and religion would be considered part of the superstructure that would get obliterated as class consciousness is strengthened.

However irrational they might seem to some, the unfortunate but hard reality all over the world is that identities do matter, and significantly so. Chapter 2 presents the economic theories, incidentally put forth within the neo-classical framework, which bring home the fact that discrimination is perfectly compatible with market orientation and with profit maximization, and that models based on discriminating agents also reach an equilibrium, albeit a different and sub-optimal (that is, not Pareto optimal) one, as compared to the equilibrium in an economy with no discrimination. Most importantly, these theories provide a motivation about why 'rational' economic agents might discriminate.

The Western imagination, familiar as it is with racial (skin colour-phenotype) divisions, has consistently sought to locate the racial roots of caste distinctions. The British systematically probed this connection, fairly convinced that there was indeed a racial basis to caste divisions. That quest threw up a very interesting body of writings on the connections between race and caste. I examine some of this literature also in Chapter 2, not so much because it has a direct bearing on the economic outcomes in contemporary India, which is the real theme of this volume, but more because my travels and interactions with audiences in several parts of the world have made me realize that the racial theory of caste continues to draw adherents, not only among non-Indians, but also among a section of educated Indians who are acutely aware of racial distinctions and the social construction of race. Thus, part of the motivation in understanding the race–caste connection (or the lack of it) was just the desire to set the record straight, as it were.[7] However, as my work on caste discrimination continued, I was very glad to have spent some time understanding the research on the question fairly early on. The belief in the racial theory of caste gives rise to a specific understanding about how caste manifests itself in contemporary, modern, anonymous settings: the simple belief, for example, that a dark-skinned person is more likely to be of 'low' caste. Chapter 6 discusses some of my research geared towards uncovering the exact pathways through which caste asserts itself, which are at variance with what would emerge if the racial theory of caste were to be valid. In other words, while caste is not ascriptive, it can be determined very easily, albeit not visually.

Chapter 3 outlines contours of caste disparity in modern, contemporary India, evidence that seriously questions the belief that caste is irrelevant in globalizing India. I present evidence spread over the last 20 years, using the largest two data sets after the national census, on a variety of indicators of material well-being. I have aggregated some of these indicators into a 'Caste Development Index' (CDI). This index, as well as other indicators, clearly shows substantial regional variation, but no reversal of traditional caste hierarchies. Those who believe in the relevance of caste (I am not referring to the apologists of the caste system, but to those who believe that it continues to be strong) might argue this is common knowledge, and thus question the

---

[7] I edited a volume called *Boundaries of Clan and Color: Transnational Comparisons of Inter-group Disparity* in 2003, along with William Darity, Jr. During the course of that exercise, I was engaged in several long-drawn-out discussions on the race–caste connection, which prompted me to read the literature on this subject, even though it is not a question that economists are particularly concerned about. The major achievement of that exercise was to drive home the fact that while there are inter-group disparities in all parts of the world, there are some that are colour/phenotype-based and others that are not. This understanding, backed by some systematic reading, gave that volume its title.

value that Chapter 3 adds to the corpus of knowledge. However, as will be clear, the chapter does not reinvent the wheel, but instead engages with the more recent, fairly widespread belief that the traditional caste hierarchy is now turning on its head and those who were marginalized earlier are no longer so: thus, the belief is that linear hierarchies are giving way to competing equalities.[8]

Chapter 3 also examines the relationship between the regional distribution of the CDI and the rate of growth of state domestic product, to address the question whether disparities are lower in richer or faster-growing states? In other words, if the size of the pie gets larger, does everyone's share remain the same (that is, the total amount for each group increases, but their proportion of the total remains the same), or do the disadvantaged castes increase their share? If the latter were to be true, then affirmative action would be considerably less important, might even be redundant, and the policy focus could be on increasing the rate of growth. It turns out that this straightforward, non-controversial, and intuitively appealing solution to reducing group disparities would not work because of the absence of a clear-cut relationship between disparities and economic growth.

What happens when there are multiple identities? Most Indians have several simultaneous identities, so the question is very obviously relevant to anyone working on India; academically, 'intersectionality' is indeed an important concept that underlies the global discourse around identity. Disentangling the web of identities into which an average Indian is trapped would be a Herculean task, if at all possible. However, a few of the strands can, and ought to, be picked up and studied. The focus of my research on multiple identities has been on the overlap between caste and gender, again focusing on the empirical dimension. It is worth emphasizing that my engagement with the gender question is not via gender disparities per se (that is, between men and women; several volumes could be written on those alone), not because I believe them to be any less important or serious, but because the overlap of identities is of special relevance to my enquiry. Chapter 4 reports the evidence on the changing nature of that overlap.

In addition to economic indicators, Chapter 4 also reports on the evidence on women's autonomy and decision-making ability within

---

[8] See, for example, Gupta (2004).

the household and on domestic violence, based on two rounds of a large survey. I use this latter evidence to directly address the question, relevant in the context of the caste–gender overlap, of the classic, oft-discussed trade-off: between material prosperity and immurement. Several micro-studies and anthropological accounts have demonstrated how upper-caste women, though materially more prosperous, face a large number of taboos on public visibility and inegalitarian spousal relations. Conversely, women from the disadvantaged castes are trapped in poverty but have relatively greater freedom in terms of public visibility and comparatively more egalitarian spousal relations. Examining data on indicators of material standard of living (aggregated across the 'Gender–Caste Development Index') along with that on autonomy reveals an interesting recent development: that several of the disadvantaged castes, as a part of the process of 'Sanskritization', seem to have adopted greater constraints on women as a part of their efforts to emulate upper-caste behaviour. Thus, recent evidence suggests that the trade-off is vanishing and women from castes lowest in the hierarchy are trapped in a cesspool of poverty, deprivation, and reduced autonomy.

Chapter 5 moves from disparity to discrimination to specifically explore the question of how economists define discrimination and how it can be measured in the labour market. It should be noted that while the quantitative estimation of labour market discrimination is based on Gary Becker's theory of 'taste for discrimination' (examined in Chapter 2), now all empirically inclined researchers (whether economists or sociologists) use these methods. The primary method is called the 'decomposition method' and is fully explained in Chapter 5. Basically, the idea is to focus on the gap in average wages/earnings between social groups. Through an econometric technique, the researcher decomposes the wage gap between groups in order to determine how much of the gap is explained by differential group characteristics or endowments and how much is due to discrimination. The chapter also discusses the critiques of this method and examines additional new techniques, such as correspondence and audit studies, which are being used to gauge the extent of discriminatory attitudes and their manifestations during economic interactions. Clearly, there is no perfect technique that could exactly measure a problem so complicated; it is interesting and instructive to understand the various methods that are continuously being evolved. It turns out that together these methods throw up a whole body of very rich and insightful literature that illustrates the pathways through which discrimination manifests itself.

MODERNITY, MERIT, AND AFFIRMATIVE ACTION

I have been fortunate to have been associated with three pioneering exercises related to the exploration of discrimination in urban labour markets in India, each with implications for affirmative action. The latter is a critical aspect of engagement with disparity and discrimination; after having established the presence of both these phenomena, the natural question is: what is to be done?

The first of these exercises, discussed in Chapter 6, was a state-of-the-art, first-of-its-kind study of urban, formal sector labour markets, designed by a team from Princeton University and conducted by the Indian Institute of Dalit Studies over 2005–7. The study had four components: one, the larger, macro picture, decomposing the wage gap between caste groups in urban labour markets, based on the largest all-India data set (Madheswaran and Attewell 2007). This study established that a significant part of the wage gap was due to discrimination: when all wage-earning characteristics are controlled for, there is still a residual, unexplained gap in wage earnings that can be taken to be a measure of discrimination. The second paper was a correspondence study conducted in Delhi, where fake resumes were sent to different private sector employers. Several matching sets of resumes were sent, where everything was identical, except the caste and religious identity of the applicant. The call backs from the companies were then analysed to test whether employers distinguish between identically skilled or equally meritorious candidates on the basis of their identity. It turned out that social or group identity does matter, even when there is no significant difference in the qualifications of the applicant (Thorat and Attewell 2007).

The third study was a college-to-work study (Deshpande and Newman 2007), where we tracked a group of students who graduated from three Delhi-based elite universities. These cohorts of students were similarly qualified and received the same quality of education; thus, from the point of view of the labour market, embodied similar 'merit'. We conducted a baseline survey on the eve of their graduation, eliciting responses about their expectations from the labour market and their notions about ideal jobs. We then tracked them for two years, with periodic follow-up interviews, and documented their experiences in the labour market and the jobs they finally landed. Most of our respondents went into the private sector, and thus these follow-up interviews revealed the process through which the social identity (caste or religion) ends up shaping the final outcome in the labour market. It is important to note that these are jobs that do not require a formal declaration of caste status, since there is no affirmative action in the private sector. Thus, these settings are supposed to be anonymous and meritocratic, and yet the outcomes are strongly shaped by social identity.

The fourth component of the larger study was an employer attitude survey (Jodhka and Newman 2007), designed to gauge what private employers in the formal, modern sector look for when they are hiring. This study confirms the findings of the other three exercises. Employers talk the language of merit and confess a deep faith solely in the merit of the applicant. However, they also believe that merit is distributed along lines of caste, religious, and gender divisions. Nowhere do employers see this as discrimination: it is as if they were describing a neutral and unbiased state of the world. Chapter 6 presents the evidence from these four pioneering studies, along with a discussion of some of the other emerging evidence on urban labour markets, and together presents a picture of enduring discrimination in urban labour markets.

AFFIRMATIVE ACTION

Chapter 7 contains a discussion of the Indian affirmative action (AA) programme, which primarily takes the form of caste-based quotas. However, AA need not be quota-based, and indeed there are many forms that AA takes across the world and is also known by different names: affirmative action (the US and Northern Ireland); positive action (UK), employment equity (Canada), Black empowerment (South Africa), reservation (India), preferences (Malaysia), and so forth. The interesting feature of debates around AA is that irrespective of the form that it takes, the anti-AA arguments are remarkably similar across contexts and histories that are widely dissimilar.[9] Typically, AA is seen as interfering in labour markets that are presumed to be meritocratic and efficient in the absence of AA. Chapter 6 demolishes the myth of meritocratic labour markets in the case of India; there are other similar studies for other countries.

Unlike in the US context, which has produced empirical studies of the productivity impact of AA, for India not a single study existed that empirically examined the relationship between AA and efficiency or productivity of the enterprise. The lack of a study, of course, never prevented anyone from making definitive claims about the negative effects of AA. The first effort to redress this gap is a study by Deshpande and Weisskopf (2010)—the second pioneering exercise that I have been associated with—discussed in Chapter 7. Examining data from the Indian Railways for 23 years over eight zones, we find that AA has no adverse effect on productivity or total output. In some cases, the presence of quota employees in the highest decision-making jobs has a positive impact, confirming the results from several of the US studies.

In India, empirical studies face a peculiar problem. While the AA programme is caste-based, the Indian census does not collect data by jati (caste)—see Chapter 2 for exact definition. The last jati-based census was in 1931. Since then, the idea of collecting jati data in the census has been fiercely debated and was rejected till recently the government modified its earlier stand. It appears that the 2011 census will have a separate exercise to gather caste data. However, the manner in which this would be done remains unclear and thus, the reliability of the figures that this exercise would yield is a moot point. Given the absence of reliable data, claims and counter-claims abound with very little meeting ground. The problem is that preferential schemes (whether quotas or in any other form) cannot be accepted unless they are based on reliable data, and reliable data cannot be collected for fear of exacerbating caste feelings. Interestingly, this argument (that collection of caste data will divide an otherwise homogeneous society) does not get invoked in the context of other social categories. For example, religion and language can be considered (and indeed have been) divisive, but the government has not stopped collecting

---

[9] For a flavour of the debates around AA in the international context, see, for example, Sowell (2004), Coate and Loury (1993), and Bowen and Bok (1998).

data on these, nor is there a serious argument that the collection of data on religious affiliation is responsible for increasing religious animosity. Given that the last census (2001) did not collect data on Other Backward Classes (OBCs), the best estimate of OBCs is available from the National Sample Survey (NSS) data (61st round, 2004–5), which indicates that overall close to 41 per cent of the population self-declares itself to be OBCs.

Given the multitude of group divisions in the country, the quota-based approach, even if it worked well, has its limitations. It is not possible to have quotas to represent all the marginalized groups. However, persistent lack of representation can cause alienation, with serious adverse consequences for social stability. It was, therefore, a privilege when in 2008 I was asked to be one of the authors of the 'diversity index' as an index to measure and increase representation in public spaces, especially of the minority groups. This index, discussed in Chapter 7, was designed to measure diversity across several dimensions: caste, gender, and religion, in the sphere of education, employment, and housing. We proposed a formula to enable each institution to calculate a diversity index, with the idea that over time, institutions should register a rise in the value of their specific index. We also suggested a system of financial rewards and penalties (via subsidies and taxes) which would be the incentive structure that would make the index self-enforcing. The index, thus, is flexible, incorporates the specific institutional structure/constraints, and contains built-in incentives. It can, therefore, be seen as an alternative form of AA, which avoids the somewhat mechanical features of the quota system. However, the operationalization of the index is not yet on the policy agenda.

Finally, the volume does not contain any overarching conclusions, other than to suggest that a multifaceted dialogue geared towards ending inequalities based on birth and descent needs to be forged urgently. It is time that the economics of caste gets linked to the politics, sociology, and the history of it. This volume is an effort in that direction.

2 Theories of Discrimination and Caste

DEFINING CASTE INEQUALITY

To start with the very basics, caste in English translates into two distinct concepts—the *varna* and the *jati*. Briefly, the varna system divided the ancient Hindu society into initially four, later five, distinct varnas that are mutually exclusive, hereditary, endogamous, and occupation-specific: Brahmin (priests and teachers), Kshatriya (warriors and royalty), Vaisya (traders, merchants, moneylenders), and Shudra (those engaged in menial, lowly jobs), and those doing the most despicable menial jobs, the *Atishudra* or the former 'untouchables'. Whether it is appropriate to consider the Atishudras as a part of the varna system is a moot point, as they are the *avarana*s (the lowliest of the low, so low that they are considered unfit to even be given a varna), in contrast to the *savarna*s (those with a varna). Thus, the Atishudras were a part of the varna system by being excluded from it.

However, the operative category that determines the contemporary social code is the jati. There exist over 6,000 jatis that are also called castes (and share the basic characteristics of the varna), but they follow a much more complex system of hierarchy and rules of conduct towards each other. In reality, the varnas provide a scale of status to which the jatis try to align themselves. If there existed a one-to-one correspondence between the two, jatis would reduce to mere subsets of the varnas. However, this scale turns out to be fluid and ambiguous for a whole range of jatis as they present claims and counter-claims of their varna affiliations (Kothari 1997: 62). Srinivas (2003) refers to the 'frequent disagreement' regarding the position of a jati in the rank order: between the rank that the jati claims for itself and the rank conceded by others.

More than 50 million Indians belong to tribal communities which are distinct from Hindu caste society. These are the Adivasis, who have origins that precede the Aryans and even the Dravidians of the south. Many have lifestyles and languages that are distinct from any of the known communities in India. Singh (1994) identifies 461 tribal communities in India and finds that they are derived from all four racial stock: Negrito (Great Andamanese, Onges, and Jarawas), Proto-Australoid (Munda, Oraon, and Gond), Mongoloid (tribes of the north-east), and Caucasoid (Toda, Rabri, and Gujjar). However, he emphasizes that concern with racial typology has given way to the study of genetic and morphological traits of the tribal population, but existing data are too meagre to permit any generalization and that typically, different population groups that are a part of the region exhibit homogeneity of traits.

Most tribals, being local communities, see their identity at the local level, at most, the state level. Only 10 per cent see themselves as national communities. Tribes have a rich oral tradition, the documentation of which has helped researchers to understand several aspects of their lives. Tribes have generally remained outside the varna system. Singh (1994) reports that only 12 per cent recognize their place in it, and another 32 per cent are even aware of the varna system. Of those who recognize their place in it, roughly 8 per cent claim to be Kshatriya, 7.5 per cent Shudra, and 0.9 per cent Brahmin. However, Ghurye (1963) points to the close similarities between tribals and Hinduism. In terms of the self-perception of a tribal community in the regional hierarchy, 27 per cent see themselves as high status, 47 per cent see themselves as middle, and roughly 25 per cent see themselves as low. This perception, however, is not shared by others in the region. Others see 11 per cent of the tribals as high, 39 per cent as middle, and 49 per cent as low (Singh 1994). This confirms the picture of marginalization of most tribal communities, which emerges from data (reported in Chapter 3).

Tribal groups share some similarities with jatis in that almost all tribals are endogamous and tribal communities have a notion of hierarchy based on ecology, descent, ranking, status, and so on. Tribal social organization recognizes principles of division into clans and lineages which regulate sex and marriage. Despite some similarities, some of the specific areas where the tribals can clearly be distinguished from Hinduism are: the dominant form of tribal family is nuclear (91 per cent), divorce is permitted (93.2 per cent), and remarriage of widows (96 per cent) and divorcees (90 per cent) is allowed. On the whole, even though the tribals report their main religion as Hinduism or Christianity, and some report more than one religion, there is sufficient heterogeneity and distinctiveness within tribal communities that they cannot be considered a part of the varna system.

Since caste divisions are not dichotomous, the meaning of caste inequality is not obvious analytically. Are we advocating pair-wise comparisons, technically possible for the varnas, but quite mind-boggling for the jatis? And, for the former, if people report the jati as their caste, then we are left with the Herculean task of unravelling the complexity of the web of relationships between individual jatis and their varna counterparts, assuming rather heroically that this is within the realm of possibilities. Or, are we making a plea for forcing a hierarchical ordering of the jatis based on an economic criterion alone, for example, on the basis of a definition of standard of living?[1] I would like to suggest a third course: that we can characterize inequality by focusing on the sharpest contradiction, that is, between those at the top and those at the bottom of the caste pyramid (using either the jati or the varna criterion). Unfortunately, the nature of data availability does not allow us to do that directly. In national data sets up to the mid-1990s, there are three broad 'caste' divisions: the Scheduled Castes (SCs), Scheduled Tribes (STs), and Others (everyone else).[2] Data sets

---

[1] This would be highly questionable, given the debate surrounding the validity of a strict hierarchical ordering of castes (see, for instance, Dumont 1980; Gupta 1984; and Chatterjee 1997, to get a flavour of the debate).

[2] At the time of formulating the affirmative action policy, jatis and tribes that were economically the weakest and historically subjected to discrimination and deprivation were identified in a government schedule as the target group of the reservation policy. These were called the SCs and STs. The former untouchable castes often identify themselves by the original Sanskrit, now Marathi, word Dalit (meaning 'the oppressed'), employed as a term of pride. While the SC/ST nomenclature has grown

after the mid-1990s further divide the 'Others' into Other Backward Classes (OBCs) and the remaining 'Others'. The national census is the exception to this, as the latest census (2001) continued to adhere to the three-way division. This volume goes to press on the eve of the 2011 census and despite the formal announcement of a caste census, there continues to be a cloud of uncertainty over it.

The objection to this classification is that these omnibus categories attempt to club a diverse set of jatis into one label that further essentializes these categories. Some would even argue, legitimately so, that these categories are meaningless, particularly the 'Others', as no Indian would self-identify her/himself as an 'Other'. Analytically, however, this three/four-way division of the data is appealing for its simplicity and for its amenability to computations. While clearly 'Others' is an unnatural, residual category, the same is not true of SC and ST categories. With all the disparity *within* them, the SCs are united in suffering the stigma of untouchability, or share a common 'stigmatized ethnic identity'.[3] The weakness of this broad classificatory scheme lies in *underestimating* the relative disadvantage of the SCs, since the 'Others' is a very large, heterogeneous category containing a whole range of castes, including jatis that are socially and economically not necessarily very distinct from the SCs. Nevertheless, if empirical studies establish inter-caste disparity between SCs and 'Others', then it is reasonable to infer an even greater disparity between castes at the two polar ends.

It is important at this point to remind ourselves that while the caste system is conventionally associated with Hinduism, all religions in India, including Islam and Christianity, display inter-group disparity akin to a caste system, leading to the hypothesis that perhaps caste was a system of social stratification in pre-modern South Asia. This is also true for the so-called egalitarian religions such as Buddhism. 'The term "Brahmana" of the Vedas is accepted by the Buddhists as a term for a saint, one who has attained final sanctification' (Radhakrishnan 2004: 177).[4] Thus, Buddhism makes a distinction between Brahmins

---

out of government policy, Dalit is a more loosely defined social category. I use both the words in the book, and the context makes their usage clear.

[3] See Berreman (1971) and Thorat (1979).

[4] Radhakrishnan (2004: 177) quotes J.G. Jennings: 'It should never be forgotten that Buddhism is a reformed Brahmanism, as is evidenced by the invariably honorific

and others. This is ironic, since Buddhism has been embraced by the stigmatized castes in large numbers with the belief that it will provide them with the equality that Hinduism denies them. Occasionally, Dalit castes (the 'untouchables') have converted to other religions, including Christianity and Islam, as an escape from discrimination and exclusion. However, such conversions do not necessarily guarantee social equality; for instance, the census label 'neo-Buddhist' indicates an ex-untouchable who has converted to Buddhism. Since this is common knowledge, it is unlikely that the social position of this person will improve significantly.

CASTE AND RACE

The caste system has fascinated Western scholarship that often sees direct parallels between racial divisions in colour-segregated societies and the caste divisions in India. While several of the manifestations of racism and casteism are identical, especially towards those at the receiving end, I would like to reaffirm the idea that there are fundamental differences between race and caste as social categories.[5] Attempts to draw parallels between race and caste have a long history, going back to the British efforts to classify castes by the alleged racial commonalities within each caste. While there are many similarities between racism and casteism as ideologies or institutions, race and caste themselves are distinct and dissimilar. To begin with, the histories of the two systems differ vastly. Racism is a direct product of slavery under colonialism: the ascriptive differences between the slaves and their masters were extended to defining group characteristics. It is important to note that the negative stereotyping of blacks truly begins with capitalism and is consolidated during colonialism.

Caste, on the other hand, represents a system of social stratification that predates colonialism by centuries. Prominent scholars of the caste system have decidedly rejected the racial theory of caste. Ketkar (1909/2002: 78) criticizes the 'invention of racial lines in the present varna system of Hindu society made by European scholars on the basis

---

use which Gautama makes of the title "Brahmin" and it therefore takes for granted certain Vedic or Vedantic postulates.'

[5] See Béteille (1971) for a concise and lucid review of the differences as well as the similarities between the two systems.

of Vedic literature'. Mincing no words, he says, 'I shall be very sorry if a superficial acquaintance with a half-developed and hybrid ethnology, and a wrong interpretation of ancient documents, and an invented tradition, should result in magnifying racial differences and in making the future consolidation and amalgamation of India more difficult and distant' (ibid.: 79). Ambedkar, in his essay 'Castes in India', suggests that 'European students of caste have unduly emphasised the role of colour in the caste system. Themselves impregnated by colour prejudices, they very readily imagined it to be the chief factor in the caste problem. But nothing can be further from the truth' (Rodrigues 2002: 261). In another essay 'Annihilation of Caste', he goes on to argue that the 'caste system is a social division of people of the same race' (ibid.: 265). A discussion of racial theory of caste inevitably involves forays into the historical origins of the caste system as well as into anthropological features of jatis; while an entire monograph could be devoted just to this topic, I am attempting here a brief summary of the issue, making reference to some of the historical literature.

In Western Europe and in the Americas, skin colour (and phenotype), or what is popularly known as 'race', forms the basis of group disparities. Even though it is established that there is greater variation in phenotype and appearance within races than between them, the concept of race has proved to be a powerful tool that is used to keep the minorities in these societies segregated, discriminated against, and oppressed. In a country that celebrates its multiculturalism, Canada's use of the term 'visible minorities' makes this distinction explicit. Visible are those whose skin colour is not white; the 1986 Employment Equity Act designated the visible minorities and other groups such as women, disabled persons as facing discrimination in the labour market. As it turns out, the racial/ethnic differentiation picture in Canada is complex and the single umbrella term of 'visible minorities' does not capture the multifaceted nature of discrimination in the labour market. However, the fact remains that skin colour or phenotype forms a crucial group marker.

However, not all ethnic disparities and conflicts in the world are based on skin colour. Take for instance, conflicts that have been particularly bloody and violent, such as those in Rwanda, Sri Lanka, or Israel, or the Ethiopian conflict that led to the formation of Eritrea. In fact, in case of African countries, ethnic conflicts not involving a group of European descent are between groups whose identities are not based on skin colour. Indeed, even in Europe, the Balkan crisis does not originate in race-based conflicts. Both in Singapore and Malaysia, inter-group disparity is based on national origins. Thus, in non-colour-based societies, the conflicting groups are not defined on the basis of skin colour or race but are based upon other social categories—religion, nationality, or other ethnic groupings. In such societies, skin colour is considered more an individual attribute than a group characteristic. Thus, it is entirely possible in these societies that individual distinctions in skin colour are noticed or that they might be considered an attribute of beauty, but the 'defining' character of social groups is not their common skin colour.

The history of present-day India does not offer straightforward answers to why the caste system ought to be colour-coded. The racial theory of Indian civilization is a formation of the late nineteenth century, when 'in the wake of slave emancipation, white–black relations in the Anglo-Saxon world were being restructured with ideological support from a rush of racial essentialism' (Trautmann 1997: 208). Another reason that the theory is erroneous is that the Indus valley civilization predates the arrival of the Aryan-speaking people; so to argue that the 'Indian' civilization is the product of the conflict between lighter skinned Aryans and darker skinned aborigines is misleading. Dealing a blow to the Aryan–Dravidian dichotomy, Ketkar (1909/2002: 169–70) argues that 'all the people of India today with the probable exception of the Bengalese [sic] and the north eastern frontier tribes are people of the Caucasian race ... excepting in the complexion [sic], the Dravidians do not differ very much from the Caucasians of Europe'. He also reminds us that the 'conquering tribe will be of a higher caste, whether it is an "Aryan" or a "Dravidian" tribe; the conquered tribes also may be of Aryan race, still it would be of low caste, because it is a conquered tribe' (ibid.: 170).

However, the racial theory of the Indian civilization was extended to the formulation of the racial theory of caste.[6] One important basis of the racial theory of caste is that one of the meanings of 'varna' is hue, and is often interpreted as skin colour. However, there is no evidence

---

[6] See Klass (1980) for an excellent critical review of the theories of the origins of the caste system.

to suggest that the varnas are racially different among themselves. Trautmann (1997: 211) analyses the British colonial quest:

In this fantastic back-projection of systems of racial segregation in the American South and in South Africa onto early Indian history, the relations of the British 'new invader from Europe' with the peoples of India is prefigured thousands of years before by the invading Aryans. But what the British encountered was not their Aryan brethren, as Max Mueller wanted to have it, but a 'mingled population' toward whom a supposed perduring prejudice of whites against interracial sexual relations (or rather a perduring mixture of repulsion and desire) structured those relations in a certain hypergamous way.

Given the ongoing controversy around the origins of the caste system, a detailed assessment is outside the scope of this brief account. However, a few comments are in order. First, the historical origins of the caste system are fuzzy and it is *not* conclusively established that a system of social stratification did not exist prior to the Aryan invasion. The implication being: if something akin to the caste system existed among the generally dark-skinned aborigines, then skin colour would have not been the basis for the various social distinctions. It also helps to remember that Aryans were truly speaking a linguistic group and not a 'race' in the current sense of the term.[7] The racial theory of caste advocates that the Brahmin might have descended from the Aryan, thus explaining his superiority in the caste hierarchy. However, it is noteworthy that the Brahmin was a professional priest without parallel in Aryan tradition elsewhere; in later India, he acquired virtual monopoly of almost all rituals (Kosambi 1985). Also, given centuries of migration and inter-marriage, there is absolutely no evidence of one particular group being descendants of the Aryan-speaking people. The word 'arya' or 'arya putra' is sometimes found in the literature to refer to the royalty, who are not Brahmins but are typically Kshatriya (though not always; there have been important Shudra kings as well). Ketkar (1909/2002: 79) suggests that 'till the arrival of European scholars on Indian soil, the people of India never meant by the word "arya" that race of invaders who reduced the natives of the soil to servitude'.

[7] The notion of the 'Aryan Race' was created by the German Sanskritist Friedrich Max Mueller in the nineteenth century. While he consistently advocated the brotherhood of the Aryan peoples, the kinship between Indians and Europeans, interestingly, he never visited India. For a critical account of his two-race theory of India, see Trautmann (1997: chapter 6).

To make the picture more complicated, Kosambi (1985) traces the pre-Aryan features of Brahminism and also non-Aryan descent of several Brahmin castes. He suggests that the Brahmin priest was an unsupported individual, often on the tribal fringe. It is with his alliance with the warrior classes that the reorganization of the caste system begins. Kosambi (1985: 107) links this to a 'higher level of production, regular settlements, the inevitable decay of tribal organization with the rise of a new type of property'.

Second, the presumed skin colours of the four varnas that are found in the nineteenth-century discourse are difficult to justify: white for Brahmins, red for Kshatriya, yellow for Vaisyas, and black for Shudras. Klass (1980: 40) suggests that varna may not refer to complexion or supposed skin colour, but rather to some kind of spiritual colouration or aura. It is interesting to note that the *Manusmriti*, a text dated between fourth century BC and second century AD that outlines the basic differences between castes and sets forth a highly detailed caste code, has no reference to skin colour as being the basis of the ranking of castes.[8] Given that today there are over 3,000 jatis in existence, a jati–colour link is close to impossible to establish.

Third, the geographical variations in skin shade differences in India seem to dominate the caste differences.[9] India is a virtual ethnographic museum, as all the major racial types can be seen in different regions of the country. Referring to the Aryans, the Dravidians, the Mongolians, and the Scythians, Ambedkar suggests that 'these stocks of people came into India from various directions and with various cultures, centuries ago, when they were in a tribal state. They all in turn elbowed their entry into the country by fighting with the predecessors, and after a stomachful of it, settled down as peaceful neighbours' (Rodrigues 2002: 242). He goes on to argue that 'the caste system cannot be said to have grown as a means of preventing the admixture of races or as a means of maintaining purity of blood' and thus 'to hold that distinctions of caste are really distinctions of race and to treat different castes as though they were so many different races is a gross perversion of facts ...'. As a matter of fact, the caste system came into being long after the different races of India had comingled in blood and culture'

---

[8] See *The Laws of Manu*.

[9] See the introduction to the National Family Health Survey (NFHS 1992–3) for broad geographical patterns.

(ibid.: 265). Klass (1980) points out how skin colour and hair colour lighten as one moves from the south-east to the north-west of the country, and finds no reason to believe that this would have been otherwise 3,000 years ago.

In its attempt to 'prove' the racial theory of the Indian civilization, the British administration had commissioned investigations into the distinctions in skin shade and phenotypical features (such as length of the nose and cephalic index). Herbert Hope Risley (1851–1911), a member of the Indian Civil Service, who served in India from 1873 to 1910, was instrumental in concretizing the racial theory of caste vide the 1901 census report (*The People of India*) and a journal article, 'The Study of Ethnology in India' (1891). One of the most well-known statements of Risley is 'The social position of a caste varies inversely as its nasal index.' Trautmann (1997), after a detailed review of the contending theories and available evidence, concludes that 'both Risley and Max Mueller show a tendency to exaggerate the significance of noses in ancient Indian evidence' (Aryans presumably with long, leptorhine noses in conflict with a 'black snub nosed—platyrhine—race'). Klass (1980) points to the near impossibility of determining with certainty the skin colour and phenotype a given group might have had 3,000 to 5,000 years ago. Ghurye summarizes the conclusions of Risley's studies and reports that a systematic relationship between jati affiliation, skin colour, and phenotypical features cannot be drawn. He finds, for instance, that a Brahmin in Uttar Pradesh has more in common with a 'Chamar' (a Dalit caste) in Uttar Pradesh than with a Brahmin in Kerala. Ambedkar concurs: 'What racial affinity is there between the Brahmin of the Punjab and the Brahmin of Madras? ... what racial difference is there between the Brahmin of the Punjab and the Chamar of the Punjab?' (Rodrigues 2002: 265).

Thus, jati is not visually ascriptive in that it is not possible to identify the jati by simply looking at the individual. Thus, one important difference that emerges between caste and race is that it is not just the body that is the source of the understanding of the self. Is it then impossible to determine a stranger's jati? Often, though not always, jati is indicated by the last name (surname) of the person. However, naming conventions differ across the country: for instance, in the four southern states, traditionally, the first name is written last. Some individuals often drop their surnames and use generic names such as

Kumar, Lal, Singh, or Chowdhary that are not jati-specific. Even when jati is indicated by the last name, since jatis are regional categories, the same surname belongs to different jatis across (even within) states; moreover, it is impossible to remember the exact placement of over 3,000 categories. However, people have a way of ascertaining the jati of an individual if they want to—either directly or by discreet enquiry. But this requires some effort and the corresponding inclination, which is typically not made with respect to *each* person that one interacts with, but is made when it matters. Ascertaining jati in rural settings is not difficult. Chapter 6 discusses how jati could be determined in relatively anonymous urban settings, if one wanted to. For a system so all-pervasive, paradoxically, it is equally possible to have lifelong interactions with individuals without knowing their jati.

In other words, one can say that skin shade does not form the basis for social stratification in Indian society, whereas caste does. Thus, there is no socially recognized group of fair-skinned individuals in opposition to another group of darker individuals that would correspond to the established castes or religions.

Having said that, we have to recognize that having a lighter skin shade (Indians use the English word 'fair' rather than 'white', the latter term typically used for non-Indian 'whites') is considered an attribute of beauty. The gender angle used to be important here, in that while darkness in men was traditionally considered erotic, darkness in women is perceived as a handicap, especially in the arranged marriage scenario. Thus, one finds women using a range of beauty products—skin lotions, soaps, sunscreens, creams, etc.—which are geared towards 'lightening' the skin ('Fair and Lovely', 'Fairglow', etc.). As 'global' standards of beauty and fashion have invaded the Indian scene, fairness has become an attribute of physical desirability for men as well (reflected in skin-whitening creams for men, e.g., 'Fair and Handsome'), but this desire is mainly a consequence of the globalization of Western standards of beauty and is not the dominant norm to assess male beauty in the Indian tradition (seen, for instance, in the celebration of Krishna's dark-skinned sensuality). A look at the matrimonial advertisements reveals a preference for 'fair' brides *across castes and regions*. However, even here a careful analysis will indicate that caste, region, and class dominate over skin shade. In other words, the girl has to match these social requirements before her skin colour becomes an issue. From the set of girls that pass these social eligibility criteria, the fairer bride *may* be chosen. But the bottom line might end up being the amount of dowry forthcoming from the girl's family. Ceteris paribus, a higher dowry could outweigh a lighter skin shade with ease.

EARLY THEORIZING OF CASTE AND THE HINDU SOCIAL ORDER

Jotirao Phule (1827–90), the nineteenth-century social reformer from Maharashtra, was India's first systematic theoretician of caste and one of its most radical opponents. Religion and caste are at the centre of Phule's thought. He was opposed not only to the varna system, but almost everything within the Hindu belief system, as he believed that the Hindu texts (*Shrutis*, *Vedas*, and the *Smritis*) rationalized and perpetuated Brahmanical dominance.[10] His writings are scathing in their attack on Brahminism. He believed that 'Brahmanism was historical, constructed over time and since it was the ideology of oppression and dominance, it had to be opposed and ultimately smashed. There was nothing sacred or divine about it' (Deshpande 2002: 6). He did not make a distinction between varna and jati. He argued that since the Brahmin derived his authority not from his jati but his varna, it was important for the others to realize that they could fight this dominance only if they asserted their Shudra–Atishudra status. Thus, Phule's central point was that the Brahmanical system is bipolar and that caste or varna is a relationship of power and dominance and has to be attacked at that level. Of course, he was cognizant of the existence of several smaller jatis within the broader varna: 'The brahmans divided the shudras into various castes, punished or rewarded them according to their loyalty and established their control over them .... And are now enjoying themselves at the cost of the shudras' (ibid.: 45).

Phule's critique of caste encompasses both the socio-religious and the economic aspects. He saw caste 'both as a category in the productive process and as something that facilitated the dominance of Brahmins in the ideological sphere' (Deshpande 2009: 53). Deshpande (2009)

[10] He rarely used the word Hinduism, but used Brahmanism instead (Deshpande 2009: 48).

believes that for Phule, caste was a category that belonged to the base as well as the superstructure of the Indian society. If one accepts this reading of Phule, then apart from providing a contrast to the standard Marxist understanding that would regard affiliations other than class a part of the superstructure, Phule's characterization would also help explain the persistence of caste-based distinctions which seem to have weathered the various manifestations of the caste system over centuries. He writes about the laws of the varna system:

Their main object in fabricating ... falsehoods was to dupe the minds of the ignorant and to rivet firmly on them the chains of perpetual bondage and slavery which their selfishness and cunning had forged. The severity of the laws as affecting the Sudras, and the intense hatred with which they were regarded by the Brahmins can be explained by no other supposition but that there was, originally between the two, a deadly feud, arising ... from the advent of the latter into this land. ('Slavery', 1873, translated and reproduced in Deshpande 2002: 30)

Thus, he puts forward a theory about the origins of the varna system and caste conflict. There is a very strong economic element to Phule's writings. As would be expected from someone who was so committed to the cause of the Shudra–Atishudras, Phule was extremely concerned about agrarian issues and about the conditions of cultivators. He wrote extensively on the subject, including some very concrete suggestions related to irrigation, animal breeding, education of children of peasants, and the role of the state towards the small peasantry, which he felt were imperative to ameliorate the condition of the cultivators. What makes Phule's analysis of this oft-discussed topic (that is, conditions of the peasantry) unique is that he intertwines this assessment with his critique of Brahmanism by outlining, in meticulous detail, the various ways in which the Brahmins deprive the peasantry of its already meagre income (Deshpande 2009: 59). Phule's understanding of caste and village society, as of other Dalit thinkers, stands in direct contrast with Gandhi's views, as the following discussion illustrates.

In 'Cultivator's Whipcord' (1883, reprinted in Deshpande 2002: 120), he writes:

Now, the first type of letter-less farmer is so exploited by the brahman under the pretext of religion that it would be very hard to find a parallel example anywhere in the world. The ancient and cunning Arya brahman scripture-writers have so smoothly machinated to tie up the farmer in their selfish religion that even before he is born, when his mother gets her menses and the *garbhadaan* rituals[11] are performed, till he dies, various things are looted from him. Not only that, but even after he dies, his son has to bear the weight of religion for the *shraddha*[12] and other rituals.

Phule's detailed elaboration of the various ways in which Brahmins extracted farmers' incomes via rituals is only one aspect of his critique; he argued that another fundamental way in which Brahmins contributed to the impoverishment of the farmers was to keep them deprived of good education.

The Arya *bhats* [priests; emphasis in original] and brahmans do not admit shudra farmers' children in their Sanskrit schools, but in their Prakrit Marathi schools they admit these children, and over and above their own monthly salaries, extract food on every full moon and moonless night, grain on many festival days, and even take a fourth from what the children bring everyday to eat in school; and teach them only the basic letters, arithmetic and *modi*,[13] some shloka in Prakrit relating to pretentious and false Puranas, and a few songs, or teach them lavanis,[14] making them educated enough to write such things. Never giving them sufficient knowledge even to keep accounts of expenses at home. So how would they enter into the mamledar's offices and become even clerks? (Deshpande 2002: 121–2).

Denial of access to education, especially to good-quality education, as a fundamental cause of caste disparity and discrimination is a theme that emerges forcefully first in Phule's writings, and subsequently in the writings of B.R. Ambedkar, which we will consider later in the chapter. However, before moving on, it is important to make a final point about Phule. In the analytical frameworks employed in India and abroad to study and discuss caste, unfortunately, Phule's writings and thought do not get the attention they deserve, given how powerful and pioneering they are. Phule is better known in Maharashtra, but attacked by the Hindu right wing, and not very often discussed outside the region, which could be due to the fact that the Indian academic

[11] To mark conception.

[12] Death rituals.

[13] This is the footnote from the original: 'Modi: A running script in which most Marathi correspondence and account-writing used to take place. It was taught in schools till well into the 1940s.'

[14] This is the footnote from the original: 'Lavani: Songs, often erotic, mostly accompanied by dance in the popular theatre of Maharashtra called tamasha.'

community overwhelmingly thinks and writes in English, and its access to vernacular writings is rather limited.

A very important aspect of Phule's life emerged out of his belief that radical thinking (on religion, caste, and gender) had to be matched by equally radical action, and thus he took steps that no upper caste or *bhadralok* (belonging to the upper classes) reformer had taken (Deshpande 2002). Phule's approach to the gender issue was by far the most radical of all his contemporaries, and was certainly the first systematic understanding of the gender question by a Shudra thinker. In *Manusmriti*, women are treated as Shudras, and accordingly Phule included all women in his definition of Shudra–Atishudras, in the sense that he viewed the subordination of women as similar to the subordination of Shudra–Atishudras in a Brahmin-dominated social order. In Chapter 4, we will examine this connection in somewhat greater detail. He established his first school in 1842 for girls. While he was deeply critical of gender oppression overall, he was especially concerned about the most ostracized section within women—the widows. Questions such as widow remarriage and banning of child marriages were taken up by other reformers as well, but Phule took the question the farthest and his actions matched his words. For instance, in 1863, he established the first-of-its-kind home for widows who were forced to abort or kill their children, fearing social ostracism. He himself adopted the son of a Brahmin widow as his own. He played an active role in the remarriage of a Saraswat Brahmin widow in 1864. He organized a barbers' strike to protest against the humiliating Brahminical custom of compulsory shaving of widows' heads. He was the only one to protest against the virulent reaction against Tarabai Shinde, who in 1882 had published a radical tract called 'Stree Purush Tulana' ('A Comparison between Men and Women'). He also vociferously defended the rights of Pandita Ramabai, a Brahmin who converted to Christianity and was bitterly attacked for that move, as he saw this as a deliberate shift away from Brahmanical Hinduism. He went on to establish the Satyashodhak Samaj (Society of the Seekers of Truth) in 1873 (Deshpande 2009: 60–1).

Another powerful early critique of the caste system is found in the writings and campaigns of Periyar E.V. Ramasamy Naicker (born 1879), whose main focus was on social, rather than the economic, aspects of caste inequalities. His view of the caste system, rather like

Phule's, was a dichotomous one: his belief being that the Brahmin–non-Brahmin was the central opposition that shaped society. He was staunchly rationalist and anti-religion.[15] He actively campaigned for temple entry for Shudras;[16] against segregation between Brahmins and non-Brahmin students, for instance, in the dining arrangements at Cheranmadevi Gurukkulam; and during his years in the Congress, for communal representation for non-Brahmins in legislatures, a proposal that was never accepted by the Congress (Pandian 2007).

He left the Congress and declared his philosophy to be 'no god, no religion, no Gandhi, no Congress and no brahmins' and founded the Self-Respect Movement (hereafter SRM) in 1926 with the primary objective of advancing a rationalist critique of caste, religion, and mainstream nationalism. The primary audience of the SRM comprised of the non-Brahmins and the SRM deliberately propagated rationalism (or opposition to god and religion) as a means that non-Brahmins could employ to gain control over their lives. In direct contrast to Gandhi, the SRM regarded the varnashrama dharma advocated in the *Manusmriti* as the backbone of casteism and as a system that legitimized the degradation of non-Brahmins. Periyar and the SRM set forth a critique of 'essential Hinduism' (a unified Hinduism represented by, for instance, diverse texts such as the *Manusmriti*, the *Ramayana*, and the *Bhagvad Gita*) and showed that caste, and hence the Brahmin, were central to this essential Hinduism. It should be noted that is a deliberate departure from the flexible view of Hinduism; Periyar did not question the flexibility of Hinduism per se, rather he read it as a Brahminic strategy of 'co-opting opposition to caste and thereby reaffirming Brahminic supremacy' (ibid.: 203). Periyar portrayed the Brahmin as symbolic of a range of identities (Brahmin, Hindu, the Aryan, upholders of Sanskrit, believers in the *Ramayana*) and allowed each of these (rather distinct) identities to represent the others by

[15] He believed, for instance, that 'he who created god is a fool, he who propagates god is a scoundrel and he who worships god is a barbarian' (Pandian 2007: 196), or that 'god and fate are direct enemies of reason' (p. 197).

[16] He staged satyagrahas in front of the Mahadevar temple in Vaikkom, so that lower castes could enter the temple streets. He provocatively and irreverentially described the idol at Vaikkom temple as a 'mere piece of stone fit only to wash dirty linen with' (Pandian 2007: 197).

assuming transitivity. This transitivity allowed him to mobilize a large number of 'inferiorised subaltern identities' against the Brahmin (based on gender, occupation, language, and region)[17] (Pandian 2007: 205). Thus, Periyar's project, in which he succeeded to a very large extent, was to create a bloc of diverse interests based on their common antagonism against the Brahmin.

In Chapter 4, we will discuss Periyar's views on the gender question and its salience in the SRM. There are two aspects of Periyar's views related specifically to the economic dimension of the caste system, which merit mention here. One, he made an explicit connection between Brahminic Hinduism and the inferiorization of physical labour (in Phule's terminology, this would be the labour of the Shudra–Atishudras), and argued that the varnashrama dharma was the institutional foundation that allowed this. Thus, he directly differed not only with Gandhi but also with the sociological concept of the *jajmani* system that views caste as a system of reciprocal relationships. Two, as a concrete expression of this view, he observed May Day, not only in the commonly accepted way as signifying workers' rights but more importantly as a symbolic opposition to caste and religious indignities. In his view, the communal and religious aspects of the caste system preceded its economic aspects and the fact that the fourth varna (the Shudra) was assigned physical labour was proof of this.

Moving to the Twentieth Century: B.R. Ambedkar

The critique of the caste system is further elaborated in Ambedkar's writings, unambiguously regarded as the ideological leader of the present-day Dalit movement. Ambedkar was a prolific writer and to do justice to the full range and diversity of his writings could easily consume not just one but several volumes. Also, the analysis of his writings by various experts has yielded very rich insights into the functioning of the caste system and of the colonial economy. While we cannot reproduce the richness either of Ambedkar's thought or of the analytical writings on Ambedkar here, it is only appropriate for us to take a glimpse of his economic critiques of the caste system.

[17] Accordingly, the SRM publications were clearly directed at the subaltern sections. They were very cheap, often free, and also used language that was coarse, often too coarse even for its own cadres, and was non-grammatical. As Pandian (2007) suggests, this was a deliberate opposition to middle-class morality and its standards of correctness.

In his essays 'Castes in India' and 'Annihilation of Caste' (see Rodrigues 2002), Ambedkar summarizes theories of the origins of the caste system and outlines his own views. Like Phule, his critique of the caste system is devastating, especially as it shapes the lives of millions of untouchables into a life of slavery, exploitation, and abuse. He, in fact, goes further and condemns the caste system for its effects on Hindu society as a whole: 'The effect of caste on the ethics of the Hindus is simply deplorable. Caste has killed public spirit. Caste has destroyed the sense of public charity. Caste has made public opinion impossible. A Hindu's public is his caste. His responsibility is only to his caste. His loyalty is restricted only to his caste. Virtue has become caste ridden' (ibid.: 275).

Refuting the specific defence of the caste system as a division of labour, he argues that it is not a division of labour, as much as it is a '*division of labourers*' (ibid.: 263, emphasis original). He points out that in no civilized society is a division of labour accompanied by a division of labourers into watertight compartments, where the workers are graded one above the other. He further argues that this division of labour is neither spontaneous nor based on natural aptitudes. The caste system attempts to 'appoint tasks to individuals in advance, selected not on the basis of trained original capacities, but on that of the social status of the parents. Looked at from another point of view, this stratification of occupations which is the result of the caste system is positively pernicious' (ibid.: 263). He goes on to argue that the essence of industry is change, but the caste system does not allow individuals the freedom to adjust themselves to the changing opportunities by being able to select which jobs they would rather perform. And there are some jobs that are always abhorred and considered despicable. The caste system assigns them to certain castes and thus makes those castes degraded as well. 'As an economic organisation, caste is therefore a harmful institution, inasmuch as it involves the subordination of man's natural powers and inclinations to the exigencies of social rules' (ibid.: 267). Therefore, the 'caste code does not result in economic efficiency' (ibid.). This point about efficiency is especially important, since it forms a link with the discussion of discrimination and efficiency in the next section.

In a sharp critique of the idealized Indian village as a model of socio-economic stability, Ambedkar concisely and with lucidity points out that the Indian village is not a homogeneous, harmonious unit. For illustrative purposes, he divides the village into two units—the touchables and the untouchables—and outlines a set of rules that govern their living and conduct in the village economy and society. In this long list are special rules dedicated to the duties and obligations of the untouchables, such as 'when the whole village community is engaged in celebrating a general festivity such as Holi or Dasara, the Untouchables must perform all menial acts which are preliminary to the main observance' and 'On certain festivities, the Untouchables must submit their women to members of the village community to be made the subject of indecent fun' (ibid.: 327). He also goes on to list duties that untouchables have to perform without remuneration. His account diverges very clearly from the beliefs of say, Gandhi, who believed in and supported the idealized view of Indian village society and of the caste system as a harmonious and benign division of labour.[18]

Thus, we see that there are very powerful critiques of the caste system from within, as it were, by individuals who were not only thinkers but also acted on their beliefs and led significant movements. These movements obviously created a mass of opinion against the predominant manifestation of the caste system, but it is important to recognize that they also affected the very evolution of the caste system in the post-colonial period, both by their intended (for example, the establishment of affirmative action for Dalits and the rise and consolidation of the anti-Brahmin movement in Tamil Nadu) and unintended (for instance, the rise of identity politics) consequences.

These critiques as well as other models of the caste system from the contemporary sociological literature (for instance, models found in the writings of M.N. Srinivas, Louis Dumont, André Béteille, or

---

[18] Gandhi's view of the caste system differed very sharply from that of Phule, Ambedkar, and the other critics of the caste system, notably Periyar. Ambedkar wrote a scathing criticism of Gandhi in his book *What Congress and Gandhi Have Done to the Untouchables*. A detailed discussion of the differences is outside the scope of this book. This quote from Gandhi illustrates the sharp contrast. In a visit to south India in 1927, seemingly oblivious to the spread of the anti-Brahmin movement, Gandhi publicly declared: 'Varnashrama dharma is not an unmitigated evil but it is one of the foundations on which Hinduism is built [and it] defines man's mission on earth .... Brahmins [are the] finest flowers of Hinduism and humanity', adding that he would 'do nothing to wither it' (Pandian 2007: 191).

Dipankar Gupta) emerge from their authors' empirical observations and their reading of history. In other words, these authors observe an empirical reality and try to articulate the complexity of its features, its mechanics, and its consequences. In contrast, the economic theories (the ones reviewed in the next section relate mainly to identity and discrimination) abstract from a very complex reality by focusing on a few key features and construct theoretical models, based on a set of assumptions, in order to understand why and how rational economic agents (producers, consumers, employers, employees) might discriminate in market settings and how, therefore, economic outcomes might be closely linked to group identities. While these two branches of the literature (economic and non-economic) are often not in conversation with each other, I believe they should be, for each can offer to the other very rich insights and together they have the power to enhance our understanding of the mechanics that produce discrimination and disparity. With this understanding, we now move to an examination of the economic theories.

IDENTITY, DISCRIMINATION, AND ECONOMIC OUTCOMES

While the bulk of economic theory is built on the assumption that social identities of agents do not matter in the market, there are powerful exceptions that show how social identities of economic agents can be central to the determination of their economic outcomes. The two main neo-classical theories that demonstrate this—'statistical discrimination' (Arrow 1971; Phelps 1972; Akerlof 1984) and 'taste for discrimination' (Becker 1957)—however, approach discrimination from opposite ends.

Statistical discrimination ascribes discrimination to the presence of imperfect information in labour markets: in a deviation from the theoretical world of general equilibrium theory that assumes perfect information that is instantaneously available, information in the real world is neither perfect nor costless. Thus, employers cannot easily gauge productivity of prospective employees and hence cannot determine what wage to offer them, without incurring a cost to measure productivity, which, despite the employers' best efforts, might end up being a guesstimate and not very accurate. One way out of this problem is the use of indicators or proxies that are derived from and based on social convention. Thus, for instance, employers might assume that women, in general, are likely to be less productive than men, and use this belief as the basis of their wage decisions when faced with the prospect of employing a male or female candidate. In other words, employers use group identity (which they can observe) of the employee as a proxy for ability (which they cannot observe).

In its simplest form, the theory suggests that employers assume that all members belonging to a given social group have equal abilities and use the dominant stereotypes about the distribution of abilities between groups (for example, beliefs such as 'whites are better workers than blacks', or that 'men are more efficient than women') to offer higher wages to groups endowed with positive stereotypes (the group that is considered more productive). In this way, workers' job and wage offers get shaped by their group affiliation and employers save the cost and effort of devising various tests and techniques to gauge individual productivities. Thus, an important neo-classical postulate which is supposed to guide efficient resource allocation in the perfect world of general equilibrium theory—workers should get paid according to their marginal productivity in equilibrium—gets violated, but the economy attains equilibrium nevertheless. Here discrimination is seen as a rational decision by the employers and occurs *because of* economic incentives (that is, the incentive to acquire productivity information in order to decide on wage offers).

This is a very powerful theory, in that, by altering just one of the assumptions of the general equilibrium model (that of perfect and costless information), the model reaches a very different conclusion, that is, profit-maximizing agents can discriminate and that the state of discrimination can continue unless there are countervailing factors, such as affirmative action policies or a coalition of employers that breaks free of social stereotypes. The general equilibrium model suggests that all employees get paid according to their productivities, whereas in a world with statistical discrimination, employees get paid according to their group identities. Also, the equilibrium attained under statistical discrimination is not Pareto optimal (at least one person can be made better-off, without anyone else being made worse-off), which makes the economy inefficient, even though individual employers might statistically discriminate on grounds of efficiency. It is important to note and highlight this distinction between private and public or social efficiency—what might be efficient for one individual could result in an inefficient outcome for the economy. Statistical discrimination demonstrates this elegantly and effectively.

Offering lower wages for the same work might be legally untenable or socially infeasible. In this situation, statistical discrimination would take the form of differential assignment of jobs to workers belonging to different social groups. Coate and Loury (1993) suggest that an employer with negative stereotypes against a particular group is less likely to assign workers belonging to that group to the more highly rewarded jobs within the firm. This would lower the expected return on investments (such as education or skill acquisition) for members of that group, and thus they will be less inclined to invest in attributes that would make them more productive on these jobs. In this case, employers' beliefs become a 'self-fulfilling prophecy', since employers' negative beliefs about a group are confirmed in equilibrium even when all groups are ex-ante identical. This is another reason why an economy with discrimination would not be efficient. It is interesting that this picture of an economy with discrimination causing a division of workers along lines of social identity, who might have similar abilities, resonates strongly with Ambedkar's view of the caste system as being a 'division of labourers' rather than as division of labour.

McCaffery (1993) points out yet another source of inefficiency in a world with statistical discrimination—it is not efficient if it works against a group with higher wage elasticity (for example, women). He also argues that we need to make a distinction between 'imperfect information' (knowable but not known) and 'incomplete information' (cannot be known). Often, statistical discrimination is used as a substitute for the former, in which case it is especially not justified. He reiterates the point made earlier: given information failure, the idea that individuals acting in their self-interest without intervention will result in the best of all possible worlds is untenable. This argument is especially relevant to discussions of policy interventions to counter discrimination, for example, affirmative action. As we discuss in Chapter 7, critics of affirmative action claim that such policies introduce inefficiencies, not recognizing that these are designed as a response to already existing inefficiencies. Coate and Loury (1993) examine the effect of affirmative action on existing stereotypes and conclude that theoretically, there could be two different impacts. One, where affirmative action policies eliminate negative stereotypes about minority workers by allowing them to demonstrate their abilities, but equally, if employers 'patronize' minority workers (assign them less challenging jobs or lower standards in their assessment), then affirmative action could end up reinforcing the negative stereotypes. They suggest that minority workers should respond to the enhanced opportunities created by affirmative action by producing evidence of greater productivity, such that the negative stereotypes attributed to their group weaken.

The statistical discrimination approach can be distinguished from the Chicago School that explains discrimination by a 'taste for discrimination' (Becker 1957: 14). According to Becker, an individual X will discriminate against Y simply because he has a taste for it. In keeping with the Chicago tradition, this theory presupposes that any market-based phenomenon should be measurable in monetary units or should have a monetary equivalent and, therefore, an individual with a taste for discrimination 'must act *as if* he were willing to pay something, either directly or in the form of a reduced income, to be associated with some person instead of others' (ibid.).[19] Becker's theory addresses prejudice directly as it defines the taste for discrimination as stemming from a set of beliefs or values that are formed without an 'objective consideration of fact'. The statistical discrimination model treats discrimination as a consequence of lack of information, and prima facie does not allow for individual prejudice. In other words, under statistical discrimination, employers simply inherit dominant stereotypes about various groups and as individuals, it is possible for them to discriminate without necessarily having a taste for discrimination. In Becker's model, information does not play a central role: he argues that individuals will discriminate even if it means a loss of income for them, or *despite* economic incentives for behaving otherwise.

Taste for discrimination, then, is measured by what Becker calls the discrimination coefficient, which is a function of several factors—the intensity, duration, and level of contact with members of the other group. For instance, a white employee might not exhibit

---

[19] Both the Chicago school (Becker) and statistical discrimination (Akerlof) have been criticized for an excessive focus on questions of efficiency at the expense of distribution. See Hoff et al. (1993) for a more detailed discussion.

any discrimination towards a black co-worker, as long as the black person is in a subordinate position, but might exercise a strong taste for discrimination if he had to work with him as an equal or, worse still, as a superior.[20] Or, individuals might not exercise their taste for discrimination in one-off or short-term interactions, but definitely would in sustained, long-term interactions. Becker also considers the effect of the numbers of individuals of the other group, and suggests that this could cut both ways: on the one hand, increase in the numbers of the other group might lower prejudice; on the other hand, it could stoke majority fears of being 'taken over' by the minority and could thus increase discrimination by the majority.[21]

Another significant difference between the two models is that in Becker's model, *any* individual could have a positive taste for discrimination: one need not belong to the dominant group in order to exercise one's taste for discrimination. This allows for interaction between discrimination exercised by different individuals (groups) and gives rise to the concept of 'effective discrimination': in a two-group society, if both groups discriminate against members of the other group (and thus suffer a loss in income), then the group which is hurt more, suffers effective discrimination. This is a powerful concept, as it allows us to identify the net losers from discrimination in a society where everyone can discriminate (that is, every individual has a taste for discrimination, whether or not they choose to exercise it). When taste for discrimination becomes sufficiently large to preclude any economic contact between two groups, it leads to 'complete segregation'. Becker's model shows that complete segregation by the minority does not avoid the bad economic effects of discrimination but only multiplies them, a proposition that he verifies with reference to data on three communities: American Indians, whites, and blacks. This is a result with widespread resonance: it suggests that ghettoization is likely to make things worse for minorities, and thus greater (rather than lesser) contact with the majority might be necessary to reduce the negative impact of discrimination. Of course,

---

[20] Chapter 5 outlines the methodology of assessing discrimination in labour markets that is directly based on Becker's theory.

[21] In India, the Hindu right often uses the myth of the exploding Muslim population to induce take-over fear among the Hindu majority, and thus further bolsters its ammunition for fostering mutual distrust and hatred between Hindus and Muslims.

these are exceedingly complex issues, inextricably intertwined with politics (international and domestic) and history; however, here is an insight that adds to our understanding of how and why communities might become segregated.

Kreuger (1963) gives a twist to Becker's model by taking forward his modelling apparatus of trade between two hypothetical societies (W and N) in order to explain how discrimination can take place even without a taste for discrimination. While in a Beckerian world, whites with a taste for discrimination will not export capital to the N economy unless compensated by higher returns, Kreuger points out that discrimination against N could take place even if the whites had no taste for discrimination. Her basic point is that Becker assumes a taste for discrimination in the white utility functions, whereas there could be several utility functions without that argument which would result in discrimination. For instance, Becker demonstrates the effect of disaggregating the white community into classes by showing that while the aggregate net income of the white community will be lower, within the community, white capitalists' income will be lower and white workers' incomes higher as a result of discrimination. Based on this, Kreuger argues that if white capitalists had no taste for discrimination and were maximizing only their income, they would not discriminate. However, if their objective was to maximize the aggregate income of the white community, rather than their own personal incomes, then that could result in discrimination against N.

She argues that another way in which a discriminatory allocation of capital may result might be in the allocation of publicly owned capital, for example, education. Since investment in education directly benefits the recipient, whites (via their majority in the ballot) might have an interest in keeping education restricted to themselves. Kreuger admits that it might not be possible to empirically test whether Becker's formulation is more valid compared to hers; however, she points out that Becker's equilibrium is Pareto optimal (N incomes can go up only at the cost of W incomes), whereas if there is no taste for discrimination in the white capitalists' utility function, we can get a non–Pareto optimal outcome, in which an end to discrimination could be managed such that both W and N incomes could increase.

These theories, powerful as they are, confine themselves to market-based discrimination, that is, to differences in wages and occupations in labour markets. However, stigmatized groups such as Dalits experience discrimination in virtually all aspects of life and the process starts much before individuals enter the labour market. Economists refer to this as 'pre-market' discrimination and recognize its importance, but unfortunately, none of the theories on discrimination address pre-market discrimination directly.

An alternative approach to discrimination, distinct from the established neo-classical theories, is provided by the work of feminist economists, whose primary concern is to assess the impact of gender identity on social and economic outcomes. The feminist argument makes a distinction between 'productive' (all the work that conventionally gets counted for the purpose of estimating the national product) and 'reproductive' (all the jobs that do not get counted: housework, reproduction, child care, nursing, caring for the sick and the elderly) economies and argues that the former cannot exist without all the work done in the latter. However, the argument goes, instead of recognizing the interdependence and the complementarities between the two economies, markets function in ways that reward those who work in the productive economy and penalize those who work in the reproductive economy. Since women predominate in the reproductive economy, they are typically disadvantaged in labour markets and often would not be offered jobs equivalent to their male peers with comparable skills and qualifications. Thus, markets are not neutral arenas, but are, in fact, 'gendered' institutions (Elson 1999) and discrimination is not an aberration or a residual, but an integral part of the way markets are organized. This approach rejects the standard econometric technique of measuring discrimination (discussed in Chapter 5), where discrimination in labour markets is measured as a residual, after all the wage-earning characteristics are accounted for.

While the feminist approach to discrimination is radical, thought-provoking, and compelling, it can be used to understand gender discrimination alone, whereas the statistical discrimination and taste for discrimination theories could be used to understand discrimination based on any definition of identity (gender, caste, religion, nationality, and so forth).

However different these theories might be from each other, what they indicate very clearly is that identity matters in the economic world, even in strongly market-oriented situations. Indeed, even a casual glance around the world based on very elementary data would confirm this: the history of the post–World War II world is replete with the increasing salience of identity as the basis of nation-building as well as national conflicts.

Models of the Caste Economy

While there is plenty of theoretical literature on discrimination per se, there are only a handful of theoretical works that especially focus on caste identity and economic outcomes. Akerlof (1984) provides, within the statistical discrimination framework, a simple explanation of why a segregated or caste economy may be self-perpetuating. Based on the assumption of all members of a given group (race or caste) perceived as having equal ability in a caste economy, 'the behavior of one member of society toward another is predicted by their respective caste statuses' (ibid.: 24). The idea here is that the identity of the agent *perceived by other agents* is seen as an indicator of merit or worth and that, in turn, determines their labour market outcomes. In a system where there are social costs (for instance, sanctions in the form of being declared an outcaste) associated with breaking traditional norms and practices, his model demonstrates how this would thwart any tendency to alter the social code of a segregated society.[22]

The motivation behind the statistical discrimination models is closer to the 'disadvantage model' that is used to explain racial disparity—insofar as construction of identity is seen to flow from a set of characteristics attributed to an individual, which either explain how others would behave towards the individual (Akerlof 1984) or how this individual would behave in society (Akerlof and Kranton 2000).[23] What these models do not address is the fundamental question of how these assessments are formed. Are they based on averages that the group is presumed to possess? Assuming, temporarily, that the

[22] An objection to this from a sociological perspective could be that the contemporary meaning of 'belonging to a caste' is not clear—for instance, to what extent caste affiliation determines the behaviour of its members? Or, what exactly is the contemporary nature of sanctions—do they apply only to marriage or to other social behaviours? All these questions are important but outside the purview of economic enquiry.

[23] Akerlof and Kranton (2000) do not talk of caste, but since they look more broadly at how identity can affect individual interactions, it finds a periodic reference in their review.

averages are 'accurately' estimated, this means that the outliers in the group, specifically those with attributes much higher than average, will suffer. More importantly, *beliefs* about the group frequency distribution and the true group frequency distribution may differ widely and this difference would in all likelihood be driven by prejudice. But the theoretical apparatus of imperfect information does not allow an evaluation of the process by which indicators are formed, left as they are to 'social convention'.

Turning specifically to these models and the Indian caste system, one finds a whole range of questions that these models leave unanswered. For instance, why are the attitudes of the upper castes towards the Dalits derogatory? Are they due to the fact that the Dalits are genuinely 'inferior'? If Dalits acquired superior human capital indicators over time, would these attitudes change accordingly? Why are the upper castes 'superior' anyway? Is it due to their inherent characteristics or due to a social institution that was created by the privileged to maintain their privilege? If it is the latter, then the existence of discrimination would have very little to do with either presumed or actual characteristics of the Dalits (in the literature on racial discrimination, this would be analogous to the white privilege model).

Also, by focusing on a given individual (Akerlof and Kranton 1998), how does one reconcile conflicting social prescriptions? Social prescriptions are defined by the authors as 'what actions are ... appropriate' and function as 'powerful motivations to behavior' (ibid.: 1). They constitute a social code. But are social prescriptions simply an aggregate of individual prescriptions? Or are there dominant prescriptions of privilege that determine what social codes or norms ought to be?

Related to this is the problem of identity formation: suppose the identity agent 'A' would like to possess is at variance with the identity that society bestows upon 'A': in the contemporary context of caste, excellently summarized by the conflict between the terms 'Dalit' (the oppressed) and 'Harijan' (the latter term, coined by Gandhi, meaning people of/close to God). By which of these two terms would an (ex-) untouchable in India be described? Official terminology prefers the latter, but the Dalits themselves find it offensive and patronizing. The point of this discussion is that construction of 'identity' itself is not unproblematic and the self-perceived identity may vary a great deal from the socially enforced one, and individuals in subaltern groups might have to struggle to get labelled in ways that conform to their notions of self-respect. What the statistical discrimination theory implicitly assumes is that there is a singular consensual identity and while that might be necessary as a simplifying assumption for the purposes of modelling, it is important to take cognizance of the fact that the construction of identity, especially for stigmatized groups, is a process marked by contestation.

Continuity and Change

What about social change? In the Akerlof (1984) model, while there is a theoretical possibility of an anti-caste coalition succeeding in breaking free of the code, this possibility falls victim to the free rider problem. Akerlof (ibid.: 44) writes, '[U]sually the greatest rewards go to those who do not break social customs. ... the models of statistical discrimination and caste explain why economic rewards may follow those who follow prevailing social customs.' Lal (1988), in developing an economic rationale for the Hindu social system, uses essentially the Akerlofian argument (indeed, his model is a variant of the Akerlof model) to explain the relative stability in the caste system.[24]

Going beyond economics for a moment, one can see other, perhaps more powerful, disincentives to the formation of such a coalition: prejudice and the desire to perpetuate their domination and the power to prevent such a coalition on the part of the upper castes, coupled with fear of a backlash on the part of the lower castes. In this context, Kuran (1987) argues that the system continues because the most oppressed are in fact its supporters. This support could either be forced because of fear of reprisal, or genuine due to a mistaken fatalism. This formulation ignores huge chapters of India's history that are replete with social reform and religious protest against the caste system (discussed briefly in Chapter 4 on the gender–caste overlap).

---

[24] Lal's (1988: 72) argument is that given a set of problems that the ancient Indians were facing, like political instability, the need for a secure labour supply for labour-intensive settled agriculture in the Indo-Gangetic plains, uncertainty concerning outputs, and so forth, the caste system was a 'second best optimal response'. An analysis of this argument necessitates forays into ancient history that are well beyond the brief of this chapter.

The Sikh revolt against Hinduism was initially anti-caste, but with the formation of castes within the new religion, Sikhism ended up with a situation not very different from before.[25] It is also argued that a strong caste consciousness prevents the formation of a class consciousness. However, through the colonial period as well as in contemporary times, India has witnessed several major class-based struggles and revolts involving the industrial working class and/or sections of the peasantry, but the degree to which they have blurred caste lines is a moot point.

This leads more generally to the question about the appropriate agency for social change. To say that this issue is exceedingly complex would be an understatement. To narrow down the discussion within the context of the models being discussed, if construction of identity flows from a set of presumed characteristics, then can social change come about if subjects of discrimination acquire the socially desirable characteristics (assuming, of course, the highly unlikely possibility that a well-formulated consensus exists on what constitutes a set of socially desirable characteristics)? Or would victims of discrimination have to resort to protest (perhaps violent)? Can either legal reform or external force (or both) be agents of change? While it would be stretching the limits of economic inquiry to expect answers to these questions (assuming that they exist), some elements of the dynamic of change could be incorporated into the framework of these models to make them richer. For instance, it would be interesting to know how the Akerlof (1984) equilibrium would change if, say, the indicators for the Dalits improved over time.

The Akerlof model assumes a market setting. But Scoville's exercise (1996: 385–6) looks at caste as a 'system of human resource allocation as one alternative to reliance on market mechanisms', arguing that this is a situation where 'strongly non competitive labor market institutions have long prevailed...occupations are hereditary, compulsory and endogamous'. In an earlier paper, Scoville (1991) sought to formalize the relationships in such a caste economy. While Akerlof's work

---

[25] Jodhka (2009) discusses the religious demography of caste in Punjab where nearly 60 per cent of the population identifies with Sikhism. Before the Partition in 1947, more than half the population was Muslim. Thus, Punjab has had a substantial presence of both these religions that theoretically reject caste. However, caste-based divisions are prominent in Punjab, with the state reporting the highest proportion of ex-untouchable castes.

focuses on the *existence* of a caste-ridden equilibrium even under competitive conditions, Scoville's (1991: 49) paper is concerned with the 'production and distribution workings of such a caste economy, much in the fashion of Leontief, and with equilibrating adjustments taking place in the size of several castes'.

Thus, Scoville (1991) constructs a 'jajmani matrix' capturing some of the reciprocal obligations of the caste system.[26] The use of reciprocity has connotations of fairness or a fair exchange. Thus, the question of production of surplus and who (which castes) appropriates it is completely outside the purview of this model, as are the hierarchy and the exploitation inherent in the caste system. By highlighting interdependence, the model takes the focus away from the hierarchical and exploitative nature of the caste system and presents a benign picture that emphasizes the role of the caste system as the facilitator of a mutually beneficial division of labour. As Mencher (1974: 470) points out, 'It is hard to see it [the Indian caste system] as being any more interdependent than any other stratification system.'

One of the basic assumptions of Scoville's model is that demand for most traditional goods and services is primarily driven by the size of the population. This ignores the role played by purchasing power (or the lack of it) as a determinant of the size of the market. Following the same assumption, the dynamic version of the model focuses on population growth of different castes as a driving force behind determining the elements of the matrix. While population growth is undoubtedly important, it is difficult to be persuaded that it provides the key dynamic behind the matrix—assuming of course, that such an exercise can adequately capture the essential features of the complex network of relationships structuring the caste system.

What is intriguing to observers is the degree of stability in caste relationships or the 'absence of institutional change' (Scoville 1996: 390), where, in terms of his earlier model, institutional change is defined as the change in the definitions of the rows/columns or changes in the elements of the jajmani matrix. He identifies three characteristics of labour market barriers that ensure that institutional change in the caste labour market will be minimal or nil. These are the

[26] The traditional caste divisions implied a hereditary work allocation, where the specified arrangement of the flow of goods and services between the individuals in the system was called the jajmani system.

features of impermeability (workers cannot easily leave their caste and enter another); inevitability (lack of alternative sources of supply); and permanence (these barriers have a long history and are expected to last into the indefinite future). However, this matrix is based on traditional occupations. In the modern occupational structure, heredity plays a much smaller direct role (in the sense of directing the exact profession that will be chosen by a given individual) and labour market barriers work differently, as we will see in Chapter 6.

Attempting to define institutional change in this way is problematic. In addition, the matrix apparatus may be inadequate in capturing the entire network of inter-caste economic relationships. One is led to ask the more basic question: unless a change is fundamental and complete, are we to conclude that there is no change at all? How does one assess change that takes place in degrees? Lanjouw and Stern (1998: 212) report on perceptions of change in Palanpur, where people they talked to felt that caste-based distinctions had become less important in recent decades. Such perceptions would find no place in the Scoville model.

Caste and Patronage

Platteau (1992) makes an interesting attempt to tread a completely different path, from the essays discussed so far, in exploring caste relationships by looking at them as a system of 'aristocratic patronage', where the patrons (the upper castes) are bound together by a kind of a class solidarity. Relations between them and the lower castes have elements of patronage.[27] He realizes that the jajmani system cannot be equated with patron–client relationships but feels that it

---

[27] He argues that patronage relationships display four main characteristics, which very briefly can be stated as follows:

(i) They are highly asymmetrical.

(ii) They contain a strong element of affection.

(iii) They are comparatively stable.

(iv) They involve multiple facets of the actors concerned and implying a set of reciprocal obligations which stretches over a wide and loosely defined domain, including some degree of social security to the client, which could be important to poor villagers deprived of significant access to land. The rationale of patronage from the point of view of the patron for this point is made explicit later—basically, they are assured of a pool of readily available trustworthy and compliant labour for agricultural tasks and for ritual, social, and political activities or duties.

contains such elements. Also, contrary to what is usually observed and assumed in descriptions of patronage, untouchable dependents may have hereditary relationships with several members of upper castes (meaning that several generations of a given untouchable family work for corresponding generations of one or more upper caste families and receive remuneration), implying the presence of non-exclusive, non-dyadic clientilist relationships.

The importance of this essay lies in the manner in which patronage has been defined, more importantly, in his introduction of caste into the cultivator–peasant proprietor relationship. Economists' work on patronage has focused on interlinked markets in rural areas, usually land and credit. Contrary to these models that assume competition, Platteau's system assumes very stable relationships, blocking the development of competition and thus formalizing a scheme of stable, hierarchical relationships based on servitude and coerced labour. The instrument of patronage in the models is the provision of land plots to the untouchable clients to ensure compliance and docility.

While this is undoubtedly seen in some instances, and while social insurance to the clients does exist, we should note that first, social insurance could take a variety of forms other than provision of land. We also should be careful not to exaggerate the importance of social insurance, in view of the antagonism and tension in upper and lower caste relations. In addition, there exists a very high degree of landlessness among the Dalits that this model does not treat.

Platteau's paper models caste relationships as an informal system of indentured servitude. The jajmani system is far more complex. In addition to the land-based work, the Dalits under the traditional jajmani system performed jobs that were completely divorced from land—especially the most menial ones like working with dead animals (removal and leather-making), scavenging, cremating the dead, and sweeping. In terms of spectrum of occupations that each of them focuses on, Platteau's work is totally opposite to that of Scoville (who does not consider land-based production at all).

Despite these limitations, Platteau does address the critical issue of the link between landownership and caste status. That, indeed, is an important facet of caste inequality. His models suggest that radical land reform would destroy the root of the untouchables' dependence on their upper-caste landowning masters. To the extent that this is valid, it suggests that the long unfinished agenda of land reform in India could provide a clue to one of the important causes of the perpetuation of caste inequality in the rural areas.[28]

However, this still leaves open the issue of low-caste status and consequent discrimination that stems from traditional menial jobs. In Platteau's (1992) dynamic models, the jajmani system does not turn out to be robust in the face of a number of changes. This result needs to be properly interpreted. In addition to all the caveats in the model, a weakening or even the end of jajmani may not mean the end of casteism. To understand this, one has to simply observe the continuation of racial prejudice, inequality, and discrimination towards those seen as descendants of slaves in a country such as the US where slavery has been abolished for over 130 years.[29]

Social Mobility

This leads us directly to the question of inter-caste mobility. At the time of India's Independence in 1947, there was a belief that modern industrial development and urbanization would gradually loosen the web of caste stratification and eventually lead to its demise.[30] Unfortunately, this expectation has not been borne out by post-Independence developments.

Let us be ambitious at the start of our quest for tracing social mobility. Have the most deprived been able to move into the uppermost echelons of the economy? Nafziger (1975), in an investigation into caste origins of industrialists in certain regions of south India, rejects the Horatio Alger model and finds a very low degree of both caste and class mobility.[31] He finds an overlap of feudal dominance and prestige

[28] Struggles for greater equality in landholdings were a part of the independence movement and their strength varied across regions. Land reform after independence has been under the purview of state governments, thus depending entirely on the political will of a given state government. These two factors together have contributed to the lopsided nature of land reforms.

[29] For a comprehensive examination of the economic consequences of contemporary racism in the US, see Darity and Myers (1998).

[30] Parallel claims have been made by Brazilian scholars about the impact of industrialization on racial attitudes in their country. For a discussion of some of the theories and the 'dissonance between theory and data', see Lovell (1994).

[31] Horatio Alger Jr., an American novelist of the nineteenth century, wrote over 100 boys' books with 'rags-to-riches' as the central theme. Thus, his protagonists from

with capitalist control of business, hence a continuation of the privilege and social prestige of the high-income upper-caste families. This is not a surprising result, as he himself points out, given the very low degree of class mobility historically and internationally.

Mayoux (1993: 556, 563) in a case study of the silk reeling industry in Karnataka—a small-scale industry, supported and promoted by the government, targeting the disadvantaged groups—finds limited evidence of upward mobility (though 'not for the poorest of the poor') and finds that 'structural disadvantages for those with little capital persist in the industry'. Those at the bottom attributed their lack of success not only to fate but also to their inability to get credit. And 'in some cases, reluctance to lend...based on prejudice... is certainly an element in the lower levels of lending to Scheduled Castes' (ibid.: 557). The significance of this finding in a programme that is supposed to be a targeted intervention to raise the economic status of the disadvantaged cannot be overemphasized. Lanjouw and Stern (1998: 37) discuss the poor access to credit for the lowest castes (Jatabs) in Palanpur and suggest that this may be the reason why 'Jatabs sometimes lease out their land on cash rent, despite the unattractive terms of cash rent contracts'.

Chandra (1997), examining the migration patterns of the Kanbis (a low cultivator caste) from Gujarat to Kenya between 1911 and 1939, argues that this caste acquired wealth abroad and, coupled with the adoption of Brahminical practices upon their return to India, managed to advance in the caste hierarchy to the middle range with the new name Patidar. This could be a case illustrating the validity of the specific process of 'Sanskritization' or a more general one of wealth leading to a higher caste status (or the Latin American claim that money 'whitens').[32] Its importance lies in the fact that it challenges the

---

very humble backgrounds ended up achieving fame and fortune, ultimately realizing the American Dream.

[32] This term is due to Srinivas (1962: 9), who believed that 'Sanskritisation is both a part of the process of social mobility as well as the idiom in which mobility expresses itself ... can also occur independently of the acquisition of political and economic power'. This is how he describes the process: 'A low caste was able, in a generation or two, to rise to a higher position in the hierarchy by adopting vegetarianism and teetotalism, and by Sanskritising its ritual and pantheon. In short, it took over, as far as possible, the customs, rites, and beliefs of the Brahmins, and the adoption of the

notion of the Indian society as rigid and inflexible, but it is not clear to what extent this kind of change permeates the lowest rung of the caste hierarchy. Jayaraman and Lanjouw (1998: 38) report that 'several village studies find that the turbulence surrounding caste relations at the middle and upper levels of the social distribution is less marked among the lowest castes'. Also, they raise the larger question of whether 'Sanskritisation should be seen as contributing to the breakdown of the caste based patterns of behavior, or rather the opposite' (ibid.: 46).

Deshpande and Palshikar (2008), analysing a sample for Pune, investigate the patterns of intergenerational occupational mobility across caste groups between 2000 and 2007. They have information for four generations of each respondent, based upon which they classify each family on a five-point scale of upward mobility, downward mobility, no mobility, skewed pattern, and others. Overall, they find evidence of great upward mobility, with great upward momentum in the fourth generation. However, for SCs, the proportion in the upper and upper-middle occupations rises from 8 per cent to 11 per cent over the period, in sharp contrast to upper castes, for whom the corresponding proportions are 47 per cent and 54 per cent respectively. At the opposite end of the spectrum, the proportion of SCs in the poor and the 'very poor' also increases from 42 per cent to 48 per cent, with the biggest increase being in the 'very poor' category (from 24 per cent to 32 per cent). For upper castes, the corresponding proportions are 8 per cent to 17 per cent, and 2 per cent to 5 per cent, respectively.

They find, therefore, that Dalits have experienced mobility, but at the end of the day, they have not overcome stagnation, as the upper occupation category shows a plateau. Also, their upward mobility could be explained by a very low starting point—for them, a move from 'very low' to 'low' is also upward mobility. Also, in their sample, all caste groups have experienced some downward mobility as well. Thus, there is some evidence of overall polarization (across all caste groups). Commenting on the role of caste in explaining these patterns, they suggest that caste is not very strongly associated with occupational

---

Brahminic way of life by a low caste seems to have been frequent, although theoretically forbidden' (ibid.: 42).

mobility in general, yet it is a strong predictor of upward mobility. Downward or horizontal mobility does not appear to be a function of caste.

Munshi and Rosenzweig (2006, 2009) examine the issue of low social mobility in India. They point out that among developing countries, India's levels of occupational and spatial mobility are especially low. They argue that low out-marriage and low out-migration in India, both manifestations of restricted mobility, can be explained by the presence of rural jati-based networks, which have been smoothing consumption in the absence of well-functioning markets, for centuries. In other words, caste networks, by providing mutual insurance, play an important role in restricting mobility. In their 2009 paper, using a data set over the last three decades, they identify which households are most likely to leave this mutual insurance agreement in wake of the increase in income inequality after the Green Revolution. They then proceed to demonstrate that it is precisely these households or vulnerable jatis that have the highest rates of out-migration and out-marriage.

In their 2006 paper, they describe how caste-based labour market networks historically assisted their members in finding well-paying jobs in particular occupations in Mumbai. They also document the restrictions on mobility that were imposed by these networks; however, in the wake of increased economic opportunities during the 1990s, outside of the traditional caste-based occupations, they find a substantial increase in intergenerational mobility, indicating a degree of flux and fluidity in the system.

The latest study on social mobility, assessed via the experience of Dalit businesses in north-west India, is Jodhka (2010). He finds that most Dalit business establishments in the area are small in size, run mostly as self-proprietorships in the informal sector. His study indicates that caste appeared to matter for business in many different ways. Some Dalits who had set up business felt they were victims of prejudice. Damodaran (2008) has discussed the caste foundation of business in modern India in extensive detail. In Jodhka's field account we find that the locally dominant communities, who have traditionally dominated the business scene, do not like Dalits getting into business. 'They hate us'; 'non-dalits do not like us being in the business' were some of the common responses that Jodhka's fieldwork elicited. Some others reported being regarded as outsiders or 'odd actors'. Many felt handicapped because of not being a part of the traditional business communities. Fifty-seven per cent of his respondents felt that caste affected their business negatively, whereas only 2 per cent felt that it affected business positively.

Dalit businessmen faced discrimination from within the business community as well as from consumers: 'Identification of my factory with my caste name tends to discourage my clients. Even when they do not have caste prejudice, they feel we may not be able to deliver because we are traditionally not the ones who have been in business or possess enough resources to run a good business' (Jodhka 2010: 47). This prejudice was in evidence even when they were in completely 'secular' occupations. Despite these problems and discrimination they encountered, Dalit entrepreneurs in the study were happy with the new choice of occupation and had few regrets. Most significantly, they were happy to be not doing subservient roles and the fact that they had escaped 'slavery'. Chapter 7 discusses how affirmative action also provides another route for some Dalits to escape traditional subservient, humiliating jobs, and lead a life of dignity, which is, and ought to be, a central feature of social mobility.

* * *

In order to gain insights into the caste system and its inherent discrimination, one needs to make a reference to several disciplines and a variety of perspectives within each. This chapter gave a flavour of what that quest might yield. Subsequent chapters will discuss more of the literature, focusing on different facets of caste and economic outcomes. But even this limited discussion clearly establishes that social identity is not irrelevant to the market and that this social identity (or multiple identities) might transcend class, that is, economic outcomes might be shaped more by social identity than by class status. We now need to see whether, and how much of, this theoretical presumption is borne out by contemporary evidence.

3 Mind the Gap

'No collection of wealth must be made by a Sudra, even though he be able [to do it]; for a Sudra who has acquired wealth, gives pain to Brahmanas.'
—*The Laws of Manu*, Chapter X, verse 129, p. 430.

THE STANDARD OF LIVING DEBATE

This chapter attempts to document the extent of caste disparity after six decades of Indian Independence in order to assess if some of the theoretical propositions outlined in the previous chapter are borne out by the empirical evidence. Before we dig deeper, however, a more basic issue needs to be settled. It might be argued that to document standard of living differences between castes is akin to reinventing the wheel, given that the suggestion of a broad, albeit not very clearly defined, correspondence between caste and economic status, particularly at the upper and lower ends, may, at first blush, appear to be conventional wisdom.

Does this imply that we are engaged in a trivial exercise? Not really, for it turns out that the traditional association of hierarchy and power, at both the upper and lower ends, is not uncontested in contemporary India. On the question of the relative economic position of caste groups, perceptions are often based on preconceived notions and inadequate data. Thus, there is a view, for instance, among upper caste Hindus that they are the marginalized, since Dalits and Other Backward Classes (OBCs) are presumably advantaged due to the special benefits of state-sponsored programmes. To support these claims, examples of influential Dalit political leaders or anecdotal accounts of rich Dalit families are given. The affirmative action programme (discussed in detail in Chapter 7), which ought to be seen as a compensatory discrimination system, is often seen as bestowing 'privileges' on the lowest castes, that are denied to the rest of the population.[1] Politically, castes are perceived as 'vote banks', and thus are presumed to hold and wield power.[2] In the discussion on the interplay of caste, class, and political power (to borrow the apt title of Béteille 1996), there is a belief that the post-Independence ascendancy of non-Brahmins in the political arena represents a fundamental change in the socio-economic conditions of lower castes.[3] A detailed appraisal of socio-political changes is outside the scope of this inquiry; we will see if claims of substantial economic mobility—a presumed result of political mobility—can be sustained.[4]

To reiterate the point made in the previous chapter, we cannot hope to, and indeed do not aim to, capture the complexities of the *varna–jati* relationship using macro data. For our purpose, the best course would be to focus on changes in the standard of living of the strata of castes that, by consensus, are recognized as being at the bottom of the hierarchy. Given the nature of data availability discussed in the previous chapter, we will focus on a three-way division (Scheduled Castes–Scheduled Tribes–Others) for data sets before 1995, with some discussion of a four-way division (Scheduled Castes–Scheduled Tribes–Other Backward Classes–Others) for the post-1995 data.

As discussed in the previous chapters, both varna and jati are hereditary categories, so that the social code that an individual is expected to follow is supposedly determined by being born into a

---

[1] See, for instance, Srinivas (1996: Introduction, p. xiii).

[2] See, for instance, Kothari (1997) for a glimpse into the interplay of parliamentary politics and caste. Indian newspapers are a good source of stories and statements by politicians that clearly indicate the use of castes (jatis) as 'vote banks'.

[3] See, for instance, Panini (1996).

[4] Panini (1996) argues forcefully that 'occupational diversification has occurred in all castes' (p. 31) despite his discussion of 'caste clustering', which means 'certain castes tend to be prominent in particular occupations' (p. 32), later in the essay.

particular jati. This social code encompasses marriage, occupation, rules of conduct towards women and members of other castes, and so on. In independent India, legally the caste code is not binding, and in actual fact its rigidity varies a great deal with respect to each of its facets across the spectrum of castes. At one end of the spectrum, particularly among upper-class urban Indians, there are individuals who lead a life completely free of caste: displaying almost no awareness of caste in their everyday lives. At the other end, there would be individuals whose life trajectories would follow a more or less pre-determined path. The village studies pioneered by M.N. Srinivas, and continued by several generations of sociologists, provide fascinating insights into these fundamental aspects of caste interactions. Being an economist, my task is limited and straightforward: to examine, at the macro level, the link between caste and standard of living, to the extent data allow. That is to say, since the jati is the socially operative category, it is obviously impossible to comment on the standard of living of each jati. But we can say something instructive about the three-way or four-way division, something that can contribute to the debate on the extent of the change in the material aspects of caste disparity.

Based not on feasibility or triviality of the exercise, but perhaps more on an Occidental–Oriental dichotomy, Dumont (1980: 164) raises the question of the 'applicability to traditional India of the very category of economics'. Articulate critiques of Dumont exist;[5] summing up those critiques is outside the scope of this chapter. However, one can reiterate the point made in Chapter 1. To believe that an economic analysis alone can uncover the complexities of the caste system would be erroneous; however, to bypass or ignore an economic analysis would present an *equally* partial, and hence possibly erroneous, picture. More importantly, the point that needs due recognition is that there are aspects of the caste system that are certainly amenable to an economic analysis. After all, jatis existed, and continue to exist, with certain associated material conditions and regardless of what the motivations of individuals might be (utility/profit maximization, self-interest, altruism, spiritualism, or whatever else), material standards of living can certainly be assessed. Finally, while care should be taken to formulate models that incorporate

---

[5] See Gupta (1984), Srinivas (1989), and Chatterjee (1997).

crucial distinguishing features of a given reality, certain economic phenomena and institutions are ubiquitous. Thus, an analysis of inequality and inter-group disparity is not out of place in any country of the world: the most prosperous, industrialized nations as well as the poorest are grappling with these extremely serious issues as ethnic divisions sharpen all over the world.

The bottom line, therefore, is that the standard of living debate is certainly not trivial. For a debate that is so easily empirically verifiable, unfortunately, the bulk of the discussion, certainly until the last few years, was divorced from any reference to the all-India macro-level data. Most of the sociological analysis is sceptical of large data sets and for the most part, refuses to engage with the macro evidence. On the other hand, most of the economic literature on poverty and inequality until certainly the 1990s was focused on individual and not on inter-group disparities.[6] As we noted in Chapter 1, it is only in the last six or seven years that we have seen a proliferation of empirical analyses that directly address caste inequalities, thus also reinforcing the validity of this enquiry that I have been engaged in for over a decade now and whose results I want to share through this volume.

Before we turn to discussing the standard of living by caste, it might be useful to state some stylized facts about the Indian economy, especially as they relate to the specific data sets that have formed the basis of the empirical analysis, for the benefit of non-Indian readers. The following section can be skipped without loss of continuity; readers familiar with these basics can move directly to the next section that presents evidence based on two large macro data sets.

Some Stylized Facts

Rural–urban disparities in India are deep-rooted and get manifested in almost all indicators. India's population is mainly rural: according to the 2001 census, only 27.8 per cent of Indians reside in urban areas. This illustrates one of the several contrasts that characterize the Indian economy. Despite the predominantly rural population, the

---

[6] This chapter, and indeed the rest of the discussion, does not deal with overall poverty and its differential incidence across social groups. There is a huge literature on poverty estimation in India, with widely divergent estimates, doing justice to the complexity of which would require a lengthy, connected but tangential discussion. Suffice it to note that irrespective of the specific estimate, SCs and STs are disproportionately represented among the poor.

value added by agriculture as a percentage of gross domestic product (GDP) has declined from 42 per cent in 1970 to 29 per cent in 1990, 23 per cent in 2000, and to 18 per cent in 2007. The corresponding proportions for industry are 21 per cent, 27 per cent, 26 per cent, and 30 per cent; and those for services are 37 per cent, 44 per cent, 50 per cent, and 52 per cent.[7] The agro-climatic diversity in the country implies that almost all the major crops are produced here and the regional differentials in the contribution of agriculture to the state domestic product (SDP) can be partially attributed to the differential cropping pattern. Industrialization, both in its geographical spread and composition, displays marked regional variation. The Indian economy has been loosening and gradually dismantling the Soviet-inspired *dirigiste* model of economic development since the mid-1980s and increasingly shifting to a market-based economy. In 1991, as a result of a foreign exchange crisis, the economy took a decisive turn towards liberalization and privatization, and thus became much more integrated with the dominant global economic order, than at any time since independence.

The states in contemporary India are the result of linguistic reorganization, done in the 1950s and early 1960s, of the provinces ruled directly by the British and the former princely states, each culturally and historically distinct. There were numerous further reorganizations of states in subsequent decades. Some states such as Chhattisgarh, Jharkhand, and Uttarakhand are a result of a recent reorganization of some of the other bigger states; some others such as Goa and Delhi were granted statehood at different times after Independence.

The pre-colonial diversity got further complicated by two factors. One was economic, in that the impact of British rule and of the consequent 'modernization' was lopsided. The second factor, unrelated to the reorganization of states or to the lopsided economic development of different regions, was that several of these regions witnessed major social movements, not necessarily connected, which led to reforms within Hinduism, and shaped the socio-cultural contours of the region for subsequent years. The social reform movements impacted the functioning of the caste systems in those particular regions in specific ways, and thus the evolution of caste inequalities took on region-

[7] See, for instance, http://databank.worldbank.org/ddp/, accessed on 14 May 2009.

specific or state-specific characteristics. For these reasons, states of India represent very diverse histories and ethnic/community inter-relationships. The north-eastern states are majority ST states[8] with significant inter-ethnic strife *within* each state, and even though there are sections here that report themselves as SCs, the proportion of SCs is actually very small.

It is, therefore, highly likely that the specific history of vigorous social reform in certain states might influence variables such as access to primary education for SCs and women: groups that have traditionally been denied access to basic education. The current data sets do not allow us to test for a set of influences that have operated through centuries; however, some broad patterns can be discerned, as we will see later. With this kind of diversity, it helps to think of India as what Europe would be if it were one country. Thus, for India, a regional- or state-level analysis of any problem is imperative: any generalization that holds true at the all-India level has to be nuanced with references to the regional diversity, some of which would confirm the all-India picture and some would question it from different angles. Given that they are products of specific historic conditions, the regional differences could additionally provide clues into the differential impact of alternative policies.

INDICATORS OF MATERIAL WELL-BEING

There is a fair amount of scepticism about using only income-based measures to assess standard of living. Indeed, there are several other spheres along which standard of living or well-being advances can be gauged.[9] In recent years, with the popularity of the human development approach and other alternative approaches (such as the capabilities approach) to measuring well-being, using income alone is almost passé.

[8] According to the 2001 census, the percentage of ST population was 64 in Arunachal Pradesh, 86 in Meghalaya, 94 in Mizoram, and 89 in Nagaland. Other states, such as Assam, Manipur, and Sikkim have large tribal populations but not necessarily STs; however, even here the share of STs is close to 30 per cent, except in Assam.

[9] The 'Kerala Model' of development, in fact, shows that it is possible for a relatively poor state such as Kerala to achieve high levels of development in social indicators, such as education and health. Thus, its population might be, relatively speaking, income-poor but is enriched in other very important ways.

I have been working with the two largest all-India data sets (after the census) to investigate the various aspects of standard of living. First, the successive rounds of the National Sample Survey (NSS), surveying over 100,000 households across all states of India. The NSS rounds that have been used to compute figures reported later correspond to the following years: NSS-38 in 1983; NSS-50 in 1993–4; NSS-55 in 1999–2000; NSS-61 in 2004–5.[10] Second, the National Family and Health Survey (NFHS), with close to 90,000 households, has three rounds of data so far: NFHS-I in 1992–3, NFHS-II in 1998–9, and NFHS-III in 2005–6. Thus, irrespective of when we believe the liberalization and globalization trend started in India (mid-1980s or early 1990s), the data reported in this chapter cover that period and could be used to discuss the impact of these changes on inter-caste disparity.

Income data in India, in fact in several developing countries, are notoriously poor and monthly per capita expenditure (MPCE) is often used as a proxy for income. It should be noted that consumption inequality is typically lower than income inequality, which in turn is lower than wealth inequality; so gaps based on MPCE will be lower than the gaps based on income.[11] The best source of MPCE data, by caste groups and by state, across time, is the NSS. In addition, both the NSS and the NFHS also provide information about several other crucial variables, such as landholding, occupational structure, and education. The principle objective of the NFHS is to provide information on health outcomes of mothers and children; unfortunately, it does not contain any information on certain variables that economists would consider basic to analysing inequality, that is, income, wages, or consumption expenditure. The absence of this information makes the standard measures of economic inequality inaccessible. While this seemed like a serious limitation at the time I started working on NFHS-I, it turned out to be a blessing in disguise since I was forced to look at some of the other variables that could be combined into an index that captures

---

[10] These are all large sample rounds. I am using NSS-38 as a shorthand notation to connote the 38th round of NSS; similarly for the other rounds.

[11] The Gini coefficients based on income data from the Desai et al. (2010) survey are higher than what researchers have estimated using the NSS MPCE data. Zacharias and Vakulabharanam (2009) find even higher levels of inequality based on wealth indicators.

standard of living more broadly than an income-based measure. Thus, I identified five indicators from the NFHS—occupation, education, landholding, assets (including consumer durables), and livestock—that I used to construct the Caste Development Index (CDI).[12] The following discussion is based on evidence from both these sources of data, finally leading to the inter-temporal comparisons of the CDI that is constructed from the NFHS data.[13] I will first discuss some of these variables individually before discussing the index. The reason I used the NFHS data to construct the index (and not the NSS) was simply that I wanted to make use of the information contained in the data set and this seemed like an interesting and potentially useful exploratory path to follow. Of course, the index could be recalculated with NSS, or indeed with any other, data set with similar information.

Occupation

This is perhaps the most important variable contained in the index, for two reasons: one, because occupational status is the closest indicator of income; two, as the discussion so far suggests, assertions about the degree of change in the caste system rest critically on the evidence on the caste–occupation nexus. For reasons discussed earlier, we will not be able to use the macro data to examine precisely the changes in jati–occupation link, since macro data on occupations by jati is not

[12] The NFHS-II independently realized the necessity of a standard of living index (SLI) that has been created using several other variables as well (NFHS 1998–9). Of course, since the SLI was not created for the first round, it cannot be the basis of comparison over time. Thus, the basis of comparison is the CDI that I have calculated for the three rounds. Having said this, the CDI, which is inspired by the HDI, suffers from certain well-known drawbacks, for instance, shifting goalposts. For comparisons over a long period of time, this could be a drawback that would need to be settled. However, for this particular three-point comparison, the maximum and minimum values do not change, and thus in this specific exercise, the shifting goalposts problem does not arise.

[13] Unfortunately, there are problems of comparability across the two rounds of the NFHS. As often happens with large data sets, variables have been dropped, added, or simply changed to address the lacunae in the first round. Thus, while the changes in the second round are an improvement, they make strict comparability with the first round difficult. In the context of the CDI, for instance, an entire set of questions based on livestock ownership is absent from the second round: the only question that is asked is 'Do you own any livestock?' The yes/no responses to this question is not strictly comparable to the question asking the number of animals owned that NFHS-I had.

available, but will instead examine the overlap between contemporary occupations (which include hereditary occupations) and caste, based on the broad caste categories. The degree to which the association between hereditary occupations and jati is intact or broken has to be examined through micro-level case studies, and that evidence might reveal a mixed picture, but it is only a broad picture from macro-level evidence that can cast light on the contemporary nature of the occupation–caste overlap.

For the three rounds of NFHS, I aggregated the various occupational categories[14] in the data set to six broad groups (to ensure comparability across time) and cross-tabulated the broad caste categories (SC, ST, OBC, or Others) with occupational status.[15] Table 3.1 shows the picture from NFHS-III,[16] and, as is to be expected in a predominantly rural sample, the largest proportions are associated with primary activities across all caste groups, but there is definite evidence of inter-caste disparity.

Primarily due to the north-eastern states, the ST distribution looks marginally better than the SC distribution at the top end of the occupational spectrum. Yet, despite the higher numbers of STs from regions where they experience relatively more favourable outcomes,

[14] On occupations of respondents, NFHS-II has a much more detailed disaggregation than NFHS-I. The total number of occupations listed in the former is close to 100, whereas the latter had only broad occupational groups. NFHS-II further groups these various occupations into broad categories, but these again are different (and more detailed) from the broad categories of the first round. I have rearranged the broad categories into the same number of categories as the first round, while roughly attempting to match the descriptions of the first round. Similar adjustments were made for NFHS-III. However, it is likely that the result is not strictly comparable, in that while I have made the number of categories the same across rounds, the occupation groupings are not completely identical.

[15] The six groups in the survey were: not working; manual labourers and farmers; clerical workers, sales workers, service workers, and merchants; creative workers and artisans; professional, technical, administrative managers (low-level); and professional, technical, administrative managers (high-level). The survey allows for very large households containing up to 41 members per household. I use the occupation of the head of the household as the proxy for the occupational and education status of the entire household.

[16] I am reproducing here the numbers from the latest NHFS survey to avoid overload of tables. All the other tables and numbers, not reproduced here, are available from the author upon request.

Table 3.1 Occupational Levels of Household Heads, Major States, India, 2005–6 (per cent)

	SC						ST						OBC						Others					
	1	2	3	4	5	6	1	2	3	4	5	6	1	2	3	4	5	6	1	2	3	4	5	6
INDIA	4.94	67.54	14.03	9.77	3.44	0.28	2.74	79.23	9.46	5.1	3.26	0.21	6.39	56.66	19.49	12.5	4.56	0.39	8.05	45.68	25.08	11.25	8.44	1.5
NORTH																								
Jammu and Kashmir	4.38	77.71	10.84	4.71	2.35	0	9.11	59.25	18.13	6.37	6.23	0.91	2.99	53.87	25.79	13.73	2.87	0.75	6.24	40.86	26.92	16.92	7.92	1.14
Himachal Pradesh	11.51	58.54	10.88	13.21	5.04	0.82	9.87	51.99	22.85	4.94	8.71	1.65	12.52	48.91	16.08	13.26	9.22	0	13.21	41.36	25.5	6.42	13.1	0.41
Punjab	8.96	61.35	12.64	13.39	3.65	0	0	66.67	0	33.33	0	0	6.43	45.9	22.6	15.75	9.32	0	8.75	46.44	22.28	13.43	8.4	0.7
Uttaranchal	4.36	63.94	14.36	11.31	5.71	0.32	5.64	68.33	16.7	3.69	5.64	0	5.96	54.72	19.88	11.73	6.81	0.89	8.67	43.49	26.4	6.07	12.8	2.57
Haryana	3.4	71.59	12.61	8.39	3.7	0.31	19.25	61.51	0	0	19.25	0	7.65	54.93	20.49	13.53	3.4	0	8.51	53.88	23.68	5.75	7.4	0.77
Delhi	5.79	36.25	30.02	22.31	3.74	1.88	7.53	41.95	27.94	9.69	12.89	0	5.75	28.35	33.37	22.42	8.1	2.01	6.9	16.17	46.57	17.31	10.08	2.95
Rajasthan	4.87	68.66	11.2	11.36	3.71	0.2	4.84	81.89	6.54	2.65	3.81	0.27	5.05	65.83	14.4	10.72	3.69	0.3	3.92	38.08	27.84	12.11	13.54	4.52
Uttar Pradesh	4.32	69.89	12.74	11.32	1.56	0.17	3.92	46.99	3.92	45.12	0.06	0.13	6.99	57.79	18.86	13.71	2.51	0.13	10.22	44.49	23.56	12.31	8.71	0.69
CENTRAL																								
Chhattisgarh	3.15	72.45	11.66	7.27	5.47	0	2.72	86.03	4.67	2.6	3.97	0	3.43	71.39	11.87	7.82	5.41	0.08	4.59	39.04	28.5	13.34	14.18	0.35
Madhya Pradesh	2.94	75.18	11.06	8.9	1.68	0.23	0.36	91.49	3.65	2.71	1.61	0.18	1.83	69.94	15.78	8.48	3.84	0.14	5.07	46.97	29.29	5.55	10.44	2.69
EAST																								
Bihar	9.12	73.53	9.63	7.06	0.54	0.11	17.89	71.55	5.28	0	5.28	0	15.23	57.88	17.9	6.28	2.71	0	22.82	47.1	16.21	4.43	8.9	0.54
West Bengal	5.73	65.4	15.76	9.51	3.25	0.35	3.58	80.76	9.27	4.29	2.1	0	2.96	53.98	28.52	10.56	3.06	0.93	8.18	51.47	21.12	11.37	7.34	0.52
Jharkhand	3.61	71.7	10.76	12.9	1.04	0	1.78	86.23	4.62	5.1	2	0.26	4.36	61.83	19.6	10.38	3.49	0.34	6.06	35.94	32.69	15.66	9.05	0.6

	1	2	3	4	5	6	1	2	3	4	5	6	1	2	3	4	5	6	1	2	3	4	5	6
Orissa	4.38	77.71	10.84	4.71	2.35	0	1.6	87.07	6.52	2.82	1.99	0	6.27	57.15	20.82	10.88	4.79	0.08	9.36	49.99	27.74	5.28	5.83	1.81
NORTH-EAST																								
Sikkim	3.85	44.12	17.43	22.98	10.5	1.13	5.82	51.1	19.14	9.2	14.74	0	5.51	52.06	19.27	9.11	13.78	0.27	9.16	29.33	33.27	14.08	14.16	0
Arunachal Pradesh	4.35	24.62	34.55	18.12	16.9	1.45	8.26	58.13	14.36	2.41	16.22	0.62	3.39	37.99	31	3.39	24.22	0	1.18	54.73	14.92	11.37	17.04	0.77
Nagaland	6.78	42.06	30.14	15.19	5.37	0.47	6.61	48.2	23.93	5.3	15.7	0.25	4.96	51.25	24.02	5.94	13.21	0.62	3.82	34.28	36.26	14.02	9.35	2.27
Manipur	2.43	56.27	18.78	10.37	12.16	0	5.47	60.34	13.74	11.37	8.63	0.45	3.9	46.45	25.95	11.02	11.9	0.78	3.55	54.02	19.97	11.74	10.19	0.53
Mizoram	0	79.34	0	0	20.66	0	3.3	53.74	24.62	5.26	12.2	0.88	14.79	13.61	71.6	0	0	0	0	10.62	63.7	10.62	15.07	0
Tripura	7.14	60.42	18.31	5.92	7.95	0.27	4.32	72.1	8.45	2.55	12.58	0	9.02	44.51	24.24	13.07	9.17	0	11.68	48.74	20.47	6.54	11.65	0.92
Meghalaya	3.72	27.69	47.46	11.94	5.48	3.72	7.73	58.15	24.83	2.97	5.63	0.7	7.15	28.97	56.54	3.57	3.77	0.7	4.24	36.59	37.14	7.88	12.31	1.85
Assam	5.81	54.46	22.07	12.43	4.42	0.81	4.48	63.37	17.7	4.74	8.47	1.24	9.16	48.93	25.93	5.68	9.53	0.78	7.34	53.39	24.73	5.84	8.03	0.67
WEST																								
Gujarat	3.79	57.88	17.97	14.53	4.8	1.02	2.27	72.66	14.18	8.62	2.28	0	3.96	60.02	18.13	12.87	3.94	1.08	4.05	35.7	24.14	22.7	8.94	4.47
Maharashtra	4.69	58.92	21.56	8.92	5.55	0.36	2.13	72.11	17.08	5.75	2.89	0.04	3.41	46.19	29.2	11.94	8.6	0.66	4.48	44.5	29.09	12.06	8.74	1.13
Goa	12.98	51.16	19.58	9.68	6.61	0	16.42	57.16	19	4.83	2.58	0	13.14	33.35	29.57	14.74	9.21	0	16.72	32.05	27.19	11.07	11.6	1.36
SOUTH																								
Andhra Pradesh	2.89	72.21	11.63	7.11	5.71	0.45	1.23	79.78	9.34	6.98	2.03	0.64	3.65	61.44	16.55	15.35	2.77	0.24	5.58	46.8	26.35	13.72	5.38	2.16
Karnataka	3.64	68.11	14.36	9.55	4.13	0.21	4.23	77.79	10.46	4.73	2.79	0	4.2	53.01	21.94	14.36	5.7	0.78	4.23	60.01	19.8	7.96	7.01	0.99
Kerala	6.41	69.03	13.89	6.4	4.27	0	2.64	76.34	10.55	7.87	2.59	0	18.81	34.78	23.01	15.98	5.76	1.67	16.5	39.69	24.7	10.33	6.33	2.44
Tamil Nadu	4.67	67.49	13.47	8.9	5.45	0.02	6.66	80.23	6.46	6.66	0	0	6.68	48.47	20.52	16.51	7.32	0.51	8.41	12.58	27.94	6.64	34.7	9.72

Source: Author's calculations based on NFHS-III data.

Notes: 1 = not working; 2 = manual labourers and farmers; 3 = clerical workers, sales workers, service workers, and merchants; 4 = creative workers and artisans; 5 = professional, technical, and administrative managers (low-level); 6 = professional, technical, and administrative managers (high-level).

looking at the bottom rung (unemployed, not working, primary activities), the SC and the ST distribution is very similar and presents a clear contrast to the 'Others' across all the three rounds, which, of course, is not evident from Table 3.1 since it focuses on NFHS-III alone (see note 14). What is interesting to note in the context of the OBC debate, viz., the claim that OBC as a category is not really 'backward', is that both NFHS-II and NFHS-III reveal that the gap between Others and OBCs at the uppermost occupation levels is positive in all states of India, except West Bengal. In other words, in no state in India have the OBCs 'taken over' or surpassed the upper castes at the topmost end of the occupational spectrum.

Across the three rounds, for all groups, the high numbers at the bottom end and the low numbers at the top end indicate occupational inequality *within* each caste category, but the clear differences between castes at the top and bottom ends of the occupational spectrum suggest that caste shapes occupational attainment, something that is confirmed by evidence in the subsequent chapters. The main point that emerges from this is the continuing dominance of upper castes in the prestigious, upper-rung occupations. It would be a reasonable assumption that these also would be better-paying occupations. Hence, we find no evidence of a substantial *reversal* of the traditional association between caste hierarchy and economic power.

It would be useful to keep this occupational distribution in mind when discussing the Dalit 'creamy layer';[17] we will have more to say on this issue in later chapters.

Changes in Occupational Distribution by the Respondents' Principal Status

What does the NSS data tell us about changes in the occupational structure? The NSS classification is not very illuminating, as it uses omnibus occupational categories (that is, self-employed, helper in household enterprises, regular salaried/wage earner, casual labour, did not work but was willing and available for work, attended educational institution, attended domestic duty, and others), which hide more than they reveal. Also, these occupational categories are not very good indicators of class or status. However, with all these limitations, here

---

[17] A term used for clustering of beneficiaries of affirmative action at the upper income ends of the SCs; see Chapter 7 for a discussion of the 'creaming' effect.

is what the picture looks like (Figures 3.1–3.4, based on author's calculations from the Employment–Unemployment Surveys of the NSS), based on the respondents' principal occupation, over four rounds of NSS, spanning a two-decade period (1983 to 2004–5). Each of these figures shows the distribution for each category, first for rural over all the rounds, and then for urban over all the rounds.

What Figures 3.1–3.4 reveal, first, is the rural–urban disparity for all the caste groups. We also see that for urban areas, all the social groups report approximately 30 to 35 per cent of workers to be in the somewhat ill-defined category of 'attended domestic duty', the proportion being the highest for 'Others', both in rural and urban areas. For reasons stated earlier, OBC data is available only in the last two rounds of the NSS. I have calculated the distribution for 'OBC+Others' category for the last two rounds, since that is comparable to the 'Others' category of the first two rounds, as well as separately for OBCs and 'Others' (as shown in the figures). It turns out that the OBC distribution does not reveal much change over the two rounds, not surprising since it is only a five-year period. The two largest categories for OBCs are 'self-employment' and 'attended domestic duty', although in comparison to 'Others', the former proportion is smaller and the latter larger.

For inter-temporal consistency, we can compare SCs, STs, and 'OBC+Others' (figures for the latter not reproduced here, but available with the author upon request). For the latter, in rural India, the next largest group after 'domestic duty' is 'self-employed' (whose proportion dropped from 28 per cent to 24 per cent), followed by 'casual labour' (whose proportion has remained roughly constant around 16 per cent). For rural SCs, however, the picture looks different. The proportion of rural SCs that reports 'casual labour' as its principal occupation is much higher than the 'OBC+Others' group, but it has declined from 38 to 35 per cent, after having reached nearly 40 per cent. The proportion of 'self-employed' among SCs has remained constant at roughly 16 per cent. The picture for STs is similar to the SCs, rather than to the 'OBC+Others'. For STs, 20 per cent are in the category 'helper in household enterprises', whereas 31 per cent are 'casual labour'.

In urban areas, the distribution across caste groups differs from the rural areas in the following respects: first, the 'regular salaried/wage earners' category is much larger for each of the groups, as compared to rural areas. Second, the proportion of 'self-employed' is the largest

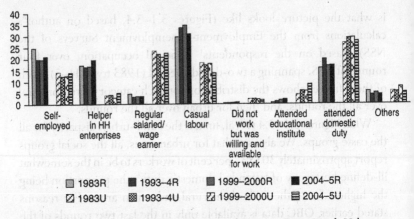

Figure 3.1   Occupation Distribution of STs over Time, Rural–Urban
(per cent)

Source: Authors' calculations based on the NSS Employment–Unemployment Surveys, various rounds.

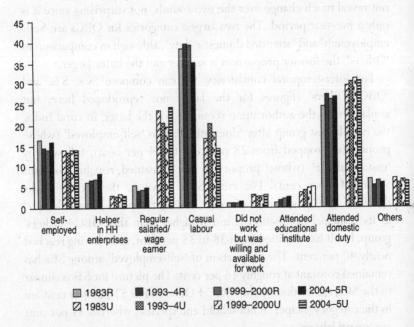

Figure 3.2   Occupational Distribution of SCs over Time, Rural–Urban
(per cent)

Source: Authors' calculations based on the NSS Employment–Unemployment Surveys, various rounds.

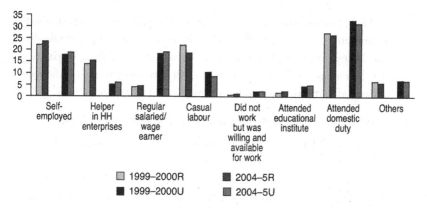

Figure 3.3   Occupational Distribution of OBCs over Time, Rural–Urban
(per cent)

Source: Authors' calculations based on the NSS Employment–Unemployment Surveys,
various rounds.

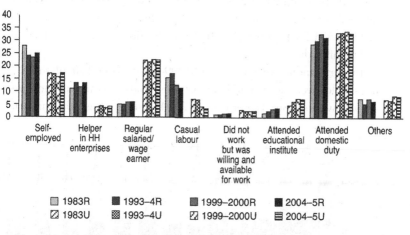

Figure 3.4   Occupational Distribution of 'Others' over Time, Rural–Urban
(per cent)

Source: Authors' calculations based on the NSS Employment–Unemployment Surveys,
various rounds.

among 'OBC+Others' (18 per cent); it is 14 per cent for SCs and STs.
Another big difference is in the proportion of 'casual labour': both SCs
and STs report roughly 14 per cent, whereas 'OBC+Others' report
around 6 per cent.

Thus, both in rural and urban areas, the patterns of occupational attainment reveal a clear difference by broad caste affiliation. While this may be less surprising in rural areas, the persistence of these disparities in urban areas needs to be noted. We will have more to say on the role of caste affiliations in urban labour markets in Chapters 6 and 7.

Changes in Distribution of Households by 'Household Type'

Another way that the NSS classifies households is by 'household type', which defines the nature and type of work from which the household derives its major income. Households are classified into different types depending on the economic activity of the members of the household, from which the major income of the house was generated, during 365 days preceding the date of survey. For rural areas, these categories are 'self-employed in non-agriculture', 'agricultural labour', 'other labour', 'self-employed in agriculture', and 'others'. For urban areas, these are 'self-employed', 'regular wage/salary earner', 'casual labour', and 'others' (note that for NSS-38, urban households were classified into only two types: 'self-employed' and 'others').

Figures 3.5 and 3.6 report that classification, separately for rural and urban India.

In rural India, we see that in 1999–2000, over half of the SC households were agricultural labour households, and that proportion went down to about 41 per cent in 2004–5. In contrast, the share of

■ Others   ▢ Casual labour   ▦ Regular wage/salary earners   ■ Self-employed

Figure 3.5   Change in Occupational Distribution by Household Type over Time, Rural India

Source: Author's calculations, various rounds of NSS.

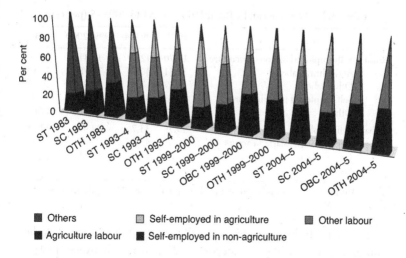

Others

Self-employed in agriculture

Other labour

Agriculture labour

Self-employed in non-agriculture

Figure 3.6   Change in Occupational Distribution by Household Type
over Time, Urban India

Source: Author's calculations, various rounds of NSS.

agricultural labour households amongst 'Others' never exceeded 24
per cent over the entire period, and was about 16 per cent in 2004–5.
The main difference between the caste groups in the urban areas is the
proportion of casual labour: for 'OBC+Others', it is less than one-
tenth (8 per cent), whereas for the SCs, even though it shows a decline,
it is nearly 22 per cent in 2004–5.

Summing up the rural–urban differences (for all groups taken
together, see Table 3.2), we see that for rural households, 'self-employed
in agriculture' and 'agricultural labour' comprise the two major
categories of employment. The proportion of the latter increased over
the first three data points but dropped by almost 7 percentage points
between 1999–2000 and 2004–5. The proportion of the former
followed exactly the opposite trend: dropped over the first three
rounds and then rose between the third and the fourth data points. It
is possible that a part of this shift might be accounted for by a change in
self-identification by households, but that is difficult to verify. It should
be noted that even a distress-driven survival strategy can be counted
as 'self-employment'; this omnibus term is not very revealing. Thus, a
part of the increase in the proportion of self-employment in rural and
urban India could represent survival activities, as it is mirrored by a
decrease in the proportions of other forms of paid occupations.

Table 3.2   Occupation, by Rural/Urban, 1983 to 2004–5 (per cent)

		1983	1993–4	1999–2000	2004–5
Rural	Self-employed in non-agriculture	11.70	12.69	13.41	15.76
	Agricultural labour	30.71	30.34	32.18	25.82
	Other labour	6.57	7.95	7.93	10.88
	Self-employed in agriculture	40.73	37.83	32.74	35.92
	Others	10.29	11.19	13.68	11.62
Urban	Self-employed	19.79	33.7	34.43	37.53
	Regular wage/salaried earners		43.36	41.76	41.29
	Casual labour		13.21	13.88	11.78
	Others	80.21	9.73	9.83	9.4

Source: Author's calculations based on the NSS Employment–Unemployment Surveys, various rounds.

In urban India, 'regular salaried' and 'self-employed' together comprise the two biggest categories. We see that between 1993–4 and 2004–5, the proportion of regular salaried households decreased slightly (by roughly 2 percentage points). The proportion of self-employed households increased over the period, again the largest increase corresponding to the time period between 1999–2000 and 2004–5. The proportion of casual labour households declined slightly during the same period.

While the variable used in the construction of the CDI is occupation, the other side of the coin is unemployment and underemployment. We have seen that there are unambiguous differences in occupational attainment, discernible even with these broad, imprecise occupational categories. Appendix 3.A presents data on unemployment and underemployment, which demonstrates clear caste divisions in the proportion of those who seek productive work but fail to find it.

Overall, therefore, irrespective of the data set and the classificatory system used to define occupation, the evidence of inter-caste disparity in occupational attainment is clear and persistent. SCs (and STs) are disproportionately clustered in the lowest rungs: casual labour, agricultural labour, and unemployed, while the 'Others' dominate the more prestigious occupations. Comparing 'Others' with OBCs, we find substantial gaps between these two groups as well. Thus, the upper castes' (loosely proxied by 'Others' without OBCs) hold over prestigious, better-paying occupations does not seem to have loosened; their fears of having been marginalized seem to be based on myth rather than reality.

EDUCATION

Underlying the occupational pattern is the educational attainment of the population. Looking at educational attainment by caste for all the categories, illiteracy is a problem, though it is declining over time but perhaps not as fast as would befit an emerging 'superpower'. Education is a state subject and the calculations indicate wide regional variations in educational attainment, reflecting a combination of two factors: the differing importance the respective state governments have given to education, especially in making it accessible to groups that were historically disadvantaged, and the respective state government's fiscal constraints.[18] A comparison of the three NFHS rounds reveals that the regional pattern in educational attainment is marked and consistent: the southern and western states displaying better educational outcomes, followed by the eastern states, and then by the northern states that continue to be laggards in educational attainment for all caste groups. The north-eastern states have been consistent in their exceptionally good performance, which is especially noteworthy given their relative economic underdevelopment, poor infrastructure, and the serious and violent ethnic strife for the last several decades.

Apropos the point made earlier about the impact of social reform being reflected in better educational outcomes, we see that states such as Kerala (which, contrary to official pronouncements, still displays some illiteracy, albeit lower than all other states), Maharashtra, and Tamil Nadu display significantly higher overall achievements, but also better outcomes for SCs. However, in these states, the gaps are substantial. The gaps in Tamil Nadu are especially noteworthy, given that it has been the arena of non-Brahmin politics for decades and Tamilian Brahmins often claim to be marginalized because of extensive reservations for non-Brahmins, much higher than in the rest of the country. It is interesting to note that despite all that, Tamil Nadu has the highest gap between 'Others' and both SCs and OBCs in higher education.

Tables 3.3 and 3.4 reveal that, first, illiteracy has declined consistently over the last two decades for all social groups across

---

[18] 'State subject' here means that it is under the purview of the state government (as opposed to the central government). This is standard terminology used by the Indian government.

Table 3.3 Education Levels of Household Heads, Major States, India, 2005–6 (per cent)

Education Level	% of SCs with						% of STs with						% of OBCs with						% of Others with					
	0	1	2	3	4	5	0	1	2	3	4	5	0	1	2	3	4	5	0	1	2	3	4	5
INDIA	47.33	11.84	7.33	25.77	3.28	4.38	55.22	13.82	5.81	19.66	1.94	3.5	38.92	10.9	8.32	30.91	4.13	6.74	25.65	10.73	6.55	35.45	6.18	15.35
NORTH																								
Jammu and Kashmir	52.73	6.98	7.67	28.75	0.98	2.89	52.96	5.36	5.52	32.56	1.34	2.26	39.37	5.9	4.97	42.55	3.74	5.61	34.34	5.18	5.1	37.37	5.61	12.24
Himachal Pradesh	39.54	8.92	10.69	34.22	2.81	3.81	35.89	3.92	11.08	41.1	3.51	4.49	29.18	7.73	9.84	44.61	4.56	4.07	22.71	5.86	9.97	41.63	6.82	12.91
Punjab	50.83	6.54	11.08	27.08	2.44	1.92	66.67	0	0	33.33	0	0	30.7	3.6	11.75	47.15	3.9	2.89	30.13	4.9	8.53	40.16	5.66	10.51
Uttaranchal	39.82	7.76	11.57	30.74	4.17	5.78	40.49	7.02	12.43	28.66	4.21	7.2	38.32	8.46	11.93	27.62	5.96	7.49	26.53	3.67	10.92	32.21	10.35	16.32
Haryana	46.68	6.56	8.38	32.46	3.67	2.24	57.85	0	0	22.87	0	19.28	39.23	4.8	8.9	38.04	3.82	5.22	27.49	4.72	6.51	43.02	6.73	11.53
Delhi	30.94	4.59	12.2	40.11	6.48	5.69	18.88	10.98	11.27	29.87	6.44	22.55	23.42	4.59	8.63	37.31	11.18	14.87	10.61	2.22	5.71	34.15	11.75	35.56
Rajasthan	54.08	8.64	9.24	21.23	2.21	4.6	58.28	8.17	7.76	18.75	1.62	5.42	48.1	7.63	9.65	26.86	2.86	4.91	21.45	5.09	10.74	29.51	5.41	27.68
Uttar Pradesh	52.37	5.92	8.87	23.24	4.86	4.55	70.55	5.06	9.01	13.97	1.36	0.04	49.64	5.47	8.77	26.04	4.87	4.97	27.28	4.98	6.97	32.04	10.27	18.25
CENTRAL																								
Chhattisgarh	39.18	19.08	9.54	22.66	4.82	4.55	54.95	14.9	7.84	16.78	2.06	3.09	41.46	17.23	11.94	20.97	3.18	4.96	15.7	14.36	6.93	30.21	5.08	27.52
Madhya Pradesh	45.01	10.5	8.34	26.41	3.98	5.76	63.77	12.06	8.84	13.39	0.54	1.4	38.02	13.96	11.71	26.28	3.89	6.15	18.21	6.38	8.31	31.7	8.96	26.44
EAST																								
Bihar	74.58	5.74	2.42	14.05	1.85	1.36	46.76	3.24	0	46.76	3.24	0	54.44	6.44	5.03	26.57	4.22	3.29	42.37	4.86	2.55	29.12	6.6	14.5

West Bengal	47.08	20.53	5.01	22.95	1.48	2.95	20.52	4.08	13.95	0	1.93	27.16	16.57	5.88	36.28	7.23	6.83	32.21	16.72	5.04	30.51	4.12	11.27
Jharkhand	52.76	15.33	4.86	20.02	3.18	3.85	9.98	3.66	26.67	2.38	3.02	42.83	9.79	6.56	32.06	3.69	4.96	25.22	5.49	4.61	36.95	7.12	20.43
Orissa	44.35	22.43	6.01	23.55	1.15	2.51	14.88	5.91	14.25	1.44	1.47	32.88	20.78	9.76	29.23	2.31	5.04	23.56	15.88	9.28	35.51	3.03	12.75
NORTH-EAST																							
Sikkim	37.09	16.69	8.4	25.51	6.76	5.56	14.36	8.56	23.68	8.21	6.99	30.33	15.39	6.61	31.81	6.88	8.98	29.64	11.31	4.58	37.05	5.55	11.37
Arunachal Pradesh	29.9	12.66	9.35	34.13	4.77	9.19	9.68	6.06	25.35	4.77	8.53	32.14	15.83	3.64	25.7	3.2	19.48	26.76	15.5	6.83	31.95	5.45	13.51
Nagaland	41.98	12.45	5.04	32.72	3.77	4.04	11.69	5.92	41.15	3.96	8.36	29.3	15.04	6.17	40	3.24	6.25	32.49	11.05	6.19	31.98	5.82	12.47
Manipur	29.69	9.88	1.96	43.12	3.91	11.43	12.98	5.01	39.62	6.02	7.79	21.44	8.65	2.4	37.3	7.85	21.1	22.49	10.05	4.45	39.57	6.47	16.49
Mizoram	44.91	9.73	0	40.27	0	5.09	23.06	6.05	45.74	4.37	11.01	25.56	17.04	0	31.84	8.52	17.04	2.88	11.52	2.88	45.81	8.64	28.28
Tripura	28.36	29.13	9	27.56	2.32	3.43	16.27	6.49	30.38	2.96	1.88	17.44	22.55	11.2	40.12	2.25	6.1	21.31	19.12	8.01	35.22	4.92	11.13
Meghalaya	28.01	14.04	5.26	34.79	8.57	9.33	15.29	3.45	27.2	3.73	8.29	22.02	19.95	6.76	38.69	6.76	5.82	31.97	8.13	5.86	33.06	3.49	17.49
Assam	29.89	20.74	4.47	38.15	2.6	3.23	18.96	4.41	36.7	6.62	5.87	15.77	16.6	3.71	48.23	5.81	9.14	33.45	19.94	3.73	31.29	3.58	7.76
WEST																							
Gujarat	29.88	13.7	7.17	40.38	5.06	3.81	16.6	4.37	21.04	2.34	4.09	32.81	17.15	4.75	36.94	2.75	5.6	13.3	9.35	5.8	47.66	5.89	17.99
Maharashtra	30.95	17.28	5.38	35.09	4.22	7.08	20.59	2.43	19.75	2.45	4.89	17.45	15.97	5.33	42.8	5.84	12.53	19.64	12.72	5.47	41.91	6.05	14.18
Goa	48.04	15.51	3.44	26.17	1.52	5.31	12.46	3.88	26.89	2.24	3.14	28.71	19.64	4.24	33.37	4.86	9.18	22.91	13.13	5.71	37.07	5.09	15.98
SOUTH																							
Andhra Pradesh	48.53	10.5	7.47	23.85	3.24	6.4	6.65	4.38	14.81	0.86	2.87	49.84	11.94	8.61	21.25	3.17	5.19	29.74	10.4	9.86	31.45	5.98	12.5
Karnataka	57.33	9.88	3.69	20.21	3.69	5.2	14.63	6.34	18.98	2.76	3.02	32.64	11.79	5.62	33.91	5.77	10.28	34.95	11.09	5.14	29.7	4.51	14.53
Kerala	23.67	26.64	7.69	34.91	1.18	5.91	27.61	8.61	36.21	0	3.44	8.96	19.53	7.55	51.13	3.24	9.49	9.57	18.32	9.1	46.61	5.32	11.03
Tamil Nadu	42	10.79	10.85	28.47	2.89	4.99	12.36	11	14.35	0.86	4.66	26.61	11.27	12.22	36.86	4.02	8.98	3.47	3.18	5.65	32.89	7.74	47.07

Source: Author's calculations based on NFHS-III.

Notes: 0 = no education; 1 = incomplete primary; 2 = complete primary; 3 = incomplete secondary; 4 = complete secondary; 5 = higher.

Table 3.4 Evidence from NSS on Education Levels, Successive Rounds

SC Rural

	00.not literate	01.literate and up to primary	02.middle	03. secondary/ higher secondary	04.diploma/ certificate	05.grad and above
38th	72.01	22.32	4.01	1.5		0.17
50th	61.2	28.31	6.34	3.7		0.44
55th	53.5	31.57	8.98	5.08		0.88
61st	46.28	35.51	10.78	6.03	0.35	1.05

SC Urban

	00.not literate	01.literate and up to primary	02.middle	03. secondary/ higher secondary	04.diploma/ certificate	05.grad and above
38th	48.09	35.51	9.6	5.73		1.08
50th	40.31	36.46	11.8	9.22		2.22
55th	34.17	35.52	14.83	12.21		3.27
61st	28.53	36.27	16.38	13.53	1.25	4.03

OBC Rural

	00.not literate	01.literate and up to primary	02.middle	03. secondary/ higher secondary	04.diploma/ certificate	05.grad and above
55th	46.26	33.82	11.41	7.41		1.1
61st	39.53	36.22	13.4	8.7	0.6	1.55

OBC Urban

	00.not literate	01.literate and up to primary	02.middle	03. secondary/ higher secondary	04.diploma/ certificate	05.grad and above
55th	25.36	35.55	16.85	17.21		5.03
61st	22.02	34.92	17.52	17.14	1.96	6.44

Others Urban

	00.not literate	01.literate and up to primary	02.middle	03. secondary/higher secondary	04.diploma/certificate	05.grad and above
38th	27.64	37.31	14.92	14.36		5.76
50th	20.73	35.08	15.22	19.96		9.02
55th	14.48	29.9	15.67	24.99		14.96
61st	12	28.15	16.09	24.62	2.33	16.81

Others Rural

	00.not literate	01.literate and up to primary	02.middle	03. secondary/higher secondary	04.diploma/certificate	05.grad and above
38th	56.18	30.93	8.03	4.09		0.76
50th	44.96	34.6	11.05	7.9		1.49
55th	33.28	36.97	14.66	12.36		2.73
61st	28.41	38.06	15.48	13.88	0.76	3.41

Source: Authors' calculations based on the NSS Employment–Unemployment Survey, various rounds.

rural and urban areas, but the rural–urban divide continues to be strong across all educational categories. However, there seems to be no convergence in SC–Others trends. In 2004–5, the proportion of urban 'Others' who were illiterate was less than half that of urban SCs. At the other end of the spectrum, the proportion of urban 'Others' who are 'graduate and above' is four times than of urban SCs. Thus, while within each caste category, the direction of change is in the desirable direction (population becoming more literate over time), the rate of change is different for each caste category, as we will see later.

Figure 3.7 shows the gap between 'Others' and SCs at each level of education over the four rounds of the NSS for rural India, followed by Figure 3.8 for urban India. For rural India, as expected, the gap is negative for illiterates (number of SCs who are illiterate is greater than the number of illiterate 'Others') and positive for all other categories of education. From 1983 to 1999–2000, the gap at the illiterate level actually increased and declined in the last phase, but the gap in 2004–5 is still higher than in 1983. This indicates that SCs continue to be dogged by illiteracy, and in this respect, their distance from the 'Others' has actually become larger.

What about those who do not declare themselves to be illiterate? Starting at the very basic category of literates, the gap has steadily narrowed. For the next higher category, the middle-school level,

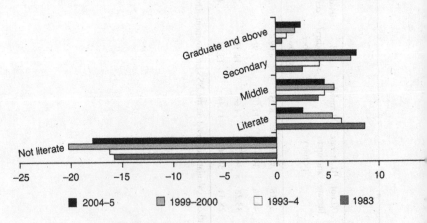

Figure 3.7 Caste Gap in Education: Rural India

Source: Author's calculations from various rounds of NSS.

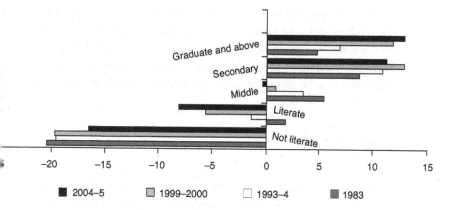

Figure 3.8   Caste Gap in Education: Urban India

Source: Author's calculations from various rounds of NSS.

the trend is similar to the illiterate category and overall the gap is increasing. For 'secondary' and 'graduate and above' categories, the gap has steadily increased. On the whole, therefore, in rural India, the educational attainment gap between 'Others' and SCs is not only persistent, but the last two decades have also shown an increase. SCs in rural India are not catching up, at least not yet. We will say more on the policy implications of this in Chapter 7, but for now it seems like there is no alternative to the urgent and vigorous enforcement of the policy of free and compulsory primary education.

In urban India (Figure 3.8), the picture looks different and more optimistic. First, the illiteracy gap has become smaller, decidedly so between 1999–2000 and 2004–5. At the other end of the spectrum, the gap at the 'graduate and above' level has increased consistently. At the secondary level, the gap narrowed in the last phase, but has increased overall in the two-decade period. Surprisingly, at the middle-school level, the gap has almost closed to become mildly negative. This is contrary not only to rural India, but also to the general understanding that the dropouts at the middle-school level shape the contours of educational disparities in subsequent years. Urban India seems to have moved a notch above: clearly, the gaps in 'secondary' level shape the disparities in subsequent years. Again, this has implications for the kinds of interventions that might be appropriate in order to close the gaps between SCs and 'Others'.

Summing up, although educational disparities by caste are persistent, they follow different patterns for rural and urban India. The latter shows some narrowing of gaps, perhaps not with the speed that would befit the urgency of the problem. It is clear that education in rural India needs to be in urgent focus, particularly at the lower levels and especially for the SCs.

LANDHOLDING

Historically, Dalits have been prohibited from owning wealth, as the quote at the beginning of the chapter indicates, and landownership is perhaps the single most important indicator of wealth, certainly in rural India. As the discussion in Chapter 2 highlighted, lack of landownership was a critical element in the servitude of Dalits. Landownership in India was historically highly unequal (even within the upper castes), and in the post-Independence period, equity and efficiency considerations led to land reforms being placed firmly on the policy agenda. However, the actual implementation was lukewarm as these reforms have been under the purview of the state governments, and only a handful of governments with a political commitment undertook land reforms that were of some consequence (most noteworthy being Kerala and West Bengal). The concentration of land was very high at the time of Independence and continues to remain high despite various land reform laws (for details, see, Sen and Patnaik 1997). The north Indian plains had a much higher initial polarization, and my calculations reveal that after over 60 years, there still is substantial inter-caste disparity in these states.

While the discussion on occupational attainment is very revealing, in that it highlights the strong overlap of caste and status, the manner in which occupational categories have been formulated in the NFHS does not reveal the full extent of the degree of rural stratification, since a very rich landlord and a landless farmer would both fall in the same occupational category ('farm, fish, hunt, or log' or primary activities). Thus, to appreciate the full extent of rural stratification, we have to look at the landholding patterns.

The three rounds of NFHS show a marked regional variation, similar to that seen for education and occupation. More importantly, even in 2005–6, land distribution is highly unequal for all caste groups.[19] States that have had a better record of implementation of land reforms, unfortunately, do not necessarily display a better record of SC access to landownership. For example, both in Kerala and West Bengal, SCs are predominantly landless and gaps between them and 'Others' are among the highest in the country. Surprisingly, Rajasthan and Uttarakhand display a relatively more equal distribution of land, both compared to the all-India distribution as well as compared to states that have been more serious about implementing land reforms. Similarly, Maharashtra displays a significantly more equal distribution and a markedly similar distribution across caste groups. Punjab has had a peculiar history in that the Land Alienation Act of 1901 classified castes as agricultural and non-agricultural, and only the former were allowed to own land. Most of the present-day Dalit castes got classified as non-agricultural, perhaps because they were traditionally not landowners (they were either scavengers, leather workers, or were engaged in agricultural labour). This Act was repealed in 1946. Kumar (1965) documents how the Brahmins were predominant owners of land in large parts of south India, and how the lowest castes were probably prevented by powerful social sanctions from owning or leasing land. One sees that the historical legacy of lack of landownership continues to manifest itself in the form of present-day disparities (see the gap between SCs and 'Others' as shown in Table 3.5).

Other Components of the CDI

There are two other components of the index: 'Assets' is an aggregate of the 12 consumer durables and livestock that were included in the NFHS survey.[20] What is common across the entire Indian population is the fact that only a very small proportion owns all 12. The larger

[19] Like for other variables, the NFHS changes the definition of landholding to include homestead land; thus the third round shows no landless, but that is slightly misleading.

[20] This is distinct from the measure that Sundaram and Tendulkar (1988) use. Their measure is based on the All India Debt and Investment Survey (1971/2), and the definition of owned assets includes, apart from productive physical assets, consumer durables, financial assets, and dues receivable. The value of productive physical assets accounts for 85–95 per cent of the value of all assets across regions (p. 321). In

Table 3.5 Land Distribution by Caste, Major States, India, 2005–6

Landholdings	% of SCs with								% of STs with								% of OBCs with								% of Others with							
	0	1	2	3	4	5	6	7	0	1	2	3	4	5	6	7	0	1	2	3	4	5	6	7	0	1	2	3	4	5	6	7
INDIA	55.74	37.36	4.81	1.56	0.43	0.11			32.87	53.52	9.41	2.98	1.12	0.11			40.98	44.82	8.9	3.83	1.22	0.24	0.02		35.57	44.06	12.3	5.46	2.26	0.35	0	
NORTH																																
Jammu and Kashmir	68.33	28.05	3.62	0					62.36	34.45	1.59	0.56	0.47	0.56			58.4	39.24	2.36	0	0	0			56.15	38.27	4.5	0.79	0.28	0		
Himachal Pradesh	74.29	24.61	0.67	0.43	0				62.88	33.87	3.25	0	0				73.18	22.99	1.55	1.42	0.43	0.43			54.85	39.04	4.45	1.03	0.5	0.13		
Punjab	49.41	39.62	6.84	4.13	0				0	100	0	0	0				43.63	37.12	11.22	8.03	0	0			19.79	47.01	20.33	9.26	3.5	0.12		
Uttaranchal	28.53	52.05	13.7	4.53	1.19				40.89	30.86	26.03	2.23	0	0			17.72	42.82	23.95	9.67	3.68	2.15			18.88	46.54	19.94	8.89	5.34	0.41		
Haryana	40.46	50.32	5.79	0	3.43				78.32	10.84	10.84	0	0				43.3	41.64	6.45	5.21	2.27	1.13			25.17	48.98	17.11	5.83	2.51	0.41		
Delhi	79.87	19.2	0.46	0.46	0				28.88	54.99	11.31	2.96	1.87				57.38	32.35	6.85	2.62	0.8	0			55.02	35.78	3.87	2.99	1.74	0.59		
Rajasthan	25.22	55.25	11.92	5.25	2.36				37.67	57.32	5.01	0	0				19.9	51.9	16.41	9.16	2.53	0.11			16.17	47.56	17.76	11.92	5.67	0.91		
Uttar Pradesh	68.27	28.41	2.78	0.46	0.09												52.38	40.45	5.33	1.25	0.4	0.2			32.96	47.49	13.26	4.83	1.47	0		
CENTRAL																																
Chhattisgarh	47.02	44.55	6.67	1.27	0.49	0			23.43	57.28	13.03	4.84	1.43				32.13	52.88	9.72	3.69	1.24	0.34			24.68	47.43	13.65	10.7	3.01	0.53		
Madhya Pradesh	33.97	56.87	7.12	1.36	0.34	0			19.34	64.12	11.09	4.51	0.75	0.19			22.77	54.75	14	5.81	2.03	0.51	0.13		13.88	58.27	16.93	7.51	2.76	0.64		
EAST																																
Bihar	81.67	17.21	1.12	0					24.19	30.33	30.33	15.16	0				58.97	33.07	4.84	2.27	0.81	0.04			33.44	38.67	16.46	6.82	3.59	1.01		
West Bengal	78.57	20.78	0.32	0	0.32				69.6	30.4	0	0	0				56.54	39.85	3.61	0	0	0			65.14	32.1	2.37	0.24	0.02	0.12		

State	0	1	2	3	4	5	0	1	2	3	4	5	6	0	1	2	3	4	5	6	0	1	2	3	4	5
Jharkhand	71.14	22.58	4.58	1.7	0		52.4	40.31	4.48	1.78	0.79	0.2		65.94	30.79	2.18	0.7	0.3	0.09		52.89	38.52	5.1	1.21	2.28	0
Orissa	59.41	36.34	3.75	0.5	0		45.62	45.21	7.3	1.24	0.63	0		48.54	42.38	6.41	2.05	0.63	0		49.59	40.09	5.54	3.67	1.11	0
NORTH-EAST																										
Sikkim	55.72	38.31	4.23	1.74	0	0	35.62	54.66	5.2	3.15	1.13	0.25	0	43.47	49.98	5.11	1.17	0	0.27		51.95	40.84	5.34	0	0	1.87
Arunachal Pradesh	66.36	26.93	2.24	2.24	0	2.24	35.97	46.52	10.04	3.97	2.81	0.56	0.13	49.74	45.29	2.48	2.48	0	0		43.16	44.25	8.57	3.43	0.61	0
Nagaland	36.15	48.36	12.91	2.58	0		25.04	46.35	15.65	6.83	3.57	2.52	0.03	39.5	45.69	5.35	5.05	1.65	2.75		52.08	32.58	10.23	4	1.12	0
Manipur	31.57	64	3.17	1.27	0		30.33	62.75	4.85	1.16	0.58	0.29	0	49.34	45.88	4.37	0.41	0	0		35.13	61.6	2.17	0.93	0.17	0
Mizoram	0	50	0	50	0		24.87	58.25	11.43	3.23	1.16	1.05	0	61.07	20.36	18.57	0	0	0		40	40	0	0	0	0
Tripura	75.48	22.18	2.34	0	0		52.73	43.51	2.78	0	0.93	0		64.25	32.72	3.03	0	0	0		67.99	31.67	0	0	0	0.34
Meghalaya	33.33	66.67	0	0	0		48.23	44.85	2.48	2.91	1.47	0		28.88	57.75	13.37	0	0	0		52.21	28.67	14.34	0	4.78	0
Assam	67.45	26.2	2.82	2.48	1.05	0	45.25	45.82	6.16	1.53	1.23	0		49.55	43.68	4.25	1.41	0.95	0.15		50.97	42.73	5.12	0.54	0.64	0
WEST																										
Gujarat	32.65	48.54	10.14	7.94	0.72	0	30.05	51.31	13.47	3.11	2.07	0		29.35	51.32	11.37	5.87	1.71	0.38	0	14.73	40.36	24.14	14.14	5.71	0.92
Maharashtra	18.42	64.44	12.7	3.72	0.19	0.53	14.99	66.6	13.05	4.11	1.24	0		15.03	52.99	16.42	8.54	2.15	0.68	0.18	19.25	52.26	16.54	7.69	3.58	0.67
Goa	48.08	46.02	2.95	0	2.95	0	35.34	51.38	6.64	3.32	1.44	1.88		41.86	46.04	8.37	1.41	2.32	0		35.87	41.93	11.88	5.94	2.85	1.54
SOUTH																										
Andhra Pradesh	58.45	36.81	3.96	0.78	0		25.23	64.04	7.7	2.28	0.76			31.91	52.33	7.61	3.14	1.01	0	100	27.7	47.9	15.52	6.74	1.81	0.33
Karnataka	34.96	54.72	6.88	2.81	0.63	0	24.73	58.34	12.36	2.89	1.67			2.22	49.25	15.68	8.16	3.24	0.45	100	36.08	52.86	7.23	2.94	0.89	0
Kerala	89.2	10.8	0	0	0		77.26	22.74	0	0	0			7.13	20	2.29	0	0.57	0	100	66.66	29.52	2.8	0.76	0.25	0
Tamil Nadu	53.51	34	1.34	0.89	1.48	0.45	32.88	62.92	0	0	4.19	0		4.62	48.13	7.72	1.89	0.37	0.27	100	40.66	45.72	8.36	2.63	2.63	0

Source: Authors' calculations based on NFHS-III.

Note: Land Classification: 0 = 0 acres; 1 = less than 1 acre; 2 = 1 to 5 acres; 3 = 5 to 10 acres; 4 = 10 to 20 acres; 5 = 20 to 50 acres; 6 = 50 to 500 acres; 7 = more than 500 acres.

part of the explanation for this is, of course, poverty. But a smaller part lies in the choice of assets that range from a tractor to a VCR/VCP. Given the high degree of landlessness or very small landholding, a correspondingly small proportion would own tractors and this ownership would be relevant only to the rural segment. Ownership of a VCR/VCP would be more common in the urban areas than in rural areas. Thus, for a combination of reasons, it is not surprising to find a negligible proportion of the sample owning all the 12 assets. Finally, the index also takes into account livestock ownership, which is clearly more relevant in rural than urban areas. The pattern in livestock ownership mirrors that in the other variables.

THE CASTE DEVELOPMENT INDEX

Following the spirit and the methodology employed in the construction of the Human Development Index (HDI) by the United Nations Development Programme (1990), we can aggregate these aforementioned five variables first into a Caste Deprivation Index that can be calculated for each of the three caste categories for the different states and for all-India.[21] The value of this index ranges between 0 and 1, with

---

the present chapter, landownership is considered separately from 'assets', which is constructed as a linear combination of consumer durables. Weighting this by prices would have been ideal but the lack of data prevents us from doing that. The 'assets' considered in the survey were: clock/watch; sofa set; fan; radio/transistor; refrigerator; TV; VCR/VCP; bicycle; motorcycle/scooter; car; bullock cart; and tractor.

[21] Following the UNDP methodology, the Caste Deprivation Index is calculated thus:

I^c_{ij} is the deprivation indicator for the jth state with respect to the ith indicator for group c

(c can take three values: SC, ST, others) and is given by the following:

$I^c_{ij} = [\max X_{ij} - X^c_{ij}] / [\max X_{ij} - \min X_{ij}]$, where the maximum (minimum) values are those that the given indicator takes from the all-India data. Thus, in the entire country, if 12 is the maximum number of assets that an individual owns, then the max value for assets is 12, which will be used for calculation of the index in all states. X^c_{ij} is the mean value of the ith indicator for the cth caste group in the jth state.

The Caste Deprivation Index is an average of the five deprivation indicators, calculated as mentioned.

Thus, I^c_j = summation over i $[I^c_{ij}]$ / 5, for the cth caste group in the jth state.

The CDI = (1 − Caste Deprivation Index).

lower values indicating lower deprivation. Subtracting the values of the deprivation index from unity will yield its inverse index, the CDI.[22] For analogous reasons, higher values of the CDI will indicate higher development. For a given state, inter-caste disparity between a pair of castes can be defined as the distance between the values of the index for the two caste groups (taking either of the indices).

Figures 3.9, 3.10, and 3.11 plot the CDI from NFHS-I, NFHS-II, and NFHS-III, respectively.[23] In all three figures, the columns for SCs are consistently lower (reflecting lower development) than those for the 'Others'. What varies is the distance between the two across states.

From Figures 3.9 to 3.11, we see that the height of the bars is increasing, indicating that on the whole the CDI for all the groups is improving with time. However, there is marked regional variation both within and between each round of the NFHS. The economic literature on regional differences in India mainly focuses on the examination of whether regional inequality is increasing or decreasing, or contains an account of differential growth rates between states or a discussion of state-level HDIs.[24] Most of the literature seems to suggest a strong to moderate increase in regional inequalities since the beginning of the 1990s, but the explanations are varied. Lopsided regional development is, to a certain extent, a legacy of the British rule in India, as industrial growth got concentrated in the richer and more accessible regions. Agricultural growth varied due to climatic factors in any case. Post-Independence, during the heyday of the planning era, lip service was paid to the lowering of regional inequalities. Attempts were made by organizations such as the Finance Commission to use the instrument of federal transfers to states in order to alleviate regional imbalances. However, with the declining role of the government in the economy, conscious interventions to reduce regional imbalances have declined

[22] The World Bank (1998) uses an 'economic status index' based on the NFHS asset data as a proxy for wealth to assess the impact of wealth or poverty on health outcomes. The Bank's primary concern is with poverty reduction and intuitively their index is very different from the one constructed here. My index focuses on the relative deprivation of the average person of a given caste group in a state compared to the maximum deprivation that is possible in the country based on this data set.

[23] The north-eastern states have been left out since most of them have no SC population.

[24] See, for instance, Jha (2002); Singh et al. (2003); Bajpai and Goyal (2004); Milanovich (2004).

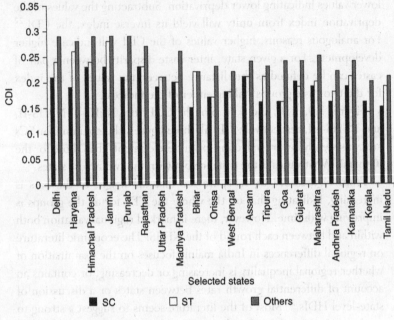

Figure 3.9   Caste Development Index, 1992–3

Source: Author's calculations based on NFHS-I.

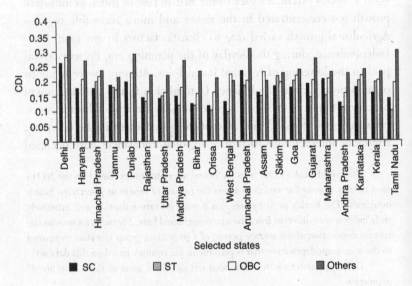

Figure 3.10   Caste Development Index, 1998–9

Source: Author's calculations based on NFHS-II.

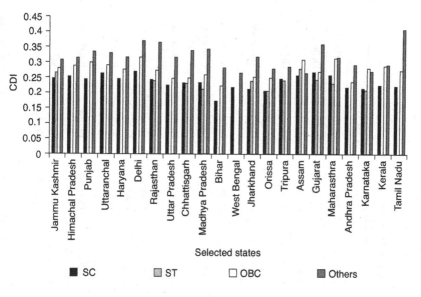

Figure 3.11   Caste Development Index, 2005–6

Source: Author's calculations based on NFHS-III.

and that could be one of the reasons underlying an increase in regional inequalities after 1990.

As one tries to investigate the underlying linkages between the regional variation in the CDI and caste disparity, perhaps the first explanation that an economist would investigate would be the relative material prosperity of the state: is it the case that SCs are better-off in richer states than poorer states? Also, do richer states have lower inter-caste disparity than poorer states? If the answer to both these questions is in the affirmative, then one can outline a blueprint for improving the material position of the Dalits as well as for lowering inter-caste disparity. However, Table 3.6 presents a picture that is mixed enough for us to wonder if a pattern can at all be discerned between these variables.

For instance, Tamil Nadu ranked number 6 in the per capita real SDP rankings in all the three years, qualifying it as a relatively richer state among the 18 states. However, with no change in its relative ranking in per capita real SDP, its ranking on disparity (gap in the CDI between 'Others' and SCs) was eleventh in 1992–3 and increased to first (implying highest disparity) in the other two years. In terms

Table 3.6 Rankings of CDI-SC, Disparity, Real PC SDP

Ranks	Real PC SDP			Disparity			CDI-SC		
	1993–4	1998–9	2002–3	1992–3	1998–9	2003–4	1992–3	1998–9	2003–4
1	Delhi	Delhi	Delhi	Haryana	Tamil Nadu	Tamil Nadu	Himachal Pradesh	Delhi	Delhi
2	Punjab	Punjab	Maharashtra	Delhi	Madhya Pradesh	Rajasthan	Jammu	Maharashtra	Gujarat
3	Maharashtra	Maharashtra	Punjab	Punjab	Karnataka	Madhya Pradesh	Rajasthan	Punjab	Maharashtra
4	Haryana	Gujarat	Haryana	Bihar	Bihar	Bihar	Delhi	Gujarat	Assam
5	Gujarat	Haryana	Gujarat	Himachal Pradesh	Andhra Pradesh	Delhi	Punjab	Jammu	Himachal Pradesh
6	Tamil Nadu	Tamil Nadu	Tamil Nadu	Jammu	Haryana	Gujarat	Assam	Haryana	Jammu & Kashmir
7	Kerala	Karnataka	Himachal Pradesh	Madhya	Orissa	Uttar	Madhya Pradesh	Himachal Pradesh	Haryana
8	Himachal Pradesh	Himachal Pradesh	Karnataka	Maharashtra	Punjab	Punjab	Gujarat	Assam	Punjab
9	Karnataka	Kerala	Kerala	Orissa	New Delhi	Andhra Pradesh	Haryana	Kerala	Rajasthan
10	Andhra Pradesh	Andhra Pradesh	West Bengal	Andhra Pradesh	Gujarat	Orissa	Uttar Pradesh	Madhya Pradesh	Madhya Pradesh

11	West Bengal	West Bengal	Andhra Pradesh	Tamil Nadu	Uttar Pradesh	Haryana	Maharashtra	Rajasthan	Uttar Pradesh
12	Madhya Pradesh	Rajasthan	Rajasthan	Karnataka	Rajasthan	Kerala	Karnataka	Uttar Pradesh	Kerala
13	Jammu & Kashmir	Madhya Pradesh	Madhya Pradesh	Rajasthan	Kerala	Himachal Pradesh	West Bengal	Tamil Nadu	Tamil Nadu
14	Rajasthan	Jammu & Kashmir	Assam	Gujarat	West Bengal	Jammu & Kashmir	Orissa	Karnataka	West Bengal
15	Assam	Assam	Orissa	West Bengal	Himachal Pradesh	Maharashtra	Andhra Pradesh	West Bengal	Andhra Pradesh
16	Uttar Pradesh	Orissa	Uttar Pradesh	Keral	Assam	Karnataka	Kerala	Andhra Pradesh	Karnataka
17	Orissa	Uttar Pradesh	Bihar	Assam	Jammu	West Bengal	Bihar	Bihar	Orissa
18	Bihar	Bihar	N/A	Uttar Pradesh	Maharashtra	Assam	Tamil Nadu	Orissa	Bihar

Source: For PC SDP, www.indiastat.com, table 51676. Disparity and CDI are author's own calculations from NFHS I, II, and III.

Note: Only those states that are common to all 3 rounds have been retained in this table.

of the CDI for SCs (the indicator for the absolute standard of living for SCs), it was the lowest among the Indian states (lower than even the notorious Bihar) in 1992–3 and rose to number 13 in the next rounds. These movements seem to be independent of the SDP levels; moreover, despite being a relatively richer state, it fares poorly on CDI for SCs and has fairly high disparity.

Take another example: Uttar Pradesh. With a ranking of 16, 17, and 16 in per capita real SDP across the three rounds, it is clearly one of the poorest states in India and has remained so across the three rounds. However, inter-caste disparity has steadily increased across the three rounds: from being the state with the lowest inter-caste disparity, it moved up to number 11 by 1998–9 and to number 7 in 2004–5, demonstrating that just as being a relatively rich state (for example, Tamil Nadu or Delhi) is no guarantee for lower disparity, being poor is not necessarily equalizing (witness Uttar Pradesh or Bihar). In terms of CDI for SCs, its ranking remains relatively stable: 10, 12, and 11, respectively, across the three rounds. One can find other examples to illustrate the basic point being made here: the relative prosperity of a state (or the lack of it) does not appear to be a good predictor either of inter-caste disparity or of the absolute level of development of the SCs.

Given that we are comparing across time, we could also look at rate of growth of real per capita SDP as an explanatory variable. Could it be that faster growing states (not necessarily richer) do better in terms of lowering low-caste deprivation *and* inter-caste disparity? It is often argued that the focus of economic policies should be on growth, such that the size of the pie gets bigger. While recognizing that there is a debate on the growth-enhancing effects of the policies of liberalization and greater integration with international markets, for our purpose we can simply note that the overall rate of growth of the Indian economy has been increasing from roughly 5.4 per cent in the 1970s to 6 per cent in the 1990s and close to 7.5 per cent in the 2000s. Despite the 2008 global economic crisis, the estimates for the rate of growth of the Indian economy remain high, though perhaps not as high as the earlier pre-crisis forecasts.

However, what is critical to our discussion is the answer to the following question: if the rate of growth increases for a sustained period of time, does it imply that all groups will share equally in the increase?

Will the gap between upper and lower castes decrease? Indeed, the pie can get bigger, but the share of the marginalized groups can stagnate, increase, or even fall. We need not speculate: Table 3.7 shows the correlation coefficients between the following variables, across selected states, over the three NFHS rounds: between CDI-SC and per capita real net state domestic product (NSDP) (in 1992–3 prices); between CDI-SC and the rate of growth of per capita real NSDP over the previous year; and these correlations are repeated between using disparity instead of CDI-SC.

Column 1 of Table 3.7 indicates that the correlation between CDI-SC and per capita state income is positive and has become stronger, suggesting that over time, SCs have better CDI values in richer states. However, the correlation with rate of growth (column 2) presents a mixed picture: it is negative for the latter two rounds of NFHS (that is, SCs have lower CDI in faster growing states) and the strength of the negative correlation seems to have declined between the latter two rounds; all three rounds considered together present a somewhat ambiguous relationship. Column 3 presents the correlation between disparity and per capita real NSDP. From a fairly strong positive correlation in the first round (disparity is greater in richer states),

Table 3.7   Correlations

	CDI-SC and per capita real NSDP (1)	CDI-SC and rate of growth of real NSDP (2)	Disparity and per capita real NSDP (3)	Disparity and rate of growth of real NSDP (4)
1992–3	0.09	0.09	0.54	0.22
1998–9	0.50	−0.27	0.08	0.25
2005–6	0.72	−0.16	−0.03	−0.27

Source: CDI-SC and disparity: Author's calculations based on NFHS data. Per capita real NSDP is in terms of 1992–3 prices from various tables in Indiastat.com.

Table 3.8   Correlation between CDI-SC and Disparity

1992–3	−0.15
1998–9	−0.36
2005–6	−0.14

Source: Author's calculations based on successive NFHS rounds.

the correlation has weakened to be almost insignificant by 2005–6, suggesting that disparity is no longer correlated with whether the state is rich or poor. Column 4 presents the correlation of disparity with the rate of growth of NSDP: the strength of the correlation is low and has increased slightly, but from a negative correlation, it moves to positive and then to negative again, thus presenting a completely ambiguous picture.

The preceding discussion indicates that CDI-SC and disparity move in opposite directions across states. Indeed, Table 3.8 shows that the correlation between the two is negative. However, the strength of the correlation coefficient is not too high and it has fluctuated between the rounds to return to its level in 1992–3.

What about overall inequality (as captured by the Gini coefficient)? For reasons explained earlier in the chapter, the Gini coefficient for India is often calculated using MPCE, rather than income. Only two of the NFHS rounds (first and the third) are close to NSS rounds (with a gap of one year), and Table 3.9 reports the correlation between CDI-SC and the Gini coefficients for selected states and that between disparity and Gini coefficients. Appendix 3.B lists the Gini coefficients for selected states. The former is small but positive, suggesting a counter-intuitive pattern: that CDI-SC is higher in states with higher overall inequality. The latter correlation moves from being virtually non-existent to a small and positive correlation (states with higher disparity also have higher Gini), a pattern that is easier to understand. Overall, the correlations in Table 3.9 are not large enough and lack a definite pattern that could enable us to confidently make any assertions about the possible relationship between overall inequality, CDI-SC, and inter-caste disparity.

Summing up, while there is some evidence to suggest that CDI-SC is higher in richer states, there is sufficient ambiguity in the correlations

Table 3.9   Correlations between CDI-SC, Gini Coefficient, and Disparity

	CDI-SC–Gini coefficient	Disparity–Gini coefficient
NFHS-I	0.21	−0.03
NFHS-III	0.29	0.16

Source: CDI-SC and disparity from author's calculations. Gini coefficient is the overall Gini coefficient for the states for the NSS rounds in 1993–4 and 2004–5, respectively, calculated from unit-level data, from Banerjee et al. (2010).

between the variables of interest to make us wonder whether standard economic solutions (material prosperity and growth) might be sufficient to simultaneously raise the material standard of living of SCs *and* to lower inter-caste disparity. For instance, while growth is no guarantee for the reduction of inter-group disparities, the lack of growth is not a solution either. Similarly, overall inequality could be lowered with marginal impact on inter-caste disparity. This suggests that the problem of inter-group disparities needs to be tackled independently through special policies such as affirmative action. Chapter 7 focuses precisely on policies of compensatory discrimination.

Unravelling Causes of Disparity

Based on NSS data, we can use the average MPCE figures for the broad caste groups for a more direct assessment of standard of living, with the caveat mentioned earlier that typically income is more unequally distributed than consumption and thus differences between average consumption levels will underestimate income inequalities between groups. I ran a set of multivariate regressions to ascertain the chief determinants of MPCE levels for each of the NSS rounds. The results reveal that education of the head of the household emerges as the key positive determinant of MPCE levels across all four rounds, both for rural and urban areas, for all states, with a higher elasticity for urban areas than for rural areas. Also, SCs, STs, and OBCs are significantly more likely to have lower MPCE as compared to 'Others'—this result is again robust across rounds and across rural–urban. Landownership is significant, but the coefficient is very small, but that could be due the presence of the caste dummy in the regression. In the indicators that constitute the CDI, landownership and education turn out to be the most significant in explaining the regional pattern.

One key confounding factor in the estimation is that of reverse causation, that is, education of the head of the household itself is a function of MPCE and more empirical work is needed to disentangle the causal effects. As a first step towards understanding the relationships, we can look at the significant regional variation in educational attainment, which both the NSS and the NFHS data document.[25] It

[25] I am not reproducing the state-level tables based on the different NSS rounds in order to avoid an overdose of evidence. However, they can be obtained from the author upon request.

Table 3.10   Correlations between Real Median MPCE and Gender and Caste Gaps

Real median MPCE	Rural		Urban	
	Gender gap	Caste gap	Gender gap	Caste gap
1983 MPCE	−0.37	0.53	−0.51	0.36
1994 MPCE	−0.45	−0.39	−0.75	−0.18
1999 MPCE	−0.41	−0.33	−0.52	−0.26
2004 MPCE	−0.33	−0.38	−0.67	0.04

Source: Author's calculations, different rounds of the NSS.

might be worth putting the two variables together to see how the gap in education between caste groups (or between men and women: the gender gap) corresponds to differences in MPCE levels. A correlation between state-level real median MPCE and the education gap at the illiterate level is shown in Table 3.10.

We will discuss the caste gap in this chapter and focus on the gender gap in the next chapter. Table 3.10 indicates that in rural India, except for 1983, the correlation is negative: the gap is smaller in states with high MPCE (note that this does not indicate anything about the causation; it is not clear whether a low caste gap causes high MPCE or the other way around, or indeed if there are other variables that cause both a high MPCE and a low caste gap). For rural India, the strength of the correlation coefficient weakened between 1983 and 1999, suggesting that over time the caste gap might be explained by factors other than MPCE levels, but then increased between 1999 and 2004 to levels that were seen in 1994. Urban India, in contrast, shows lower and fluctuating levels of correlation (as is perhaps to be expected) between 1983 and 1999 and then a sharp decline to almost zero correlation in 2004, once again highlighting rural–urban differences.

Das (2010) estimates the determinants of the probability of being in different employment categories compared to salaried work based on data from the employment–unemployment schedule for the 61st round of the NSS for 2004–5. She finds that in urban areas, where the real non-farm jobs are located, Dalit status makes urban men 12 per cent less likely to be self-employed. In rural areas, where Dalits are disproportionately concentrated, they have a 25 per cent greater likelihood of being casual labourers and a similar, though slightly smaller, likelihood of being out of self-employed farming. Her most instructive results reveal that Dalit men with post-primary education have distinctly lower returns in the form of formal jobs compared to other men. This suggests discrimination in the labour market, which is the theme of the subsequent chapters. Das's results indicate that for educated Dalit men, setting up businesses may not provide the requisite escape out of labour market discrimination, since they are even more disadvantaged in non-farm self-employment than they are in formal employment.

LIBERALIZATION AND CASTE DISPARITIES

The time span covered by the NFHS surveys is crucial in that it marks nearly 15 years of liberalization in India. Invoking the evidence on gaps in educational attainment, presented in an earlier section, we see that there is no clear trend towards a closing of the gaps. More broadly, looking at the disparities based on the CDI, the regional picture is mixed but there is no evidence suggesting that overall the disparities might be reducing. On the whole, therefore, this suggests that over two decades of liberalization have not started to close the inter-caste gaps.

It needs to be pointed out that this is not a trivial observation. Because caste and gender oppression are rooted in an antiquated tradition, there is a serious belief that an opening of the economy and its integration with the world economy, entry of foreign multinational companies that are outside the framework of this tradition, and greater penetration of the market can serve as catalysts of change. 'Foreign' agents, the argument goes, are more likely to be guided by the expediency of profit maximization rather than be mired by local constraints; thus, these can actually serve as 'liberating' influences. This view cites, in its support, the period under British rule, where mass education was for the first time made available to Dalits who were, for centuries, denied education on the grounds that the scriptures permitted only upper castes to be educated. Exposure to education and to English and the subsequent opening of channels of employment, which would have been unimaginable earlier, prompted some important Dalit thinkers and leaders, for instance Phule, to endorse colonial rule or at least to see some positive aspects of that period. We have already referred to the portrayal of English as the new Dalit goddess. In addition, important contributors to the writings and thought on Dalit issues—for instance, Gail Omvedt and Chandra Bhan Prasad—have argued that liberalization and the changing economic ethos can actually provide opportunities to Dalits by opening up new avenues of employment.[26]

However, more rigorous research is needed to establish liberalization and globalization as vehicles for Dalit emancipation. Evidence from rich and strongly market-oriented economies suggests that discrimination and a strong market orientation or 'modernity' can co-exist with ease and for long periods of time. In the Indian context, both under the British rule and in the present experience with globalization, foreign interests may find it easier to adjust to, and hence perpetuate, pre-existing patterns of inequality rather than break them. Certainly in the last two decades of liberalization and globalization of the Indian economy, there seems to be scant evidence of a break in patterns of caste inequalities, as the evidence presented earlier in the chapter demonstrates. The findings of a study where I was one of the authors (Rao et al. 2010) show that the initial period of high growth had some positive effects in that it showed a reduction in caste and gender inequalities, but the narrowing of disparities has tapered off with time. The report also found that the faster growing the sector, the less likely it is that women and marginalized groups participate in it; thus women from marginalized groups are found to be doubly disadvantaged (see Table 3.11).

Table 3.11   Female Participation in the Workforce, by Sector and Social Group (per cent)

	Growth	Scheduled castes	Of which female	Scheduled tribes	Of which female	Others	Of which female
Agriculture	17.7	20.5	38.2	11.2	49.8	68.4	32.5
Industry	36.1	18.6	29.2	6.5	42.7	74.9	23.4
Services	46.1	14.0	22.2	3.6	29.4	82.4	17.0
Total		18.5	33.7	8.5	46.8	73.0	26.6

Source: See Rao et al. (2010: 32).

[26] See, for instance, Shyam Babu (2004) and the conference report contained in Shyam Babu and Prasad (2009).

Privatization of education and jobs has been one of the prominent features of the 1990s. Affirmative action directed towards SCs, STs, and later OBCs, which is confined to government jobs and educational institutions, has correspondingly become weak. In addition, there is evidence of increasing casualization of jobs, with women bearing the brunt of this change. Given the established caste hierarchies, it is not difficult to imagine that low castes, women, and especially low-caste women would be the first to bear the adverse impact of these changes. Indeed, evidence presented in the chapter shows how in the first half of the current decade, the unemployment rate for SCs has increased sharply. Conversely, it would not be unreasonable to imagine that beneficiaries of the process of liberalization would predominantly be upper-class, upper-caste sections not only because of the historical advantages they have enjoyed, but also because they disproportionately possess the skills necessary for jobs in the new economy. For the new kinds of jobs that liberalization and globalization have generated (for instance, those in business processing outsourcing industries, or the outsourced jobs), fluency in English and computer literacy are critical requirements, in which Dalits, even urban ones, are seriously disadvantaged. Thus, Dalits are not only battling historical prejudices but are, in fact, dealing with contemporary, modern forms of discrimination. Chapter 6 documents the contemporary nature of caste discrimination in urban, formal sector, upper-end, supposedly merit-based labour markets.

* * *

This chapter makes a case for examining stratification patterns of India's population through the lens of caste. A preliminary investigation into the relative economic status of the SCs based on three rounds of NFHS data and four rounds of NSS spanning over two decades indicates that there is strong evidence of persistence of inter-caste disparity within the more general problem of overall inequality or deprivation. Also, it appears that the SCs continue to belong to the lowest rung of the economic ladder after over 60 years of Independence, calling into question any notion of substantial upward caste mobility. The spatial and inter-temporal variation in the CDI suggests that while the problem has persisted, its magnitude has not remained uniform.

There is wide variation across time and regions. Also, regional rankings have changed substantially over the last two decades. This provides a glimmer of hope: the condition of inter-group disparity need not be considered endemic; a combination of particular policies, social reform movements, and focused interventions could lead to different, more positive outcomes for Dalits. The difficult question is: what policies and interventions are optimal? Chapter 7 offers a discussion of the possible policy interventions.

APPENDIX 3.A

Table 3.A.1   Measures of Unemployment

Unemployment rate	No. of persons unemployed per 1,000 persons in the labour force (which includes both employed and unemployed)

Four Types of Unemployment Rates

Type	Indication
1. Usually unemployed by principal status	Indicates the magnitude of persons unemployed for a relatively longer period during a reference period of 365 days. Approximates to a measure of chronic unemployment.
2. Usually unemployed, excluding subsidiary status workers	Indicates the magnitude of persons unemployed for a relatively longer period during a reference period of 365 days. Excludes people employed in subsidiary status.
3. Unemployed based on weekly status	Indicates the magnitude of people unemployed during the week. Approximates a measure of both chronic and intermittent unemployment caused by seasonal fluctuations in the labour market.
4. Unemployed based on current status	Indicates the average level of unemployment on a day during the survey year.

Table 3.A.2 Unemployment Rates

Rural Unemployment Rates

ST	1983	1993–4	1999–2000	2004–5
Usual (ps)	0.58	0.88	0.94	1.19
Usual (ps+ss)	0.34	0.57	0.71	0.8
cws	2.44	2.13	2.38	3.01
cds	5.53	4.09	5.09	6.47
SC				
Usual (ps)	1.7	1.49	1.79	2.43
Usual (ps+ss)	0.91	0.88	1.46	1.57
cws	5.78	3.54	4.34	5.12
cds	12.82	8.09	9.58	12.04
OBC				
Usual (ps)			1.67	2.37
Usual (ps+ss)			1.29	1.62
cws			3.14	3.67
cds			6.19	7.71
Others				
Usual (ps)	2.22	2.06	3.02	3.26
Usual (ps+ss)	1.34	1.42	2.25	2.27
cws	3.6	2.98	5.38	3.79
cds	6.99	5.14	7.72	6.6

Urban Unemployment Rates

ST	1983	1993–4	1999–2000	2004–5
Usual (ps)	4.09	4.61	4.26	3.83
Usual (ps+ss)	3.52	3.84	3.84	3
cws	5.86	5.33	5.11	5.08
cds	9.49	7.5	7.15	7.53
SC				
Usual (ps)	5.94	5.13	4.95	6.22
Usual (ps+ss)	4.51	4.55	4.46	4.99
cws	7.03	6.31	6.47	7.59
cds	11.89	9.65	9.79	11.39
OBC				
Usual (ps)			4.82	4.79
Usual (ps+ss)			4.38	4.11
cws			5.74	5.69
cds			8.02	8.47
Others				
Usual (ps)	6.15	5.25	5.71	5.55
Usual (ps+ss)	5.17	4.54	5.28	4.58
cws	6.81	5.77	6.21	5.83
cds	9.16	7.08	7.21	7.11

Source: Author's calculations based on the NSS Employment–Unemployment Surveys, various rounds.

Table 3.A.3 Measures of Underemployment

Usually employed (ps+ss) but unemployed by Current Weekly Status

Rural	1983	1993–4	1999–2000	2004–5	Urban	1983	1993–4	1999–2000	2004–5
All	2.31	1.47	2.16	2.10	All	1.67	1.09	1.09	1.46
Male	2.29	1.53	2.21	2.16	Male	1.71	1.13	1.13	1.45
Female	2.35	1.36	2.06	1.99	Female	1.52	0.94	0.93	1.51
ST	1.84	1.41	1.5	2.02	ST	1.76	1.22	0.96	1.89
SC	4.08	2.2	2.58	3.26	SC	2.44	1.56	1.86	2.31
OBC			1.64	1.9	OBC			1.17	1.53
Others	1.89	1.25	3.02	1.44	Others	1.53	1.01	0.8	1.08

Usually employed (ps+ss) but unemployed by their Current Daily Status

Rural	1983	1993–4	1999–2000	2004–5	Urban	1983	1993–4	1999–2000	2004–5
All	5.54	3.66	4.84	5.6	All	4.12	2.6	2.63	3.55
Male	5.81	4.02	5.25	6.12	Male	4.17	2.65	2.73	3.66
Female	5.09	3.01	4.09	4.7	Female	3.93	2.39	2.21	3.14
ST	4.4	2.99	3.75	4.75	ST	4.73	3.18	2.84	4.11
SC	9.56	5.92	6.88	8.89	SC	6.7	4.67	4.76	5.82
OBC			4.17	5.22	OBC			3.22	4.08
Others	4.58	3.08	4.79	3.76	Others	3.68	2.25	1.69	2.26

(contd...)

Table 3.A.3 (contd...)

Usually employed (Current Weekly Status) but unemployed by their Current Daily Status

Rural	1983	1993–4	1999–2000	2004–5	Urban	1983	1993–4	1999–2000	2004–5
All	3.95	2.48	2.97	3.89	All	2.74	1.61	1.62	2.2
Male	3.83	2.63	3.2	4.16	Male	2.64	1.58	1.65	2.3
Female	4.23	2.17	2.5	3.33	Female	3.21	1.72	1.5	1.82
ST	3	1.85	2.48	3.1	ST	3.54	2.14	1.94	2.43
SC	6.99	4.3	4.8	6.37	SC	4.93	3.33	3.11	3.73
OBC		2.04	2.8	3.65	OBC			2.16	2.71
Others	3.28	2.04	1.93	2.54	Others	2.37	1.32	0.93	1.22

Source: Author's calculations based on the employment–unemployment survey, NSS, various rounds.

APPENDIX 3.B

Gini coefficients: The following Gini coefficients (calculated in Banerjee et al. 2010) were used in the chapter:

Table 3.B.1   Gini Coefficients

	Gini 1993–4	Gini 2004–5
Jammu & Kashmir	0.27	0.26
Himachal Pradesh	0.32	0.33
Punjab	0.29	0.35
Uttaranchal	*	0.31
Haryana	0.31	0.36
Delhi	0.4	0.34
Rajasthan	0.28	0.3
Uttar Pradesh	0.3	0.33
Chhattisgarh	*	0.37
Madhya Pradesh	0.32	0.35
Bihar	0.25	0.24
West Bengal	0.31	0.35
Jharkhand	*	0.31
Orissa	0.19	0.32
Tripura	0.26	0.28
Assam	0.37	0.24
Gujarat	0.28	0.33
Maharashtra	0.38	0.39
Goa	0.3	0.37
Andhra Pradesh	0.31	0.35
Karnataka	0.31	0.36
Kerala	0.32	0.39
Tamil Nadu	0.34	0.38
Total	0.33	0.36

Note: * Represents states that did not exist at the time of the corresponding NSS round.

4 Overlapping Identities
Caste and Gender

The previous chapters, and a host of case studies across the world, firmly suggest that identity matters in the real world, even in strongly market-oriented situations. What happens when there are *overlapping identities*? There are several contexts where identity has multiple contours and every individual simultaneously has multiple identities: race, religion, nationality, gender, and so forth. Indeed, the overlap between race and gender has been studied in the context of other societies.[1] In this chapter, I focus on two important definitions of identity in the Indian context—caste and gender[2]—while being acutely aware that there are several other, crucial ones that I am not considering, simply in order to retain expositional clarity. When overlapping is such that an individual is disadvantaged according to one identity (gender) but not according

---

[1] For instance, Sokoloff (1992), Ayers (2001), and Lovell (2003), to mention a few from a huge body of literature.

[2] There is substantial literature on gender disparities in India that examines the phenomena of the declining sex ratio, educational disparities, differential labour market outcomes between men and women, health outcomes for women, with a special focus on reproductive health, and so forth. Similarly, the caste system has been widely researched, as the other chapters in this book demonstrate. The literature on the *overlap* between caste and gender is much smaller, and within that, economic analyses of this overlap are very few indeed.

to another (caste), it turns out that making assessments about relative well-being is more complicated compared to the exercise in the previous chapter when only one identity was considered.

WOMEN AND THE CASTE HIERARCHY

From *varna* to *jati*, from the ancient to the colonial and to the contemporary, the common theme underlying the various manifestations of the caste system is that it is inegalitarian and oppressive towards the Dalits and women. Sociologists and historians have extensively analysed the treatment of women under Brahmanical Hinduism, which is the dominant version of Hinduism. I will not attempt to summarize the numerous and complex issues that the literature raises, but here is a glimpse into some of the connections between gender and caste. In the *Manusmriti* as well as in other texts, women and Shudras are treated identically—the caste system places similar restrictions on the two, especially in terms of denial of religious privileges or denial of access to education.

Sociologists have also argued that the caste system not only determines the social division of labour, but its sexual division as well. For instance, in agriculture, women can engage in water regulation, transplanting, and weeding, but not in ploughing. The literature suggests that endogamy (a crucial feature of the caste system) should be seen as a mechanism of recruiting and retaining control over the labour and sexuality of women; the concepts of 'purity' and 'pollution' segregate groups and also regulate the mobility of women. Indeed, the prescribed social sanctions against *anuloma* marriages (upper-caste men marrying women of lower caste) are not as censorious as those against *pratiloma* marriages (the reverse), since the 'purity' of the upper-caste women is not violated in the former.

'The subordination of women was crucial to the development of caste hierarchy, the women being subject to increasing constraints the higher the caste in the hierarchy' (Liddle and Joshi 1986: 50). Thus, the caste–religion nexus is strongest amongst the upper castes, as they view themselves as custodians of the established religious tradition and hence strictly conform to the caste code as part of their duties towards religion. On the other hand, the Dalit castes have historically been relatively more egalitarian towards women. Since the Shudras and *Atishudra*s were denied access to the scriptures, their versions of Hinduism are distinct from the upper-caste versions.[3]

Can we, therefore, postulate a dialectical relationship between caste status and womanhood? A lower-caste woman is trapped in the cesspool of relative poverty, deprivation, and sexual abuse with comparatively fewer restrictions on her public visibility. Among the upper castes, poverty level varies across the spectrum of castes (although upper castes as a group are economically better off than the lowest castes). However, the lives of the women are shrouded in a mass of taboos. Does this enable a judgement about which section of women is better off?

A unilateral answer to this is problematic, since there is a trade-off between material well-being and autonomy and mobility. In reality, for Dalit women, this trade-off is more illusory than real. The fewer restrictions on working outside their homes could be more due to compelling poverty and less due to a radical belief in the fundamental right of women to work. Thus, subject as they are to prejudice, deprivation, discrimination, and oppression, this section of women might turn out to be the worst off.[4]

I would like to suggest that the distinction between the two caste rungs, based on the public visibility of women, is increasingly redundant. While the actual upward mobility of Dalits has been negligible, there has been a tendency to emulate upper-caste traditions, perhaps as a part of the oft discussed phenomenon of Sanskritization.[5] Since

---

[3] It is important to note that Hinduism is not a monolithic religion and religious practices and worship of deities vary with region and jati. However, certain common features mark the religious practices of the 'twice born' castes and certainly constraints on women and a derogatory and discriminatory attitude towards the Dalits is inherent in the upper-caste religious code.

[4] Kapadia (1995) discusses how within each caste, the status of women is lower than that of men. So Dalit women, being at the bottom of the caste hierarchy, would be subject to the dual burden of exploitation that their sex and caste exposes them to.

[5] This term is due to Srinivas (1962: 9), who believed that 'Sanskritisation is both a part of the process of social mobility as well as the idiom in which mobility expresses itself ... can also occur independently of the acquisition of political and economic power.' This is how he describes the process: 'A low caste was able, in a generation or two, to rise to a higher position in the hierarchy by adopting vegetarianism and teetotalism, and by Sanskritising its ritual and pantheon. In short, it took over, as far as possible, the customs, rites, and beliefs of the Brahmins, and the adoption of the

'constraints on women are an essential part of a rise in caste hierarchy' (Liddle and Joshi 1986: 59) (the rise could be real or presumed), this has meant the spread of practices that undervalue the role of women in the family and in the workplace (such as disinheritance from land, exclusion from the productive economy, removal from public life, and seclusion inside the home) to castes that were known for their relative egalitarianism. This has been seen to be responsible for the spread, among other things, of the now ubiquitous practice of dowry. Kapadia (1995: 66) discusses the decline in the status of women in traditional matrilineal societies and argues that 'earlier valorization of women in non-Brahmin cultures [was] due to earlier participation in productive work outside the home ... when work opportunities outside home became restricted to the women, the traditional bride price system became reversed to give way to "dowry" ... women [began to be] viewed as burdens both by their natal kin and marital kin'.

Also, since women are seen as 'custodians of purity of the house and its members' (Srinivas 1976: 229), this may imply tremendous pressure on them to conform to antiquated and conservative traditions that could, in reality, work against their desires. This spread of the undervaluation of women could well have altered the egalitarian nature of marital relationships among the lower castes. An observation that was valid 30 years ago—'among the less Sanskritised "low" castes, conjugal relations appear to be more perceptibly egalitarian than among the Sankritised high castes, and this is true of all the regions, including the Hindi-speaking areas' (ibid.: 231)—now needs to be re-examined.

This chapter seeks to explore if the trade-off is vanishing or persistent, and suggests that those who are disadvantaged according to *both* identities, that is, Dalit women, bear the brunt of the burden of disadvantage. Shah et al. (2006: 117) document how Dalit women are 'weighed down by the oppressive hierarchies of caste, class and gender'. Note that the acceptance of the vanishing trade-off is not critical to this argument: even if one believes in the persistence of the trade-off, we could hold one identity constant and vary the other, that is, look at castes *within* women, and arrive at the same conclusion that low-caste

---

Brahminic way of life by a low caste seems to have been frequent, although theoretically forbidden' (ibid. 42).

women are at the bottom of the hierarchy. Elsewhere (Deshpande 2004) I have examined the relationship between 'within-caste' and 'between-caste' inequality using the Theil Index; while clearly, within-caste inequality exists, there are strong reasons to focus on 'between-caste' differences.

GENDER AND CASTE EFFECTS

From an economist's perspective, this section narrows down the enquiry into disentangling the gender and caste effects shaping women's lives, by looking at some indicators of the standard of living of women in different caste groups as a first step. Since a large part of the devaluation of women is explained by their role, both perceived and actual, in productive work, the chapter focuses on that in some degree of detail.

In the previous chapter, we examined the variation in the overall pattern of caste inequality. The results I report in the present chapter are from the all-women sample of the three rounds of NFHS. However, now we are interested in two facets of disparity—caste disparity and gender disparity. Roughly 90 per cent of all household heads in NFHS-I and NFHS-II data were male, but in the third round this proportion was 86 per cent. Deshpande (2001b, 2007) extended the CDI framework to the women's survey to calculate and analyse the Gender–Caste Development Index (GCDI) (disparities between different caste groups among women).

Of the five variables in the index, two are individual-specific (education and work) and the other three are household-specific.[6] The household-specific indicators are either owned explicitly by the men or the ownership is of the 'household'; in either event, the women in the household would seldom have full or equal control over these assets, but the data do not allow us to isolate the relative control between men and women. It follows, therefore, that the difference between results based on GCDI and CDI respectively would actually *understate* the relative disadvantage of women relative to men. We

---

[6] Thus, when the women respondents in the survey were asked for information on the five variables comprising the index, they reported their own educational and occupational levels, but reported the household ownership of the three asset-related variables—land, consumer durables, and livestock.

will discuss the two individual-specific variables—education and occupation—separately, before moving on to the index. Also, for these two variables, I will present evidence both from the NFHS as well as from the NSS, as in the previous chapter.

EDUCATION

NFHS-I indicated an appallingly high level of illiteracy among women and the presence of inter-caste disparity. For India as a whole, in 1992–3, 77.3 per cent of SC women and 69.7 per cent of ST women reported no education, as compared to 51.6 per cent of 'Other' women. Moving to the other end of the spectrum, 0.74 per cent and 0.88 per cent of the SC and ST women, respectively, had higher education, compared to 5.39 per cent of 'Other' women. The northern states had a distribution worse than the national average, with the exception of Delhi (the national capital) and Himachal Pradesh. While Delhi had lower illiteracy across the board, the disparity between castes was the highest. The western states of Goa, Gujarat, and Maharashtra also reported lower illiteracy levels. The significant outlier was the southern coastal state of Kerala, which has subsequently achieved full literacy.

Evidence from NFHS-II and NFHS-III indicates that there has been an improvement in women's education level in general, which is the least of the outcomes expected from an economy in the twenty-first century. At the all-India level, in NFHS-II, as many as 68 per cent of SC women, 55 per cent of OBC (Other Backward Class) women, and 40 per cent of upper-caste women reported 'no education', and these figures further declined to 51 per cent, 44 per cent, and 26 per cent in NFHS-III. Another aspect of educational disparities is seen in male–female differences in education, which are significant both in rural and urban areas. I have discussed them earlier in Deshpande (2002), and in this chapter, I will use the evidence from the four rounds of NSS to discuss the changing nature of gender gaps.

The regional pattern in educational attainment that was seen in NFHS-I remains virtually unaltered in NFHS-III (Table 4.1) and is consistent with the pattern that we saw in the previous chapter: the northern part of the country, with the consistent exception of Himachal Pradesh (and now Uttarakhand), continues to lag behind the educational attainments of western and southern India. That

Table 4.1 Education Levels of Women, by Caste, Major States, India, 2005–6

Education Level	% of SCs with						% of STs with						% of OBCs with						% of others with					
	0	1	2	3	4	5	0	1	2	3	4	5	0	1	2	3	4	5	0	1	2	3	4	5
INDIA	50.67	8.58	6.68	27.78	2.83	3.47	62.11	8.72	4.37	20.92	1.97	1.91	44.12	7.62	7.17	31.46	4.14	5.5	25.6	7.88	6.81	39.88	6.98	12.85
NORTH																								
Jammu and Kashmir	42.44	4.37	8.01	37.54	6.44	1.21	69.09	3.74	4.16	20.25	2.05	0.71	46.29	4.13	5.71	37.39	3.91	2.57	37.06	4.32	4.1	37.1	6.01	11.4
Himachal Pradesh	26.26	4.35	15.37	43.29	5.41	5.32	33.82	3.41	11.91	40.07	7.94	2.85	15.97	4.35	13.44	49.71	10.96	5.57	15.2	3.14	10.11	44.44	13.84	13.27
Punjab	44.44	4.4	10.96	32.11	5.48	2.6	66.67	0	0	0	33.33	0	23.06	2.03	9.75	47.27	9.1	8.8	20.74	2.75	10.35	40.98	11.5	13.67
Uttaranchal	45.3	3.99	8.83	31.86	4.14	5.89	43.15	9.9	9.78	19.56	1.96	5.01	43.15	5.42	10.86	26.9	6.57	7.1	23.95	2.38	10.49	33.65	11.44	18.09
Haryana	52.11	5.3	7.12	29.2	4.09	2.19	80.75	0	0	19.25	0	0	41.19	2.82	10.54	36.27	5.31	3.87	29.46	1.82	9.52	39.05	8.53	11.62
Delhi	37.53	2.69	10.9	37.69	7.01	4.18	49.75	1.2	2.99	19.17	5.98	20.91	33.59	2.11	9.78	33.45	9.48	11.59	14.11	1.46	3.3	33.58	13.54	34.01
Rajasthan	70.34	6.55	6.05	14.39	0.5	2.17	78.59	4.87	5.25	9.92	0.38	0.98	66.29	4.25	8.09	17.65	1.4	2.33	32.32	5.69	10.16	29.55	4.69	17.6
Uttar Pradesh	64.81	4.28	7.67	19.22	1.86	2.16	81.81	2.44	4.82	9.65	0.04	1.24	59.26	3.73	8.03	22.01	3.46	3.52	31.5	2.98	10.71	30.61	9.57	14.64
CENTRAL																								
Chhattisgarh	51.62	8.71	7.37	28.01	2.23	2.07	65.06	7.38	6.4	18.69	1.42	1.04	47	10.15	10.99	25.13	2.68	4.06	18.65	6.82	8.27	38.25	6.41	21.6
Madhya Pradesh	54.88	8.38	8.82	22.07	1.87	3.98	71.82	7.47	6.26	13.44	0.55	0.45	49.86	9.52	10.52	24.39	2.84	2.86	25.3	4.11	10.42	35.68	6.91	17.57
EAST																								
Bihar	83.16	3.92	2.8	9.48	0.19	0.44	42.19	22.54	9.82	25.45	0	0	63.5	6.04	5.02	22.26	1.61	1.57	44.04	4.87	4.55	34.48	6.37	5.68
West Bengal	46.92	17.21	6.24	25.93	1.42	2.29	73.58	11.48	3.53	10.13	1.28	0	25.69	14.83	5.23	45.93	3.86	4.46	29.86	15.74	6.13	37.05	3.61	7.6

Jharkhand	67.17	8.11	2.86	16.58	2.24	3.04	71.1	5.12	2.59	18.8	0.99	1.39	59.32	6.2	6.01	23.08	3.16	2.23	31.75	5.47	4.48	34.15	8.35	15.81
Orissa	49.89	14.63	5.76	27.01	0.92	1.78	73.66	6.94	3.22	14.39	0.8	0.99	33.69	14.47	8.1	36.39	3.22	4.13	19.29	14.44	5.61	45.3	6.13	9.24
NORTH-EAST																								
Sikkim	30.84	13.16	6.77	42.31	3.52	3.4	29.24	15.22	6.72	36.11	6.76	5.96	23.02	15.09	6.18	42.76	7.61	5.35	28.39	11.34	7.07	39.11	7.57	6.52
Arunachal Pradesh	42.07	13.97	5.41	27.73	4.36	6.46	42.14	12.84	5.33	32.44	3.32	3.93	47.16	11.79	2.29	17.43	10.22	11.11	40.15	11.41	5.63	29.56	6.74	6.51
Nagaland	46.37	9.65	3.01	34.17	2.37	4.43	18.2	12.7	6.29	51.09	4.97	6.74	25.64	13.77	7.8	47.04	2.12	3.62	34.72	8.38	3.03	39.05	6.26	8.58
Manipur	15.96	5.58	1.86	51.81	11.42	13.37	26.23	12.56	5.61	43.25	6.61	5.74	27.24	8.07	2.55	42.4	5.92	13.82	19.42	6.82	3.14	46.35	7.21	17.06
Mizoram	23.96	0	11.98	64.07	0	0	5.42	14.5	6.05	59.91	6.91	7.21	28.82	0	0	56.47	0	14.71	0	6.66	13.87	52.01	10.4	17.06
Tripura	21.92	20.33	10.6	43.39	1.33	2.43	45.47	14.57	5.2	31.99	1.38	1.38	14.23	16.9	11.08	52.62	1.1	4.06	17.3	13.56	9.36	48.63	4.03	7.13
Meghalaya	29.71	13.77	5.49	38.07	2.69	10.28	29.4	14.43	4.73	38.43	5.16	7.85	8.25	15.37	2.99	52.44	4.98	5.98	34.82	6.8	4.71	35.32	7.03	11.32
Assam	30.32	16.96	4.45	41.42	3.96	2.9	34.74	12.52	2.53	41.72	3.87	4.61	9.09	11.93	2.95	51.79	5.93	8.3	33.95	14.89	3.86	37.58	3.59	6.13
WEST																								
Gujarat	36.88	8.75	4.75	41.46	4.59	3.58	55.24	7.14	3.99	26.47	2.66	4.49	40.83	10.6	6.14	36.72	2.69	3.03	15.27	6.29	5.18	48.32	8.9	16.04
Maharashtra	29.71	10.82	3.9	45.15	4.31	6.11	48.51	13.08	2.15	30.13	3.97	2.16	17.12	10.79	3.1	50.84	7.25	10.91	19.59	8.36	4.26	48.1	6.39	13.31
Goa	31.08	7.38	6.43	41.1	7.65	6.36	24.2	13.1	3.46	51.01	6.35	1.87	10.62	9.94	4.09	50.02	11.35	13.98	11.26	6.91	3.79	46.88	11.42	19.74
SOUTH																								
Andhra Pradesh	47.64	7.96	7.37	27.72	3.47	5.84	72.12	9.48	3.76	11.68	1.97	0.99	51.17	8.57	7.87	26.32	2.21	3.86	27.16	6.84	10.26	41	5.34	9.39
Karnataka	48.87	6.03	4.67	33.78	3.02	3.63	55.48	8.8	3.17	28.09	2.76	1.71	29.85	8.68	4.12	43.18	6.07	8.09	26.18	9.14	4.95	40.04	6.63	13.05
Kerala	10.17	8.85	4.94	61.22	3.65	11.17	25.8	24.23	6.03	37.86	0	6.08	2.49	6.88	2.32	61.9	8.84	17.57	2.77	7.59	3.43	58.2	8.26	19.75
Tamil Nadu	29.88	11.05	9.66	36.15	6.55	6.7	41.75	6.99	15.75	24.95	6.45	4.11	19.33	10.07	10.6	39.91	8.01	12.07	3.75	0.3	4.56	34.42	14.36	42.6

Source: Author's calculations based on NFHS-III.

the regional effect is important in explaining patterns of education in general is also suggested by the fact that for all three rounds, the states that have high male literacy rates are also those with high female literacy rates. Median years of schooling, literacy rates, and school attendance vary substantially by state. These vary significantly by age cohorts as well, indicating the well-known problem of dropouts in primary/middle school.

Evidence from NSS

Table 4.2 shows that illiteracy has been declining consistently over the period, for males and females, across urban and rural India. Urban women have better educational outcomes than their rural counterparts, but almost a quarter of urban women were illiterate in 2004–5, 4 percentage points below rural males (nearly 29 per cent were illiterate). For both rural and urban women, there is a sharp drop in percentages from 'literate, up to primary' to 'middle' (see Table 4.3). The proportions in both categories have been increasing over the last two decades, but the gap remains substantial and larger for rural women than urban.

Table 4.2   Illiteracy over Time, by Gender and Rural/Urban (per cent)

	Rural males	Urban males	Rural females	Urban females
1983–4	47.93	21.25	74.67	41.14
1993–4	37.83	16.00	63.44	31.92
1999–2000	33.98	14.63	56.86	28.54
2004–5	28.85	12.48	49.84	24.92

Source: Author's calculations based on the NSS Employment–Unemployment Surveys, various rounds.

Table 4.3   Difference between 'Literate up to Primary' and 'Middle' Levels, by Gender and Rural/Urban

	Rural males	Urban males	Rural females	Urban females
1983–4	26.34	22.66	16.33	23.01
1993–4	25.85	20.25	19.76	20.8
1999–2000	24.17	15.94	20.63	17.44
2004–5	24.56	14.69	22.51	15.8

Source: Author's calculations based on the NSS Employment–Unemployment Surveys, various rounds.

Figures 4.1 and 4.2 show the gender gap in education over the four NSS rounds for rural and urban areas, respectively. In rural areas, we see that the biggest gap is at low levels of education, but that the gap is, in general, declining. The gap at the 'graduate and above' level has, however, increased. It is clear that urban education is associated with a much lower gender-based disparity. Furthermore, this has been declining at a steady rate at most levels.

Figure 4.3 depicts the trends in the gap between completion of primary- and middle-level education of rural and urban women. As the figure shows, this gap has been increasing for rural girls, primarily on account of the fact that while middle school completion rate has risen, it has increased in lesser proportion than primary school completion rate. In urban areas, on the other hand, the gap has been closing, but not necessarily for all the right reasons. Primary school completion rates have been declining, whereas middle school completion rates have been increasing, thus leading to the closing of the gap.

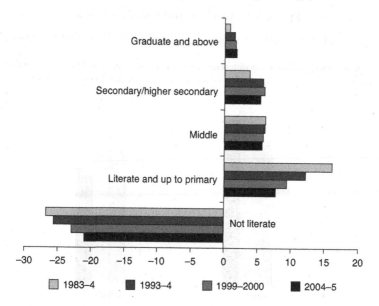

Figure 4.1   Gender Gap in Education, Rural

Source: Author's calculations based on the NSS Employment–Unemployment Surveys, various rounds.

Note: Gender gap defined as difference between the number of males per 100 in that level of education and the number of females per 100 in that level of education.

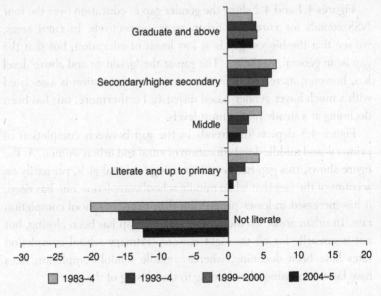

Figure 4.2   Gender Gap in Education, Urban

Source: Author's calculations based on the NSS Employment–Unemployment Surveys, various rounds.
Note: Gender gap defined as difference between the number of males per 100 in that level of education and the number of females per 100 in that level of education.

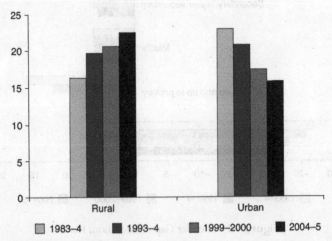

Figure 4.3   Gap between 'Literate up to Primary' and 'Middle' Levels for Girls

Source: Author's calculations based on NSSO Employment and Unemployment Surveys, various rounds.
Note: Gap between levels of education defined as difference between number of girls per 100 at 'literate up to primary level' and number of girls at middle level.

Table 4.4 shows the breakdown of these educational achievements and disparities by social group, gender, and rural/urban. It reveals a very clear gender divide within each caste category. So, for instance, the proportion of rural SC women who were graduates and above was a virtually non-existent 0.52 per cent in 2004–5. Given the high dropout rates at the middle-school level, this is perhaps only to be expected, but the final outcome is a cause for concern. Also, middle school dropouts cannot provide the entire explanation, since these can be seen across all caste groups, and yet we find gaps between castes at higher levels of education. Prima facie, this suggests that both gender and caste matter as far as dropouts are concerned. It is highly likely that financial constraints might be particularly severe for SC families, but these data do not allow us to test the validity of this hypothesis. Further investigation, either through specifically focused surveys and/or through longer in-depth interviews, can give us insights into understanding the role of financial constraints as a factor explaining dropouts, both for women and SCs. Also, research such as that by Nambissan (2010) demonstrates the pathways through which Dalit students face discrimination in schools on account of their stigmatized identities and Dalit girls bear the double stigma of gender and caste. The variety of ways in which the stigma manifests itself, and if there is any regional variation in this stigma, can only be established by more in-depth qualitative investigation.

Table 4.4   Gender Differences in Education, by Caste, 2004–5 (per cent)

	Not literate		Literate up to primary		Middle		Secondary/ higher secondary		Graduate and above	
	W	M	W	M	W	M	W	M	W	M
ST Rural	60.6	39.8	29.6	41.6	6.6	11.4	2.8	5.8	0.3	1.2
ST Urban	34.3	17.2	28.8	34.6	14.6	18.5	15.5	19.7	5.5	8.0
SC Rural	57.5	35.5	30.4	40.4	7.5	14.0	3.8	8.2	0.5	1.6
SC Urban	39.3	18.7	33.3	39.0	13.4	19.1	10.1	16.6	2.9	5.0
OBC Rural	51.2	28.2	31.7	40.6	10.2	16.5	5.9	11.4	0.7	2.4
OBC Urban	29.6	15.1	34.1	35.7	16.1	18.8	14.6	19.5	4.6	8.1

Source: Author's calculations based on the NSS Employment–Unemployment Surveys, various rounds.
Note: W = Women; M = Men.

Another noteworthy difference between SC and 'Other' women is that for the latter, outcomes for urban women are clearly better than their rural counterparts, especially in the 'graduates and above' category. The proportion of urban 'Other' girls who are 'literate, up to primary' has been declining over the period. That could be due to the fact that a larger number of girls are proceeding on to the next stage, as indeed Table 4.4 indicates.

Figure 4.4 shows the great disparity in literacy across states, something we know already from the NFHS data: the largest gap is almost 20 per cent between states. In the previous chapter, we had looked at the correlation between state-level real median monthly per capita expenditure (MPCE) and the caste gap. We can refer to the same table again (Table 3.10 in Chapter 3) to examine the correlation between MPCE and gender gap: unlike the caste gap, the gender gap at the illiterate level in both rural and urban areas is negatively correlated with MPCE levels: states with higher MPCE levels have lower gender gaps. This is more in keeping with the expected effect of material prosperity on illiteracy. The correlation in urban areas is stronger

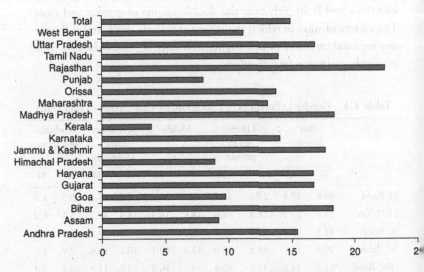

Figure 4.4   Gender Gap in Literacy, by State, 2004–5 (no. of girls)

Source: Author's calculations based on the NSS Employment–Unemployment Surveys, various rounds.

than in rural areas, and while it has fluctuated over the period, it has increased in urban areas and slightly decreased in rural areas.

WOMEN AND WORK

The results on women's occupational distribution are perhaps one of the best illustrations of how a pure quantitative analysis, divorced from a feel for the underlying social structure, can lead to misleading conclusions. Data from both NFHS and NSS show that the majority of women self-report themselves to be 'not working'. These responses are not in sync with the evidence from numerous case studies as well as our prima facie expectations: given the high rates of absolute poverty and near-poverty, could so many women afford not to work?

NFHS-I reveals that at the all-India level, 60.1 per cent of SC women, 48.31 per cent of ST women, and 70.26 per cent of 'Other' women self-reported themselves to be 'not working'. The majority of the remaining women (those who self-report themselves to be working) are associated with primary activities. Again, with the exception of Himachal Pradesh, all the northern states reveal a percentage that is noticeably greater than the all-India average of women not working. The eastern and north-eastern states' 'not working' averages are slightly higher than the national average, with the western numbers lower and the southern numbers substantially lower than the national average.

NFHS-II reveals that there has been a decline in the proportions reporting 'not working' for SC and ST groups, such that at the all-India level, 53.65 per cent of SC and 36.8 per cent of ST women self-report to be 'not working'. It is not clear if the same trend can be seen in the 'Others' category. The erstwhile 'Others' are now divided into OBCs and upper castes, and the latter actually show a greater percentage of 'not working' (72.38 per cent) than the combined 'Others' category of the previous round. The decline in the 'not working' proportions for SCs is registered despite the trend in north India, which continues to be a problem zone as far as women's work is concerned. Most of the states from this region report an increase in 'not working' proportions, and it is the proportion in the rest of the country that defines the national trend. NFHS-III proportions for SCs and STs 'not working'

Table 4.5 Occupation Levels of Women, by Caste, Major States, India, 2005–6 (per cent)

	SC						ST						OBC						Others					
	1	2	3	4	5	6	1	2	3	4	5	6	1	2	3	4	5	6	1	2	3	4	5	6
INDIA	51.53	35.43	6.21	4.69	2.12	0.02	29.66	63.29	3.47	2.22	1.36	0.01	54.48	33.36	4.63	5.4	2.09	0.04	70.75	14.21	5.02	5.92	3.99	0.11
NORTH																								
Jammu and Kashmir	79.25	8.63	4.15	6.21	1.76		65.85	30.23	1.14	1.57	1.21		60.57	30.58	1.29	6.51	1.05	0	58.63	22.94	2.72	12.15	3.47	0.08
Himachal Pradesh	71.06	22.39	2.04	2.97	1.54		71.28	22.65	2.64	2.4	1.04		73.95	20.09	1.41	2.43	2.12	0	69.62	19.98	2.45	3.56	4.38	0
Punjab	67.9	15.4	8.06	6.06	2.59		66.67	0	33.33	0			73.11	8.63	6.3	7.89	4.06	0	79.81	5.4	5.18	5.31	4.3	0
Uttaranchal	54.58	36.3	3.63	2.76	2.73		35.21	58.31	4.28	0	2.2		62	27.4	4.43	4.67	1.49	0	54.7	35.2	2.7	2.68	4.6	0.11
Haryana	63.33	28.87	3.42	3.43	0.95		100	0	0	0			75.51	18.68	2.26	2.08	1.47	0	73.67	17.7	2.63	2.08	3.85	0.08
Delhi	73.32	5.63	12.82	6.72	1.51		79	3.61	16.18	0	1.2		78.39	2.25	6.22	7.93	5.21	0	79.17	1.24	7.78	3.78	7.75	0.28
Rajasthan	45.46	44.72	3.8	4.59	1.42		19.98	76.81	1.53	1.51	0.17		40.08	52.51	2.3	4.06	1.01	0.05	67.99	17.23	3.25	5.41	5.73	0.39
Uttar Pradesh	58.62	33.57	4.34	2.78	0.69		54.29	26.5	2.37	15.69	1.16		60.92	31.47	2.26	4.54	0.81	0	82.61	6.48	2.82	4.85	3.19	0.05
CENTRAL																								
Chhattisgarh	31.78	59.59	3.26	3.68	1.7		15.1	80.15	2.77	1.05	0.93		33.89	59.17	4.06	1.73	1.15	0	61.87	21.79	6.1	3.78	6.46	0
Madhya Pradesh	39.85	47.44	3.63	7.06	2.02		22.74	73.89	1.39	0.78	1.21		44.74	45.24	2.8	5.67	1.54	0	76.3	14.57	3.13	1.84	4.13	0.02
EAST																								
Bihar	39.22	55.52	2.54	1.55	1.16		90.18	9.82	0	0	0		65.64	29.25	2.29	2.01	0.8	0	85.88	9.43	2.01	1.23	1.45	0
West Bengal	57.15	20.12	10.32	9.84	2.56		27.72	64.81	3.06	3.53	0.88		69.04	13.89	6.99	6.33	3.74	0	70.74	8.17	5.56	11.89	3.63	0.01

Jharkhand	48.55	41.07	4.67	4.48	1.23		18.47	75.09	4.07	1.41	0.96		45.25	47.34	4.07	2.2	1.14		71.92	13	4.71	6.09	4.14	0.14
Orissa	54.14	37.51	5.64	1.86	0.85		31.93	62.14	3.15	1.86	0.93		70.97	21.56	3.32	2.81	1.34		82.76	9.42	3.6	1.14	2.88	0.2
NORTH-EAST																								
Sikkim	68.9	15.87	8.24	1.48	5.23	0.25	63.27	19.86	10.02	0.91	5.93	0	70.73	13.87	9.38	0.55	5.46	0	79.88	5.47	9.64	0.5	4.51	0
Arunachal Pradesh	65.44	11.16	18.16	1.05	4.19	0	36.68	48.9	8.79	1.46	4.17	0	70.44	19.68	5.47	1.23	3.18	0	47.41	39.82	7.72	0.46	4.59	0
Nagaland	78.8	8.39	4.91	1.58	6.33	0	49.61	33.01	9.4	1.39	6.58	0.02	58.58	29.27	5.41	1.62	5.02	0.11	77.09	11.61	4.24	0.81	6.05	0.2
Manipur	32.88	26.28	18.44	17.99	4.4	0	30.9	43.65	8.97	12.22	4.26	0	42.33	21.29	11.42	19.34	5.5	0.13	37.55	18.46	11.98	25.76	6.17	0.09
Mizoram	88.02	11.98	0	0	0	0	54.01	23.55	15	1.36	5.89	0.18	70.59	0	29.41	0	0	0	76.01	3.47	17.34	0	3.19	0
Tripura	72.53	11.06	9.15	1.73	5.52	0	48.57	44.9	2.92	0.81	2.79	0	70.82	15.25	6.08	3.05	4.8	0	76.34	10.06	4.75	1.83	7.02	0
Meghalaya	78.17	11.09	6.43	0	4.32	0	55.05	29.08	10.89	0.62	4.26	0.11	80.08	1	13.94	1	3.98	0	77.37	10.96	7.77	0.35	3.55	0
Assam	69.36	20.39	5.13	1.86	3.26	0	66.24	23.21	5.72	1.81	3.01	0	70.98	15.66	3.99	274	6.56	0.07	72.07	17.27	4.2	1.69	4.77	0
WEST																								
Gujarat	42.43	42.76	5.42	7	2.2	0.2	27.81	65.28	1.6	3.99	1.32	100	42.96	42.97	4.44	8.09	1.41	0.13	60.42	19.56	3.95	11.25	4.38	0.45
Maharashtra	51.35	31.42	10.33	4	2.89	0	26.39	67.58	3.68	1.33	1.02	100	51.33	33.35	8.31	3.12	3.74	0.15	57.67	25.91	7.84	4.17	4.36	0.05
Goa	58.24	20.03	16.98	3.3	1.45	0	50.63	32.14	13.56	3.18	0.48	100	62.02	16.3	12.66	4.17	4.85	0	64.02	10.83	14.72	3.37	6.89	0.17
SOUTH																								
Andhra Pradesh	42.78	43.1	5.63	3.98	4.39	0.11	25.58	64.28	3.59	5.25	1.3	0	42.36	40.33	6.86	8.33	2.11	0.01	66.7	18.87	5.23	6.73	2.31	0.16
Karnataka	48.11	38.26	6.16	5.38	2.1	0	39.24	52.73	3.86	3.05	1.13	0	55.42	27.45	5.53	8.04	3.54	0.03	58.45	24.42	7.79	5.84	3.41	0.09
Kerala	48.71	26.35	11.68	7.29	5.98	0	45.44	37.94	7.58	4.51	4.54	0	72.2	5.85	8.9	7.9	5.06	0.09	73.74	5.46	8.32	5.7	6.42	0.36
Tamil Nadu	40.93	44.49	7.37	4.16	3.03	0.03	35.01	49.84	10.16	3.94	0.36	0.69	52.82	25.76	8.5	8.92	3.85	0.15	74.78	6.1	7.26	0.88	8.45	2.52

Source: Author's calculations based on NFHS-III.

are 52 per cent and 30 per cent, respectively, with the proportions for the OBCs and 'Others' being 55 per cent and 71 per cent, respectively (Table 4.5).

Prima facie, these numbers confirm the widespread notion about the majority of Indian women not engaged in productive work; but it is difficult to accept these results at their face value. Also, given the high incidence of landlessness in the sample (in NFHS-I, for instance, 61 per cent of SCs own no land), the assertion that most women are not 'working' seems untenable. In order to track this anomaly, I first went back to the questionnaire. The section that deals with work starts with a series of questions about the husband's/partner's work. These are followed by questions about the woman's work, the first of which is, 'Aside from your own housework, are you currently working?' If the response to this is negative, then the entire subsequent section is skipped; thus no information is gathered on what kinds of work these women may be engaged in.

A whole lot of agricultural tasks are done by women at home and it is likely that the respondents may have discounted their own contribution as a part of normal household chores. Kapadia (1995) reports on research that has found that not only do men tend to minimize the contribution of the women in their families towards productive work, but how women are socially conditioned to undervalue and under-report their own work. So even if they are engaged in work that would otherwise be a part of the productive economy, it would not be socially recognized and therefore would not show up in economic surveys. It is worth noting here that in rural India, household enterprise is the predominant form of organizing economic activity, which is defined as the following: 'Working members of the household act as a collective unit in employing the household asset base for generating gross income, which, after intermediate costs are netted out, is shared among the members of the household, including non workers' (Sundaram and Tendulkar 1988: 318). However, it is easy to see that the women, as part of the household enterprise, may not be paid for their labour, thus reinforcing the belief that their contribution is not productive. Srinivas (1976: 225) discusses how agriculture is a 'familial activity', with 'clear and self understood division of labour between the sexes among agriculturists and this includes both activities inside and outside the household. Each set of activities is seen as supportive of the other...'.

Thus, a deeper look at this question indicates that the self-reporting by women as 'not working' could well be the result of a combination of several factors: the low worth they attach to their own contribution, reflecting the low worth that society attaches to their work; how productive work is defined in their own minds; and the perception that working for wages is a mark of low status.

A number of case studies confirm the suspicion that, certainly in rural areas, far greater numbers of women are engaged in productive work than the 'not working' responses indicate.[7] Kanungo (1993: 486), in two decades of her observations in Rajasthan and West Bengal, found that 'transplanting is done solely by women, by bare hands...planting, weeding and hoeing are done by both men and women...major part of processing of paddy, wheat, jowar, bajra etc. are done by women...allied agricultural activities like animal husbandry...tending the milch cattle, keeping cattle feed ready as well as milking the cattle are done by women'.

Mencher (1996) discusses the sexual division of labour in the rice-producing districts of Tamil Nadu and finds that the type of work that the women do differs by region, caste, training, etc. Among the small landowning households and tenant households, women (low caste) work on their own lands and sometimes for others, and are involved with the purchase of inputs, preparing food for labourers, frequently supervising field operations. Kapadia's (1995) study confirms these trends and in her study of low-caste Pallar women of Tamil Nadu, she finds that it is the women who form the major part of the workforce. They contribute a far greater share of their incomes to the households than their husbands, and do so far more regularly. For this reason, Kapadia (ibid.: 199) believes that these women are 'major providers and breadwinners'. She also reports Mencher's (1974) research that shows that the differential pattern of high contributions from women earners and low contributions from male earners is typical and widespread

[7] Mencher (1996) argues that the census materials have tended to under-report the involvement of women in agriculture, and one of the reasons for this is that the census enumerators are males, who mainly talk to the male members of the households and that the census is taken at a time in the year when there is relatively little activity in agriculture. In the NFHS data that I use, it is not clear if the enumerators are male or female, but the respondents for this data set were women, so the reasons for underestimation would be different.

not only in Tamil Nadu but also in the neighbouring state of Kerala and elsewhere. Deliege (1996: 85), in a case study of a village in Tamil Nadu, finds that 'among the low castes, the wages of women represent an important part of the household income and therefore basically all the women work as coolies or agricultural labourers'.

The case studies also confirm the evidence of inter-caste disparity in women's work. Due to greater restrictions on their public visibility and fewer economic compulsions, accounts of participation in the labour force differ depending upon which caste the women belong to. Srinivas (1976: 229) argues that '[Sanskritization] alters the life-style of those who have "arrived", and in particular, it has radical effects on the lives of women. It immures them and changes the character of the husband-wife relationship.' For our present purpose, the immurement aspect is more relevant. Our results, while they are in all likelihood underestimates of labour force participation rates, do reflect the inter-caste differences correctly, with higher caste women having lower rates of participation. However, immurement does not imply the luxury of idleness; Mencher's (1996) study finds that among the higher caste landowning households, women do not work in the fields, but are involved very closely with a variety of day-to-day supervisory operations. Srinivas (1976: 226) outlines the variety of tasks that fall into the domain of the upper-caste women, including cleaning and processing of grain and several food processing jobs. He also points out that these women additionally may be involved in some economic activity of their own, such as pawnbrokers for needy relatives and neighbours, selling paddy on the sly, or running a chit fund (monthly contributions by members paid to a fund that accumulates over time).

Mascarenhas-Keyes (1990) in her study of Goa found that women from a few elite Brahmin families that had good incomes from large estates did not work in the fields. However, in most other Brahmin families, women contributed to sowing, weeding, and harvesting of paddy; cultivation of vegetables; and the rearing of farm animals such as pigs and chickens. But the Brahmin women, unlike the Shudras, did not sell their labour and worked for other households on a reciprocal basis. Desai (1996) reports a study that shows that production work outside the house is considered of secondary importance for women. 'The higher the caste status, the more important it becomes for women to remain secluded (ibid.: 103).

Kapadia (1995) finds that among the Muthurajas of Tamil Nadu, an agricultural caste that spans the spectrum of low, low-middle, and upper-middle class, socially aspiring men tend to withdraw their wives or sisters from wage work. 'The women themselves are not always happy to withdraw from agricultural wage work, even though it is hard and back breaking, because it is their only source of independent income' (ibid.: 250). In fact, for both men and women, working for wages is seen as an indicator of low status (Srinivas 1976; Epstein 1996), even though few can afford the 'luxury' of keeping women at home. This has resulted in gender-based specialization within agricultural work, as the aforementioned case studies indicate. However, the attitudes towards women's work are derogatory, irrespective of the existence of specialization.[8] Mencher (1996: 61) discusses how 'when an activity is done by women, it is considered easy work, but when the same activity is done by men, it is regarded as hard work'. She also finds that the reason why women are excluded from certain activities, for instance, applying pesticides, is not out of concern for their health (since they are exposed to pesticides while weeding and transplanting anyway), but because of the perception that women should not be trusted with such costly items.

There is an added dimension to characterizing work in an activity such as agriculture that is marked by seasonal fluctuation in intensity. Palriwala (1996) discusses the practice of 'aaoni-jaaoni' in Rajasthan, which describes women moving between their natal and marital homes, depending upon where their labour is more in demand. Despite doing double the work, their contribution is undermined in both the homes.

Turning to urban women, the caste–class interaction has interesting implications for the participation of women in the employment arena. While the constraints arising from caste have not disappeared, an upper-class background often enables urban women to break free of the traditional caste dictates and that is reflected in their presence in higher education, professional occupations, marriage choices, and so on. Their absolute numbers could be deceptive, since in proportional terms they remain a small minority.[9] Even here, with significant

[8] Agarwal (1997: 10), in her discussion of bargaining power of women, believes that 'a person's contributions may be undervalued because of her gender or race'.

[9] Liddle and Joshi (1986) discuss various aspects of this interaction through their study of urban, professional women.

exceptions, it is true that an urban educated girl is expected to marry within her jati and is expected to be less educated than her husband. Working couples in urban areas often could simply reflect the economic benefits of two incomes.

Dube (1996) discusses another dimension of the importance of women's work, again not captured by the classification that this data set relies upon. In a number of cases, continuity of a caste's traditional occupation may be dependent upon the women carrying on that task— traditional crafts, petty trading, scavenging, and, of course, midwifery (the last is exclusively a woman's job). She also discusses how, when the male members of that caste leave their ritual status on account of its low status or low pay, it falls upon the women to continue the traditional occupation.

Summing up, given the vast amount of qualitative evidence on women's work, it can be argued that the quantitative estimates reflect the underlying social tendency to under-report and devalue women's work.[10] However, having said that, this is not sufficient to conclude that since women are working, they enjoy the privileges that are presumed to be associated with economic independence. NFHS data has no information on wages or salaries, but the NSS does: we will see in the following that poor earnings, for *paid* work, seem to characterize women's remuneration. The lack of control over the meagre earnings is also a reflection of the subordinate social status of women inside the family. In addition, studies indicate dismal working conditions, occupational hazards, and long working hours (when hours are defined at all).

LABOUR FORCE PARTICIPATION RATES: EVIDENCE FROM NSS

The much-discussed phenomenon associated with globalization is that of feminization of the labour force, which argues that starting in

[10] Notice here that for the sake of clarity, we are focusing on work that is conventionally regarded as productive; in other words, work that would be counted in the calculation of the national product of a country. This excludes the entire range of work that is not counted as productive (conventional housework) and the exclusion of this kind of work is controversial, to say the least, and of course it undermines a major part of women's work in all societies. But a discussion of this controversy would involve a digression, and so here we would have to confine ourselves with noting this problematic manner of defining productive work and move on.

the 1980s, as labour markets were deregulated, there was a rise in female labour force participation rates (LFPRs) and a fall in men's employment, as well as a 'transformation—or feminization—of many jobs traditionally held by men' (Standing 1989: 1077).[11] Evidence from India does not support the feminization thesis in the aggregate: male LFPRs have marginally risen in the last 20 years while female LFPRs have marginally fallen—which is exactly the opposite of what is predicted. Other evidence on women's employment indicates a decline in self-employment and a clear increase in the casual labour category. Agriculture continues to be the main provider; however, the share of agriculture in employment has declined much more for men than for women.

Figure 4.5 and Table 4.6 show LFPR by gender, caste, and rural/urban. Over the two decades, rural female LFPR has virtually remained the same with negligible fluctuations. The same is true for male LFPRs; thus, the overall picture is that of very little change in the LFPRs in rural India over the two decades. Urban LFPRs show a similar trend,

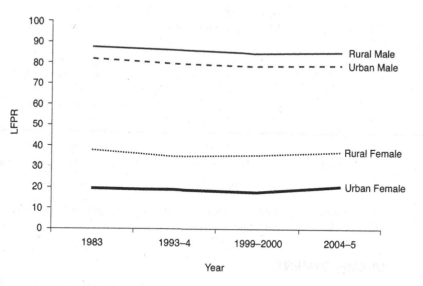

Figure 4.5   LFPR, by Sex and Urban/Rural over Time

Source: Author's calculations based on the NSS Employment–Unemployment Surveys, various rounds.

[11] Ashwini Deshpande (2003) discusses this issue in detail.

with the difference that urban female LFPRs are roughly half that of their rural counterparts.

The figures also reveal that LFPR by subsidiary status is considerably higher than that by principal status. This suggests that a lot of women enter labour force for short periods during the year, balancing constraints of domestic work such that they are out in the labour force when conditions at home are more favourable. While seasonality in entering the labour force is better understood in the context of rural agricultural work cycles, its presence in urban areas is intriguing, but further research is required.

Table 4.6 reveals that overall, SC LFPRs are greater than those for 'Others' for all definitions of LFPRs (based on principal, subsidiary, weekly, and daily status), and we can see that SC women have substantially higher LFPRs than 'Other' women. This is completely in sync with the preceding discussion and evidence from NFHS.

Table 4.6   LFPRs, by Gender and Social Caste, 2004–5

Gender and LFPR types		Urban				Rural			
		ST	SC	OBC	Others	ST	SC	OBC	Others
Women	Principal	58.49	38.20	38.12	26.67	30.69	25.66	23.05	16.18
	Subsidiary	69.77	52.19	50.09	38.52	35.67	30.17	27.66	19.56
	Weekly	59.95	44.44	43.32	33.54	30.73	28.70	25.73	18.69
	Daily	50.84	36.56	36.00	26.98	28.33	25.70	23.00	16.85
Men	Principal	88.78	86.00	84.66	82.76	77.20	80.99	80.71	76.42
	Subsidiary	89.68	87.05	85.77	83.95	77.69	81.38	81.47	76.96
	Weekly	87.63	85.49	84.37	82.72	75.63	80.79	80.82	76.63
	Daily	84.85	82.91	82.39	80.91	74.43	79.50	80.00	76.10

Source: Author's calculations based on the NSS Employment–Unemployment Surveys, various rounds.

Note: 61st round only. 'LFPR types' refers to whether participation is measured on a daily or weekly level, and so forth.

UNEMPLOYMENT

What happens to those who enter the labour market? Not all those who seek work end up being employed: to enter the labour force is one issue, to get employment is quite another. From Table 4.7 we can see the daily and weekly status unemployment rates. These are much higher than the usual status ones and with lower rural–urban

Table 4.7 Unemployment Rates

Rural

Males	38th	50th	55th	61st	Females	38th	50th	55th	61st
Usual (ps)	2.12	1.96	2.09	2.15	Usual (ps)	1.42	1.4	1.5	3.13
Usual (ps+ss)	1.41	1.43	1.71	1.6	Usual (ps+ss)	0.66	0.8	1.04	1.78
Weekly	3.71	2.98	3.92	3.8	Weekly	4.26	3.01	3.66	4.19
Daily	7.51	5.64	7.19	7.98	Daily	8.98	5.55	7.01	8.73

Urban

Males	38th	50th	55th	61st	Females	38th	50th	55th	61st
Usual (ps)	5.86	4.54	4.81	4.42	Usual (ps)	6.92	8.21	7.05	9.25
Usual (ps+ss)	5.08	4.05	4.51	3.74	Usual (ps+ss)	4.85	6.24	5.71	6.89
Weekly	6.69	5.17	5.61	5.24	Weekly	7.45	8.42	7.33	8.99
Daily	9.22	6.72	7.29	7.47	Daily	11.01	10.52	9.39	11.66

Source: Author's calculations based on the NSS Employment–Unemployment Surveys, various rounds.
Note: ps = principal status; ps+ss = principal status and subsidiary status. See Appendix Table 3.A.1 of Chapter 3 for definitions.

differentials than those for usual status. For 2004–5, women have higher unemployment rates than men for corresponding definitions of work for both urban and rural India. For the other three NSS rounds, the urban female unemployment rates are greater than the male unemployment rates for all definitions of work; however, in rural areas, the female unemployment rate for weekly and daily status is higher than that for males.

Figure 4.6 reveals a sharp contrast between rural and urban trends. In rural India, for both men and women, the unemployment rates declined from 1983 to 1993–4 to rise by 1999–2000, with a sharper rise by 2004–5. The unemployment rates for men were higher than those for women in all years except in 2004–5, when the unemployment rates for women overshot that for men. The urban unemployment rates show a different pattern. First, for both men and women, the urban unemployment rates are far greater than the rural unemployment rates, with the unemployment rates

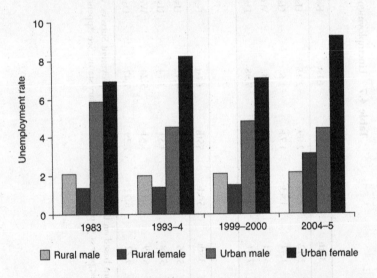

Figure 4.6   Unemployment Rate, 1983 to 2004–5

Source: Author's calculations based on the NSS Employment–Unemployment Surveys, various rounds.
Note: Unemployment rate is defined as percentage of persons unemployed among those in labour force.

for urban women over 3 percentage points higher than those for rural women. Second, for men, the rates show a steady downward trend over the two decades, whereas for women it is almost a steady upward trend, with a blip in 1999–2000 from the previous round, but still higher than the first round. But overall urban unemployment rates show a downward trend because of the downward trends in the male unemployment rates. Third, for all the years, the female unemployment rates are higher than that for the males. Thus, overall, we see much higher unemployment rates for urban India compared to rural India. However, the trend in the former is that of a decline, sharply differentiated by gender, whereas the latter shows an increasing trend, with a smaller gender differential and not always in the same direction as the urban.

EMPLOYMENT AND EARNINGS

Figure 4.7 shows women's principal activity in urban and rural areas according to NSS-61. As expected, women are far more often regular

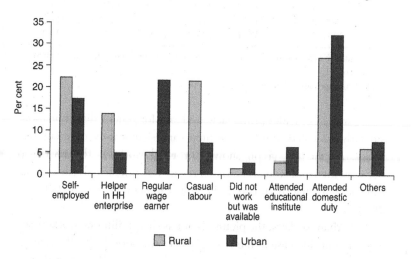

Figure 4.7   Women's Principal Activity, by Rural/Urban

Source: Authors' calculations based on the NSS Employment–Unemployment Surveys, various rounds.
Note: Only the 2004–5 data is used.

wage earners in the urban than in the rural areas, and far more often casual labourers in the rural than in the urban areas.

Table 4.8 shows daily wages by gender and social groups. By this measure, gender disparity is larger than that of social group, and part of the reason could be that a far higher proportion of women do domestic work (mostly unpaid) as compared to men. The rural gender pay differential remained nearly proportionally constant, at a half, despite wages doubling in real terms. Urban wage differential narrowed only slightly in proportional terms.

Table 4.8   Daily Wage Earnings, by Gender, Caste, and Rural/Urban, 1983 to 2004–5 (Rs)

		Male	Female	ST	SC	Others & OBC
Rural	1983	9.91	5.42	6.91	7.13	9.67
	1993–4	13.64	7.40	9.32	10.12	13.25
	1999–2000	17.55	10.27	11.80	12.82	18.66
	2004–5	22.12	11.98	14.44	16.36	21.88
Urban	1983	20.65	12.04	14.52	13.77	20.33
	1993–4	27.73	18.43	22.19	18.48	27.62
	1999–2000	36.71	27.18	29.96	25.92	41.45
	2004–5	32.16	23.03	26.82	20.95	32.72

Source: Author's calculations based on the NSS Employment–Unemployment Surveys, various rounds.
Note: Real wages are calculated using base 1983.

Figure 4.8 provides prima facie evidence for gender discrimination: similarly educated men and women earn significantly different real wages. As the last graph shows, for rural workers, the wage gap between men and women has been rising over time for all educational categories, with a sharp rise in the wage gap between 1999–2000 and 2004–5.

For urban workers, the picture is not as sharp. Illiterate workers see a continuous increase in the wage gap over the period. The 'literate up to primary' category sees an increase and then a decline, such that in 2004–5 the gap is almost the same as in 1983. For workers who have studied up to middle school, the gap increases over the first three data points and then declines, but is still higher than in 1983. Secondary and higher secondary pass workers have the smallest absolute gap

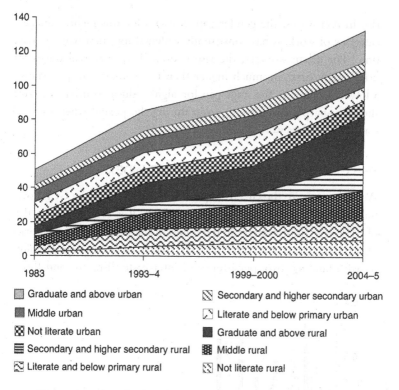

Graduate and above urban

Middle urban

Not literate urban

Secondary and higher secondary rural

Literate and below primary rural

Secondary and higher secondary urban

Literate and below primary urban

Graduate and above rural

Middle rural

Not literate rural

Figure 4.8 Gender-based Wage Differential for Salaried Workers,
by Education and Rural/Urban

Source: Author's calculations based on the NSS Employment–Unemployment Surveys,
various rounds.

(across all categories of workers), but the trend is increasing over the
period, with the gap remaining more or less constant over 1999–2000
and 2004–5.

The evidence of discrimination is more persuasive when we look
at highly educated workers, since these workers would apply for
jobs where 'merit' should matter the most, and presumably their
own merit should be the most obvious owing to their high levels of
education. For the category 'graduate and above', rural wages have
been rising steadily for men and women, and the rise of urban wages
from 1983 is arrested by a decline over 1999–2000 and 2004–5 for
both men and women. Even though both groups have experienced a

rise in real wages, the gender gap in wages for this highly educated category of workers has consistently widened for rural workers over time. For urban workers, the rise is even sharper as real wages for urban men, first, are much higher than for women and have shown a lower decline; so the wage gap for highly educated urban workers shows a sharply rising trend, even during the period when the real wages themselves were declining.

THE GENDER–CASTE DEVELOPMENT INDEX

We now return to the GCDI. Figures 4.9 to 4.11 show the GCDI over the three NFHS rounds. The pattern of GCDI is very similar to that of CDI: one, improvement in the values of the GCDI for all categories of women across the three rounds, issues of strict comparability notwithstanding; two, persistence of inter-caste disparity; and three,

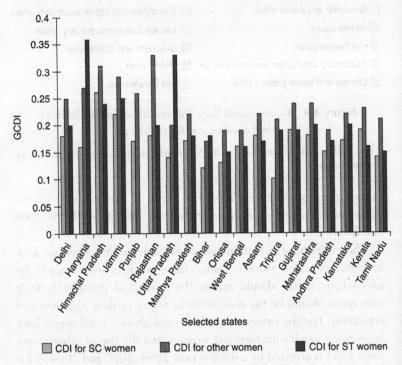

Figure 4.9   The Gender–Caste Development Index, 1992–3

Source: Author's calculations based on NFHS-I.

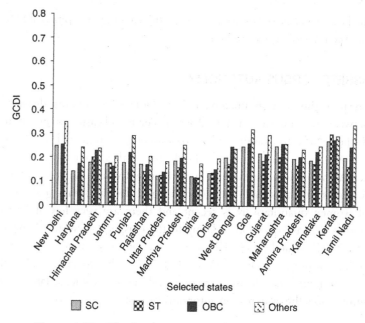

Figure 4.10   The Gender–Caste Development Index, 1998–9

Source: Author's calculations based on NFHS-II.

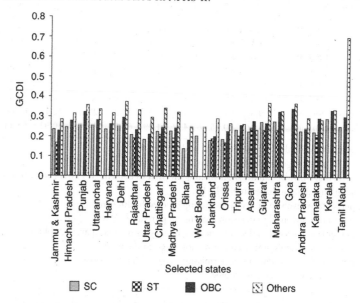

Figure 4.11   The Gender–Caste Development Index, 2005–6

Source: Author's calculations based on NFHS-III.

the lack of a clear relationship between the GCDI, per capita real SDP, and the rates of growth of SDP.

ASSETS VERSUS AUTONOMY

The preceding sections unambiguously establish the economic disparity between men and women as well as between broad caste groups within women. Now, to examine the second aspect of women's lives: What the Dalit women lose in standard of living, do they make up by greater autonomy? Before we examine the evidence, I would like to state that the quest to investigate the autonomy and decision-making abilities of women quantitatively is recent and there are very few all-India studies that ask questions relating to these aspects of women's lives. The NFHS-II and NFHS-III[12] have a section on women's autonomy and, as of now, it is only data set of its size with information related to autonomy and decision-making abilities of women. Table 4.9 summarizes the evidence on autonomy by caste.

Table 4.9   Women's Autonomy and Decision-making Abilities, by Caste

Caste/Tribe		1	2	3	4	5	6	7	8
SC	1998–9	9.1	86.2	49.7	51.8	47.4	31.3	23.7	56
	2005–6	14.37	61.66	63.01	52.95	60.13	53.24	38.66	56.12
ST	1998–9	7.6	87.6	49.8	52.9	48.8	30.7	26.2	50.7
	2005–6	15.27	62.2	59.17	54.58	61.97	49.55	35.1	61.96
OBC	1998–9	10.2	84.4	51.3	52.5	48.4	34.7	26.6	62.4
	2005–6	17.39	59.38	60.22	51.82	58.99	49.75	35.21	53.98
Others	1998–9	9.3	84.7	53.3	53.3	48.2	29.6	22.7	61.0
	2005–6	13.26	60.75	65.43	54.29	63.24	53.42	40.92	54.11

Source: Author's calculations, NFHS-II and NFHS-III.
Notes: 1: percentage not involved in any decision-making
2: percentage involved in decision-making on what to cook in NFHS-II and decision-making on daily purchases in NFHS-III.
3: percentage involved in decision-making on own health care
4: percentage involved in decision-making on purchasing jewellery etc.
5: percentage involved in decision-making on staying with her parents/siblings
6: percentage who do not need permission to go to the market
7: percentage who do not need permission to visit friends/relatives
8: percentage with access to money

[12] The questions in NFHS-III are slightly modified compared to NFHS-II, but there is sufficient common ground to enable comparison across time.

In NFHS-II, the percentage of women not involved in any decision-making does not vary between the SCs and 'Others'. In fact, this proportion is marginally higher among the OBCs, providing some support to the Sanskritization hypothesis, albeit weak. Looking at the nature of decision-making, it is only in the decision on 'what to cook' that the SC and ST women report higher percentages than OBCs and 'Others'. In other areas, especially the crucial one of 'own health care', the proportion of women involved in decision-making seems to increase in the higher castes. We can see a similar trend in 'purchasing jewellery', indicating that these aspects are a function of material conditions. This distinction is the sharpest in the case of 'percentage with access to money', where 56 per cent of SC women report yes, as compared to 62.4 per cent of OBC women and 61 per cent of 'Other' women. The 'freedom of movement' variables, or the percentage of women who do not need permission to go to the market or visit friends/relatives, are only marginally higher in the case of SC women compared to the 'Other' women. In this area, the OBC women report the highest percentages, which could result from their having a low-enough caste status coupled with marginally better material conditions.

NFHS-III figures indicate that SC women seem to have lost the comparative advantage in terms of freedom of movement, as the proportion of SC women involved in decision-making on visiting family and relatives is lower than that for 'Other' women. Proportion of SC women involved in making daily purchases is slightly higher than the 'Other' women, but this slight difference is counteracted by all the other indicators according to which SC women are worse-off than 'Other' women. The pattern regarding OBC women that the NFHS-II revealed seems to be further strengthened, thus providing some support for the view that the emulation of upper caste practices towards women might be the strongest among OBCs. The positive feature of this data is that 'Other' women seem to be improving their indictors of relative autonomy; whether that is due to higher levels of education among their families or some other influences, it is difficult to say.

Domestic Violence

Some other figures from NFHS-II give further clues on whether SC women have, relatively speaking, more egalitarian spousal relations.

Table 4.10   Women's Experience with Beatings and Physical Mistreatment, 1998–9 and 2005–6

	1	2	3	4
SC: 1998–9	25.2	2.2	3.3	27.4
SC: 2005–6	35.37	1.32	8.61	35.33
ST: 1998–9	20.8	1.8	3	23
ST: 2005–6	33.83	0.84	8.13	33.82
OBC: 1998–9	20.7	1.7	3.6	23
OBC: 2005–6	28.85	0.99	7.37	28.84
Others: 1998–9	13.6	1.6	2.6	15.7
Others: 2005–6	21.23	0.72	6.58	21.21

Source: Author's calculations, NFHS-II and NFHS-III.
Notes:
1. % ever physically mistreated by husband
2. % ever physically mistreated by in-laws
3. % ever physically mistreated by other family members
4. % ever faced any violence

The percentage of women who discussed family planning with husbands and family members, etc., is almost the same for SC and OBC (at 24.1 per cent and 23.9 per cent, respectively), but is 26.4 per cent for 'Others'. However, a greater blow to the presumed egalitarian relations among the SCs comes from the figures on domestic violence across castes. Table 4.10 shows self-reported figures for percentages of ever-married women beaten or physically mistreated since age 15, which shows that 27.4 per cent of SC women reported physical mistreatment as compared to 15.7 per cent of 'Other' women (and 23 per cent of OBC women). The question always arises whether the incidence of physical violence is actually lower among upper castes or whether the SC women are more candid in reporting about the incidence of domestic violence. That is difficult to settle without supporting qualitative data. However, NFHS-II reports that 'the prevalence of domestic violence decreases substantially as the standard of living increases' (p. 76). To the extent this is true, there is reason to believe that the incidence of domestic violence might be greater among the SCs than for upper-caste women. However, it could equally be the other way round and thus figures might reflect greater reluctance to admit to domestic violence on the part of women as their class status increases. Thus, the issue of domestic violence is extremely complex and intractable, and thus we really need more in-depth studies to capture the various dimensions of the deep-rooted problem.

NFHS-III data establish quite decidedly that SC women are subject to greater violence than their upper-caste counterparts within the family, or at least report it in greater numbers. In addition, these data indicate that SC women face greater violence from individuals outside their families. Incidents of dominant caste men raping, beating, and terrorizing Dalit women are known to be a regular feature. All these factors contribute to a situation where Dalit women are quite decidedly at the bottom of the economic ladder, and in addition face constraints and violence in greater measure than the upper-caste women.

Thus, the evidence in this section, read together with that in the preceding sections, suggests fairly conclusively that the material gap persists between Dalit and upper-caste women. On the other hand, it is not the case that Dalit women enjoy much greater autonomy to compensate for their greater poverty. Thus, it seems reasonable to infer that the trade-off between material conditions and autonomy is no longer in evidence in contemporary India. The caste gender overlap, therefore, unambiguously suggests that Dalit women are worse off than upper-caste women.

EXPLOITATION AND ABUSE

At this point, it is worth reminding ourselves that the preceding numbers, while revealing some aspects, do not capture the multifaceted tyranny of exploitation, abuse, and discrimination that is an integral part of a Dalit woman's everyday life (see, for instance, Meera V. 1979; Human Rights Watch 1999; Shah et al. 2006). It is not possible to do justice to the enormity of the problem in a couple of paragraphs, but to not refer to it at all would be a grave omission. Despite being abolished in 1976, bonded labour continues to exist in several parts of India and the majority of the bonded labourers are Dalits, including women and children.[13] The inhumanity of this modified form of slavery has been well documented and that has prompted the legislation for its abolition. Its indifferent implementation and hence the persistence of

---

[13] Bonded labour refers to work in slave-like conditions tied to the landlord/ employer (most often the same as the moneylender) in order to pay off debt.

bonded labour reflects the social and political clout of the upper-caste landlord employers.

Despite being outlawed, large parts of India (both rural and urban) continue to have toilets that are cleaned by manual scavenging, a practice that is entirely the 'preserve' of some of the Dalit castes. Not surprisingly, these castes face greater social discrimination than other Dalits and live in completely segregated colonies. Subject to one of the worst forms of indignity for their entire lives, these meagrely paid workers (comprising of very large numbers of women) battle with disease and ailments arising from the appallingly unhygienic conditions; their condition made worse by virtually non-existent labour legislation and social ostracism.

Parts of south India, particularly in Andhra Pradesh and Karnataka, still have the *devdasi* (literally, female servants of god) system, where pre-pubertal young women are 'married' to the lord. The devdasis typically are Dalit girls from very poor families and socially the initiation ceremony is performed as if an honour was being bestowed upon the girls. While some of the devdasis are excellent artists (performers of classical music and dance, some of whom are highly renowned), most end up as victims of this system of ritualized prostitution in the service of upper-caste patrons. Some are eventually auctioned into urban brothels. Their social position offers them very little protection from the police or the judiciary. 'When a *devdasi* is raped, it is not considered rape. She can be had by any man at any time' (Human Rights Watch 1999: 150). This system works over and above the 'regular' prostitution, that is, the degrading compulsions of poverty, illiteracy, ignorance, and abuse pushing Dalit women into prostitution.

Unarguably at the bottom of the socio-economic ladder, Dalit women are subject to attacks by upper-caste men with impunity. Terrifying tales of sexual abuse, rape, torture, mutilation, murder, and massacre of Dalit women by upper-caste men are reported, and accounts of police brutality compound their vulnerability. In general, the combination of caste, class, and gender bias in the police and the judiciary implies that these women have minimal protection, if at all. Shah et al. (2006) elaborate on how there are two aspects of Dalit women's lives that are of special concern: the gendered division of labour that exposes women to specific forms of untouchability, and the sexualized forms of oppression.

RESISTANCE OR ACCOMMODATION?

Far from being mute sufferers, women in India have a long and continuing tradition of resistance and struggle, both in organized movements and in their everyday lives (see, for instance, Kumar 1993). The Indian women's movement is large, vibrant, and encompasses a variety of streams—some very similar to Western feminism and some that are culturally and ideologically distinct (in other words, not a direct offshoot of Western feminism). In analysing the Indian women's movement, it is important to avoid the fallacy of equating Indian tradition with patriarchy and oppression and Western exposure (especially the influence of British colonialism) with modernity and progress. As Liddle and Joshi (1986: 49) point out, 'Women's resistance to oppression in India neither began nor ended with the British women's intervention, but had its roots in the Indian social structure and cultural heritage...the two movements had very different starting points and developed in different directions.'[14]

In fact, the earliest questioning of Aryan or Brahminic dominance is found in women's writing that precedes British colonialism by centuries. Tharu and Lalita (1991: 52) suggest that 'women often found opportunities for involvement in literary creation in the context of powerful historical movements that questioned Aryan or Brahminic dominance and represented rival political groups and emerging social classes' and 'both the Buddhist [roughly 500 BC] and Bhakti [meaning devotion, roughly speaking from the 8th to the 17th century] poetry came from movements that opposed caste discrimination and ritualised Hinduism dominated by Brahmin priests'. In fact, there is a thesis (Chattopadhyay 1959, quoted in ibid.: 54) that 'Vedic idealism itself was shaped by the struggle against

---

[14] This perspective on the women's movement is not the starting point of all analyses; often accounts of the women's movement in India begin with the nineteenth century (for instance, Radha Kumar's [1993] analysis) that coincides with the spread of Western education and the corresponding ideas of equality.

matriarchal materialist cultures and still carries the marks of that engagement.' Tharu and Lalita (1991) find that very little that has been written by women has survived from Vedic Sanskrit or from the later Sanskrit classical literature.

The Bhakti movement, a medieval movement against religious and caste orthodoxy, is not only an extremely crucial indicator of the long-standing resistance to conservative tendencies, but also demonstrates how a struggle against orthodoxy is as much a part of Indian tradition as orthodoxy itself. It was 'characterised by the abandonment of the self in devotion and love for a personal God, and by the deprecation of all man-made social and religious distinctions' (O'Hanlon 1985: 224).The earliest expression of this was in the eighth century in Tamil Nadu and from there it successively spread to other parts of present-day India, a remarkable achievement for a period preceding the idea of the nation-state and nationalism. The poets composed in regional languages, 'deliberately breaking the literary and religious hold of Sanskrit', thus ensuring accessibility to low castes and women (Tharu and Lalita 1991: 57).[15]

[15] Illustrating the remarkably progressive content of the Bhakti compositions would take volumes. I have a couple of examples to show how bold this movement was in terms of its attack on the religious establishment. In the first verse, this woman poet is strikingly candid in questioning and rejecting the orthodox view of women (Tharu and Lalita 1991: 107):

The Vedas cry aloud, the Puranas shout,
'No good may come to a woman.'
I was born with a woman's body
How am I to attain Truth?
'They are foolish, seductive, deceptive—
Any connection with a woman is disastrous.'
Bahina says, 'If a woman's body is so harmful,
How in this world will I reach the Truth?'

—Bahinabai (1628–1700)

Taking another illustration, the following, written even earlier by a Shudra woman poet, reflects the dual hardship of being a woman and a Shudra; by transforming the deity into a friend, a companion who lightens up the burden by sharing all the menial work that defines her lot, with her sensitive poetry, she literally takes the divine off the pedestal and places him at par with the outcasts—an incredible act of heresy and rebellion (ibid.: 83):

The movement arose in different parts of the country apparently independently, and developed various idioms, but they also had several things in common. In each place these artisan groups led what has been called a people's revolt against the domination of the upper castes and the lifeless ritual of vedic Hinduism practiced by the brahmin priests. Washerpeople, leather workers, oil pressers, stonecutters, potters, weavers, silversmiths, artisans, and small tradespeople of all kinds swelled the movement's ranks. And, what is perhaps most significant from our point of view, the path of devotion set up no barriers of caste and sex. The women poets of the Bhakti movements did not have to seek the institutionalized spaces religion provided to express themselves, and women's poetry moved from the court and the temple to the open spaces of the field, the workplace, and the common woman's hearth. (Tharu and Lalita 1991: 57)

Of course, it would be naive to view the Bhakti movement simply as a utopian upsurge since, like all social movements, it is marked with considerable complexity. Degrees of radicalism within the movement varied across time and space, and in the ultimate analysis, the extent to which this movement succeeded in breaking the dominant orthodox religion—caste mould is a moot point. The earlier phases of the movement, especially in Tamil Nadu, Karnataka, and Maharashtra, were more radical in terms of both the number of women who took part and in the rejection/questioning of patriarchy, the caste code, and constraints on sexuality, than the later seventeenth-century movements that developed in the north. These and many other caveats notwithstanding, the movement is an important landmark in the struggle against caste hierarchy and women's oppression, since even if orthodoxy ultimately triumphed, the Bhakti movement succeeded in building a fundamental critique of the Aryan philosophy, from within

---

[Jani sweeps the floor]
Jani sweeps the floor,
The Lord collects the dirt,
Carries it upon His head,
And casts it away.
Won over by devotion,
The Lord does lowly chores!
Says Jani to Vithoba,
How shall I pay your debt?

—Janabai (ca. 1298–1350)

as it were, which was at the root of the subordination of women and the Dalits.[16]

The contribution of women in the anti-colonial nationalist movement is better documented, both as illustrious leaders and as participants in the numerous mass movements. The particular dimension of the women's movement in this period that is relevant to the present chapter is the renewed attack on the restrictive practices of the caste orthodoxy with a demand for a life of dignity for women and low castes. Again, no attempt is made here to summarize the efforts of numerous individuals in the struggles, agitations, and movements that were either directly attacking religious orthodoxy (and thus advocated Dalit and women's rights) or confronted these issues more tangentially in the wider focus on imperialism and class struggle. However, a few illustrations would be useful.

From the western state of Maharashtra alone, one can think of several instances. Savitribai Phule (1831–97), wife of the progressive Dalit social reformer from Maharashtra, Jotiba Phule, became a 'poet, scholar and activist in her own right' (Tharu and Lalita 1991: 211) by first educating herself and then going on to become a crusader for the rights of women and the Dalits in general. Together they founded the Satyashodhak Samaj (loosely translated, 'Society for the Quest for Truth') in 1873, based on the 'desire for a form of social organisation that would reflect the merits and aptitudes of the individual, rather than enforcing birth as the basis both for occupation and for religious status' (O'Hanlon 1985: 223). 'By insisting that God was available to all his human creatures and that no intermediary was necessary for the invocation of divine power, the society attempted to remove any justification for the special sanctity of the Brahmans' (ibid.: 237). Pandita Ramabai (1858–1922), author of *High Caste Hindu Woman* (1888) among other writings, and Muktabai (1841–?), a student in the school founded by Jotiba and Savitribai Phule, were other significant figures in the movement for women's

---

[16] In the fifteenth–sixteenth centuries, there were other important movements that were stridently anti-caste. For example, two very powerful movements developed around the teachings of Nanak (the founder of the Sikh community, a monotheist, and bitterly opposed to the rigid hierarchies of caste) and Kabir, who abandoned his religion by birth, Islam, and worked for the formation of a new religion in which there would not be a man-made barrier between the individual and god.

emancipation and against caste divisions. The history of the freedom movement is replete with instances from all parts of the country (see, for instance, Kumar 1993).

The contemporary Indian women's movement is highly complex, both in its ideological leanings and in the method of struggle. Women's organizations span the entire ideological spectrum from extreme left to extreme right, thus indicating the awareness of this issue from all quarters. The extreme right organizations function mainly as mouthpieces of the conservative forces and thus their place in the movement for emancipation of women is questionable. However, it is important to note that their capacity to mobilize women is not insubstantial, and thus they present a serious challenge to the other organizations that question orthodoxy. During the violence in Gujarat in 2002, it was reported that many women were mobilized by the right-wing to support the violence, or at least participate in it as voyeurs.[17] Also, the influence of the conservative organizations implies that the orthodoxy-versus-emancipation dichotomy cannot be equated with the men-versus-women one, since we now see powerful women, with mass following, advocating the path of conservatism.

* * *

The most obvious implication of low educational attainment for women is the persistence of a low income-earning capability. There might be a circularity in relationships, as low earnings, in turn, cause further material deprivation, which leads to a further neglect of women. However, there is also evidence of discrimination in earnings: women with comparable education earning less than men. While this pattern is true for all women, the inter-caste divisions suggest that this vicious cycle may be the hardest to break for SC women. Thus, while a section, small in terms of proportion of the Indian population, but large in absolute size of Indians (of both sexes) can claim that caste does not matter, either because it does not affect their lives or because they personally do not discriminate on the basis of caste, this freedom from caste is impossible for Dalit women, who endure a combination

---

[17] For a discussion of the anti-Muslim sentiment among Hindu women, see, for instance, Nonica Datta (2002).

of poverty and gender discrimination that keeps them illiterate, low paid, malnourished, and unhealthy—all linked in an iniquitous cycle. The relatively low degree of autonomy is relevant here in that higher levels of autonomy for women could perhaps ensure that the meagre resources of poor households are distributed more equitably, thereby ameliorating some implications of poverty. However, it is important to note that the greater constraint on the well-being of Dalit women, if one had to choose, might be material deprivation rather than lack of autonomy, given that the size of the cake to be distributed within the household is itself very small.

Both Chapters 3 and 4 have presented a range of evidence on material disparities over a two-decade period that highlights, first, that traditional broad hierarchies persist, in all states of India, in varying degrees; and second, that the relationship between growth, SDP, and material conditions of Dalits is not straightforward. We now need to turn to an examination of whether the gaps between Dalits and 'Others' are due to current discrimination against Dalits or due to educational disparities between Dalits and non-Dalits, which may or may not be discriminatory. The next two chapters attempt precisely that, by first defining discrimination, explaining how it could be gauged, and then by summarizing studies attempting to gauge discrimination in the Indian context.

5   Measuring Discrimination

'Racial discrimination pervades every aspect of a society in which it is found':
Arrow (1998)

'Disparity in market outcomes does not prove discrimination': Heckman (1998)

'Discrimination is a hellhound that gnaws at Negroes in every waking moment
of their lives to remind them that the lie of their inferiority is accepted as truth
in the society dominating them': Martin Luther King, Jr.

WHAT IS DISCRIMINATION?

The evidence in the preceding chapters has established that disparities
are shaped by social identities; in the present discussion, by caste
and gender. However, as the quote by Heckman suggests, the existence of disparities is not sufficient to establish discrimination.[1]
Initial differences in education or poverty levels can lead to disparate
outcomes and those differences could be the result of very specific,
individual-level factors, and not necessarily reflect systematic discrimination, whether between individuals or groups.

---

[1] In theory, disparities are not even necessary for discrimination. Consider a hypothetical world where women are more qualified and productive than men. If women
are discriminated against, their average wages would be lower than productivities
and could conceivably be equal to those of men.

This leads to the very basic question: what is discrimination and how can we measure it? The word discrimination per se has both positive and negative connotations. For instance, to be a 'discriminating listener of music' or a 'discriminating art critic' would be considered a positive attribute, since it implies an ability to discern fine gradations in quality. When the word is used in a negative sense, it has the sense of (arbitrary) subjective judgement: discrimination in this sense would entail applying separate standards to two individuals when objectivity demands that they should be evaluated by the same standards. For example, a common complaint a child might have against his/her sibling—how come I get scolded for not doing my homework but he does not—indicates a feeling of being discriminated against. Here, discrimination embodies the notion of unfair treatment. It is in this sense that we will use the word. However, it is worth repeating that the theory of statistical discrimination defines discrimination more neutrally as a valuation of personal characteristics unrelated to productivity and thus eschews any normative judgement on whether discrimination should be viewed positively or negatively. The discussion in Chapter 2 demonstrates that statistical discrimination is far from neutral in its consequences, even though it might be used as a neutral tool by employers, and negative stereotypes about groups can end up becoming self-fulfilling prophecies.

We also saw in Chapter 2 that under taste-based discrimination, prejudice is the cornerstone of discrimination. As Becker (1957) has demonstrated, if prejudice is strong enough, individuals can discriminate against others in market settings even at a cost to themselves. It is important to reiterate that even when *all* individuals can discriminate (and earn less than if they had not discriminated), we can still talk about effective discrimination: groups/individuals who are the victims of net discrimination and thus might be conventionally regarded as groups discriminated against. If one believes that in contemporary settings, taste-based discrimination is passé and discrimination in market settings mainly takes the form of statistical discrimination, then of course, it is employers who discriminate, and identification of groups that are discriminated against is much more straightforward. The simple point is that irrespective of our views on the causes of discrimination and all the ambiguity surrounding the concept, given the salience of social identities in a variety of material outcomes, it is typically not difficult to identify groups that, on balance, are discriminated against.

Of course, discrimination among economic agents or in market settings constitutes only a part of the overall discrimination in society. Social or non-economic discrimination is harder to define precisely and judgements about whether a given situation is discriminatory or not might differ widely. Thus, when Dalits or women are denied entry into temples on account of their social identities, this is commonly understood as a discriminatory practice. Understanding this as discrimination does not necessarily imply that people would be opposed to it: there would be several who would justify this blatant discrimination on the basis of archaic, doctrinaire religious beliefs. Thus, understanding a situation as discriminatory (the objective characterization) could be distinct from the normative judgement about it (the subjective belief of whether it is justified or not).

However, there could be other situations where the objective and the subjective may not be as easily separable. For example, in India, when Muslims are denied membership in residential apartment complexes that are dominated by Hindus, opinions will differ about whether this is discriminatory or not. Or when young Muslim men, irrespective of nationality, are disproportionately denied US visas post-9/11, is that 'discriminatory' or 'rational'? In these instances, opinions about whether these actions are justified are inextricably linked with perceptions of whether these are discriminatory. This is difficult terrain and some of these debates are virtually impossible to settle; in keeping with the tone of this book, this chapter will discuss how economists seek to measure discrimination not only in market-based interactions, the traditional domain of economics, but also how experimental methods are being used to assess discrimination in non-market interactions.

DISCRIMINATION IN LABOUR MARKETS: EARLY STUDIES

Concerns about racism as well as about male–female differentials in wages and occupational attainment in the US prompted the early econometric attempts to quantify labour market discrimination.

These differentials were not confined to the US alone; however, they became subjects of investigation in the US much earlier than in other countries. Consequently, both in terms of method as well as in terms of databases, the US academic fraternity—economists, sociologists, social psychologists, and demographers—has made very rich and pioneering insights into the study of group-based discrimination.

The overwhelming majority of the econometric studies are based on Becker's analytical framework. Ashenfelter (1970), in a study of post-war US, attempts to quantify labour market discrimination against non-whites by linking discrimination to overall labour market conditions, as captured by the unemployment rate (overall, as well as separately for whites and non-whites). He finds, for instance, that discrimination, as defined by the log of relative earnings (non-white to white), increased significantly during the Great Depression. Disaggregating by gender, he finds that the relative earnings of non-white women increased primarily by a movement between occupational categories, whereas non-white men apparently gained by changes *within* occupational categories. Ashenfelter's contribution lies not as much in the findings as in the methodological framework that consisted of studying the relationship between three main variables— ratio of non-white to white earnings; market discrimination against non-white labour; and the ratio of non-white to white productivity— and then estimating the relationship by finding operational, estimable equivalents to these three variables.

He also tests the hypothesis that the extent of discrimination is negatively related to aggregate labour market activity. The prima facie basis for this hypothesis is that in a tight labour market, the perceived cost of discrimination against non-whites might increase because of the general scarcity of labour as well as because a tight labour market might provide a better environment for dissolving the restrictive practices in unions and some crafts. However, he finds that the state of the labour market hardly has an appreciable effect on the relative earnings of non-whites. Even though Ashenfelter does not interpret it as such, this could be interpreted as evidence of a strong taste for discrimination. On the whole, he finds that non-white females have gained, whereas non-white males have lost, in terms of relative earnings in post-war US.

Decomposing the Wage Gap

Before we come to the predominant econometric method of estimating labour market discrimination, it should be stated that a very preliminary exercise to establish whether or not group membership matters in determining the level of wage earnings would be to estimate a standard wage equation with the addition of a dummy variable to capture group identity. In the standard wage equation, earnings are postulated to be a function of several wage-generating characteristics, such as age, education, sector of occupation, whether the job is in rural or urban areas, whether it is full- or part-time employment, whether it is in the formal or informal sector, and experience level. Thus, the estimation consists of a regression of the log of monthly wage on all the possible measurable characteristics that could explain the monthly wage, such as the ones mentioned earlier.[2] The idea is that the set of explanatory variables should be as broad as possible. Once this equation is specified and estimated for the entire population relevant for the particular study, it is re-estimated with all the explanatory variables plus a dummy variable that captures group identity.[3] If the group dummy turns out to be significant in the presence of all the other explanatory variables, we can conclude that group identity is not only one of the several predictors of earnings, but also that it matters after controlling for all other wage-earning characteristics.

However, this is not sufficient to establish discrimination and certainly yields no insights into the extent of discrimination. The reason it is not sufficient to establish discrimination is that the wage equation with a group dummy implicitly assumes that the wage structure of groups (say, Scheduled Castes [SCs] and non-SCs) is the same. In other words, except for the dummy variable in the equation, all other characteristics have the same coefficient, whether the individual is SC or not. This means that the returns to characteristics, or the way in which the labour market values these characteristics (such as

[2] Individual studies add variables specific to the study: for instance, a study of wage gap among migrants will add a variable to control of the length of residence in the city of employment and age at arrival, the latter as a proxy for pre-migration experience.

[3] For example, in the present context, we could define the dummy variable to take the value 1 if the individual belongs to SC, and 0 otherwise.

experience, skill, or education), are the same for the two groups. This, as we will see later, is untenable in the presence of discrimination. Hence, the estimates from this equation will produce biased estimates of the effect of caste membership on wage earnings.

If the group dummy is significant or even if we simply observe, without estimating the wage equation, that average wages of two groups differ, there is a prima facie case to investigate whether, and to what extent, the gap can be explained by discrimination. The gap could be due to differences in education or skill levels or simply due to the fact that the groups might be concentrated in different segments of the occupational spectrum (which in turn could also be due to skill differences). Thus, it is necessary to separate the effects of the differential educational or skill levels from the discriminatory component, which could be, of course, zero.

In two independently written pioneering papers, Blinder (1973) and Oaxaca (1973) outlined the econometric methodology to do precisely this, that is, separate the effect of the endowment/skill effect in the wage gap from the discriminatory component. Thus, the *Blinder–Oaxaca decomposition method* is the main established method for econometrically measuring labour market discrimination. Essentially, this method involves explaining the wage earned by a standard wage equation regression, as explained earlier. This regression is done for each of the groups (say, men and women, or blacks and whites, or non-SCs and SCs). Then, the regression coefficients from, say, the 'white' equation (measuring of the rate of returns to each of the white characteristics) are substituted in the estimated 'black' equation to yield the wages that blacks would have earned if they had been treated as an average member of the white community. The difference between this wage and the wage that blacks actually receive is the measure of discrimination. Similarly, 'black' coefficients could be substituted into the white equation to yield wages that whites would have earned if they had treated as average members of the black community. In this case, however, the difference between these hypothetical wages for whites and actual wages would measure 'nepotism' in favour of the white community.[4]

---

[4] Following Becker (1957), in the discrimination literature, nepotism is seen as the opposite of discrimination.

The basic belief behind this approach is that average wages of groups differ both because of productivity or skill differences between groups as well as because the market treats the same characteristics differently. What can be observed are only the actual wage differences; we need to artificially separate the endowment/productivity/characteristics differences from the treatment effect, and the way in which the Blinder–Oaxaca method estimates the treatment effect is by pairing the estimated rates of returns for one group with the characteristics of the other group.

CRITIQUES OF THE DECOMPOSITION TECHNIQUE

While this method is widely used, there are several critiques in the literature that have also paved the way for subsequent refinements. We will discuss some of the main points of criticism in the following.

Index Number Problem

One of the problems with the decomposition method is that it yields two different estimates of discrimination depending on which wage structure is used as the base: for instance, in the two-group case, the white rates of return could be substituted into the black equations or the other way round (see Appendix 5.A). There is no prima facie reason to prefer one over the other.

This has been addressed by researchers in a variety of ways. Some calculate both estimates and treat the two as upper and lower bounds, within which the 'actual' estimate of discrimination lies. This implies that even with the best method we cannot estimate the 'true' value of discrimination with accuracy. Thus, for instance, Banerjee and Knight (1985: 290) find that the gross wage gap between SCs and non-SCs in their sample is 17 per cent, of which the discriminatory component accounts for roughly between half and two-thirds, depending on which wage structure is used as the basis of the decomposition. Oaxaca's (1973) study of the male–female wage differential finds that for whites, the discriminatory component of the gap lies between 77 per cent and 78.4 per cent. Thus, both the extent of the discriminatory gap as well as its break-up between the 'explained' and the 'residual' are a function of the particular data set being estimated.

In their defence, the proponents of the decomposition technique can argue that as long as we can get a rough order of magnitude of the discriminatory component, the actual value may not add too much extra information. Those interested in a single value use an average of the two (for instance, Banerjee and Knight [1985] use a geometric mean). Some believe that it is the wage structure of the dominant or high-wage group (men, whites, non-SCs, etc.) that is more likely to prevail in the absence of discrimination, and therefore it should be the base for the decomposition (Madheswaran and Attewell [2007] use this approach).

Selection Bias

Heckman's (1979) famous critique has now decisively refined the decomposition method. He argued that wage estimates based on samples in which some individuals are more likely to self-select themselves than others (or those based on non-randomly selected samples due to the research design) would be biased, that is, will not correctly estimate the underlying population wage estimates. In the context of the wage equation, this would mean the following. The sample on the basis of which the wage equation is calculated consists only of those individuals who decided to work at the given wage. If an individual decided not to work because the wage offer was too low, that person will be excluded from the sample, because she will self-select herself out of the workforce. This self-selection makes the sample non-random and estimates based on the sample cannot be taken to be representative of the population from which the sample is drawn.[5]

In order to correct for the sample-selection bias, he suggested a two-step procedure. To understand the intuition behind his procedure, suppose we want to estimate the determinants of wage offers based on a sample. The wage data would come from a sample in which all individuals would be working, that is, those who decided to accept the wage offers. However, there would be individuals in the population who would not work at a given wage offer, and thus would be naturally

[5] This self-selection problem is also encountered in other contexts. For example, in studies that are based on a sample of migrants, wage estimates based on the migrants' sample will not correctly estimate the wages of the underlying population (or what the non-migrants would have earned if they had migrated) because some individuals are more likely than others to migrate for a variety of reasons.

excluded from the sample. Therefore, Heckman suggested that as a first step, the probability of working should be estimated. In the second stage, a transformation of the predicted individual probabilities should be included in the wage equation in order to correct for self-selection.

Omitted Variable Bias

If the residual wage gap is supposed to be a measure of discrimination, it is important to make the wage equation as comprehensive as possible. Otherwise, the residual might simply be measuring the effect of omitted variables on wages, rather than discrimination. However, even if the wage equation is carefully specified and data collected on all the measurable variables, there are some factors that can never be measured, and thus cannot be included in the wage equation. For instance, a more confident job applicant, who is more fluent and articulate, can get a higher wage offer, since he/she might come across as more competent and promising. There is, therefore, always a question mark over the interpretation of the residual as a measure of discrimination, since it is highly likely that there would be the confounding presence of omitted variables, and to the extent this is true, this method is likely to *overestimate* the discriminatory component. This criticism is valid and the best response to this would be to minimize omitted variables to the extent possible.

However, Yinger (1998) points out that the bias can work in the opposite direction too. He cites an example from a study of housing prices: when neighbourhood variables, such as the quality of the surrounding housing, are excluded from the regression, the regression underestimates discrimination against blacks. Neighbourhood quality is, on average, poorer for blacks; thus, leaving out this variable biases the coefficient of the variable indicating black households towards zero—suggesting little or no discrimination against blacks in housing markets.

While the omitted variable bias is a serious problem, the best solution is to consciously minimize it. However, given that it can never be completely eliminated, should this be reason enough to abandon the decomposition method? No, since given the index number problem, this method does not yield a unique number in any case, and thus there is an inherent cloud of uncertainty about the precise quantitative value of discrimination. What it does is to provide an order of magnitude that is instructive especially for inter-temporal comparisons: measured by the same yardstick, we can examine if discrimination is going up or down over time. Further, as the later discussion suggests, it is not clear if *any* method can measure a concept such as discrimination with absolute precision.

Included Variable Problem

This is a kind of an endogeneity bias: if variables that are included are influenced by the actions of the agents whose behaviour is being studied, then it is possible that discrimination might be underestimated. Yinger (1998) cites the examples of car dealers who might refuse to give loans to minorities. In that case, a variable indicating which buyers received loans could produce a downward bias in an estimate of discrimination in car prices. Similarly, if whites are offered a greater trade-in price relative to the market price of the vehicle, a similar bias can be seen if a control for trade-in allowance is added.

Diverting Variable Problem

This bias arises when a variable that is not a legitimate control variable, but that is correlated with race or ethnicity, is included in the regression. Of course, it is difficult to decide which variables are 'illegitimate', and the possibility of the omitted variable bias does lead most researchers to include as many variables as possible. But if some of the variables are illegitimate, then this could have the effect of lowering estimates of discrimination. In other words, the race or ethnicity effect might get picked up by the unnecessary controls and the final estimate of discrimination might end up being lower. How does one decide which the legitimate controls are? Strictly speaking, only the variables that are critical in the particular market being studied should be used as control. Thus, in the wage regressions, only the variables that affect the workers' wages should be included as controls. However, the reason this decision (which variable to include) is complicated and not as straightforward as it appears at first sight is because economic agents can base their decisions on variables that are not, strictly speaking, relevant to their decision. To use Yinger's example, suppose landlords are not only concerned about profit but also believe that people from certain occupations make better tenants and should be charged lower rent. If blacks are underrepresented in these occupations, then a control for occupation in explaining rents will underestimate discrimination against blacks. Ultimately, it is extremely difficult, if not impossible, for researchers to determine which variables are legitimate. Thus, researchers tend to keep all the controls that are significant.

Butler's Critique

This is perhaps the most fundamental critique that has not yielded a refinement yet, except Cotton's method, described later. Butler (1982) argues that by estimating a single wage equation, this method is unable to separate the demand-side coefficients from the supply-side coefficients, since the single equation is a reduced form equation that combines the effects of both sides of the labour market. He demonstrates the following: suppose blacks have been discriminated against in the provision of schooling. In that case, a black worker and a white worker with identical years of education and number of years of experience will embody different amounts of human capital and different elasticities of substitution with other inputs. Thus, if the training received by white workers makes them more complementary with capital as compared to black workers, then the demand for white labour will be less elastic than the demand for black labour and the coefficients of the reduced form equation for blacks will be smaller than those for whites, even if blacks and whites were otherwise identical. On the other hand, if blacks have a less elastic supply or demand curve in any market, the reduced form equation is likely to underestimate market discrimination against blacks. Butler's main point is that unless one can identify structural demand or supply equations, very little about market discrimination can be learned from the reduced form, except perhaps when for both blacks and whites, the demand curve is perfectly inelastic and the supply curve is perfectly elastic. Butler further shows that if the Oaxaca decomposition is done on the demand equation, then the discriminatory component reduces drastically.

Cotton (1988) says that while Butler is correct in pointing out the confounding of the demand- and supply-side factors, he is wrong in assuming that these are the coefficients that will prevail in the absence of discrimination. He argues that over time, in the absence of discrimination, the discrepancy between the rates of return to the two groups (the two betas) will disappear and the labour market will, in fact, treat the coefficients of the two groups identically. The question is: what coefficients will prevail in the absence of discrimination?

THE NON-DISCRIMINATORY DECOMPOSITION AND OTHER ISSUES

Cotton (1988) argues that it is neither the white wage structure nor the black one that will prevail in the absence of discrimination. In fact, he argues that the most fundamental flaw in the Blinder–Oaxaca procedure is 'the failure to portray adequately the most critical of Becker's original conditions, that is, the wage structure that would prevail in the absence of discrimination'. If the black wage structure prevails, then blacks would continue to receive the same wage, whether or not there is discrimination in the labour market. Barring malice towards the whites (whites will receive a lower wage under the black wage structure), blacks would then have no incentive to desire an end to discrimination. Similarly, if the white wage structure prevails, then whites continue to receive the same wage and the black wage goes up in the absence of discrimination. Again, barring malevolence towards the blacks, whites would have no incentive to end discrimination. With these assumptions, a central aspect of discrimination gets missed: not only is one group undervalued (and the other overvalued) under discrimination, but that the undervaluation of one group subsidises the overvaluation of the other group. Cotton suggests a method to estimate the non-discriminatory wage structure—the rates of return that would exist in the market in the absence of discrimination, which lie somewhere in between the rates of return to the two groups.

The method described so far does not make a distinction between 'job discrimination', where the wage gap arises because of otherwise comparable workers from different groups being concentrated in different kinds of jobs, and 'wage discrimination', where comparable workers receive unequal pay for the same job, if they happen to belong to different groups. Refinements of the basic decomposition method (Banerjee and Knight 1985) have provided a method for further breaking up the unexplained gap between job and wage discrimination.

There are several other issues that arise from the decomposition technique. Baldwin and Johnson (1992) argue that the technique of decomposing wage differentials into 'explained' and 'unexplained' components assumes that the supply curves of labour are completely inelastic, that is, insensitive to wage offers. This assumption precludes the measurement of yet another consequence of discrimination: the loss of income to workers from the minority groups who are currently not working but would work at a non-discriminatory wage. They specifically look at the effects of discrimination on the employment of women, using Becker's conceptual framework: employers have a taste for discrimination against women and hence incur an extra cost from employing women (arising out their disutility). Thus, employers will hire men till the wage offered to men equals the sum of the wage offered to women and the disutility to the employer of hiring women.

Thus, they use information from the wage equations and correct for discrimination in the male–female differences in wage offers. They then calculate the probabilities of employment for men and women at non-discriminatory wage offers. These non-discriminatory probabilities are applied to the populations of the two groups to estimate gains or losses from discrimination: jobs not taken by women (loss) and gained by men as a result of discrimination.

Applying this method to a sample from the US for 1984, in addition to measuring wage discrimination between men and women (separately for blacks and whites), they find that roughly 5.7 million women were discouraged from working due to wage discrimination. And, approximately 1 million men were employed as a result of discrimination. It should be noted that this loss in employment represents a loss in income for women because they choose to completely withdraw from work, rather than work at the non-discriminatory wages. However, not all women withdraw—many women do also end up working, albeit at the lower (discriminatory) wages. Thus, this employment effect measures a loss in addition to the wage loss of those women who end up working at the discriminatory wage structure. This supports Becker's basic contention that employers who discriminate sacrifice on output and profits by using the wrong combination of the two groups of workers (black and white or men and women). Also, this provides yet another justification for believing that wage discrimination estimates, important as they are, might be underestimates of the total magnitude even of economic discrimination.

In Chapter 2, we had briefly discussed the feminist theory of gender discrimination that would completely reject the 'residual' approach to measuring gender discrimination. Even if one is not completely persuaded by the feminist framework, the decomposition technique leaves several issues related to gender discrimination unresolved. McCaffery (1993) argues that typically, an analysis of whether gender discrimination is increasing or decreasing is done taking as the norm the male-dominated workplace model, that is, the terms of reference are not gender neutral; they are, in fact, biased against women to begin with. Thus, for instance, even when one finds evidence of narrowing wage gaps or a reduction in occupational segregation, the structure of work and typical work–family dynamics have not changed very much. He argues that full-time work remains the norm and an increase in part-time work is typically involuntary. The absence of flexible work arrangements perpetuates a gendered division of labour. In this scenario, women are more likely to be the secondary or lesser earners in two-earner families. Further, married women, even when they are in full-time work, continue to do the vast majority of house work. Thus, his argument is that even when we might find evidence of a quantitative reduction in gender discrimination, it does not necessarily imply a qualitative change in gender equality.

CORRESPONDENCE STUDIES

Despite the fact that the decomposition method is riddled with some intractable problems, it remains the leading econometric technique of estimating labour market discrimination. One of the reasons for its predominance is that although imperfect, it is the only method that gives some rough idea of magnitudes; if data are available over time, it additionally allows an assessment of changes in the discriminatory component over time. However, it is true that it does not specifically examine the demand-side factors—what is it that employers are looking for in their hiring and wage decisions? Attempts to capture and measure discriminatory attitudes in the labour market are continuously evolving and the newer methods are designed specifically to gain insights into hiring decisions of the employers.

One such field-based method is the 'correspondence study', which is simple and straightforward in its design and telling in its conclusions. It has now become fairly widespread it its usage to a variety of contexts.

In the next chapter we will discuss the evidence from correspondence studies of urban India and what they reveal about contemporary caste and religious discrimination. Here we will discuss the design of correspondence studies in general.

Bertrand and Mullainathan (2003) designed a field experiment to test whether employers respond only to the quality of the applicant or whether race also matters independently. They wanted to understand if racism was really a thing of the past and also if reverse discrimination (ceteris paribus, employers will prefer blacks over whites) existed at all, and if yes, how widespread it was. In order to test these questions, they responded to 1,300 advertisements in Boston and Chicago newspapers and sent out over 5,000 resumes to clerical, sales, administrative support, and customer services job categories. They experimentally manipulated the perception of race via the name on the resume by using very white-sounding names such as Emily Walsh and Greg Baker to half the resumes, and very African–American names such as Lakisha Washington and Jamal Jones to the other half. They sent four resumes in response to each ad—two high quality and two low quality, and randomly assigned African–American names to both the categories.

They found a statistically significant racial difference in call-back rates: a white applicant needed to send 10 applications to receive one call-back offer, whereas an African–American applicant needed to send 15. This 50 per cent difference in call-back rates was equivalent to additional eight years of experience. Race also affected the rewards to having a better resume: the gap between whites and African–Americans *widened* with resume quality. They point out that 'discrimination therefore appears to bite twice, making it harder not only for African Americans to find a job but also to increase their employability' (ibid.: 3). Their experiment also revealed other aspects of discrimination. By randomly assigning postal codes to a resume, they found that whites living in a better neighbourhood received increased call-back offers, but that African–Americans were not helped more than whites by living in a better neighbourhood. They also found that there is no statistically significant difference in the amount of discrimination by industry; federal contractors who are supposed to be governed by affirmative action laws or large employers or those claiming to be 'equal opportunity employers' did not discriminate any less than the others.

As they themselves point out, there are several advantages to correspondence studies. Since race is arbitrarily manipulated, the same resume is sometimes associated with a white name and at other times with an African–American name. Thus, the difference in call-back offers is solely due to race. About the design of the experiment, it can be argued that it only records call-back offers and not actual job offers, and hence it is not a true assessment of employers' hiring and wage offer intentions. However, the authors claim that this is actually one of the strengths of the study since the 'use of paper resumes insulates us from demand effects' (ibid.: 5). Also, the low marginal cost allows the researchers to send out a large number of resumes.

They also discuss the weaknesses of these studies. One is that race is made salient only through last names, not explicitly. Theoretically, it is possible that employers may not associate the last names accurately with race. Second, newspaper ads represent only one channel of job applications. In actual fact, social networks provide a much stronger channel of recruitment (discussed more in the next chapter) and given that those are likely to be organized by race, these studies will underestimate discrimination. Heckman and Siegelman (1993) endorse the latter point by arguing that a major limitation of this approach is that many jobs are not found through this route, but via networks of family and friends. However, as the studies discussed in the next chapter point out, a study of job networks actually strengthens evidence of discrimination rather than diminish it.

AUDIT STUDIES

One step ahead of correspondence studies are audit studies, where trained volunteers (testers) are actually sent for job interviews or meetings with potential employers.[6] These teams of testers are selected such that they are almost completely identical in their characteristics, including appearance, and what distinguishes one tester from another is their race. The difference in outcomes is gauged in terms of job offers, terms of employment, and the level at which the testers are hired. Audit studies are also used for assessing discrimination in rental

[6] Audits have been adapted by social scientists from techniques employed by legal activists who were studying enforcement of fair housing laws during the 1960s.

markets (discussed later in the section on housing) as well as in the provision of health services.

Pager and Western (2005) sent teams of testers to apply for 1,470 real entry-level jobs in New York City over 10 months in 2004. The testers were well-spoken young men, between 22 and 26 years, college educated, between 5 feet 10 inches and 6 feet in height, had similar verbal skills, 'interactional styles', and physical attractiveness. All the testers were put through a training programme to standardize their self-presentation in job interviews. Like in the correspondence studies, the testers were assigned matched fictitious resumes to ensure that they had identical job qualifications, quality of high school, work experience, and residential neighbourhood. These testers presented themselves as high-school graduates with steady work experience in entry-level jobs.

Positive Responses

They first report the results from a three-person team consisting of a white, a black, and a Hispanic tester applied to the same set of employers presenting identical qualifications. For each set of visits, they recorded the 'positive responses': job offers on the spot, or at some later point, or called back for a second interview. The positive responses depend strongly on the race of the applicant, with whites in the lead, followed by Hispanics, with blacks trailing far behind. In their study, blacks are only slightly more than half as likely to receive consideration by employers relative to equally qualified white applicants. This difference is very comparable to the 50 per cent difference reported in the correspondence study mentioned earlier. In addition to documenting the numerical differences, Pager and Western also document interview experiences of the testers that reveal a great deal about racial attitudes and stereotypes at workplaces. For example, a black tester is told that he might not be '[company X] type of people'. In another case, the black, the Hispanic, and the white tester applied for the same job sequentially, in that order. The first two testers were told that the position had been filled; the white tester was asked to start work the next day and was introduced to the person (another white) who would be training him. Pager and Western point out that normally, this act of discrimination would remain completely undetected, since the black and the Hispanic applicants would normally have believed the employer's response that the job was filled. It is only because the white tester followed in their footsteps and *walked away with the job* that we can see this as an act of discrimination.

The study compared the magnitude of race discrimination with that of another stigma among low-wage workers: criminal background. In order to see whether it is the racial or the criminal stigma that dominates, the white tester presents evidence of felony conviction whereas the black and Hispanic testers have no criminal background. Expectedly, the number of positive responses for the white tester comes down, but surprisingly he does just as well or even better than the black tester with no criminal background. Blacks, thus, 'remain at the very end of the hiring queue, even in relation to white applicants who have just been released from prison' (ibid.: 7).

Race-coded Channelling

The basic outcome discussed so far is whether a tester gets a positive response or not. However, often employers have several types of jobs on offer and an examination of which applicant is suited to which type of job reveals a great deal about employers' assumptions about the abilities of different groups of workers and the inherent racial biases in these views. The study documents 96 cases of channelling, which were individually coded as downward, upward, lateral, or unknown channelling, by comparing the original job title to the suggested job type. The authors define downward channelling as (1) a move from a job involving customer contact to a job without; (2) a move from a white-collar position to a manual position; or (3) a move in which hierarchy can be clearly discerned.

Blacks were channelled down in 10 cases and never channelled up, whereas whites were channelled down only in four cases, and only when showing a criminal record. It is worth reminding ourselves that these results are observed when the resumes of the applicants were perfectly matched. The extent of racial biases and stereotypes are most tellingly revealed in these experiences of channelling: in one case, a white tester who applied for the position of a cleaner was encouraged to apply for a clerical position. In one case, a white applicant was even encouraged to apply for a management position, despite virtually no experience.

DEBATE OVER THE AUDIT METHOD

The audit methods are not without controversy. Heckman (1998) and Heckman and Siegelman (1993) offer strong critiques of the audit methodology. These papers point out that audit pair studies are not experiments or matched pair studies: race or ethnicity cannot be matched by randomization. Instead, race is a personal characteristic, and hence in an audit study, adjustments are made on 'relevant' observed characteristics to 'align' audit pair members.

The problem arises, they argue, because these studies do not account for unobservables that affect outcomes. In fact, they suggest that matching on observables may exacerbate the problem of non-alignment of audit pairs by accentuating differences in unobservables among audit pair members. Heckman further argues that one of the main reasons that the method is questionable is because it operates by controlling for systematic observed differences across pairs of testers, but there are unobservable or unmeasurable differences that it cannot control for. Given the limited state of knowledge of the determinants of productivity within firms, it is not possible to match *all* the possible characteristics that affect productivity. The implicit assumption in the audit method is that the effect of the unobserved characteristics averages out to zero across firms for the same audit pair. Heckman proves that the condition of zero mean of unobservable productivity differences across race groups is not compelling and requires a priori knowledge that is typically not available. In view of this, they suggest that since in housing markets, far fewer characteristics (for example, wealth, income, race) are relevant as compared to the labour market, audit studies might be better suited to studying discrimination in housing markets as compared to labour markets.

Heckman's (1998) critique rests on the distinction between discrimination at the level of the individual firm versus market discrimination. He argues that a well-designed audit study could uncover many individual firms that discriminate, but the marginal effect of discrimination on the wages of employed workers could be zero. This is based on Becker's insight that the impact of market discrimination is not determined by the most discriminatory participant in the market, or even by the average level of discrimination among firms, but rather by the level of discrimination at the firms where minorities actually end up working, buying, borrowing, that is, by the marginal firm with which the marginal minority member deals with.

Heckman and Siegelman raise the issue of 'experimenter effects: the experimenter is not simply a passive runner of subjects, but can actually influence the results of an experiment' (1993: 189). They suggest that this influence may not be due to conscious or deliberate action. They believe that since the auditors (testers) have already been coached about the problem of discrimination in American society, as an explicit part of the training, they find what the 'audit agencies wanted to find'. They would prefer an experimental design in which the testers themselves were kept ignorant of the hypothesis being tested (discriminatory hiring) and the fact that they were operating in pairs.

It is not clear how coaching (or what the audit agencies call training of testers) is responsible for the evidence that they gather, unless the suggestion is that the evidence is a combination of fact and fiction to produce a picture already anticipated by the researcher. Yinger (1998) discusses the debate over whether or not audits should be double blind: there is an argument in favour—making the testers blind could help in protecting the integrity of the audit results; however, the discriminatory treatment that minority testers face could upset them severely if they have not been trained. In that case, making them aware of the purpose of the study would help in reporting their experiences accurately. The jury is still out on whether audits should be double blind or not: Yinger (1998) argues that there is not sufficient evidence to compare double blind audits with regular ones.

A related assumption behind the audit method is that it typically assumes that the outcome being studied is a linear function of the relevant variables or the outcome can be transformed to be so, that is, more skills lead in a linear way to a greater probability of being employed or to higher wage offers. However, Heckman (1998) points out that in general, the decision to offer a job is a non-linear function of relevant characteristics. For instance, often it is the case that productivity has to be above a threshold before a job is offered. Thus, when the threshold is set the same for the two groups, which of the two groups gets selected more often depends on the degree of heterogeneity in a group. He uses the analogy of a high jump competition, where the jumpers have to clear a bar set at the same height. He makes the assumption implicit in the audit literature: that the mean jumping technique is the same for both groups. Thus, if the variance in the two groups is also the same, then both groups have the same likelihood to clear the bar. If variances differ, which of the two groups will more likely clear the bar depends on the height of the bar (relative to their common height) and which group has a higher variance in jumping technique. If the bar is set at a low level so that most people of the given height are likely to clear the bar, then the group with lower variance will more likely clear the bar. If the bar is set very high relative to the given height, then the group with a higher variance will more likely clear the bar. Thus, even when there is no discrimination, the two groups have different probabilities of clearing the bar. Equally, when there is discrimination, that is, when the bar is set higher for blacks, if blacks have a higher variance, they could end up clearing the bar more often—that is, the method could fail to detect discrimination when it does exist. Thus, depending on the distribution of the unobserved characteristics, Heckman argues that the audit method could show discrimination, reverse discrimination, or no discrimination, even with the same average observable characteristics. Heckman's conclusion is that audit methods are inherently fragile to the 'untested and unverifiable assumptions about the distributions of unobservables' (1998: 111).

Heckman and Siegelman (1993) analyse the outcomes of two specific audit studies. One issue that they raise is about the outcome of interest. For instance, one outcome that might be of interest would be the number of times that two potential employees who are otherwise identical are treated differently by employers. The authors give a hypothetical example where the two testers are treated differently (in that, one gets the job and the other one does not), but this difference could also arise because the two testers are actually quite close, and the choice between them is based on purely random factors across the two firms.

The choice of the measure of discrimination vitally affects the interpretation of the evidence, as they demonstrate using the evidence from two studies. Also, they raise the question of whether it is possible to pool the data across audit pairs within sites. They argue that such pooling is valid if there is homogeneity in the selection of firms across pairs and if audit pairs are comparably matched (which means that any discrepancies between majority and minority members are uniform across pairs—not that each pair is uniformly matched). Achieving homogeneity on skill across pairs is not necessarily a desirable characteristic. If one did that, one will get only one slice of the labour market and not observe employer behaviour across the diverse set of jobs that typically characterize the labour market.

Despite all these objections, Arrow (1998: 93) believes that evidence from audit studies is decisive: 'while one can always invent hypotheses to explain away these results, there is really no reason not to draw the obvious conclusions'. Also, he suggests that 'racial discrimination pervades every aspect of a society in which it is found' and thus raises the question: 'can a phenomenon, whose manifestations are everywhere in the social world, really be understood, even in only one aspect, by the tools of a single discipline' (ibid.: 91). What this indicates is that it may not be possible to devise an error-free, unambiguous method of gauging discrimination, but that cannot be, or should not be, the reason for rejecting the entire body of evidence on discrimination. Arrow also reminds us that this quest for measuring discrimination has acquired meaning only in the contemporary context where discrimination is illegal in most settings. Before any legal steps were taken to address discrimination, it existed in perfectly open form, with no need for any subtle economic analysis. In the era of Jim Crow laws in the US, for instance, by law, blacks were segregated in all public spheres and one would not have needed to debate the subtlety of various methods to gauge a phenomenon that was so apparent. As Arrow (1998: 92) points out, where such blatant discrimination or segregation is seen, 'estimating wage equations would have been beside the point'.

Audit versus Econometric Studies

Both these methods provide alternative ways of estimating market-based discrimination, and before moving on to other issues, it is worth comparing them briefly.

1. Econometric estimation or the decomposition technique, as explained earlier, is based on Becker's analysis and focuses on wage and occupational differentials. Thus, it does not explicitly consider the hiring process. The advantage of audits is that it explicitly considers the hiring process.

2. Audits allow more control for characteristics that are thought to be relevant for employment than the conventional post-regression analyses. For instance, when controlling for education, number of years or educational attainment (the variables used in econometric estimation) might be inadequate, whereas in audit studies, the two testers can be given educational levels that are completely identical in numbers of years as well as in quality (same high school or college).

3. By sending a pair of auditors to the same firm, Heckman and Siegelman (1993: 171) argue that there is greater control over 'idiosyncratic differences in firms valuation of common bundles of characteristics that plague ordinary observational studies'. However, they argue for further consideration of the attributes of the testers by suggesting that the difference between each tester's characteristics and the employer's stereotype or belief about the characteristics of the average applicant of that race may also matter—should both the testers resemble the black applicant or the white applicant?

4. Following up on their critique, Heckman and Siegelman (1993) offer concrete suggestions to make the audit studies empirically more rigorous. For instance, they strongly support sending more than two testers at each firm to allow the experimenters to distinguish between random and race-based explanations for differences in treatment. They also suggest that more attention should be paid to firm-specific variables: what, if anything, distinguishes firms that discriminate against blacks or Hispanics from those that discriminate against whites or do not discriminate at all? Are some firms operating under a quota constraint, while some others are free to practise discrimination against blacks?

5. In terms of their statistical aspects, econometric studies are more clear-cut, using established techniques. Heckman and Siegelman (1993) point out that since audit studies are expensive to conduct, samples tend to be small. Most of the outcomes are discrete (either the tester gets the job or he/she does not). They, therefore, suggest that researchers should make use of small sample, multinomial statistical techniques in sample design and hypothesis testing, rather than rely on large-sample normal approximations. This would make the results of the studies more rigorous and, hopefully, more acceptable.

ATTITUDES AND ACTUAL BEHAVIOUR: VIGNETTE QUESTIONS AND AUDITS

Attitude surveys are increasingly being used to gauge public opinion on sensitive topics such as prejudice and discrimination. In the US, these surveys find a consistent and steady decline in the support to racist or prejudicial behaviour. They show that increasingly, respondents see themselves as fair, unbiased, and as responding to merit of individuals rather than to their race (or more broadly, which group they belong to), suggesting thereby that actual discriminatory behaviour and barriers to employment for stigmatized groups are on the decline. The literature on the correspondence between attitudes and behaviour is not very large. Pager and Quillian (2005) designed a study to test for this correspondence that had two components. The first component consisted of a vignette question, asked via a telephone survey, that described a hypothetical situation to an employer and asked how the employer would respond if faced with that situation in real life. A typical vignette question was: 'Chad is a 23 year old [black/white] male. He finished high school and has steady work experience in entry-level jobs. He has good references and interacts well with people. About a year ago, Chad was convicted for a drug felony and served 12 months in prison. Chad was released last month and is now looking for a job. How likely would you be to hire Chad for an entry-level opening in your company?' Employers were asked to rate their likelihood of hiring this person with responses ranging from 'very likely' to 'very unlikely'.

This was then followed by an audit where the situation described in the vignette question was replicated using testers. In a study of Milwaukee metropolitan area in 2001, they found that employers' responses to the vignette questions differed sharply from their actual behaviour when confronted with those situations face-to-face. The audit study showed large effects of race and criminal behaviour on hiring decisions of employers, such that in the survey, employers showed a significantly greater willingness to hire blacks or ex-offenders than they exhibited in the audits. Not only were the levels of willingness revealed through the two methods different, there was in fact very little correlation between the attitude survey results and actual willingness to hire as revealed through the audit studies. This suggests that either due to social desirability bias (political correctness) or because individuals genuinely think of themselves as intrinsically fair, attitude surveys end up underestimating employers' propensity to discriminate and, consequently, the barriers to employment faced by the stigmatized groups.

RACIAL PROFILING

One of the arenas in which implicit attitudes and prior beliefs (the intensity of which most respondents would deny or certainly underestimate) very closely correspond with behaviour is police action. Racial profiling in a variety of situations in the US has received a lot of attention; in particular, the phenomenon of motorists being more likely to be stopped by policemen looking for illegal drugs or weapons if they are black has given rise to a term called 'driving while black' (DWB).[7]

Persico (2002) examines the phenomenon that motorists on highways are much more likely to be searched by police looking for illegal drugs if the motorists are African–American. Knowles et al. (2001) report that in a stretch of inter-state highway in Maryland from 1995 to 1999, 63 per cent of all motorists searched were black, whereas only 18 per cent of all motorists were black. There are similar allegations of racial profiling in searches at airports. The theoretical literature on this subject points to the tension between the principle of equal treatment under the law and the practical consideration of law enforcements. Persico's (2002) model shows that there need not be a trade-off between these two objectives. Constraining police to behave in a fair manner—searching both groups with the same intensity—need not per se result in more crime.

Knowles et al. (2001) develop a model to test whether racial profiling is due to statistical discrimination (the police have no inherent racial prejudice, yet one race is searched more than the other) or racial prejudice (the police have a taste for discrimination in that, ceteris paribus, they prefer searching one race over another). In their data set, which consists of 1,590 observations on all vehicle searches on I-95 in Maryland from January 1995 to January 1999, the probability that black drivers are searched is higher than that for whites. However, the probability that a searched driver is found with

---

[7] This is a variation on DUI or 'driving under the influence', which is a legitimate offence.

contraband is the same across races. They conclude that this indicates statistical discrimination, not racial prejudice. These data pertain to motorists who were stopped and searched—not to those who were stopped and not searched.

However, the finding of no racial bias should not be taken to indicate fairness. They point out that even if drivers of one race end up being searched more often due to statistical discrimination (and not racial prejudice), it still imposes a cost to innocent drivers of the race that is searched more often and can thus be regarded as unfair. In another research, they discuss colour-blind searches and find that it does not compromise with efficiency.

Durlauf (2006) discusses equity-efficiency considerations in the context of profiling. Efficiency in his model is defined as the minimization of the aggregate crime rate. He argues that costs of racial profiling to individuals have two aspects. First is the harm inflicted on individuals by stops, especially on the innocent. Second, there are the social costs associated with strategies where stop rates differ across races. Using Glenn Loury's (2002) argument that the major impediment to racial equality in the US is stigma rather than overt discrimination, Durlauf interprets stigma as the systematic tendency to ascribe the least favourable view to individuals of a group consistent with available information. If racial profiling contributes to their stigmatization, it induces costs to blacks in spheres far outside the domain of traffic stops.

The equity dimension revolves around the extent to which a profiling strategy is consistent with some conception of justice. Durlauf argues that one such conception could be fairness in the treatment by government. He cites the literature on equality of opportunity according to which, fairness requires that individuals not be held responsible for things outside their control. In the profiling context, he suggests that this leads to the idea that fairness requires equal treatment of the innocent with respect to race. And that this can be consistent with profiling. He points to the ambiguity of translating these concepts, which lend themselves to neat modelling, into clear-cut public policy. Ambiguity also arises from the fact that the available empirical studies do not identify the effects of profiling studies on crime. There is some evidence on arrest maximization of blacks, but arrest maximization does not equate with crime minimization, when the crime rate of the over-sampled group exhibits relatively less sensitivity to the stop rate.

There is virtually no assessment of the magnitude of costs, especially the disproportionate burden placed on innocent blacks by profiling. In response to a claim that harms in a traffic stop are small, Durlauf argues that the marginal harm is increased by the occurrence of other racial incidents, quite apart from the fact that these costs cannot be quantified based on current knowledge. He goes on to point out that there is no credible empirical evidence on profiling and stigma, just as there is not sufficient empirical evidence on stigma and socio-economic outcomes.

He, therefore, argues that the ambiguity can be resolved by requiring that there exists a burden of proof to justify policies that, whatever the notion of fairness, diminish it by their implementation. Reading this along with the evidence on efficiency suggests that profiling is not justified, since there is no clear evidence of a gain in efficiency (data does not point to crime minimization), but there is an unambiguous violation of fairness.

Myers (2002) discusses a case study of the battle in 2001 in the Minnesota legislature based on the demands of the two largest municipalities in Minnesota (Minneapolis and St. Paul) which supported a bill on race data collection on traffic stops. As Myers points out, this battle has wider implications; for instance, for airport security, drug dealing, gang activities, and shoplifting. He indicates that the basic problem is what the theoretical literature is attempting to model: having to make efficient decisions based on incomplete information and on unobservables. Specifically, we have data on arrests and incarceration, but not on underlying rates of participation in illegal activities. Based on an exercise conducted on several cohorts of University of Minnesota, Myers finds that while the notions of efficiency are often transparent, the assessment of fairness or equity is left ambiguous. Using monetary data for expected costs and benefits, he finds that racial profiling is efficient, in the sense that it generates a higher expected profit as compared to random stops and searches. However, here the cost to innocent drivers is not considered. This is related to the point about stigma that Durlauf raises—that racial profiling can, and does, have secondary costs to innocent minorities in the form of indignities and psychological and emotional damages, but does not get counted in a simple cost–benefit exercise.

EXTREME DISCRIMINATION: SEGREGATION

Measuring discrimination by any of the methods discussed earlier is meaningful only if both groups have some presence in a given market (labour, land, credit, or housing). As Arrow (1998: 93) points out, often black–white wages do not differ by a big margin but that discrimination takes the form of 'limiting the range of jobs in which blacks are hired at all'. Similarly, in housing, discrimination does not take the form of higher rents for blacks, but exclusion of blacks from certain neighbourhoods. Becker (1957) suggests that segregation is a limiting case of discrimination: situation that results when tastes for discrimination become so large that each community is in economic isolation and would have to get along with its own resources. Since members of groups would be working only with each other, complete economic isolation would also involve complete economic segregation. His theoretical device consists of imagining two societies, each inhabited by only one type of group, which trade with each other. He shows that an increase in discrimination is accompanied by a decrease in trade between the two societies, and since a decrease in trade implies greater segregation, it follows that an increase in discrimination leads to greater economic segregation.

HOUSING MARKETS: DISCRIMINATION OR SEGREGATION?

Becker (1957) argues that discrimination and segregation are often confused, and a good example of this confusion can be seen in the discussion on minority housing. Many whites do not want to live near blacks, and 'this is a primary cause of residential segregation, not of residential discrimination (as is often believed)' (ibid.: 160). According to the taste for discrimination theory, the latter would occur only if many whites were willing to forfeit income in order to avoid renting or selling a residential property to blacks who would live near other whites. Becker believes that this is perhaps not that common in housing markets: what is observed is segregation, and not discrimination.

However, Yinger (1998) argues that legally, discrimination is defined with respect to two standards and a violation of either standard by an economic agent constitutes discrimination. The first standard uses the notion of 'disparate treatment', and according to this, any economic agent who applies different rules to people in protected groups is practising discrimination. The second standard involves the use of practices with an adverse impact on the members of a protected class. Under the Fair Housing Act,[8] economic agents are discriminating whenever they use practices that have an adverse impact on a protected class without any 'business necessity'. Thus, if a particular practice can be shown to have an adverse impact on a protected class, then the burden of proof shifts to the business, which must then support a business necessity claim. Yinger emphasizes that some types of behaviour are illegal according to both standards, but the two standards are logically separate: disparate treatment is illegal, regardless of whether it can be shown to have an adverse impact. Similarly, business rules that have an adverse impact on a protected class and are not a business necessity are illegal even if applied equally to all groups. He also uses this to point out one further limitation of the audit study: audits may not detect practices that have an adverse impact but do not involve disparate treatment.

Massey and Lundi (1998) implicitly use an analytical definition of discrimination that is very similar to the legal definition stated earlier. They conducted an audit study to examine how pervasive racial exclusion continued to be in housing markets in the US. Whereas racial segregation was institutionalized in the American real estate industry, after the passage of the Fair Housing Act in 1968, outright refusals became rare but black renters continued to battle subtle ways in which they were excluded. They also point out that while the methods of exclusion were small and subtle, the combined effect turned out to be very powerful in terms of stalling the spatial assimilation of blacks. In order to test for the persistence of the prejudice in real estate

---

[8] In the words of the 1968 Fair Housing Act (Section 804), 'it shall be unlawful ... to discriminate against any person ... Because of race, color, religion, sex, or national origin'. This Act covers many types of discriminatory behaviour, including refusal to sell or rent, differential terms or conditions, differential advertising, and the provision of inaccurate information (Yinger 1998: 25).

markets, their experiment was based on linguistic cues: their audit was conducted over the phone with the use of black vernacular English and black accented English, both of which are spoken by African–Americans in the US. Their study first of all confirmed that most of the discrimination was conducted over the phone before the white rental agents and black clients ever met. The audit results showed that privilege in access to housing exhibited the following hierarchy: white males, white females, males and females of middle class blacks, followed by males and females of lower class blacks. The study controlled for the amount of rent, time of call, and the number of rental units in the building or complex. They found that most intense prejudice was reserved for lower class black women.

Similarly, Turner et al. (2002), using 4,600 paired testers, conducted a nationwide audit in 23 metropolitan areas. The results confirmed that discrimination still persists in both rental and sales markets of large metropolitan areas nationwide, but that its incidence had declined since 1989. The discrimination in the sales market against blacks was stronger than that seen in rental markets. Again, they found that whites received more encouragement, information, and assistance with financing than comparable black home buyers. Confirming Becker's premise, the study finds that while discrimination against blacks had declined, geographical steering had increased, which means that blacks and whites are likely to be shown homes in different neighbourhoods. The limitations of this study, which the authors themselves note, are that one, it is based on house searches using newspaper advertisements (not all buyers or rental agents are likely to use newspaper ads) and two, that the study does not encompass all phases of a housing transaction.

EXPERIMENTAL METHODS

So far, we have discussed methods of estimating market-based discrimination mainly in labour and housing markets. However, we referred in Chapter 2 to pre-market discrimination that is pervasive but not easily measurable. Lately, there have been several methods to gauge pre-market discrimination using experiments conducted on, say, school-going children. Hoff and Pandey (2004: 3) seek to test the possibility that long after the 'legal barriers to economic and social advancements by oppressed groups have been abolished—or the conditions that gave rise to those barriers have changed—the expectations that the historical conditions created may remain and give rise to behaviors that reproduce the effects of those historical barriers'. Thus, a prolonged history of inequality and discrimination might lead to expectations of prejudice and discrimination and, therefore, to behaviours that reproduce the historical inequality.

To test for this, they ran controlled experiments on male junior high school students, asking them to solve mazes. The students belonged to different caste groups and did not know each other at the start of the experiment. Three different settings were provided to the subjects in order to test for the salience of caste. In the first setting, the caste of students was not publicly disclosed. In the second setting, the experimenter publicly announced the caste of each student before the experiment began. In the third setting, caste was publicly announced and the subjects were segregated into groups according to their caste status—all high-caste students were put in one room and all the low-caste students were put together in another room. If the student solved the maze, he would get a pre-announced reward that was, in the first round of experiments, not subject to experimenter's discretion. In other words, there was no possibility of unfairness in rewards.

The results of the experiments revealed that when caste was not announced, there was no statistically significant difference in the performance of upper-caste and low-caste students. When caste was publicly announced, it lowered the performance of low-caste students significantly and this result is robust to controlling for the class background of the students. The performance gap was the highest under conditions of segregation—designed to invoke feelings of being 'outcasted' for low-caste students. The authors interpret these findings to suggest that when caste is announced publicly, low-caste students expect to be treated prejudicially, and this mistrust lowers their motivation and performance. They extend the experiment to offer a gamble to the students and consider two alternative settings. In the first setting, when the link between performance and reward is purely mechanical, making caste salient does not affect performance. However, where the reward is subject to experimenter bias, there is a significant effect on the behaviour of low-caste students. Based on this, the authors suggest that one of the reasons why individuals fall so easily into caste roles is because they expect to be treated according to those roles. This provides powerful evidence for another reason, in addition to unequal access to resources and opportunity, why social inequalities will tend to reproduce themselves.

There is a growing literature that assesses the role of trust in segmented societies, based on the belief that trust (or social capital) is essential in the operation of markets and institutions and also that trust may be linked to group affiliations, with trust being inversely related to the social distance between groups (see Burns [2006] for a concise review of this literature). Burns (2006: 806) investigates how exactly 'expectations and social meanings created by apartheid persist', specifically gauging this question by using the experimental method of 'trust games', to see to what extent the racial identity of participants affects trust relationships, particularly those involving black South Africans, as it was this group that was most severely marginalized by apartheid institutions.

Here the trust game was played by showing photographs of participants to transmit information about the race of the individual in the game, and racial identity was mutually known. In the trust game, the proposer is given an endowment and asked what portion (if any) of this endowment they would like to pass on to their partner (the trustee), who is at a separate location. The offer of the proposer is tripled before passing it on to the trustee, who needs to decide how much, if anything, to send back to the proposer. The amount sent by the proposer is an indication of trust, while the amount returned by the trustee/responder is an indication of reciprocity or trustworthiness.

Burns conducted this trust game with high school students and indicated that 'in a limited information setting where contracts are incomplete, race may affect exchange in different ways for different race groups' (ibid.: 816). Her results reveal what she terms a 'rich tapestry of behavior by individuals towards Black South Africans in a strategic setting' (ibid.: 819). I would like to draw attention to some of the behavioural patterns that she uncovers. For non-white students, being paired with a black partner does not prevent them from engaging in an interaction, but instead affects the nature of the interaction through the size of the offer made. For white students, however, being paired with a black partner prevents, for the most part, any interaction from taking place at all. 'In short, trust towards a Black partner elicits different behavioral responses for proposers from different race groups' (ibid.: 816). Also, she finds that non-white responders are significantly less likely to make any return at all when they are paired with a black partner. Thus, she finds in her experimental setting that the widespread belief among blacks participants that 'most people will take advantage of you if they get the chance' appears to be borne out by her results. Coloured students are both less trusting and less trustworthy towards blacks and they exhibit a strong insider bias in behaviour, making significantly higher offers and returns to coloured partners. White students behave differently, either choosing not to engage in an interaction at all with black partners (indicating racial stigma), or choose to engage in the strategic interaction presented in the trust game, in which they do not treat black partners different from partners from other race groups. Burns suggests that this might indicate 'the confounding influence of altruism on strategic behavior'. The heterogeneity in results notwithstanding, Burns persuasively demonstrates the importance of racial identity in exchange behaviour.

* * *

This chapter has reviewed the various methods that attempt to capture discrimination in its multilayered and multifaceted dimensions. It is clear that all methods have some shortcomings; indeed, it would have been surprising and suspect if that had not been the case, given the complexity of the phenomenon. The point is that we can attempt to gauge it and over time, these attempts have become sharper and more nuanced. Let us see what some of these attempts have yielded in their application to contemporary India.

APPENDIX 5.A[9]

Consider a simple exposition of the decomposition method based on Becker's discrimination coefficient, D. Becker (1957) defined the discrimination coefficient in competitive markets for labour with different productivity as the difference in the actual wage ratio and the one that would prevail in the absence of discrimination. For two groups, w and b, expressing this ratio in percentage terms:

$$D = \frac{\overline{W}^w / \overline{W}^b - MP^w / MP^b}{MP^w / MP^b} \tag{5.A.1}$$

where $\overline{W}^w / \overline{W}^b$ is the observed white–black wage ratio, and MP^w / MP^b is the ratio of the white–black average marginal products, which by assumption is the average wage ratio in the absence of discrimination. Expressed in logarithmic form, (5.A.1) becomes the white–black average wage differential:

$$\ln \overline{W}^w - \ln \overline{W}^b = \ln MP^w - \ln MP^b + \ln (D+1). \tag{5.A.2}$$

The difference between the marginal products, $\ln MP^w - \ln MP^b$, is that part of the wage differential that is due to differences in white and black productivity, and $\ln (D+1)$ is the treatment, or discrimination component.

Now, in general, $\ln \overline{W}$ can be estimated by $\sum_j B_j \overline{X}_j$, where $\overline{X}_j$'s are average productivity determining characteristics, and B_j's are the least-square regression coefficients. Thus, (5.A.2) can be rewritten as

$$\ln \overline{W}^w - \ln \overline{W}^b = \sum_j B_j^w \overline{X}_j^w - \sum_j B_j^b \overline{X}_j^b \tag{5.A.3}$$

$$(j = 0, \ldots, K \text{ implied}).$$

With some elementary manipulations, the terms on the right-hand side of (5.A.3) could be rearranged either as

$$\ln \overline{W}^w - \ln \overline{W}^b = \sum B_j^b \left(\overline{X}_j^w - \overline{X}_j^b \right) + \sum X_j^w \left(B_j^w - B_j^b \right) \tag{5.A.4}$$

---

[9] This is based on Cotton (1988).

or

$$\ln \overline{W}^w - \ln \overline{W}^b = \Sigma\, B_j^w \left(\overline{X}_j^w - \overline{X}_j^b \right) + \Sigma\, X_j^b \left(B_j^w - B_j^b \right) \qquad (5.A.5)$$

The first terms on the right hand sides of (5.A.4) and (5.A.5) are estimates of $\ln MP^w - \ln MP^b$, and the second terms are estimates of $\ln (D+1)$. As we can see, depending on which of the wage structures is used as the base (equation [5.A.4] or [5.A.5]), this method yields a lower and an upper bound for the discrimination operating in the market.

6   Merit, Mobility, and Modernism
Discrimination in Urban Labour Markets

A popular belief about the caste system in India is that the present-day inequalities are a result of *past* discrimination, primarily confined to rural areas. The notion is that labour markets in urban areas, especially in the formal private sector, are essentially meritocratic. Also, given the difficulties of identifying caste in the relatively anonymous urban settings, some would argue that the bulk of caste discrimination occurs mainly in rural, traditional parts of the country. For instance, it is often believed that urban disparities might reflect the impact of past discrimination (for instance, as embodied in the lower educational attainment of the Dalit students[1]); barring exceptional cases, urban markets have no mechanisms (and possibly no desire) to replicate and perpetuate caste discrimination. However, the evidence in Chapters 3 and 4 is to the contrary—we have seen that standard of living differences between social groups have persisted in urban areas (not only in rural) over the last two decades and, using some of the methods outlined in Chapter 5, we can explore whether and to what extent inequalities in urban India are a result of discrimination.

---

[1] Indeed, in the US, this is a commonly held view that labour market-earning disparities are due to lower educational attainment of blacks, rather than due to discrimination (for example, Heckman [1998]).

There is very important emerging research that is uncovering patterns of discrimination in urban, formal private sector, highly skilled labour markets in contemporary India. The evidence indicates that lip-service to merit notwithstanding, these markets show a deep awareness of caste and religious (not to mention gender) cleavages and indeed perpetuate caste discrimination *in the present*. The body of evidence on urban labour market discrimination in India, as of now, is not very large; in this chapter, I will summarize the evidence that exists as well as the findings of a pioneering multifaceted study that tried to uncover pathways of discrimination in urban areas using some of the leading methods described in the previous chapter.[2] In addition, recall that Chapter 2 reviewed some recent work on occupational and social mobility of Dalits in urban India.

WAGE GAPS: DISCRIMINATORY OR MERIT-BASED?

In the sphere of recruitment as wage labour, presumably the classic capitalist incentives of profit maximization should override all other non-economic considerations, such as the caste identity of the worker. The international evidence very clearly indicates that the social identity of workers does matter in determining their labour market outcomes. What is the evidence from India? Bhattacharjee (1985) tries to assess caste discrimination, over and above 'institutional factors' such as unequal access to education and industrial training, and finds evidence of discrimination in the form of unequal pay for equal work in the modern urban labour market. It could be argued that human capital characteristics (such as education) could explain earning differences and that the discrimination against Scheduled Castes (SCs) begins earlier—in unequal access to education. This is the so-called 'pre-market' discrimination, which is almost universally acknowledged. But what is really powerful is the finding of 'in-market' discrimination. Dhesi and Singh (1988), in a sample study of Delhi, not only examine precisely this question but also find evidence pointing to differential

---

[2] This study was conducted jointly by the Princeton Institute for International and Regional Studies and the Indian Institute for Dalit Studies. The findings of this study in the form of four papers (referred to in the text) were presented at conferences in Princeton University and New Delhi in 2007 and are contained in two volumes: Thorat and Newman (2010) and Centeno and Newman (2010).

access to education among various religious and caste categories, but they also find evidence of wage discrimination. According to them, the high incidence of illiteracy among SCs explains a significant portion of their lower earnings.[3]

While both these studies capture important facets of discrimination, the story does not end here. There are other *economic* avenues through which discrimination is expressed. Banerjee and Knight (1985) examine the crucial issue of whether discrimination in the labour market takes the form of wage discrimination or job discrimination. They find evidence of significant difference in the earnings functions for SCs and non-SCs that cannot be explained entirely by characteristics and this they take as a measure of wage discrimination. Their data also suggests that caste discrimination may be a formal sector phenomenon because of the fact that formal sector jobs are prized jobs and hence resistance to hiring SCs is greater. Further, they find that 'it is in the allocation of workers to jobs that discrimination is most likely to be practised. An employer would have no aversion to employing an untouchable provided that he worked in an untouchable's job' (ibid.: 301).

In a similar vein, Lakshmanasamy and Madheswaran (1995) examine data on technical and scientific manpower in the four southern states of India. The paper looks at evidence of discrimination in a sample of 67,927 workers. What they fail to point out is that the fact that the SCs were only 5.3 per cent of the sample—much below their proportion in the population—thus indicating discriminatory exclusion. They find a statistically significant difference between the earnings of the SCs and of the others in this highly qualified and educated sample. They also suggest that the level of earnings of the SCs may be due to the reservation policy, implying that without the reservation policy the earnings disadvantage would be even greater.

The odd note in the paper comes in the authors' apparently uncritical acceptance of statistical discrimination: 'It is possible that profit maximizing employers use caste as a screening device for differences in productivity in the absence of perfect information' (Lakshmanasamy and Madheswaran 1995: 75). What needs to be asked is why this imperfection of information becomes critical only vis-à-vis an SC employee. What if, due to the same imperfect information, an

---

[3] The main results of this paper are summarized in Dhesi (1996).

upper-caste employee turns out to be less productive than expected? Clearly, prejudice plays a role in motivating the employers' actions, as the employers do not feel the need to insure against this risk. In other words, part of the motivation for discrimination might come from taste for discrimination.

Discrimination could take other forms too. Banerjee and Bucci (1994), in an analysis of on-the-job search, after entering urban employment find that SC migrants displayed a greater propensity than non-SCs for on-the-job search in the formal sector but not in the informal sector. At first sight this seems surprising in view of the fact that the government policy of reserving jobs for the SCs applies in the public sector establishments of the formal sector.

But they interpret this as evidence of discrimination, based on the results of an earnings function analysis of the same sample that found that in the formal sector, earnings were lower for the SCs. They point out that 'the continuation of the search efforts shows that the SCs did not necessarily have lower expectations and were not prepared meekly to accept their economic lot' (ibid.: 42). Ceteris paribus, this can be used to question negative stereotypes that are usually associated with Dalits, especially when it comes to assessing their preferences for affirmative action–based formal sector jobs.

Jayaraj and Subramanian (1994) propose a number of real valued indices of discrimination and link them with measures of inequality. They also provide estimates for caste-based disparity in the distribution of consumption expenditures in rural India, based on National Sample Survey (NSS) data. Their findings, in their own words, 'perhaps constitute not so much "findings", properly speaking, as a confirmation of one's worst suspicions—namely, that in the matter of caste discrimination in India, there is much cause for disquiet' (ibid.: 19). In other words, they find evidence of 'systematically inferior status experienced by the Scheduled Castes and Tribes' (ibid.: 14).

Madheswaran and Attewell (2007) is the most recent macro-study that reveals the contours of urban discrimination using the decomposition method on NSS data. In order to address the view in the opening paragraph of this chapter, they specifically focus on urban, formal sector jobs and examine income gaps among highly educated employees. Their study estimated a wage function with age, level of education, gender, sector, marital status, job tenure, union membership, occupation, and region as explanatory variables. The findings show that for all caste categories, the marginal wage effects to education are significantly positive (holding other things constant, an increase in education level increases wages) and monotonically increasing with education level (the greater the education level, ceteris paribus, the higher would be the earnings). However, across the three rounds of NSS that they consider (1983, 1993–4, 1999–2000), they find that SCs–STs have lower returns to education than the rest ('Others' and Other Backward Classes [OBCs]); thus, an additional year of education for SCs–STs yields a smaller increase in wages than it would for the non-SCs–STs at the same level of education. Additionally, they find that in contrast to the other categories, the percentage rate of return for education for SCs–STs at each level of education is declining over the period, implying that in order to maintain the same rate of return, the average education level of SC–ST employees has to keep rising. It is interesting to note that this is happening during the liberalization phase of the Indian economy when there is compelling evidence to indicate that the premium to education is rising in the formal sector.

Their decomposition exercise suggests that the large part of the earnings gap is accounted for by endowment (or education and skill) differences, yet 20 per cent of the earnings gap between SC and non-SC workers is accounted for by discrimination. We have to remind ourselves here that the education gap itself embodies pre-market discrimination which cannot be directly measured. Also, the authors point out that over the entire period, the endowment difference has decreased, reflecting the positive achievements of the reservation policy and rising education levels of SCs–STs. The affirmative action policy (discussed in the next chapter) has quotas in public sector employment. The study compares discrimination in the public sector versus the private sector and finds that SC employees face discrimination in both sectors, but that the discriminatory effect is much smaller and decreasing in the public sector, as compared to the private sector, where the discriminatory effect is higher and unchanged. The authors explain that despite quotas at all levels of employment, the reason that we find any discrimination at all in the public sector is because quotas are far from filled in the more senior-level positions.

What is noteworthy in their results is the very clear evidence of discrimination in the private sector, calling into question its meritocratic image. Following the Cotton method (outlined in the previous chapter), they find that the treatment advantage or 'over-payment' to 'Others' because of discrimination is 5.2 per cent (Others' wages would have been 5.2 per cent less in the absence of discrimination) and the corresponding treatment disadvantage to the SCs is 13 per cent (SC wages would have been that much higher in the absence of discrimination, all else being equal). Finally, they also decomposed the total earnings gap into job and wage discrimination, using the methodology discussed in the previous chapter. They find that of the gross wage difference, 24.9 per cent can be explained by education and experience, 18.6 per cent by occupational difference, 20.9 per cent by wage discrimination, and 35.4 per cent by job discrimination. Thus, the larger part of the wage gap is explained by discrimination and also it is occupational segregation, rather than wage discrimination, that explains the larger part of the earnings gap between SC and 'Other' employees in the urban, formal sector labour market. These findings have important implications for policy that we will discuss in the next chapter.

CORRESPONDENCE TESTS

In a first-of-its-kind correspondence study of Indian labour markets, Thorat and Attewell (2007) focused on jobs in the highly educated segment. They responded to newspaper advertisements placed by private sector firms in English language newspapers, both national and regional, for entry- or near-entry-level positions, jobs that a fresh college graduate could apply for. The advertisements represented a diverse collection of firms: securities and investments, pharmaceuticals and medical sales, computer sales, support and information technology (IT) services, manufacturing, accounting, automobile dealerships, mass media, marketing jobs, veterinary and agricultural sales, construction, and banking. All the responses were sent by mail and in order to isolate the effect of caste backgrounds alone, all the applicants were male. For each job, three sets of matched applications and resumes were sent. The resumes indicated a degree from a reputed university, and where the advertisement required it, the necessary job experience and skill specific to the job. No explicit mention of caste or religion of the applicant was made in the application. However, of the three matched applications, one had a clearly identifiable, stereotypical Hindu upper-caste name, second had a Muslim name, and the third a Dalit name. Two sets of applications were sent to each firm: one set for a job that required a bachelor's degree—lower level job—and the other that required a master's degree—the higher level job. For each job, three applications were sent with names as described earlier. However, they added a 'discordant' application to each set: for a job that needed a master's degree, they sent an upper-caste application with a bachelor's degree (that is, under-qualified for the job) and for a job that required a bachelor's degree, they sent a low-caste application with a master's degree (that is, over-qualified for the job).

The paper defines a 'successful' response as one where the applicant gets called for the second stage of the selection process—either for an interview or for a written exam. They made a total of 4,808 applications to 548 advertisements over 66 weeks. Their results indicate that both caste and religion have an important bearing on whether the response is successful or not. Appropriately qualified Dalit applicants' odds of a successful response were 0.67 that of upper-caste applicants, and those of Muslims were 0.33 that of upper-caste applicants. The two discordant applications provide further evidence on the likelihood of a successful response. The odds of a successful response for an under-qualified high-caste applicant were significantly lower than that of an appropriately qualified high-caste applicant, but were not significantly different from an appropriately qualified Dalit applicant. The odds of a positive outcome for an over-qualified Dalit were larger than the odds for an appropriately qualified Dalit, but were lower than that of an appropriately qualified high-caste applicant. However, the results on the discordant applications are not statistically significant and thus do not provide conclusive proof of the effect of caste versus academic qualifications. Despite this caveat, the study captures the discrimination that highly educated Dalit and Muslim job applicants face at the first stage of the job search process in urban, formal, private sector labour markets.

Siddique (2009) conducted a correspondence study in Chennai during 2006 for jobs posted online, which confirms the Thorat and Attewell (2007) findings. This study sent out two resumes to each job, for a total of 523 jobs, one with typically high-caste names and the second with low-caste names. She found that high-caste applicants had a 20 per cent higher chance of being called back. Testing for the interaction between caste and gender, she found that the effect of being low-caste for female applicants reduces the call-back probability by 37 per cent. She further tests for differences in call-back by job types and finds that the highest reductions in call-back due to low caste are observed for female applicants who respond to jobs in front office and administration.

The study treads new ground by identifying the name of the contact person in the firm (called the recruiter) and differentiating the recruiter by gender and religion, and finds, for instance, that the ratio of number of cases in which high-caste applicants are favoured to the number of cases in which low-caste applicants are favoured is 2.1 for male recruiters and 1.5 for Hindu recruiters. It is 0.9 for female recruiters and 0.4 for non-Hindu recruiters. Siddique assesses the significance of these differences both using a test for homogeneity as well as using a probit regression. The effect of low caste on call-back is negative for male recruiters (low caste reducing call-back by 0.34 for male recruiters) and positive (increasing call-back by 0.22) for female recruiters. The effect of low caste is negative for Hindu recruiters (reduces by 0.21), but positive for non-Hindu recruiters (increases by 0.62). Interacting religion and gender of recruiters, she finds that the largest effects associated with low caste are found among Hindu recruiters who are male—low caste reduces call-back by as much as 0.51 among this group of recruiters, and this reduction is statistically significant.

It suggests that social identity of recruiters is important. This also highlights the role of networks in labour markets, discussed in detail later. Overall, based on her results, Siddique discusses whether this represents statistical or taste-based discrimination. Given that a pair of candidates has identical resumes and yet faces differential call-backs, further influenced by the social identity of the recruiter, prima facie, this would support taste-based discrimination. However, as Siddique points out, audit or correspondence studies cannot distinguish between taste-based and statistical discrimination explicitly. This is because the differential call-back could be attributed to differences in unobservable productivity that the firm infers from the resumes. So, for instance, the recruiter could believe that high-caste applicants are likely to be more productive, and thus practice statistical discrimination. However, given that resumes are perfectly matched, it seems likely that at least some of the difference in call-backs is due to employer prejudice. Whatever the motivation and the exact mechanism, the evidence of caste-based discrimination in white-collar, urban, formal, private sector jobs is unambiguous.

FORMAL SECTOR JOBS: THE SUPPLY-SIDE STORY

The studies reported so far rely on surnames to identify caste; however, as discussed in Chapter 2, last names do not always reveal caste. Thus, given the apparent anonymity of caste in urban settings, how do employers determine caste? More broadly, what are the pathways through which caste-based discrimination operates in the modern sector in India? Granovetter (2005, among his other writings) has analysed the impact of social networks on economic outcomes, and argues persuasively that in contrast to economic models that typically assume that workers and jobs are matched through a search whose costs and benefits are equalized at the margin, in real labour markets, social networks play a key role. Prospective employers and employees prefer to learn about one another from personal sources whose information they trust. This is an example of social capital. This is clearly brought out in the college-to-work study, again the first for India, which investigated the pathways through which caste enters the calculus of modern labour markets. Deshpande and Newman (2007) identified a group of educationally comparable university students from different caste backgrounds (in particular, 'reserved category' [SCs] or Dalit students and the 'non-reserved category') on the eve of their entry into the labour market and compared them in terms of job expectations, job search methods, actual placements, and the differential role that social networks (friends and family) play in determining their options in the world of work. The students in question had similar educational credentials, although they came from divergent personal backgrounds. The focus was especially on those aspects of differential experience that came to distinguish these two groups of students if/as they encountered discrimination in higher education and the sorting process in the labour market. The full study was published first in the *Economic and Political Weekly* in 2007 and then subsequently in two book collections (Deshpande and Newman 2007; Newman and Deshpande

2010). Given that the study is primarily interview-based, this chapter and the next reproduces verbatim selected parts of the study, since any attempt to summarize would not convey the complexity of the respondents' replies.

This study was inspired by sociologist Deirdre Royster's (2003) longitudinal study, which investigates the role that race plays in creating divergent and highly unequal patterns of employment and mobility among equally qualified blacks and whites. Royster followed 50 graduates (25 blacks and 25 whites) from Baltimore's Glendale Vocational High School to examine the school-to-work transition for working class black and white men.[4] She finds that in her carefully matched sample, race continued to be a powerful predictor of wages and employment. Black and white men's trajectories began to diverge only two or three years after high school graduation. Despite equal or greater effort to develop marketable skills and work experience, black men were unable to either successfully pursue the trades they had studied in high school or to recover successfully after switching trade preferences, as their white peers seemed to do easily.

Was this due to racial bias in hiring or due to unmeasured differences in human capital? Royster (2003) argues that the most powerful explanations for the differentials lie in the constitution of social networks that can be mobilized in pursuit of employment. 'Other things being equal—and in this study they are,' she points out, 'the stronger one's network, the better one's chances of making stable labor market transitions' (ibid.: 176).

Royster finds that there is very little information provided by schools on training or career options. For this reason, most work-bound students tend to rely on friends and family, rather than schools, for help in finding training and jobs. However, for black youth, who are more likely than white youth to lack ties to employers, job trainers,

[4] She uses the case study method (in contrast to the existing studies that rely on survey and archival data) to answer, what she calls, the 'how' and 'why' questions: causal factors in processes or events that develop over time. As she points out, the case study approach, which differs from aggregate-level surveys and intimate ethnographic methodologies, nevertheless combines aspects of both. This is because it relies on semi-structured interviewing techniques that use some of the same questions with all subjects but allow for considerable unstructured discussion between the interviewer and the respondents.

and other employed people in general, schools may provide the *only* available information about and connections to employers or other post–high school options. Thus, school-based connections could be a potentially equalizing resource between white and black students but, in fact, seem not to be operating in this fashion because they do relatively little for students in either race group. Here, though, at every turn, white men are at an advantage compared to black men. Black men mainly know workers, while white men know bosses as well as workers.

Granovetter (2005) suggests that since pre-existing networks which individuals tend to use predominantly are unevenly distributed across individuals, whatever social processes led to these networks will create an uneven playing field in the labour market. Thus, white contacts can recommend young men for jobs for which they had little or no training, whereas black men recommend young men only when there was evidence of training or expertise in the field. White men with contacts would be hired for desirable blue-collared jobs without interviews; black men would face screening interviews for all but the most menial jobs, sometimes even for those.

Royster (2003) finds that young white workers are neither permanently ejected from nor unduly stigmatized within networks if they 'act out' or get into trouble. Young black men have to be extra careful not to confirm widely held stereotypes regarding their alleged irresponsibility and unfitness as workers. Young white men get many of their first experiences working in the small businesses of family members or neighbours, where mistakes can be quickly and quietly corrected. Young black men's first jobs may be in white-owned firms where early mistakes confirm racially biased suspicions.

While these major racial differences in early employment outcomes are clear, Royster considers two questions that could be raised about these results: (a) that these findings could indicate progress over an even worse situation—'things are bad but getting better'; and (b) these unequal outcomes may not reflect discrimination but hidden differences in school performance, motivation, and character. Based on detailed and pointed questions to measure the latter, she finds that in this sample, black and white men demonstrated similar academic, character, and motivation/preparedness levels.

Tragically, these are the young men who have done everything society could have asked of them and still they face rampant inequality in life chances, as Royster (2003: 102) explains:

These findings are even more troubling when we recall that these are the young people who have done what society suggests they should: they have stayed in school, taken the 'dirty' jobs, gone to school regularly, performed at a satisfactory level, stayed out of police trouble, and impressed school personnel. They have followed the rules, and yet they have been unable to get returns on their educational and behavioral investments comparable to those of their white peers.

She terms this situation as 'ghetto results without ghetto residence', that is, 'the three black disadvantages—lack of networks, lack of transportation, and the presence of discrimination—operate irrespective of class and residential advantages associated with being a member of the stable working or lower middle class' (ibid.: 103).

Was the pattern of black disadvantage and white success recognized by the men she followed into the labour market? Interestingly, the answer is not only 'No', but a folk theory of white disadvantage developed instead. White men, who were extremely successful compared to their black peers, thought that racial quotas had limited their occupational options, giving their black peers an unfair advantage over them. None of the white students saw themselves as uniquely privileged compared to their black peers, not even those who admitted to having seen black workers put up with harassment on the job.

White men described the job process as meritocratic if they got the job but as biased in favour of blacks if they did not or suspected that they would not get the job. These convictions created disincentives for whites to incorporate blacks into their more effective networks. Why let the 'disadvantaged' into that tent? The answer is that they did not.

The purpose of our study was to understand the extent to which similarly qualified Indian students diverge in the labour market according to their caste backgrounds and, secondarily, whether a similar interpretation develops of 'caste advantage' through reservations.

Research Design

Our sample was drawn from the three national universities in Delhi, the capital of India—University of Delhi (DU) (masters' students in economics), Jawaharlal Nehru University (JNU) (different disciplines), and Jamia Milia Islamia (JMI) (different disciplines). DU, JNU, and JMI would be considered among the best universities in India by any yardstick. It would be a reasonable guess that these universities enjoy a 10 per cent acceptance rate. Even more gruelling would be the Indian Institutes of Technology (IITs).[5] But the institutions out of which we recruited our sample are next in line in the hierarchy of Indian higher education.

There were significant differences in undergraduate academic background between Dalit and non-Dalit students. Fewer Dalit students had first class honours in their undergraduate degrees than non-Dalit students (40 per cent versus 46.3 per cent), but this gap was not as large as one might have expected, owing no doubt to the selection pressure induced by minimum scores on the post-secondary entrance exams. For both groups, most had entered their postgraduate training with second-class undergraduate degrees (57.14 per cent of Dalits, and 53.7 per cent of non-Dalit students).

Over half of non-Dalit students reported previous job experience, compared to about one-third of Dalit students. Non-Dalit students were also more likely to report various computer skills. Most students had computer word-processing skills, but nearly 13 per cent of Dalit students (and only 7 per cent of non-Dalits) lacked that skill. Most students knew how to use Excel spreadsheet, but 27 per cent of Dalits and 13 per cent of non-Dalit students lacked those skills. Non-Dalit students were also much more likely to have skills in constructing computer presentations with PowerPoint (79 per cent compared to 55 per cent of Dalit students).

Since Royster's respondents were in several ways atypical, she believes that her sample may have reflected 'creaming' because the 'sample may reflect those who were most likely to rise to the top

---

[5] Indian Institutes of Technology (IITs) are extremely prestigious engineering schools. They were established explicitly with the purpose of providing cutting-edge training in engineering and other science programmes. Admission into the IITs is highly competitive: the acceptance rate for undergraduate courses is about 1 in 55, with about 300,000 annual entrance test-takers for 5,500 seats across the seven IITs. For SC/ST students, the cut-off for the entrance exam is lowered by 5 per cent. The IITs are not bound to fill the quota: in 2004, 112 of 279 seats for STs and 11 of 556 seats for SCs were left vacant.

or be seen as the cream of the crop, rather than those of average or mixed potential' (2003: 58). This is an advantage in her study since she deliberately sought to compare black and white men with as much potential for success as possible. Our sample is also creamed; it too captures students with a very high potential of success, given their educational background. However, the selection is operating at different levels of human capital. Our study is looking at the very top of the educational hierarchy, where students are all aiming for the professional labour market.

Our research design consisted of administering a baseline questionnaire that respondents completed while they were still students but were very close to graduating. These students were then tracked with a follow-up questionnaire at periodic intervals that had more focused questions about their job search efforts, interview experiences, and if they had found a job, details about their job, about their job satisfaction, and their overall views about the affirmative action policy (reservation policy).

The baseline questionnaire was administered to an initial sample of 108 students from DU (all in economics), JNU, and JMI (in mixed disciplines) in April 2005. Given that Dalit students were a small proportion of the DU sample (owing to a low number of Dalit students who met the rigorous minimum entrance standards and the high dropout rates from the economics programme[6]), we added a second cohort of students in April 2006 from DU (again in economics) and from a mix of disciplines at JNU and JMI, with matching Dalit and non-Dalit students in each disciplinary 'cell', such that our final sample consisted of 172 students. Over half (53 per cent) were graduating from the MA programme in economics from DU. Most of the remaining students (38 per cent) were completing degrees at JNU. About 35 per cent were women and 65 per cent were men.

Nearly 28 per cent were reserved category or Dalit students. Dalit category students were disproportionately men: 83 per cent of the reserved category students, compared to 58 per cent of non-Dalit students who were men. In terms of religious or communal

[6] Because the dropout rate of Dalit students is very high, by the time they reach the final semester, it is impossible to match the non-Dalit numbers with Dalit numbers.

background, for the sample as a whole, 71 per cent were Hindus and 12.7 per cent were Muslims. The rest of the students were Sikhs, Buddhists, Christians, and Jains. Dalit students were found in all the religions other than Jainism. All the Buddhist students, 60 per cent of the Sikhs, 27 per cent of Muslims, 25 per cent of Hindus, and 14 per cent of Christians self-reported themselves to be Dalit students students. These percentages are based on respondents' self-reporting about their eligibility for reservations. These percentages diverge from what we would obtain based on official reservation policy. As noted earlier, reservation applies mainly to Hindu and Sikh SCs and not to Muslims and Christians, even if they are marked by caste internally within their faith.[7]

On the Eve of Entry into the Labour Market

Diverging Expectations

Long before our sample confronted the labour market, their expectations of what they will find diverged by Dalit/non-Dalit status. These students were in the final months of their postgraduate studies, so that they had given considerable thought to their job prospects. Comparing the two groups on a variety of indicators, graduating Dalit students had significantly lower occupational expectations than their non-Dalit category counterparts. The average expected monthly salary for Dalit students was Rs 19,510, while non-Dalit students expected to earn about Rs 24,470. The median salary for the non-Dalit students was Rs 22,500 and that for the Dalit students was Rs 15,000. While the average salary for the Dalit students was lower, the variability (spread) of expected salary was higher.

We asked each student to describe their ideal job, and also to tell us what job they realistically expected to find. The contrasts between reserved category and non-reserved category students in terms of expectations were sharp. The majority of Dalits listed jobs in the public sector: 45 per cent mentioned administrative services/Indian Police Service, and another 28 per cent would ideally seek jobs as teachers or

[7] In several surveys, Christians and Muslims report themselves as OBCs and/or deserving of reservations. It needs to be noted that this reflects their self-perception about their relative disadvantage and/or discrimination towards their communities rather than the actual reservation policy. In the case of Muslims, it is more complicated because the government OBC list does include some Muslim *jatis*.

academics or researchers. This reflects the operation of the affirmative action policy that is applicable only to public sector enterprises and leaves the private sector completely untouched.

Non-Dalit students were much more likely to report an ideal job as a business analyst or corporate planner (19 per cent of non-Dalit students compared to 9 per cent of Dalits) or in the social or development sector (15 per cent compared to 2 per cent for Dalits). Relatively few non-Dalit students viewed the administrative services as an ideal job (12 per cent compared to 45 per cent of Dalits).

The largest area of overlap in terms of ideal job was in teaching, academic, and researcher jobs: many non-Dalit students thought that ideal (30 per cent), as did 28 per cent of Dalits. Also confirming the lower expectations of Dalit students, a small minority of Dalit students (2 per cent) thought of clerical-type office jobs as ideal whereas none among the non-Dalits did.

There was a big disparity for both categories between their ideal job and the job they realistically expected to get. This is hardly surprising in view of the enormous glut of well-educated but unemployed or underemployed men and women in India.

A large number of non-Dalit students expected to find work as business analysts and planners (19 per cent), while only 9.2 per cent of Dalits had this expectation. Many non-Dalit students also expected to find work as teachers, or academics, or researchers (29.5 per cent), but the proportion of Dalit students expecting to find work in those occupations was slightly higher (30.5 per cent).

Surprisingly, even though few Dalit students had listed planning or development as their ideal job, only about 2.4 per cent listed this as the most realistic kind of job they would actually find.

The expectation among Dalit postgraduates that they would find jobs in the public sector is further confirmed by the proportion who had taken the requisite civil service exams. At the time of the baseline survey, far more Dalit students (nearly 67 per cent) had taken the civil service exam than non-Dalit students (34 per cent).

Family Businesses, Family Connections, Parental Education

The differential ability of Dalit and non-Dalit students to benefit from family resources—ranging from business where they might find employment, to social networks that could be activated in the search for employment, to the cultural capital (or 'know how') that will help inform a student of advantageous options—was very pronounced. For example, nearly 18 per cent of non-Dalit students said that someone in their family owned a business where the student might be employed compared to only 8.5 per cent of Dalit students.

Students were asked whether they expected to rely on family connections in finding a job. About 20 per cent of non-Dalit students said they were likely to use family connections for this purpose, compared to about 10 per cent of Dalit students. These two findings parallel Royster's observations about the advantages white men can call on and turn to friends and family members for employment in the small business sector.

Differences in family background (measured by parents' occupations) for the two groups of students were quite stark. The occupational distribution of fathers of the non-Dalit students showed that the single largest category (16.5 per cent) was either self-employed or in big business. Thereafter, we found fathers who were managers or in the banking sector; or who had opted for the voluntary retirement scheme or VRS (11.5 per cent each). Ten per cent of the fathers were doctors, engineers, software engineers, or in the IT sector. Another 10 per cent were farmers. Smaller proportions (around 5 per cent each) were lawyers or chartered accountants or academics/researchers.

In contrast, the fathers of almost 33 per cent of Dalit students were farmers. This was followed by 15 per cent of the fathers who were academics/researchers, and lawyers, chartered accountants and VRS holders (9 per cent each). Another 8.6 per cent were government servants or members of the civil service. Other than farming, all the other professions either have reservation quotas for public sector jobs or the courses that lead to these occupations (medicine, engineering, law) can be pursued in government institutions via quotas. There was a small proportion, roughly 4 per cent each, in the development sector and manager/banking.

We asked the students if their mother was working outside the home. Fifty-eight per cent of the non-Dalit students had non-working mothers compared to 81 per cent of Dalit students. Thus, an overwhelming majority of Dalit students in our sample came from single-income families. The distribution of occupations for mothers who are working was much wider for the non-Dalit students as compared to the Dalit students.

Reading this together with the disparities in the parental education level, we can get a sense of how different the family background for the two sets of students was. As the qualitative section shows, family background plays a huge role in the selection process during job interviews.

Job Search

Both Dalit and non-Dalit students searched for jobs in similar ways, using university-sponsored placement cells, answering newspaper advertisements, submitting resumes by mail and over the web, and turning to family connections and off-campus 'head hunters' or placement firms. However, Dalit students were significantly less likely to use campus job fairs or placement cells and were significantly more likely to depend on newspaper ads than their non-Dalit counterparts. Again, this illustrates the preference for public sector/government/university jobs on the part of Dalit students, as a lot of private sector jobs are not advertised and government/public sector organizations cannot recruit without advertising.

Time to Find a Job

About 47 per cent of the non-Dalit students expected to find their jobs in two months. Seventy-five per cent expected to find their job in eight months. Ninety-two per cent expected to find the job within a year. The maximum time quoted was two years. The average expected time was 5.25 months.

The expected time was, on the whole, longer for Dalit students than 'general category' students. Forty-five per cent of the Dalit students expected to find their ideal jobs in eight months. Eighty-two per cent of this category expected to find their jobs within a year. Ninety-one per cent of the sample expected to find a job within 18 months (as compared to 12 months for the general category). The average time expected was 9.6 months.

MOVING INTO THE LABOUR MARKET

These group differences are clearly reflected in the follow-up interviews we conducted to learn more about their subjective experience of the educational process designed to prepare them for entry into the professional labour market, as well as their initial experiences with employment, often taken during their final years of education. I am presenting some elements from the larger study: first, the perceptions and experiences of the Dalit students, and then their perspectives on educational opportunity, labour market entry, and the political conflicts surrounding the extension of reservation policy to the private sector, would be contrasted with those of their non-reserved category counterparts.

Entry into the Labour Market

Several of the Dalit respondents had intermittent labour market experience even during their student life, since they had to take up jobs in order to support themselves and their families. We can see that their experiences to date lay the groundwork—both in terms of expectation formation and actual employment—for the more intense exposure to the competitive matching process to come when they later seek positions commensurate with their educational credentials.

The first point to note is that despite their position as students from elite universities seeking employment, they are reminded at every turn that caste matters in the eyes of hiring managers. For many civil service positions, the lists of candidates to be interviewed are organized by caste and the information is not received in a neutral or respectful fashion. Om Prakash,[8] a sociology student at JNU, applied for a teaching position—one of the 1,500 positions advertised that year. 'They had written in the list ... in a bracket [next to my name] "SC".'

Some [interviewers] were asking something of the SC candidates, but some other person was talking like this, 'yeah one knows how much talent they are having and what they can do' [sarcastically, derisively] [sic].

Many complained that they would present themselves for job interviews only to discover that they were never given serious consideration, that the selection process had been unfair. Some said that the interview had clearly been a formality as the selection committee members had already made up their minds, and hence the questions they were asked were over irrelevant matters having no bearing on the job at issue.

Several of the Dalit respondents explained that because they lack 'push' (pull), it was clear that they had no chance. An influential network

---

[8] The names of the respondents have been changed to protect their privacy.

of supporters is required to push ahead of the crowd for desirable jobs both in the public and the private sectors. At times money is the issue. Bribery is reportedly quite widespread. One respondent reported giving Rs 10,000 for a job he did not get and explained that he was unable to get the money back. For most of these students, jobs known to require bribes are simply off limits: they do not have the money and cannot apply. Vijender, a politics student at JNU, applied for a civil service position in a panchayat (council) in the district headquarters of home village. He was required to submit the application at the home of the council's headman rather than the office. But when he tried to get information on the requirements of the post through his father, the headman excoriated his father for thinking that this highly qualified son would be seriously considered:

He told my Papa, 'Why is [that boy] going for that job?' Actually, some influential people were going for that job, he told me. You cannot give money; you need to give a lot of money. That was really a shock for me. Someone like me goes for a job, then you get such a response [sic].

Even perfectly legal hiring practices impose barriers on Dalit students from poor backgrounds. For example, travelling to an interview may be prohibitively expensive. Rakesh sat three examinations for jobs with the Indian Railways and when called for interviews, could not afford the expense of staying overnight or paying for his food. 'One interview was in Calcutta,' he explained, 'another was in Guwahati. I had to go there and stay there and have meals there. For this, I need money that I was not having, so I could not attend that interview [sic].'

The signals of persistent caste barriers can be subtle as well as direct. Employers recognize the signal of surnames that are caste identified and know that names trigger questions during interviews that non-Dalits are never asked. In particular, when private sector employers raise pointed questions about the legitimacy of reservation policy, a policy that presently does not apply to these firms, students are placed on the defensive. They are being asked, in so many words, to defend their own biographies.

Kabir, a Dalit student in political science at JNU, went for a job interview in a Delhi hotel in which this topic dominated the conversation:

They asked me ... what is the caste system in India? I answered that Indian society is divided by caste and religion. So they asked me ... should there be reservations for SC/ST. I answered because SC people are facing problems, they are being discriminated against; their positions is not good, they are backward. Why should there be this difference? ... They said they have got reservation for fifty years, why should [this] continue? I said because they want to be equal with others, so that is why reservation should be there for some more years.

They said it is not fair because some SC/ST people are getting privileges. They don't have knowledge, they don't have talent. Taking admissions in good universities/colleges and then coming out [as if they were equivalent to] general category students. I said, madam, they are working hard because they are not in good position economically and socially. But it will take time to be equal to the others [sic].

As the study by Jodhka and Newman (2007), reported later, confirms, employers are given to asking questions of all applicants about their 'family background'. For students from non-Dalit caste backgrounds, the questions appear innocuous, and indeed they are regarded by everyone as normal human resources (HR) practice. For Dalit students, however, the answers they have to give, unless they are willing to lie, point directly to stigma. Their fathers do not have the kinds of occupations that confirm the student's suitability for professional jobs; their families are too large; and most of all, the students are burdened by demands for support from their families.[9]

Nathu Prasad, a politics student at JNU, applied for a job at a national research centre. He expected to be asked 'about my NET exam[10] or my MA, but there was no need to ask about my background, income source and all these things [sic]'.

They asked me about my parents, what they do. So I said they own a small bit of land, they are farmers, but they also do small business. I got the feeling that I was being singled out for these kinds of questions. I later asked some other boys who were there and they said that they had not been asked. The psychological effect of those questions is very negative. Suppose you get selected. Then even after that, you will remain conscious since the person knows about your family background and that person may try to ... exploit you.

[9] A quality that might be regarded as positive in the US, for it denotes a responsible child, but seems to signal distraction or lack of flexibility in the Indian context.

[10] Passing the NET (National Eligibility Test), an all-India examination conducted by the University Grants Commission, is a necessary condition to apply for a lecturer's (assistant professor) job. For higher level teaching jobs (reader, professor), one is exempt from this examination.

I don't think that these questions were neutral ... I knew the topic that I had to speak on, they knew my qualifications, so if they had asked about that I wouldn't have had any problem. Problem is that by asking other questions, they can find out about our 'low label' [sic].

Nathu Prasad got the job, but felt awkward that his family background factored into the equation; instead of being taken solely on his own merits, personal information that did not pertain to his qualifications was known by 'company strangers'.

Bidyut faced a harsh barrage over his family's circumstances following an equally discomfiting litany of remarks about the reservation policy from the director of the firm. Everything from his regional origins to his parental occupation was at issue:

Explain where you belong to [I was told]. I said I am from Orissa. So how did you come here to Delhi? ... He asked me so many questions about my caste, my family, about my background. First he asked me, if you are from Orissa, why don't you settled down there ... I said that in Orissa, the opportunities are very less, there is no chance [to make it]. I have been in Delhi already for one decade, so I want to join a job here because there are more opportunities. I am very interested in joining a good institute like yours. Then he asked: tell me about your background, what does your father do? I told him I come from a very poor background. My father was a farmer, he died recently. Now my mother is there, my elder brother is there. I am very much responsible for my family, so I want to earn some money [sic].

The director went on to imply that someone from his background should be applying elsewhere, forcing Bidyut on the defensive to make the case for why he should be considered at all. It was made clear that people with a family background similar to his were not welcome:

You people are struggling for life, so you are not that competent, [he told me]. I answer that is not true .... They don't like SC/ST candidates in the private sector [sic].

Dalit students are aware that these barriers are out there in the labour market well before their graduation from higher degree courses. For some, concern runs so high that they decide to conceal the truth in hopes of landing the jobs they want. Arshad, a computer science student at JMI, knew that he would face discrimination on this basis and hence reconfigured his biography to look less stereotypically lower caste:

Family background was asked, but I did not tell them reality, that we are six brothers and sisters. I told them that I have one brother and one sister. They asked me 'What is your father?' I told them he is a teacher. I thought it could have some positive impact because my family background will look like a small family and father is a teacher [sic].

It is a sad irony that in order for the reservations policy to work in education and public employment, caste identity must be affixed to qualify. SC status is made clear in official records from high school graduation certificate to university files. If this knowledge was merely part of a bureaucratic record, the story would stop at that. But it becomes part of a moral narrative in which the student's right to the education he/she has received, his/her genuine talents, and his/her fitness for a job are questioned by those who hold negative assumptions on all three counts. In a society where educational opportunity is extremely scarce relative to the demand, in which good jobs are highly coveted since there are too few for all of the qualified people seeking them, the job interview becomes more than a means of matching applicants to positions. It becomes an occasion for political debate that throws Dalit students on the defensive.

THE OTHER SIDE OF THE FENCE

Royster's book chronicles the embittered views of white working class students in the US who also face a competitive labour market in which opportunities have been shrinking, even for skilled blue-collar labour. Lacking much of a grasp of the structural dimensions of this shift, her white interviewees relapse into a politics of blame, focusing on affirmative action and unfair racial preferences for minorities to explain declining opportunities. They certainly saw no particular advantages to being white, either in terms of the social networks they could rely on or in terms of employers' preferences.

Indian students—Dalit and non-Dalit alike—also face extraordinary competition for spaces in higher education and public/private employment. At the same time, India's unparalleled growth has opened up opportunities for university graduates, and the sense throughout our interviews was that students with advanced degrees can look forward to a much better future than might have been true in the past. These truths coincide and help to explain the fractured nature of non-Dalit students' opinion on their own opportunity structure, the legitimacy of quotas in higher education and employment, and their views on the best use of available resources for creating equal opportunity. The fractures are best understood as a consequence of deep and pervasive inequality in primary and secondary education (acknowledged by virtually all non-reserved students) and the inherent competition for scarce 'mobility resources', coupled with pronounced advantages in India for those at the top of the educational hierarchy.

Those inequalities are powerfully reflected in the overall experience of non-reserved (henceforth 'general') students in the labour market. These respondents reported far more favourable interviews and selection procedures when job hunting than reserved students, as well as a more positive 'interpretive disposition'. By this we mean that matching procedures that reserved and general students *both* experience are interpreted by the former as indicative of questionable intent, while experienced as neutral or even positive by general students.

Few non-Dalit students were asked about their caste or religious background. This was clearly a difference that mattered, but it must be noted that many Dalit students were not asked about caste either. Their last names signal their caste membership in many instances, and questions on family background reveal the rest. When asked about their family background, non-Dalit students saw the questions as neutral in intent and/or an opportunity for them to shine because their families were more upper-middle class in size and occupational background. They were able to bring to bear on the job interview, fluency in English, confidence in their academic skills, and advanced knowledge of what they would be expected to demonstrate in the way of 'fitness for the firm' than Dalit students, whose cultural capital was weaker.

Non-Dalit students did not see themselves as privileged because of these qualities, even if they recognized that the distribution of these skills was differential. These are merely the talents that firms are looking for, including ease in social situations like interviews. This parallels one of Royster's findings that white men did not see themselves as advantaged, but rather as the neutral case.

Job Interviews

Bharat, a sociology student at JNU, typified the reaction of general students to their job interview experience. It was an occasion overlaid with tension, because an evaluation is in progress. But on the whole, interviews are a learning experience, not a test of cultural fitness:

[T]he interview ... teaches you a lot to handle the tension ... Just adjusting to the ambience, the environment of the interview, helps a lot. So many questions are asked and one question is followed by another. You need to keep your mind cool enough in special circumstances.

The only negative experience Bharat could remember from his many rounds of interviews was one where he was 'asked to come at 10 am and the interview began at 1:30 pm'. This was a 'bitter experience', he noted.

General students experienced a problem that many reserved students interpreted as caste discrimination: the wired interview. For general students, the idea that a job has already been handed over to an inside candidate or someone with social connections superior to their own is a recognized fact. It happens all the time. Preeti, an economics student in Delhi School of Economics (DSE), described the experience in detail:

I went to another college [for an interview]. There was an internal candidate, so she was given the job and my interview lasted only 2–3 minutes. It was virtually decided that she had to be taken in. [The interview] was a formality for me. I did ask my professor [who was on the interview board] 'You won't ask anything else? 'He said, "Yes, I won't ask anything."' They were not treating me seriously. I know because just 15 days [before] I faced [an interview at another college] and the interview lasted a complete half-an-hour and I was asked lots of questions.

Preeti did not regard this experience as a commentary on her fitness; indeed, she regarded herself as perfectly well qualified, but outmanoeuvred. The wired interview does not lead general students to believe that they will be shut out of upward mobility. If anything, it indicates to them that they too must cultivate their networks. For the Dalit student, a wired interview is one more piece of evidence that they are going to face a very long uphill struggle for mobility because they do not have easy access to the 'inside track'.

The value of cultural capital, of understanding the social skills that need to be on display in an interview, cannot be overstated. With so many applicants qualified on the grounds of skills and knowledge, Indian firms are looking for people who 'fit', a matching process noted by American researchers of the labour market as well (Kirshenmann and Neckerman 1991). For general students, a university education is often a continuation of a lifelong process of cultivation, not unlike what elite students in American Ivy League universities experience.

They move into the task of job hunting with a degree of confidence that they have the social skills to function appropriately, to avoid being overly nervous, to project an air of cosmopolitanism that may be the final element that distinguishes them from other students with similar technical credentials.

Abhijit, a general category economics student of DSE, described his experience with job interviews in tones strikingly different from even the most positive encounters among the Dalit students:

Most of my interviews are very relaxed. No one was assessing my knowledge or anything, but ... seeing how well and efficiently I contribute to the company. So, positive feedback purely in fact that I had high success rate in terms of clearing interviews that is making me feel good. I was competitive enough to get a job later if I wanted to ...

None of my interviews were stressful at all. They were all very friendly for me. For example, when I had my interview with [information firm], he asked me why I want to work in Bombay. That is one of the cities that never sleeps and lots of stuff to do there. So the interview was more in terms of what I like, what I dislike and general chit chat about what I was looking to do in the future rather than quizzing me about, let's say what particular topics I had done in a particular [academic] subject or something like that.

None of the Dalit students we interviewed expressed this kind of confidence. Even those who managed to get jobs were apprehensive and stressed by the interviews. They never had the feeling that their interest in the nightlife of the city where a firm was located was a centrepiece of conversation. Instead, they were often interrogated about their command of the academic subjects they had studied, and put on the defensive about the impact of the quota system.

Lacking cultural capital when they arrive in elite universities, Dalit students—most especially those from rural backgrounds—are not in a position to improve their cultural exposure beyond what they acquire inside the university itself. This is not minimal. Indeed, coming to a place like JNU from a remote tribal region does indeed create opportunities for exchange and personal growth in a cosmopolitan direction. But if one must work at the same time, it will be hard to take this any farther. Not so for the general category students who may have many opportunities to widen their horizons outside of the university during their years as students. Ajit, an economics student of DSE, commented on the ways in which he had been able to move outside of the university context to broaden himself:

What I expected, I got from my study at Dehli School ... Other avenues ... like travel, I got enough chances to travel around India or other places through the university. After some time, university education helped me to form a general [overall] understanding and also a social circle. Also helped me to gain general skills ...

There are so many ingredients [to being successful]. The most important thing is the peer group. There is a circle of friends/acquaintances in which one gains confidence, learns skills. A person like this will get access easily and he can be identified as a suitable candidate. Now here the background is equally important. So things other than intelligence matter a lot. Most of these ingredients are acquired with money. So [a person's] economic background gives a lot of privileges and it becomes a requirement to access several things. But someone who is less qualified at entry can be trained and learn the requirements of the job.

The Family Background Test

Virtually all of our study subjects reported being asked about their family backgrounds during employment interviews. Questions about where they come from, what their parents do for a living, the types of jobs their siblings do, and the like, were very common. However, as noted earlier, general category students can offer biographies that are much closer to the upper-middle class, professional ideal. Hence, the questions are rarely interpreted as offensive or prying. And the answers are almost always in line with positive images of family life, as Ramesh, a Delhi School, recounted:

Couple of people asked me about my family background, about what my father does, whether I have any siblings or what my mother does? No one asked me about my religion or caste. I told them that my dad is a government servant, he is working in the Indian Railways and my mom is also in the Bank of [my region]. My sister is a doctor. So that was more courtesy, interested kind of questions that the interviewer broached up. They made me more comfortable rather than judging me on what my parents do or not do. I am sure I did not make any negative kind of influence at all in my case. It might have had positive impact to see in terms of my parents are well educated and my sister is also well educated and everyone is doing well [sic].

While Dalit students often perceive a hidden agenda in family background questions, for non-Dalit students the same questions appear to be innocuous or sensible inquiries from an HR perspective. They are not 'gotcha' questions designed to discredit an applicant who is presenting himself/herself as an educated, highly trained proto-professional.[11] When asked, in our interviews, what these questions were there for, these student invariably had answers that made the whole subject seem completely uncomplicated. For example, Ashok, a general category student of economics at DSE, noted:

Yes. I was asked about family background. Where do you come from? What is your family business? I tell them I come from UP and my family is in agriculture ... [sic].

What do you think they were trying to get at?

Maybe they were trying to understand if I will stay on in the organization or leave soon. Because the one major problem that companies face is attrition. So, they do need a bit of an idea ... They try and gauge if I will stay or not looking at a variety of factors. The way I told them, it should have been positive information for them. Or at least I felt that way. They must have thought that I will work there [sic].

It is impossible to judge who has the 'right story' on family background from these interviews and it is not clear that they are contradictory either. It is entirely possible that family background questions are used to identify caste or other background information that would be disqualifying in the eyes of employers who are unwilling to employ Dalit applicants, or applicants with particularly needy families. It is also quite possible that HR practice inclines firms to ask questions that help them ascertain the risks of attrition. The questions themselves do not provide a window on what they are used for when the winnowing process begins.

Yet, if we couple these findings with the observations from studies of employer interviews (Jodhka and Newman 2007), there is some reason for concern that family background is used to 'ratify' the claims presented on the surface by a job candidate to be a 'suitable person' for a position, with siblings whose trajectories confirm his/her own 'impression management' (to use Erving Goffman's [1961] well-known term). To the extent that this is the case, being able to give a socially acceptable answer about parental occupation or family size will be helpful. The converse could knock an otherwise qualified candidate out.

Summing up, we see that as was true in Royster's study, students from these two groups bring very different levels of resources—in the form of family connections, financial security during their university

[11] Goffman (1961) uses the term 'discrediting' information when describing the fault lines in an interactive setting that occur when someone makes a gaff and inadvertently reveals that their claims to a particularly identity are false.

years, obligations to support parental households, and the like—to the starting gate. Hence, while the training they receive in the university world and the credentials they can claim when they finish are quite comparable, Dalit students lack many advantages that turn out to be crucial and are subject to scepticism on the part of employers who doubt the legitimacy of reservations (and by extension, the legitimacy of the credentials they present during the job search).

Perhaps as a result, Dalit students from comparable degree programmes as their high-caste counterparts have lower expectations and see themselves as disadvantaged because of their caste and family backgrounds. Because they arrive in college with weaker skills on average, they are 'playing catch up' and often do not succeed in pulling even with more advantaged students, and hence enter the job markets with weaker English language and computing skills. This has important policy implications that we will explore in the next chapter.

Non-Dalit students do not see themselves as relatively advantaged. They display a sense of confidence and optimism about the job opportunities that the rapidly growing, globalizing Indian economy is providing to them. In sharp contrast to the Dalit students, their experiences during job interviews, on the whole, are extremely positive, even in cases where they do not get the job. Even though they regarded the question as neutral, their family background places them in a favourable setting during the interview.

THE DEMAND-SIDE STORY: WHAT ARE EMPLOYERS LOOKING FOR?

The evidence presented so far, especially from the correspondence studies and the college-to-work study, gives a fairly strong indication of prejudice in the hiring process. However, the first study for India that directly assesses employer attitudes is Jodhka and Newman (2007). Their study is a qualitative one, based on in-depth interviews with 25 HR managers of large firms based in New Delhi and the surrounding National Capital Region. The HR managers were asked to talk about a variety of issues: overall characteristics of their firm, the nature of their labour force, challenges in the hiring process, and their views on issues such as why unemployment among SCs is high, or on the 'reservation policy', and whether they felt the reservation policy should be extended to the private sector.

As the authors caution, the interviews reported in their study are by themselves not decisive confirmation of discrimination, but read in conjunction with other evidence, they provide a critical piece of the whole labour market story, about which, ordinarily, very little is known. The most striking finding in their study was that every single interviewee expressed the view that *workers should be hired strictly according to merit*. This was seen as especially important in an age where India is poised to join the group of global superpowers, and the unanimous view was that hiring practices should appropriately reflect a commitment to meritocracy.

A media company expressed a preference for cosmopolitanism and declared that prejudice played no role in their hiring practices; any applicant who displayed the required characteristics would be hired, irrespective of caste or creed. As the authors point out, 'in principle, individuals with this kind of cultural capital could come from any background. In practice, the institutions and experiences that produce cosmopolitanism are rarely available to SCs' (ibid.: 4126). Some of the respondents admit to caste-based preferences in hiring but declare that these trends are old-fashioned, typically seen in smaller companies and have no place in large, modern corporations. The language of merit dominated the conversation, regardless of the kind of activity that the firm was engaged in. Jodhka and Newman (2007: 4127) state: 'It (the language of merit) assumes that we begin from the same starting point (regardless of evidence of deprivation), enter equally efficacious credentialing institutions (despite the clear inequalities in schooling that take a heavy toll on the poor and low caste), and come out ranked objectively in terms of sheer quality.'

The other important finding from their study is that Indian employers see no contradiction between seeking individual merit and valuing 'family background'. Virtually all the respondents confirmed asking questions about family background, a loose term encompassing any personal information not related to a candidate's educational or skill background. This fully complements the students' accounts in the college-to-work study reported earlier. When questioned what they were looking for via information on family background, some managers gave loose, amorphous answers, others had very specific ideas in their minds. It did not occur to them that focusing on characteristics other than the qualifications required for the job was actually moving away from the concept of merit. This was because they believed that 'merit was formed within the crucible of the family' (ibid.: 4127). As the authors point out and as the college-to-work study confirms, screening on the basis of family background is bound to be detrimental to the stigmatized and deprived groups, as their family backgrounds would seldom reflect qualities that are considered desirable for jobs in modern companies. Regional stereotypes also play a prominent role in the hiring process (this was again confirmed by our interviews, not reproduced in this chapter, in the college-to-work study).

* * *

All available evidence suggests that social and cultural capital (the complex and overlapping categories of caste, family background, network, and contacts) plays a huge role in urban, formal sector labour markets, where hiring practices are less transparent than they appear at first sight. While Dalits are severely disadvantaged in this setting, an effective affirmative action programme has the potential to turn things around. Whether this will be possible in the context of highly charged political opinion is hard to know. As Royster's book makes clear, white students enter the labour market with significant advantages that they do not recognize and instead perceive black students as unfairly rewarded by racial preferences. Black students see very clearly how tilted the playing field is and are often called to account personally for social policies designed to redress historic and contemporary inequality. In India, we see very similar divergence of views and differential interpretation of disadvantage in the voices of the Dalit versus non-Dalit students. This is not a recipe for social harmony. In the concluding chapter of the book, we turn to an assessment of the affirmative action programme as one of the important remedies for caste discrimination and disadvantage, along with a discussion of other possible measures.

7 What is to be Done?

The preceding chapters clearly establish the twin, interconnected, and persistent problems of inter-caste (and gender) disparity and discrimination which, for the most part, do not bear a clear and unambiguous relationship with aggregate income levels or with its rate of growth. Thus, a policy focus on increasing the latter two might be desirable for other reasons, but it is unlikely to tackle the problems of disparity and discrimination. Evidence from around the world additionally indicates that the 'trickle-down effect' does not quite work; it is, therefore, extremely unlikely that benefits of high growth are going to automatically percolate down to the most marginalized, that is, the Dalits and the tribals. This brings to the fore the critical question of policy response to persistent disparities: do we need special policies to tackle discrimination and disparities or are universal anti-poverty or redistributive policies enough to close the caste gaps? Since India already has in place an affirmative action (AA) programme, the more relevant question is about the appropriateness/sufficiency of the existing AA programme, and the overarching question is whether any AA is needed at all. It is only natural that the concluding chapter of this volume should focus on these questions, especially in the context of the special challenges and opportunities that globalization has brought in its wake.

INTER-GROUP DISPARITY

Inter-caste disparity in India manifests itself in many different dimensions with several parallel layers of discrimination, which makes the formulation of an ideal plan for compensatory discrimination difficult, if not impossible. As if this was not complex enough, what makes matters infinitely more complicated is that there are deep inter-group fissures on lines other than caste, perhaps the most potent being religion. It is beyond the scope of this volume and the expertise of the author to analyse all of these fissures in depth, and there is abundant literature that examines these aspects with great depth and rigour. Additionally, gender intersects all the group divisions; Chapter 4 has examined some contours of contemporary gender disparities in India. It needs more than a volume to encapsulate gender disparities in their various dimensions; suffice it to note for the purpose of this chapter that the demand for AA for women now has a caste dimension (quotas-within-quotas), discussed briefly in Appendix 7.D.

THE INDIAN AFFIRMATIVE ACTION PROGRAMME

The AA programme in India is primarily caste-based and is two-pronged: involving separate quotas for Scheduled Castes (SCs)/Scheduled Tribes (STs) and Other Backward Classes (OBCs). Of all government jobs, seats in educational institutions that have complete or partial government funding, and electoral constituencies at all levels of government, 22.5 per cent are reserved for SC and ST persons. This quota is roughly proportional to their share in the population at the national level. At the state level, the proportion varies, not necessarily in proportion to the population shares. For instance, Tamil Nadu has close to 70 per cent quotas, with 18 per cent for SCs and 1 per cent for STs; Rajasthan has 68 per cent, including 14 per cent for forward castes. These are the only two states that violate the 50 per cent rule, discussed later. Andhra Pradesh has now introduced 4 per cent quotas for Muslims, affecting the OBC numbers, since several Muslim *jatis* are included in the OBC category. In addition, 27 per cent seats are reserved for OBCs at the national level—this figure, however, is not proportional to their population share. As mentioned earlier in Chapter 2, in the absence of a caste census, we do not know the exact OBC population, but indication from surveys such as National Sample Survey (NSS) and National Family and Health Survey (NFHS) puts the figure at approximately 42 per cent. The OBC quota is discussed in detail later in the chapter.

The principle of reservations was enshrined in the Indian Constitution, adopted in 1950, via Article 16(4) (reservation of government jobs). Although the Constitution does not mention explicit quotas in education, but mentions 'special provisions',[1] the AA programme has taken the form of quotas in both education and employment. The use of quotas for socially and economically backward communities,[2] however, originated during the colonial rule. In some areas, such as parts of present day Kerala and Karnataka, the British introduced quotas almost a hundred years ago. Making AA for SCs and STs a part of the Constitution, a move mainly due to B.R. Ambedkar, who was the chairman of the drafting committee of the Constitution of independent India, ensured that it became mandatory and could not easily be undone or violated. He viewed reservations as *exceptional* and *temporary*—believed that the State may make adjustments to the roster of classes being given preferential treatment and may even cease making special arrangements when it feels that it is no longer necessary. However, despite being mandatory, in practice, quotas remain unevenly filled due to two reasons. One, due to the upper-caste predominance in various institutions, the implementation of AA is often indifferent. Two, due to the imposition of minimal test cut-off scores for reserved jobs or seats, often there are not enough candidates

[1] The Constitution contains two specific references related to education of SCs–STs: Article 15(4) talks of 'special provision, by law, for the advancement of any socially and educationally backward classes of citizens or for the Scheduled Castes or the Scheduled Tribes in so far as such special provisions relate to their admission to educational institutions including private educational institutions, whether aided or unaided by the State, other than the minority educational institutions ...', and Article 46: 'The state shall promote with special care the educational and economic interests of the weaker sections of the people, and, in particular, of the Scheduled Castes and the Scheduled Tribes, and shall protect them from social injustice and all forms of exploitation.'

[2] Also called the 'Depressed Classes' during the British rule.

from beneficiary groups that qualify for the reserved positions. Thus, for a combination of reasons, completely fulfilled quotas at all levels have never materialized for any length of time to create conditions where abolition of quotas could be considered.

The rationale for AA for SCs and STs is based on the following set of arguments:

1. Inter-group economic disparity: As Chapter 3 has documented, the disparities are persistent and systematic, regional variation notwithstanding. Dalits continue to suffer from a 'stigmatized ethnic identity' due to their untouchable past and remain mired in corresponding social backwardness. There is sufficient evidence that amply demonstrates the various aspects of stigmatization, exclusion, and rejection that Dalits continue to face in contemporary India.[3]

2. If equality of opportunity between groups is considered desirable, then AA is needed to provide a level playing field to members of SC/ST communities, given that most members of this group have to carry a heavy load of disadvantage in initial conditions.

3. All the evidence in the preceding chapters makes it clear that disparities are neither mainly a hangover from the past, nor are they mainly a result of educational or skill gaps. Thus, members of SC–ST communities will face worse employment outcomes *even if they were similarly qualified as the 'Others'*, given discrimination in labour markets.[4] In view of the unambiguous evidence on discrimination, AA becomes essential to guarantee representation to Dalits in preferred positions.

[3] See, for example, Human Rights Watch (1999) for an excellent documentation.

[4] Chakravarty and Somanathan (2008), in a study of one of the elite management institutions, find that the grade point average (GPA) of students in the first three semesters is a good predictor of their employment outcomes after the fourth and final semester, and that SC and non-SC students with similar GPAs perform similarly on the job market. Thus, their study indicates no discrimination in labour markets: if SCs' outcomes are worse, they can be explained by lower GPAs, not discrimination. If this happens in small pockets, it is heartening indeed. However, there are several reasons why their study cannot be generalized, including, for example, the ambiguity over the predictive ability of GPA scores for labour market outcomes. Also, their results are conditional on Dalits who join the placement programme. Experience from the University of Delhi, where I teach, indicates that several Dalits do not even join the placement programme, anticipating discrimination in markets for private jobs.

4. Finally (arguably), social policy ought to compensate for the historical wrongs of a system that generated systematic disparity between caste groups and actively discriminated against certain groups. However, given the complex history of the Indian subcontinent, this argument should be used with extreme caution, as several right-wing outfits invoke completely unsubstantiated, often manufactured injustices against the so-called indigenous inhabitants and ask for compensation for historical wrongs. It is extremely difficult to define what the historical 'wrongs' are and, therefore, what the compensations could be. But while the argument of compensation for historical wrongs could be used as one of the elements in the case for AA, fortunately, the case itself does not rest on this argument and can be made just as forcefully even without this particular element.

Founders of modern India, who gave the policy of AA decisive shape, had two approaches to social justice. One was the principle of 'equality in law' whereby the State should not deny any person equality before the law. The second was the principle of 'equality in fact' which gives the State an affirmative duty to remedy existing inequalities. While opponents of AA see these two as contradictory, it can be argued that, on the contrary, the two constitutional doctrines supplement each other. True equality can be achieved only if the State maintains an integrated society but adopts unequally beneficial measures to help those previously disadvantaged.

The OBC Quota

Reference has been made to OBC quota earlier in the chapter. There has been considerable debate, again going back to the British times, over whether AA should be extended to castes or communities that have not suffered the stigma of untouchability but are sufficiently economically and socially backward. In a number of states in British India, educational benefits were given to such groups, variously called 'Depressed Classes' or 'Other Backward Classes', and in some major states, such as Madras, Bombay, and Mysore, preferential treatment was given to these groups that included reservations and welfare schemes.

Post-Independence, the OBC quota has been mired in controversy. Unlike in the case of Dalits, where identification is relatively easier and non-controversial, the assignment of the OBC status to jatis is an exercise fraught with considerable difficulty. Undoubtedly, there are several jatis that are very low in the caste hierarchy and therefore face serious material deprivation. However, since the jati–*varna* link is fluid, it is not clear that each of the jati that tries to get the OBC status is, in fact, a descendant of the Shudra varna, or indeed, is *currently* facing serious deprivation, as several landowning, otherwise prosperous jatis have claimed OBC status. However, as Guhan (2001: 214) argues: 'The caste system in India represents a wide spectrum of graded inequalities extending from the lowliest 'untouchable' at one end to the Brahmin at the other and it is erroneous to view it as a sharp dichotomy between the SCs and all other Hindus.'

As a part of the ongoing quest for documenting and understanding the social and economic backwardness of the OBCs, in 1981, yet another report, called the Mandal Commission Report (MCR) was tabled.[5] The MCR used a large set of social and economic criteria to identify the backward castes. In its estimation, OBCs formed 52 per cent of the Indian population, an estimate that is in contradiction with the NSS estimate. The announcement of its implementation was made in 1990 by the then prime minister, V.P. Singh. Subsequently, the Government of India enacted the National Commission for Backward Classes Act (Act No. 27 of 1993) that set up a National Commission for Backward Classes (NCBC) as a permanent body.[6]

[5] In 1918, the Maharajah of Mysore appointed the Miller Committee to recommend steps for adequate representations for non-Brahmins in the services of the state. This was followed by another committee in 1928, set up by the Government of Bombay to identify backward classes and recommend special provisions for their advancement. At the all-India level, the first systematic attempt at the welfare of 'depressed classes' was made with the introduction of Montague–Chelmsford Reforms of 1919, when separate representation on a number of public bodies was given to their members. After Independence, the First Backward Classes Commission, under the chairmanship of Kaka Kalelkar, was set up in 1953 and it submitted its report in 1955. Consequently, a number of state governments set up their own commissions or committees for defining criteria for backwardness and recommending measures for its removal (Report of the Backward Classes Commission [Mandal Commission] 1980, Government of India, First Part, various pages).

[6] Article 340 of the Constitution provides for the appointment of a commission that investigates the conditions of and the difficulties faced by socially and educationally backward classes and to make appropriate recommendations.

The OBC quota is perhaps the only instance of AA in the world where the designated beneficiary category is not counted in the national census. As Chapter 2 pointed out, despite agreement on the principle of a caste census, there is a cloud of uncertainty over the exact mechanics of this exercise, and at the time of writing, it appears as if it will take place as a separate count, along with the main census but distinct from it. Given that there has been no jati-based census since 1931, most of the commissions set up to examine the conditions of the backward classes since then have had to rely on extrapolations from the 1931 census or conduct their own surveys to identify who the backward classes are. The NCBC (as did the MCR) set out guidelines for inclusion into the central list of OBCs. These guidelines are listed in Appendix 7.B. As is clear, the NCBC uses a composite set of social, educational, and economic criteria to identify backwardness, with four criteria being considered decisive to the identification of backwardness: 2(e) to 2(h). The MCR had its own criteria which it used to formulate OBC lists. The NCBC re-created the central OBC list afresh, irrespective of whether castes and communities that it designated as backward were included in the MCR list or not. One of the noteworthy features of this list is that sections of religious minorities are also identified as OBCs, if they fulfil the backwardness criteria as laid down by the NCBC. The NCBC functions like a tribunal that decides the validity of the claims made by caste groups for inclusion in the OBC list. Thus, the NCBC has handled 1,221 claims so far, 766 of which were included in the Central List and 455 cases were rejected.[7]

Under the recommendation of the MCR, based on its list as well as the various states' lists to identify the OBCs, reservations were extended to include an OBC quota of 27 per cent with effect from August 1990, taking the total quota (SC/ST/OBC) to 49.5 per cent. The Constituent Assembly in Article 335 states 'maintenance of efficiency of administration' as a specific objective. Based upon this,

[7] Interestingly, it is not always the case that the number of claims that are included are greater than those that are rejected. For example, in Bihar, 12 cases were included as against 22 that were rejected. Orissa had an equal number of rejections and acceptances (45), and for Pondicherry (now Puducherry), 8 were accepted with 81 rejections. For details, see NCBC website: http://www.ncbc.nic.in/html/faq7.html, accessed on 15 February 2010.

there is a limit on reservations that prohibits reserving a majority of the seats, thus limiting quotas to less than 50 per cent. The figure of 27 per cent for OBCs, therefore, is not in accordance with its share in the population, but is the residual, after accounting for the 22.5 per cent SC–ST quota.

The announcement was followed by a massive public protest and widespread violent and virulent student agitations across university campuses in the country. Interestingly, despite the disruptions caused by the agitations, public sympathy was fully with the striking students with no evidence of the usual middle class disdain for and impatience with agitational activities. Also, while the agitation was caused by the announcement of the MCR and the extension of reservations to OBCs, the protest was against AA in general, with openly derogatory casteist slogans directed against the Dalit castes.[8] V.P. Singh was widely demonized as having created the OBC monster. However, as the preceding discussion suggests, the problem has been in the public domain independently of, and decades before, V.P. Singh.

Chapter 3 has documented various dimensions of caste disparities based on NSS and NFHS data. A comparison between OBCs and 'Others' is striking for several reasons. First, this comparison challenges the notion of OBCs as the new elite who have presumably displaced the economic dominance of upper castes. As an economist, I am not qualified to comment on the nature of the political change (several of the country's important political leaders and elected representatives are OBCs); however, there seems to be no indication of a *reversal* in the relative *economic* position between upper castes (in our data, non-OBC–SC–ST Hindus) and OBCs *considered as a whole*. It is important to note that this aggregate picture could be compatible with evidence from micro studies that indicate the dominance of specific OBC jatis in different parts.[9]

---

[8] For instance, during the agitation, upper-caste student protestors blocked busy streets and started polishing shoes (imitating shoeshine boys) with placards that read, 'This is what we will be reduced to because of the reservation system.' Notice the implication: the occupation that they (read upper castes) would be reduced to is a Dalit occupation. In other words, it is all right for Dalits to continue to do the menial jobs, but if upper castes have to descend to this low level, it is unacceptable. Needless to add, the belief that reservations would push the upper castes down to the menial jobs was only a presumption—not supported by any evidence.

[9] See, for instance, Gupta (2004).

Second, there is a view that the preparation of the OBC list, despite very detailed objective indicators of backwardness listed in the MCR, has been influenced by lobbying such that fairly prosperous and dominant jatis have managed to get themselves labelled as 'backward'. Again, I am not competent to comment on the validity of these claims. However, assuming such errors have occurred, these would bias the standard of living indicators for the OBCs *upwards*. It follows then, that the gap between the truly disadvantaged OBCs and the upper castes would only be larger than what our estimates indicate. Indeed, these comparisons are based on the OBCs as a whole without any distinction between the creamy layer and the more disadvantaged OBCs. It follows then that if we exclude the 'creamy layer', then the disparities would be even sharper. The NCBC has several criteria to define the creamy layer among OBCs that ought to be excluded from the proposed reservations (See Appendix 7.C for the creamy layer criteria).

Finally, my limited experience with fieldwork in rural Uttar Pradesh indicates that not only is the dividing line between purity and pollution critical, but that the distinction between 'dwija' (twice-born) and 'non-dwija' (Shudra) jatis matters too. Thus, the OBCs that are low in the hierarchy face a significant amount of exclusion and are, in many ways, truly backward.

IMPLEMENTATION OF AFFIRMATIVE ACTION

Unlike, for instance, in Malaysia, in India there is no national enforcement mechanism for AA. Civil action is not an available remedy for denial of due benefits (Nesiah 1997: 165). However, there is an alternative in the form of a writ jurisdiction under Articles 32 and 226 of the Indian Constitution, but given the dominance of upper castes in the judiciary, there is allegedly an upper caste/elite bias in the redressal mechanism. A formal writ application and subsequent appearances by lawyers in a court are too expensive for most potential petitioners. The central government does have a National SC/ST Commission, but so far it has not played a proactive role in ensuring implementation of quotas. Most of all, the law does not lay down penalties for non-fulfilment of quotas, and thus institutions can easily violate (constitutionally mandated) quotas and not suffer any negative consequences.

While evaluating how many members of the target group have benefited from quotas, the following must be kept in mind. The quota-based scheme in India is similar to a guaranteed minimum scheme, in that quotas are supposed to be filled first and the rest of the seats are allocated on 'merit'. Thus, as Galanter (1991) points out, the total number of SC–ST individuals in a job or educational institution will overestimate the actual amount of preference, if some members of the target groups get in without availing themselves of AA.

The one area where caste-based quotas are completely fulfilled is the electoral sphere. Thus, constituencies that are designated 'reserved' can elect only SC/ST candidates, as the case may be. Again, a detailed analysis of the political changes is a task best suited to a political scientist. However, given the enormity of this change, a few generalized comments are offered here. The reserved constituencies have led to a noticeable change in the caste composition of the elected representatives that even 40 years ago were dominated totally by upper castes. There are major Dalit political parties as well as key political players, ensuring that Dalit issues remain in the foreground in some fashion. There is now a sizeable literature that examines the impact of political reservations empirically. To cite a few important works, Pande (2003), Besley et al. (2004) (both examining SC–ST reservation), and Chattopadhyay and Duflo (2004) (for women) demonstrate how political reservation for a group leads to a higher incidence of policies preferred by and/or targeted towards that group. Besley et al. (2004) empirically evaluate the extent of targeting of SC–ST households due to reservations at the lowest level of government: the gram panchayat, or the village council. They find that on average, an SC–ST household is 6 per cent more likely to receive a public good than others. Further, relative to living in a non-reserved gram panchayat, living in a reserved gram panchayat increases an SC/ST household's likelihood of getting a public good by 7 percentage points. Their results suggest that enhanced targeting of SC/ST households comes only from reservations.

However, as the previous chapters show, despite the positive effects of reservations in the electoral sphere, disparities persist. There could be several reasons for this. Most of the Dalit candidates from the reserved seats are members of mainstream political parties and are thus committed to the overall agenda of their parties, which may or may not include the reduction of caste disparity or, putting it differently, might be committed to a pro-Dalit agenda to varying degrees. Also, even in reserved constituencies, the voters arc both SC/ST and upper caste, and in order to appeal to the latter, the candidates often have to tone down their pro-Dalit agenda. The issue is considerably more complex: it could be argued, for instance, that the most significant contemporary Dalit political party, the Bahujan Samaj Party (BSP) is no different from the other non-Dalit parties, in that its main objective is the capture of power, first at the state level and eventually at the national level. It has now demonstrated enough number of times that if the pursuit of this goal requires political compromises with upper-caste-dominated parties (something that could result in toning down the Dalit rhetoric), it would not hesitate in doing so. The statutory disclaimer, made several times earlier, is valid here as well: these are extremely complex issues, not given to easy generalizations and outside the scope of this volume, but important to note nevertheless. Finally, along the political spectrum, there is a strong tendency for elected representatives to be opportunistic and self-seeking; thus Dalit or not, often those elected work primarily to consolidate their own power rather than transfer any real benefits to the people whom they seek to represent.

Coming to the two other spheres of AA, government jobs and education, the picture is more complex. Xaxa (2002) attempts an assessment of reservations in the University of Delhi, one of the premier institutions in the country. In 1999–2000, of all the undergraduate students, only 8.6 per cent were SCs (with a quota of 15 per cent) and 1.8 per cent STs (quota of 7 per cent). Of the postgraduate students, 5.5 per cent were SCs and 2 per cent STs (with actual quotas the same as those at the undergraduate level). Thus, quotas are grossly under-fulfilled and if this could happen in the capital city, things might be worse in other parts of the country. The situation in teaching posts is even worse. Teachers in the University of Delhi have bitterly opposed the introduction of AA, even though it is a constitutional provision. As a result, reservations were introduced as late as 1996. At that time, out of the 700 teachers in postgraduate departments, seven were SCs and two STs. Out of the 4,512 teachers in university-affiliated undergraduate colleges, 11 were SCs and none was ST.

The picture in the non-teaching posts conforms to the overall pattern in other government jobs: the higher the representation of SCs/STs, the lower paying the job. Xaxa's figures for 1998–9 show that whereas only 3 per cent of Group A jobs were filled by SCs/

STs combined, the corresponding proportions for Groups B, C, and D were 7.4 per cent, 13 per cent, and 29 per cent, respectively. The menial jobs (cleaners, sweepers, and so on) are often performed almost exclusively by Dalits, in particular those jatis whose traditional occupation was cleaning/scavenging. In all the opposition to AA, there is never any protest against *over-representation* of low castes in low-paying jobs. In other words, as long as Dalits do not compete in traditional upper-caste bastions or 'stay where they belong', it is obviously considered acceptable.[10]

Coming to government jobs, during 1953–75, on the whole about 75 per cent to 80 per cent posts in lower levels were filled.[11] However, in the higher categories of officers (called Classes I and II), quotas remain unfulfilled, revealing a picture quite like the University of Delhi earlier. This can be attributed to 'indifference/hostility on the part of the appointing authorities, insufficient publicization of vacancies and the sheer expense of application'. At the higher levels or promotion stages, formal and informal procedures had operated to keep out the SCs, such as ad hoc and temporary positions, elimination through personal evaluation procedures like interviews, personality tests, and unfair adverse entries in confidential records (Guhan 2001: 213). Tables 7.A.1 to 7.A.5 in Appendix 7.A demonstrate that significant gaps in the implementation of quotas in various spheres persist. What is noteworthy is that these gaps exist in central government jobs after over five decades of implementation of the quota system. Also, as one goes down the hierarchy, the representation of SCs–STs increases, with as many as 83 per cent of the cleaners (referred to as 'safaiwalas' in Table 7.A.3) being SCs. The idea of abolishing quotas can meaningfully be mooted only after they have been implemented

---

[10] In 2006, the University of Delhi took some symbolic steps to redress these gaps. It set up an Equal Opportunity Cell, which is mainly geared towards providing equal opportunity of employment and physical access to the differently abled, but also states in its list of objectives 'the implementation of affirmative action towards SC, ST, OBC'. However, its mission statement and list of activities for the last three years of its existence are mainly geared towards the inclusion of physically handicapped and differently abled individuals, which is welcome, but its activities do not indicate any specific attempts to ensure enforcement of AA.

[11] For details, see www.indiastat.com.

in their entirety and have been in place for a decade (to follow Ambedkar's original timeline).

SOME MAJOR CONTROVERSIES

As with AA all over the world, there is a huge debate in India both over whether AA is needed at all, and if needed, if it should be caste-based. Three major constitutional issues have arisen in the court cases over AA:

1. How many places ought to be reserved? Ambedkar was of the view that reservations, in order to be effective, ought to be limited to a minority. In two different rulings, the Supreme Court enacted a ceiling of 50 per cent with the belief that if reserved seats exceed 50 per cent, then some other qualified candidates would be excluded. Galanter (1991) disagrees and argues that 50 per cent is a mechanical rule. It will 'not resolve the tension between the right of all to open merit competition and the right of some to merit selection'. Currently, the combined SC/ST/OBC reservations are less than 50 per cent.

2. Designation of beneficiaries: Quotas for SCs and STs are constitutionally sanctioned and may not be challenged in court. However, it is not so for OBCs, which explains the huge debate and attack over OBC reservations. Constitutionally, caste is not in itself a permissible criterion for discrimination. The Indian Constitution seeks to establish a society that is egalitarian, casteless, and classless, where untouchability has been abolished and caste hierarchy is viewed as a retrograde institution that should not be perpetuated. However, the reality is very different, necessitating caste-based AA for SCs/STs. For OBCs, on the other hand, since the issue is not so straightforward, the MCR, NCBC, and the Supreme Court have developed a set of neutral (that is, not related to caste) criteria: poverty, place of habitation, occupation, income level. But the criteria do not end up remaining completely 'neutral', that is, caste-free, since these get examined for each of the OBCs, so caste does get included.[12]

---

[12] I would like to thank Tom Weisskopf for pointing out that the so-called neutral criteria are not actually neutral.

The announcement of the OBC quota revived the old debate over whether caste should be an indicator of backwardness, or whether other criteria should be used. There is a belief that reservations should be class-based for two reasons. First, if the state accepts caste as the basis for backwardness, it legitimizes the caste system that contradicts secular principles. Second, the traditional caste system (the *jajmani* system) has broken down and contractual relationships have emerged between individuals.[13] Thus, the argument goes, the life chances of an individual in contemporary India are determined by his/her economic condition and not by the membership of any social group. Thus, this position argues that a poor Brahmin and a poor Mahar (a Dalit caste in Maharashtra) would have similar social and economic outcomes that would be in contrast to a rich Brahmin and a rich Mahar. Based on data from Gujarat, Shah (1985) demolishes the latter argument and demonstrates how the objective conditions of different castes are indeed disparate. For instance, controlling for landholding, there is wide diversity in educational attainment by caste. As for the former argument, there is some concern that eventually our goal should be the effective abolition of the caste system and so any system of AA should work towards a weakening of traditional caste ties and affinities.

A variant of this argument is that given the widespread poverty in India, AA only bestows privileges on the beneficiaries that are denied to the rest of the population. Thus, AA is seen not as compensating discrimination, but as the pampering of certain groups for narrow political ends. Needless to state, this view implicitly denies systematic inter-group disparity and discrimination. A more plausible variant of the argument would say that AA policies in practice benefit a relatively privileged set of people within the beneficiary group—that is, the creamy layer. This is the clustering argument, which we will discuss later in the chapter in the section assessing the AA programme.

The Rajasthan state government introduced a proposal to extend quotas for poor upper castes,[14] openly questioning and flouting the raison d'être of the established AA programme. Interestingly, this did

---

[13] For an exposition of this position, see Desai (1984).

[14] Rajasthan Reservation Bill, 2008, extended the spread of quotas by granting 5 per cent quotas in jobs to Gujjars, and 14 per cent to economically weaker sections among the forward castes.

not provoke any seriously adverse media/public reaction, in sharp contrast to the hysterically violent reaction to the announcement of the OBC quota, when an extension of quotas was seen as a deliberate lowering of merit. The implicit assumption underlying this differential reaction would be that poor upper castes are intrinsically meritorious, just backward due to adverse circumstances. It is instructive to note that none of the usual rhetoric about pampering/vote-bank politics accompanied this announcement either.

There is the additional argument that caste matters only in rural areas. In urban areas, the argument goes, due to the possible anonymity and to the prevalence of modern, industrial and service sector contractual relations, labour market outcomes will not be affected by caste affiliation. Indeed, for caste to matter in urban labour markets would be irrational. However, the preceding chapters, notably Chapters 3 and 6, have provided sufficient evidence to bust this myth. To reiterate the points made earlier in the book, the occupational distribution reported in Chapter 3 indicates that while some jatis may have moved away from the traditional occupations, Dalits tend to be overwhelmingly concentrated in the lower end of the occupational spectrum. Additionally, studies (see Chapter 6) confirm the presence of both wage and job discrimination in the private sector, which employs most of the industrial workforce and which is free from the purview of AA.

On the whole, evidence suggests that caste remains an important indicator of backwardness in the present. However, for OBCs, since the varna–jati link is more fluid, and because they did not suffer historical discrimination in the form of untouchability, and also because sections of the OBC community are fairly prosperous (the creamy layer), the caste criterion must be combined with an income ceiling.

3. Is AA by the state permissible outside Sections 15(4) and 16(4)? This leads to the larger question of what kind of AA might be optimal. For instance, should AA be quota- or non-quota-based? If it is quota-based in educational institutions, should qualifying marks be lowered to accommodate beneficiaries?[15] The current position is that

[15] See, for instance, the two points of view in Pinto (1999) and the rejoinder by H. Srikanth (2000).

for admission to most courses, qualifying marks for SC/ST students are lower. While this is done in order to increase the presence of SC/ST students, the long-run merit of this move could be questioned in view of the fact that these students tend not to be able to cope and hence drop out before the course is over. This could be potentially avoided by special assistance during the course, such as remedial teaching programmes, but these exist in very few institutions, most notably at the Indian Institutes of Technology and some university departments, but their reach can and should be expanded.

AFFIRMATIVE ACTION IN THE PRIVATE SECTOR

Another implication of this third question is whether AA should cover only government institutions or should it extend to the private sector as well. This is an increasingly pressing question, in the wake of liberalization and privatization of the Indian economy. The growth rate of organized sector employment has been declining between 1997 and 2004. This has happened mainly due to the decline in employment in the public sector. According to the latest *Economic Survey* of the Government of India (2009–10), employment in establishments covered by the Employment Market Information System of the Ministry of Labour grew at 1.20 per cent per annum during 1983–94 but decelerated to –0.03 per cent per annum during 1994–2007, and this decline was mainly due to a decline in rate of growth of employment in public sector establishments from 1.53 per cent in the earlier period to –0.57 per cent in the later period, whereas the private sector showed acceleration in the pace of growth in employment from 0.44 per cent to 1.3 per cent per annum (p. 275).

Neither the private sector nor the new fully private educational institutions are inclined to implement quotas. Thus, if AA remains confined to Articles 15(4) and 16(4), then steady privatization can, and indeed has, erode AA significantly.

The Prime Minister of India, Manmohan Singh, during the first term of the United Progressive Alliance Government in 2004, set the ball rolling on this question by asking if and how AA could be introduced into the private sector. This was, in the same year (2004–5), followed by another bout of intense public criticism of AA in the media and by the intellectual class, and a restatement of all the ills that AA is supposed to have brought in its wake. In response, the Confederation of Indian Industries (CII) and the Associated Chamber of Commerce (ASSOCHAM) drafted a set of policies in 2008, more as a part of its package of measures designed to ensure 'corporate social responsibility' rather than specifically to implement any kind of AA (defined as specific policies designed to increase representation of under-represented groups). Here we see a classic Catch-22 situation: such measures cannot be implemented until there is data on the social and demographic composition of the employees. And such data will not be collected for fear of exacerbating caste feelings.

EMPIRICAL ASSESSMENTS OF AFFIRMATIVE ACTION

In every country with AA, the opposition to AA in principle is essentially based on meritocratic principles, with the implicit belief that labour markets and other social institutions reward merit and efficiency if allowed to function without hindrance in the form of AA. The preceding chapters have outlined the evidence that busts this myth. There is extensive literature on the international debate and no summary will be attempted here, except to emphasize the following point. Cross-national comparisons in Darity and Deshpande (2003) reveal that, first, in the presence of inter-group disparity, labour markets do not function efficiently. Indeed, there are strong discriminatory losses in earnings among the subaltern groups, the theoretical bases for which can be seen both in the 'statistical discrimination' and the 'taste for discrimination' theories, discussed in Chapter 2.

Second, while nowhere in the world has AA proven to be sufficient to close the gaps between the privileged and the oppressed groups, there is enough evidence to suggest that the gaps would be larger in the absence of AA.[16] A good example is India's northern neighbour, Nepal, the world's only 'Hindu' state until the Maoists captured power in 2008 and established a republic, ending 239 years of monarchy. Its caste composition is dominated by Brahmins and Kshatriyas (Bahun and Chhetris); the number of castes is much smaller than in India. Nepal abolished caste-based discrimination formally in 1963, but had no system of AA and thus, despite the growth of civil society organizations

[16] See Darity and Deshpande (2003).

since the 1990s, many 'hierarchical institutions, especially powerful informal networks, behavioural norms, and expectations remained unchanged' (Bennet 2005: 7).

Though they comprise over 20 per cent of Nepal's population, Dalits possessed only 1 per cent of the country's wealth in 2005 (Center for Human Rights and Global Justice [CHRGJ] 2005: 8). Collectively, Dalits represent 80 per cent of the 'ultra-poor' in Nepal and are highly vulnerable to exploitation (ibid.). Together they own just 1 per cent of arable land, while only 3 per cent of Dalits own more than a hectare of land.

Unlike in India, labour market data are available by caste and the disparity in the occupational distribution is striking. In 2004, Dalits in the rural areas were basically extremely poor, subsistence farmers, and in the urban areas were concentrated at the lowest end of the ladder. There was virtually no Dalit middle class in existence. Interestingly, because Nepal's government is the country's largest employer, discrimination at the workplace directly indicts the government. This suggests that while AA may not be the ideal remedy, its absence, that is, letting labour markets function without hindrance, does not correct for exclusion either. This should not be surprising any more, given the evidence on discrimination presented in the earlier chapters.

Lately, particularly with the announcement of the OBC quota in India, there has been a spate of interventions by economists, some to question the legitimacy of quotas, most to question AA altogether.[17] However, it is interesting that none of these contributions are based on an actual empirical assessment of AA. Thus, until the Deshpande and Weisskopf (2010) study, there was not a single empirical assessment of AA jobs in India. Galanter (1991) has attempted one of the most comprehensive explorations of the Indian AA programme. A monetary cost–benefit evaluation is not possible because of the manner in which the Indian programme is formulated. However, he undertakes a crude assessment of the SC/ST AA programme and some of his major findings are as follows:

• The programme has shown substantial redistributive effects in that access to education and jobs is spread wider in the caste spectrum

---

[17] See, for example, the arguments of Somanathan (2006) and Sundaram (2007).

than earlier, although redistribution is not spread evenly throughout the beneficiary groups. There is evidence of clustering, but Galanter believes that these reflect structural factors, since the better situated enjoy a disproportionate share of the benefits in any government programme, not just in AA programmes.

• The vast majority of Dalits are not directly affected by AA, but reserved jobs bring a manifold increase in the number of families liberated from subservient roles.

• In the short run, beneficiaries might get singled out and experience social rejection in offices, college hostels,[18] and other set-ups where they are introduced through AA. However, in the long run, education and jobs weaken the stigmatizing association of Dalits with ignorance and incompetence. Moreover, 'resentment of preferences may magnify hostility to these groups, but rejection of them exists independently of affirmative action programmes' (Galanter 1991).

• AA has kept the beneficiary groups and their problems visible to the educated public, but it has not motivated widespread concern for their inclusion beyond what is mandated by government policy.

Thus, Galanter concludes that AA has been a partial success. It has accelerated the growth of a middle class and SC/ST members have been brought into central roles considered unimaginable a few decades ago.[19]

PRODUCTIVITY IMPACT OF AFFIRMATIVE ACTION

In an attempt to empirically study the effects of AA in the labour market, Deshpande and Weisskopf (2010) chose to focus on the Indian Railways to assess if AA has impacted productivity negatively. The study covers the period from 1980 to 2002 for eight of the nine railway zones in existence during the period, and uses a variety of econometric

[18] There is no explicit AA in college hostels (dormitories); AA in colleges leads to entry of SC/ST students in college hostels.

[19] However, even this crude calculation will not work for assessing OBC reservations because, first, OBC quota is much more recent, and two, OBCs are not stigmatized in the same way as SCs because their traditional occupations do not put them in humiliating and subservient roles like the SCs. Thus, OBC reservations have to be assessed very differently from SC–ST reservations.

techniques to examine the impact of AA on total output and on total factor productivity. The paper contains all the details on data and methodology; I am outlining the broad methodology for the purposes of this chapter. One of our methods consisted of estimating a Cobb–Douglas production function with a variety of specifications for all the inputs as well as the output. The key input of interest for assessing AA would be labour, which we specified in many different forms: separating SC–ST and Other workers; using all workers and additionally using total SC–ST proportion and SC–ST proportion in A and B category jobs, which are the top administrative and managerial positions,[20] as independent explanatory variables; and using all workers as one of the explanatory variables and correlating the residual from this regression with the total proportion of SC–ST and with the proportion of SC–ST employees in A and B category jobs.

We also tried an alternative approach to investigate the impact of AA on productivity in the Indian Railways: a two-stage procedure in which the first stage was the use of the non-parametric method called Data Envelopment Analysis (DEA) of productivity changes, and the second stage was an econometric analysis of factors potentially influencing those productivity changes. DEA allows one to analyse productivity in the context of a pooled data set of time series data on inputs and outputs for multiple production units within a given industry. It does not require specification of any particular functional relationship between input and output variables; and it allows one to work with more than one output variable as well as multiple input variables. Essentially, it fits a frontier, representing technical efficiency, enveloping the outermost data points. Because the frontier is generated from the data, it is not based on stochastic processes and therefore does not produce any measures of the statistical significance of the results obtained.

For the first stage of our alternative approach, we tried two different variants. In Variant One, we initially used DEA to estimate annual changes in total factor productivity ('tfpch') from 1980–1 to 2001–2 in each railway zone, and for the second stage we sought to explain our estimated 'tfpch' values (for each zone and pair of years) in terms of several variables that appeared likely to influence annual total factor

[20] Indian government jobs are categorized into four types: A, B, C, and D, with A at the top.

productivity change. The independent variables consisted of three that were designed to capture the quality of the three types of inputs ('effective' labour, capital, and fuel) and one to reflect the scale of production. For labour quality we used 'proportion of SC–ST in A+B jobs', since our primary focus was on the impact of SC–ST as opposed to other labour on productivity.

In Variant Two, for the first stage we did a new DEA run, in which we used the 'effective' measures of the capital stock and fuel input variables instead of the unadjusted 'raw' measures of the first variant. For the second stage of this variant we simply correlated the estimated 'tfpch' values from the first stage with the various SC–ST labour variables.

Analysing an extensive data set on the operations of one of the largest employers in the public sector in India, the Indian Railways, we found no evidence whatsoever to support the claim of critics of AA that increasing the proportion of SC and ST employees will adversely impact productivity or productivity growth. On the contrary, some of the results of our analysis suggest that the proportion of SC and ST employees in the upper (A+B) job categories is positively associated with productivity and productivity growth.

Our finding of such positive associations in the case of A and B jobs is especially relevant to debates about the effects of AA on behalf of members of SC and ST communities, for two reasons. First, the impact of AA on productivity is likely to be much more affected by the efficacy with which high-level managerial and decision-making jobs are carried out than the efficacy with which lower-level semi-skilled and unskilled jobs are fulfilled. Thus, critics of reservations are likely to be, and indeed are, much more concerned about the potentially adverse effects of reservations at the highest decision-making levels that at lower levels. Second, it is precisely in the A and B jobs—far more than in C and D jobs—that the proportions of SC–ST employees would not have risen had it not been for quotas. Indeed, reservations have been indispensable for raising the proportion of SC–ST employees. Even without reservations, one would expect substantial numbers of SC–ST applicants to be hired into C and D jobs, especially the D category cleaning staff; but without reservations, very few SC–ST applicants would have been able to attain jobs at the A and B levels.

While the focus of our paper is on productivity, it also examines some other issues. For instance, critics of AA have alleged that the frequency of Indian Railway accidents is likely to be linked to quotas because reservation policies result in a larger proportion of less competent railway officials and lower overall staff morale.[21] Railway accidents are obviously an important indicator of poor railway performance; they generate adverse consequences that go far beyond the loss of damaged equipment and the failure to complete a planned passenger or freight trip. We, therefore, thought it useful to see if trends in Indian Railway accident rates could be related in any way to trends in SC–ST labour proportions.

Correlating the all-India yearly railway accident rate (the total number of accidents per million train km) over the period of our study (1980–2002) with the corresponding all-India figures for the proportion of SC–ST employees in total employment, we found correlation coefficients of –0.69 for all employees and –0.93 (both correlations significant at 1 per cent) for employees in the upper-level A and B categories.[22] The second, higher correlation is the most relevant both because Indian Railways' employees serving in management and professional positions are especially responsible for guarding against accidents and because the data on SC–ST employees in the C and D categories fail to count many SC–ST employees who do not declare themselves as such.

Our finding of a highly significant negative correlation between the all-India accident rate and the SC–ST proportion of A+B category employment results from the fact that the former has been declining and the latter rising (both fairly steadily) over the last few decades. This is strong evidence that higher SC–ST employment proportions are not resulting in higher accident rates—unless, of course, there are other likely determinants of the accident rate that have also shown steady trends (and the appropriate sign) over the same period. The most plausible alternative explanations for decreasing accident rates are increasing electrification of signals, improvement in track quality, and safer track crossings (including better-guarded level crossings and more

---

[21] See, for example, 'Job Reservation in Railways and Accidents', *Indian Express*, 19 September 1990 (cited by D. Kumar 1990: 301).

[22] Source: Government of India, Ministry of Railways, *Annual Statistical Statements*.

bridges over tracks). There is indeed evidence of positive time trends in each of these alternative determinants.[23] There is insufficiently detailed data, however, to include such variables in a multivariate regression analysis of accident rates. While such an analysis might well counter the notion that higher SC–ST employment proportions actually promote greater safety, it seems unlikely that it could undermine the conclusion that higher SC–ST employment proportions do no harm.

The results[24] that we have obtained from our analysis of productivity in the Indian Railways are consistent with the results from productivity studies in the US, in that there is no statistically significant evidence that AA in the labour market has an adverse effect on productivity. Our results are stronger, however, in that we do find some suggestive evidence that AA in the labour market actually has a favourable effect—in particular, that the growing proportion of SC–ST employees hired into high-level A and B category railway jobs, largely through India's reservation policies, has contributed to greater overall railway productivity.

It was beyond the scope of our paper to explain just how and why AA in the labour market may have such a favourable effect. We believe, however, that the answer may be found in one or more of the following suggestions that others have advanced to explain such a finding. Individuals from marginalized groups may well display especially high levels of work motivation when they succeed in attaining decision-making and managerial positions, because of the fact that they have reached these positions in the face of claims that they are not sufficiently capable—in consequence of which they may have a strong desire to prove their detractors wrong. Or individuals from marginalized groups may simply believe that they have to work doubly hard to prove that they are just as good as their peers. Having greater numbers of SC and ST managers and professionals working in high-level A+B positions in the Indian Railways might also serve to increase productivity because their community backgrounds make them more effective in supervising and motivating SC and ST workers in C and D jobs.[25]

---

[23] See Ministry of Railways (2007), esp. pp. 18–25.

[24] From this paragraph to the end of this section, the material corresponds very closely to the paper since the conclusions of our paper need to be stated clearly to readers who might otherwise not access the original paper.

[25] This recalls the arguments in favour of AA in the US educational institutions

Finally, improvements in organizational productivity may well result from the greater diversity of perspectives and talents made possible by the integration of members of previously marginalized groups into high-level decision-making teams.[26]

ASSESSING AFFIRMATIVE ACTION IN HIGHER EDUCATION

Weisskopf (2004) provides a comprehensive comparison of AA policies in the US and India. A substantial part of that discussion is focused on AA policies in Indian universities. From his evidence, as well as from other studies reported in this chapter, it is clear that a large majority of SC–ST candidates owe their presence in institutions of higher education to reservation policies. In other words, these students would not be receiving higher education if it were not for AA policies. While empirical studies on effects of AA in higher education are very few due to lack of data, the few studies that exist point towards the fact that SC–ST students find it hard to succeed in competitive entrance examinations due to past handicaps (lack of good-quality schooling, lack of access to special tutorial or coaching centres that prepare candidates for open competitive examinations, and so forth).

Evidence presented in Weisskopf (2004) suggests that at least half the seats reserved for SCs and at least two-thirds of the seats reserved for STs remain unfilled, if all institutions of higher education are considered together. He argues that this is because of 'wastage' (dropping out) as well as 'stagnation' (repeating courses because of failure or attendance gaps) at *prior levels of education*. While these are very serious problems, the real pity is that a mechanical approach to the issue of AA means that no effort is made to understand the basic underlying factors that cause dropouts and stagnation (which are discrimination and deprivation and lack of access to good-quality education at prior levels), and thus no serious efforts are made to remedy them. Since the overwhelming opinion remains anti-AA, the larger the proportion of dropouts, the more it 'proves' the contention of the anti-AA

---

made to the Supreme Court by US military officers, who want to avoid having just white men in charge of troops that are disproportionately of colour (see Weisskopf 2004: preface).

[26] Page (2007) shows convincingly how groups that display a wide range of perspectives outperform groups of like-minded experts.

opinion—that quotas are costly and useless. As a matter of fact, there are specific remedial measures that could be applied to address these problems: bridge courses, special courses in mathematics and English (the two areas with the maximum gaps between SCs and Others), summer courses, and so forth. The University Grants Commission, a government body designed to regulate higher education, has special funds allocated for these courses, but these funds remain unutilized for the most part, both because of lack of awareness about these sources of funds and, more seriously, because of a lack of serious will to make the AA programme succeed. Given that there is no monitoring and no penalties for lackadaisical implementation, institutions, even those at the feet of the central government, can turn a blind eye to the issue of unfilled quota seats.

So far, the only substantive quantitative study of the impact of AA in higher education is by Bertrand et al. (2008). They focus on individuals applying to an engineering college, via a competitive entrance examination, in one Indian state in 1996. Engineering colleges are among the most prestigious educational institutions in India. They first took a census of all students applying to this engineering college and found that the qualifying scores for admission were roughly 480/900 for upper-caste individuals, 419 for OBCs, and 182 for SCs. These score disparities provide elementary support for the hypothesis that lower-caste students would not be able to perform in colleges and will not benefit from AA because of the mismatch between their basic skill levels and the skill requirements of engineering education (the mismatch hypothesis). This could lead to wastage and dropouts. To better understand the outcomes across caste groups, the authors then interviewed about 700 households from the census of all applicants between 2004 and 2006 (approximately eight to ten years after the entrance examination). They surveyed both the applicant and their parents to gauge life outcomes including income and occupation, job satisfaction, social networks, and caste identity.

Their first finding is that contrary to popular belief, caste-based targeting does result in the targeting of individuals who are more economically disadvantaged—the parental income of upper-caste students displaced by AA is Rs 14,088, compared to Rs 8,340 among displacing lower-caste students. Similarly, 41 per cent of displaced students come from a household in which the head holds at least a master's degree, compared to only 14 per cent of displacing students. Fifty-nine per cent of displaced students attended an English private school, compared to only 35 per cent of displacing students.

Their second finding is in terms of labour market outcomes. They find that despite much lower basic skills (as measured by scores on the entrance exam), those who are admitted through AA economically benefit from attending engineering college. Depending on the specifications, attending engineering college increases lower-caste members' monthly income by Rs 3,700 to Rs 6,200. This corresponds to an increase of 40 per cent to 70 per cent. In other words, they find no evidence of the 'mismatch hypothesis'. In addition to improving earning potential, they find that AA could also increase access to more satisfying careers, measured in terms of job quality and satisfaction. These two findings (of higher earnings and better job quality) resonate with the findings contained in Bowen and Bok's (1998) seminal study of long-term benefits of AA in the US context.

However, they also find evidence of the 'creamy layer' phenomenon, discussed in detail later. Specifically, they find that those from higher socio-economic backgrounds within the lower-caste groups benefit more. Finally, they also test for AA's effect on applicant attitudes and, somewhat surprisingly, find that upper-caste students displaced by AA do not end up with more negative attitudes towards lower castes or towards AA in general. However, the lower-caste students who benefit from AA programmes end up being stronger supporters for AA, something that my own study, reported later, also finds.

QUALITATIVE ASSESSMENT OF AFFIRMATIVE ACTION

Before I embarked on the quantitative exercise, I was also involved in qualitative assessments of AA. The Deshpande and Newman (2007) study (discussed in detail in Chapter 6) specifically elicited respondents' views on the AA programme, both from the Dalit and the non-Dalit students. This section reports some of the responses and, in the process, brings to the fore the deep divisions on this question. For reasons stated in the previous chapter, I am reproducing a part of the paper here, since it is based on interviews that cannot be paraphrased.

Reservations are Critical

Almost without exception, the Dalits in the sample endorsed the
purpose of reservation policy and were convinced that without it,
they would have had no chance to obtain a higher degree. 'I am here
because of reservations,' noted Mukesh, a political science student at
Jawaharlal Nehru University (JNU).

Because of my background, even though I had the talent, I could not study
because of financial problems. We never got a chance to buy books, to get tuition.
But we got through because of reservations. I am ahead by a few steps because of
reservations. There is nothing wrong with that.

Indeed, for Mukesh, quotas in higher education not only enabled
his ascent in the university world, they literally enabled him and his
fellow reservation students to 'open their mouths', meaning speak their
minds and 'go to the centre of society', where they can 'meet other
people ... and get a platform'. The silence imposed by marginality,
caste prejudice (enforced by atrocities, especially in rural areas), and
poverty is broken by introducing these Dalit students to another world
and a different future. They are well aware that without this social
policy intervention, they could have remained stuck in a life that would
never provide the kind of options they see before them now.

For those aware of the history of the political struggle that resulted
in the creation of this quota system, reservation is seen as a noble
commitment to equality, struck by the hero of the Dalit social
movement, B.R. Ambedkar. This history is sacred to Dalit students,
for it represents the first victory in a long and unfinished struggle for
human rights and full equality. As Bir Singh, another politics student
at JNU explained, that campaign remains as vital as ever as a source of
inspiration for the poor and excluded:

Ambedkar ... used his education to free the SC/ST and OBC and to ... solve their
problems ... on the basis of equality, liberty and fraternity. He wanted to make
them live with self respect and why he was able to do that? Because of education,
because of the participation in this society in the form of reservation in every
sphere of life.

Education has created an ideal image in the minds of those people who are
illiterate, an example where a person (girl or boy) who comes from a rural area
[can] enjoy taking reservation in education institutions. He is learning, reading
and becoming a very high status profile person. That gives an example which ...

gives courage and pride to the rest of the illiterate, poor people, who are not getting [an] education, who are suppressed socially and educationally.

These opportunities are critical not only because they promote social mobility, but also because reservations literally rescue Dalits from a lifetime of exploitation at the hands of landlords, abusive employers, and neighbours who can turn on them without provocation and remind them forcefully of their subordinate status. Legal guarantees in the form of anti-atrocity regulations mean nothing in the context of weak enforcement.

Karunanidhi, a student of history at JNU, comes from a rural area near Madurai in Tamil Nadu and is all too familiar with life under the heel. 'I am from a very remote background,' he explained. Without reservations, he would have been stuck in a community where his safety was at risk.

In my [native] place ... [it] is very brutal, very uncivilized. They can kill anybody for a simple reason ... Because of reservations in higher education, I am here. I could not even imagine being here at JNU without reservations ...

After my graduation [from undergraduate school], I worked continuously from 6 to 8 hours [in a factory near his home]. If there is work, we have to work, we cannot delay. 'Sir, I am tired I worked so long!' You can't say that. If they call you, you have to go and work there whether you are sick or not, whether your father is sick or not ... This kind of exploitation is there ... I was working in Tiruppur[27] [and the] rules and regulations of the company were on the wall ... in English and Tamil. But whatever goes on in the company is just the opposite ... There is no clean toilet ... no hygienic environment [in the factory] for the workers.

The girls are really exploited by the [hiring] agents and higher positioned people in the factory. If these people asked girls to go to bed with them, they cannot [be] denied. They force the girls, though these people are educated. I think educated people do this kind of exploitation more than others.

Reservations rescued Karunanidhi from a future of this kind.

The policy has always been important to those at the bottom of a social pecking order that was resistant to change, grounded as it was in abiding caste hierarchies and the traditional, pernicious practice of pollution taboos that surrounded the lives of untouchables, especially in the more remote rural regions of India. Today, however, the importance of reservations—and the fear that their impact may diminish—is

[27] Tiruppur is a rapidly growing, important garment production/assembly centre in Tamil Nadu.

heightened by the recognition that the public sector is shrinking. The one sphere where these students could hope to find respectable employment is shedding jobs as liberalization puts pressure on government budgets. Globalization is creating enormous opportunities for the Indian economy, all of which fall into the private sector. High growth rates in corporate India have opened opportunities of the kind rarely seen before and it is common knowledge that the big money is to be made there. The public sector is often seen as a backwater of inefficiency, and students who can manage it would be flocking to the high technology sector. This perception altered substantially with the onset of the global economic crisis, even though the Indian private sector did not experience the magnitude of retrenchments and lay-offs as its counterpart in the developed industrialized world. In the last couple of years, public sector jobs have regained some degree of desirability as they offer income and tenure security.

Our interview subjects were well aware of this trend of the increasing economic might of the private sector and worried by it since reservations do not presently apply to the private sector. Even if they are willing to trade lucrative opportunities (that may or may not be available to them on the grounds of bias or skill) for the accessibility and security of the public sector, this alternative is disappearing. The solution, they argue, is to see reservations extended to the private sector, to continue Ambedkar's mission of social justice to the domain where all the action is for the foreseeable future.

Amit, a political science student at JNU, argued that 'both sectors should have reservation'.

Now in India, it is the private sector that is getting bigger. Even in Delhi, just see the size of the public sector, it is very small. So SC/ST, OBC and minorities should all get reservations. If they don't ... where will these people adjust?

This view was universally shared by the Dalit students for whom reservations policy is nothing more than a form of social engineering designed to address centuries of oppression and discrimination, extreme inequities in the distribution of educational opportunity, and the formation of a huge class of Indian citizens who are not equipped to compete without this assistance. These are not matters of history. Students cite countless examples from their own experience where they have been interrogated about their caste identities, castigated by prospective employers for their support of reservations, subjected to harassment or disrespect, and denied jobs (as far as they know) solely on account of their caste background.

As long as this injustice persists, they argue, reservations will be needed. The policy levels the playing field at the vital choke points of social mobility. They are not special privileges that unfairly advantage; they are compensation for historic and contemporary injustice that creates some measure of equality in outcomes. As Bhim, a reservation student studying Korean at JNU, points out, social engineering is necessary to modernize the country, to move it past a traditionalist, antiquated social system ridden with superstitious beliefs that are themselves anti-meritocratic. 'Because of reservations,' he notes, 'people of backward classes are developing.'

I think there should be reservation in both private and public sectors. Upper caste people are holding important positions in both sectors. In public sector all the positions at the top level are held by upper caste people and they are also filling these positions with their relatives. If we are getting any jobs, we are getting only low level jobs.

Reservation is being misused by some people like one of my classmates, who was from the general category [but] made fake certificates [for himself] of SC/ST and captured one seat that [was supposed to be] for SC candidates. So there is need of proper implementation of policy. [Still], because of this policy, people are coming from remote areas, they are getting admission, doing their courses and progressing well in their lives.

Of course, these students are aware that their sense of legitimacy is not shared by the dominant classes and castes in India. Reservation policy is condemned for punishing innocent non-reservation students for the damage done in the past, reinforcing caste lines rather than striving for a caste-free society, and exempting Dalits from the rigours of market competition. Critics argue that reservations replace one form of discrimination (against Dalits) with another, equally pernicious form (against general category students or workers).

These perspectives are unconvincing from the viewpoint of the Dalits in our sample, though, who argue that the most powerful special privileges actually accrue to high caste Hindus who can tap into exclusive social networks, bank on the cultural capital their families bequeath to them, or pay the bribes that are demanded by employers for access to jobs. As Rajesh, a student of Korean language and culture at JNU, notes these forms of advantage are never criticized as unfair:

Some people get admission in medical [school] after giving Rs 25–30 lakh [in bribes] ... They don't get admission on the basis of capability. The entry of these people is not ever opposed, but people are against the SC/ST/OBCs who get in on quota. They say that these SC/ST/OBC doctors are [incompetent], leaving their scissors and thread inside the patients' bodies during surgery. But people who [gain] admission through capitation fees, paying huge donations, why are these things [not] said about them?

The Creamy Layer and the Rural Dalit[28]

Although reservation quotas are based on caste identity, one of the most striking findings from our first round of follow-up interviews was the recognition of a pronounced 'class divide' within the Dalit student population. Many of the students we interviewed complained about the advantages accruing to what they call the 'creamy layer'. Specifically, the term was used to refer to the advantages accrued by Dalits from urban backgrounds, whose parents had already been the beneficiaries of quotas in education and employment. This creamy layer is composed of students who are in the second and third generation to benefit from the existence of reservations. Their parents are civil servants or teachers and they have grown up in a more cosmopolitan setting than their rural counterparts. We are not speaking here of absolute wealth or prestige, bur rather relative advantage. As Ashok, a Dalit student of Sociology at JNU, pointed out, 'there is a gap'.

Urban people, or those whose parents are well placed and well to do family, they used to get public school education and all. In comparison of all these rural background people, urban people are getting more advantage. They are securing most of the reserved seats in higher education ...

From the perspective of the poorest Dalits in our study, the more advantaged seem to take the opportunities afforded by reservation for granted. Jai Singh, a politics student at JNU, comes from a rural area where few students have been able to compete for the reserved spaces in urban universities.

Only few people are getting benefits from the reservation. OK, from my region, I don't know it was at all expected that I could come to this place [JNU]. I belong

---

[28] Although this emerged out of our study, this section is not contained in any published version of Deshpande and Newman (2007), or Newman and Deshpande (2010).

to such a background that it was just not possible for me. But as I worked hard, I could know about all things and started teaching tuitions and all.[29] Only few people can come here even though there is reservation. You will find drop outs and all. Only giving reservations and making no other provisions, like financial assistance or remedial teaching—that are leading to this [dropping out].

SC/STs are getting 15% reservation ... They will recruit only in that 15% category, where most competitive reserved people are getting admission and others ... are getting eliminated. In the reserved category only few people are getting benefits.

There are some who because of their financial crisis or other things like humiliation ... are entering a very different mind set. Frustrated ... and not able to do their work.

The gap between urban and rural Dalits is particularly problematic for girls, as Jyoti sees it, because rural parents tend to be culturally conservative and withhold their daughters if they think they will be exposed to unacceptable conditions in order to get an education:

There is a gender discrimination also, social taboos, you can say ... Particularly girls. Here they generally get urban exposure and being in cities, they can't cope all of a sudden because they come from a rural cultural background ... Their parents come to see places like this and they think that this place is not suitable for higher education.

Dalits from remote areas see themselves as doubly disadvantaged, by caste bias and by poverty. In comparison to Dalits from civil service families, it is harder for poor, rural Dalits to attend secondary school in the first place, since their families need their labour, and the school fees and costs for books or boarding are prohibitive. They struggle out of rural areas burdened by social isolation, ill equipped in terms of cultural capital to navigate an urban megalopolis like Delhi, lacking social networks that more privileged caste-makes rely on. The cosmopolitan panache that can make or break a job interview is harder for them to acquire and they see barriers before them as a result as they try to move in the labour market. Although most of the reservation students recognized that their fluency in English—an important skill for success in higher education and later in professional employment—is weak relative to high-caste students, those of rural origin see themselves as even farther behind in this regard.

---

[29] University-educated middle-class individuals often give private lessons to school students to earn some extra money. This is a fairly common practice, irrespective of the caste background of the tutor.

Yashpal, a Dalit student in political science at JNU, understands very well how his background has placed him in a difficult position relative to others who arrived at the university with stronger academic backgrounds. He is under pressure to make the most of the credentials he is trying to obtain and to have fallback plans in case his dreams do not materialize. His family is depending on him to make it for his own sake and for theirs:

For the last several years, I was not able to read properly and I could not score a good division like a general category student. Because of backwardness, we have to struggle for money and to study. So I think we need some special technical knowledge, computer knowledge so that in case the academic career fails, we have something. I am trying for an academic career but I don't have sufficient training for that .... I need so many books. I need to purchase so many things, travel to so many places.

Although reservation policy may help to gain them entrance to a university programme, it is not a financial aid programme and students are on their own when it comes to paying the costs of a university education. University fees are nominal, but the cost of living on or near the campus, of feeding themselves, of paying for books can simply outstrip the resources of students from poor, rural families. Indeed, they often find themselves under pressure to send money home as they are usually the most privileged members of their families.[30] Karunanidhi, the history student at JNU from Madurai discussed earlier, points out that he has to bear his family's needs in mind as he scrambles to take care of his own financial needs:

My family condition is very poor, so I had to work for my family as they're thinking I am the responsible person to take care of the family. I had to work, but I wanted to do further study.

For Karunanidhi, the provision of admissions quota has made the difference between a life of poverty and a life of possibility. Yet the financial hardship he faces threatens to derail his studies, or put him at a disadvantage when out of necessity he has to search for work during his university years. Facing additional academic burdens—often the need for remedial education to come up to par—while bearing additional

---

[30] We are reminded here of parallel findings in *The Source of the River*, which points to the differential impact of financial distress, medical problems, death in the family, and other problems that beset minority students more often than white students in American universities. See Massey et al. (2003).

responsibility is a recipe for failure, and many reservation students fail to graduate for these reasons. Students from a more comfortable background face fewer challenges and, in the view of their poorer counterparts, may even come to take reservation seats for granted, as something of a birthright. Narender, a reserved category political science at JNU explains:

> If I have got reservation and I have become an IAS officer, my son will think that, I have every resource. People like my son, they will get this benefit, the so-called creamy layer. They become complacent because they have everything; they are not struggling now.
>
> You need to have good relations with certain people, who can become mediators. If you don't have that, and to do that you need to come from a very well to family, those whose fathers, mothers are quite well off. But for people like me, whose father, mother are completely illiterate, no one from the family has ever gone to big places like Delhi. No one is working in any public sector or private sector. All are daily laborers. It is a very, very big problem.

Here the poorer reservation students echo sentiments expressed by Indian employers who argue against the continuation of reservations on the grounds that they have become an inherited privilege, not a source of 'uplift' for those who are struggling against the odds. Karunanidhi certainly notices people who take their university placements for granted and do not work very hard and contrasts them sharply to students like himself, for whom the quotas represent the chance of a lifetime:

> After getting admission through reservation, people [from my background] study a lot, they are getting jobs ... Some people are also there [who] got admission through reservation. They don't study properly, they think in higher courses we [will] also get reservations and in jobs too. So there is no need of hard work. The problem lie[s] here ...

Students in our study are universally in favour of reservations, but are on the fence over whether caste alone should be the qualifying characteristic. They see a new elite (again in terms of relative advantage) developing through multi-generational usage of reservation and wonder whether this is truly fair or sufficiently appreciated. At a minimum, they argue for the critical addition of financial aid and the provision of more remedial education in order to make it more likely that the 'truly disadvantaged' will succeed.

Equal Opportunity

Two distinct positions were evident among the general category students with respect to quotas aimed at increasing the representation of Dalits, STs, and OBCs in higher education and employment. The first simply rejects the notion that this is appropriate at all, since the reservation policy is deemed a violation of fairness principles and therefore an unfair tipping of the scales in what is meant to be a competition on the basis of merit. A variant of this view sees quotas as perfectly appropriate, but not if given along caste lines. Instead, economic deprivation or social backwardness should be the appropriate test. Here we see lines of convergence with many Dalit students from rural areas who also resent the application of reservation to 'the creamy layer' within their own caste.

The second recognizes the legitimacy and purpose of reservation and seems to be enhanced by the interactive relations between Dalit and high-caste students. The more conservative posture falls in line with Royster's findings among white working-class students. The more liberal position emerges from contact and social relations of the kind that would develop as a positive by-product of desegregation. Indeed, when advocates in the US argue for diversity in higher education, they make the point that mixing students up and ensuring that classrooms represent a rainbow of experience will enrich learning and create tolerance. Both outcomes are clear in our sample.

Akhilesh, a sociology general student from JNU, exemplifies the conservative reaction to quotas. 'I am not very happy with the Indian government actually bringing in such reservation,' he complained.

I feel that the people who actually need it the most do not get it. There should be a proper identification of who needs it. Since it is absolutely impossible for the Indian government to develop the skill to look for such people, they are giving it to the wrong people. Implementing it means they are actually dividing society. When we are looking for harmony, we are looking towards unity being in the same country.

I think such barriers should not be allowed because when we are competing, we should compete on the basis of merit. Today one person is getting into IIT [Indian Institute of Technology] with no brains whatsoever, just by virtue of reservations. Whereas certain excellent students are not getting into IIT because general quota is full ...

In jobs, also the same thing. Somebody who is an SC ... gets the job and somebody like me who is not getting a job because I don't have any caste certificate ... It should be equal because we are all living in the same country. If you can really identify the poorest people who have very low annual income ... I think then there is some reason to support reservation.

As this quote suggests, Akhilesh objects to reservations on a number of grounds. First and foremost, they are benefiting a generation whose parents have already moved up in the social structure and have been able to give them benefits denied to other, much poorer and more remote young people. Second, unqualified students are displacing highly qualified students in the race to the top of the educational heap. Many who share this view argue strenuously that the application of reservations will destroy the competitiveness of the Indian economy and drive away foreign investors because of the privileges insured by reservation. Hence, they fuse personal exclusion with a national downfall in the making.

Other critics of reservations argue that the policy may indeed be positive—in the sense that it redresses tremendous inequities—but ends up being a colossal waste because the high dropout rates that SC and ST students suffer from negate their impact. These places could have been taken by non-reservation students who would complete their demanding courses, but instead are taken by people who had almost no chance by virtue of poor preparation. Kavita, an economics student at the University of Delhi, was sympathetic in many ways to the cause of reducing inequality, but discouraged by the outcomes on both sides. 'When I was a student,' she explained, 'there were about 80 of us in college. Out of these, about 20 were from the quota.'

But by the time we reached the third year, virtually all of the reserved students dropped out, because they could not clear [pass] the courses ... Reservation should be given to them only in things that help them gain employment. If the cut off [on entrance exams] is 90% and you are admitting a person with 35% or 40% in a course like econ, medical or engineering, you very well know that he/she cannot be. He is not fit to clear the course.

This student went on to explain that forms of social segregation inside the universities did not help matters. 'They are not treated well,' she remembered, 'when they go to colleges.'

[SC/ST students] have separate tables to lunch in college [dorms]. They get separate treatment. I don't know whether these people actually gain out of these quotas because [of] lots of stress. OK, there have been people who completed their degree, but see in our college, there were hardly any ... General category students who were eligible could not get admission and had to go to other colleges or get into worse courses ... So this reservation policy is not achieving its objectives at all.

What is the value, she asks, of a policy that produces dropouts and deprives the capable of a place because they lack a quota on their side? This is a view many non-reservation students embrace.

But they are not a monolithic voice. On the other side of the equation are non-reserved students for whom equality is a high principle and the barriers to achieving it for historically oppressed peoples clear enough. They embrace the purpose of reservation and see in it the possibilities of upward mobility. Among these supporters, there are differences of opinion nonetheless about the effectiveness of reservations for some of the same reasons that critics voice: high dropout rates. The lesson to be learned for these more progressive students, though, is not to abandon reservations, but redouble efforts to address educational inequality at much younger ages. Without a massive commitment to improving primary school education, they argue, we cannot really expect reservations to succeed. If not for reasons of equity, then for reasons of efficiency, differential investment is required.

Dalit support for AA in both higher education and jobs is unanimous and overwhelming, against the backdrop of discriminatory tendencies and their relative handicaps. At the same time, many (though hardly all) join many of their general category counterparts in arguing that either reservations should be more targeted (towards poor and rural Dalits, rather than second- or third-generation recipients of quota admissions, who are viewed as an internal 'creamy layer') or that reservations should be coupled with generous financial aid. The search for the 'truly disadvantaged' continues in India (as it does in all countries with AA), with complex political agendas in the mix.[31]

---

[31] Were this to be explored fully, one would have to take seriously the claim that urban Dalits from civil servant families are relatively advantaged over their poor, rural counterparts, but still as a significant disadvantage in competing for managerial and professional jobs compared to their high-caste counterparts. The parallel point has been made in the US context. Some have complained that middle and upper class black students are given the benefit of affirmative action, while poor whites are not. Yet proponents of affirmative action have argued that middle class blacks continue to face racial barriers and are less economically secure than their middle class white

Expectedly, the ideal jobs for the Dalit students are either administrative/civil service or teaching jobs, which are subject to reservation quotas, while high-caste students tend to look to the private sector where wages are quite a bit higher. This may reflect an anticipatory sense of where reservation students will be welcome, or at least find a 'fair shake'. It may also reflect family traditions. In any case, the implications for earnings over the life course are non-trivial. Dalit students who find themselves in public service will undoubtedly see more security, but at much lower wages.

Reservation students experience their employment interviews in a far more negative vein than their non-reserved counterparts. Dalit students often felt that these interviews were pro forma or were put on the defensive because of their caste background, even for private sector jobs which are not subject to quotas and where caste is not supposed to matter.

Direct questions about caste affiliation are rare for both Dalit and non-Dalit students, but the catch-all question on 'family background' is extensively used by employers to gauge the social and economic status of the applicant. One sees a clear class divide among Dalits, with those from rural backgrounds with relatively less educated parents at a clear disadvantage compared to their urban, second- or third-generation AA beneficiary counterparts. Financial constraints are a serious stumbling block for rural Dalits and the good fortune of admission to the university is followed by significant financial burdens both for self-support and for contributions to their natal families' survival.

There are two clear views on quotas among the non-Dalits. One, expectedly, in sharp opposition but the other, the more progressive view, more cognizant of disparities and discrimination, recognizing the need for reservations but arguing for better focus and outreach.

LIMITATIONS OF A QUOTA-BASED APPROACH

Given the nature of India's AA policy, quotas are naturally more relevant in urban areas, even though their existence provides the possibility of

---

counterparts, owing to wealth differences (controlling for income). See especially Conley (1999), and Oliver and Shapiro (2006).

obtaining formal sector government jobs that rural educated Dalits can aspire to. However, not all rural Dalits might be interested in this avenue for their livelihoods. They, more often than not, might not have the desire or the opportunity to secure the education levels necessary to obtain jobs via quotas. Thus, if economic and social marginalization of Dalits is to be countered, other welfare-improving measures in rural areas have to be as much on the agenda as quotas are. Noteworthy among these are land reforms and rapid generation of non-farm employment, especially in the small-scale manufacturing sector. The Chinese experience demonstrates the tremendous potential of both these measures—land reforms during the 1949 to 1978 era and rural industrialization, via the township and village enterprises (TVEs)—to transform the lives of the rural peasantry, especially the landless agricultural wage labourers. In a large, labour abundant, predominantly rural economy such as India, the importance of these measures cannot be overstated. If the existence of a quota system is regarded as the beginning and end of the AA programme, large sections of the rural poor, an overwhelming majority of whom are Dalits, would continue to remain marginalized.

In any event, even if we limit the discussion to quotas, given the demands of other marginalized sections to be included in the ambit of reservations, it can be argued that the Indian policy is reaching the limits of the quota-based approach to counter discrimination and exclusion, even if the Supreme Court relaxed its 50 per cent rule. As the preceding discussion suggests, quotas have been successful in enabling the creation of a Dalit middle class, which is an important ingredient of inclusion, and in liberating several families from the tyranny of traditional stigmatizing and oppressive jobs. However, there is a large section, especially of rural Dalits, which is untouched by quotas in government-provided jobs and education. Thus, quotas are not a universal panacea for caste-based discrimination.

There is an additional related issue that warrants concern. What is often loosely called a 'quota mentality' can be interpreted to engender a certain brand of identity politics which draws sustenance from the existence of caste-based fissures. The proponents of this brand of identity politics—for example, the current chief minister of Uttar Pradesh and leader of the Bahujan Samaj Party, Mayawati—would much rather keep caste divisions alive, as it justifies their existence.

Quotas then become a tool for mobilizing their constituency, rather than an instrument of genuine empowerment of Dalits. This brand of identity politics is therefore inimical to the idea of annihilation of caste, and though the leadership might use Ambedkar's iconic value to further its case, its actual practices are antithetical to Ambedkar's vision and goal of a casteless society.

THE DIVERSITY INDEX

Given the multiplicity of fissures discussed at the beginning of this chapter, it could be argued that India should address caste disparity but not at the cost of ignoring other, very pressing, dimensions of group divisions. Contemporary India offers plenty of examples of how a state of persistent exclusion generates resentment and hostility that manifests itself in violent, secessionist forms. The urgency of increasing diversity in a variety of spheres cannot be overemphasized. The Sachar Committee Report, accordingly, recommended that concrete steps should be taken to increase diversity in public spaces. Accordingly, the Ministry of Minority Affairs appointed an expert group to create a Diversity Index (DI) to measure diversity in public spaces, with a focus on education, employment, and housing. I was privileged to be a member of this group, and thus, was one of the authors of its report that was submitted in 2008.[32]

Here is how we thought of the DI. To begin with, the DI should measure the gap between the proportion of the group (say, Muslims or women, or Dalits) in an institution and its proportion among the 'eligible population'. Thus, for a bachelor's degree course, all those who have passed high school constitute the eligible population. This gap would then be calculated as a proportion of the share of the group in the population. The gap could be positive (for over-represented groups) or negative. The DI only takes into account negative gaps, since the idea is to quantify under-representation. There are three broad dimensions across which the DI is calculated separately—caste, religion, and gender—and the different numbers are integrated *horizontally* (across the three social categories of caste, religion, and gender, using semi-

---

[32] The group was constituted in April 2007 and the report submitted in August 2008. For details, see http://minorityaffairs.gov.in/newsite/reports/di_expgrp/di_expgrp.pdf, accessed on 15 June 2009.

flexible weights, reflecting the needs of the institution) and *vertically* (across the different tiers in an institution, say categories of employees, like managerial and clerical if one were to calculate the DI for the workforce, or categories of students like undergraduate, postgraduate, and diploma if one were to calculate the DI for students) to yield one single number that is a composite measure of diversity in that institution. The detailed methodology is explained in the report cited in the Bibliography.

The next step is to classify institutions (whether public or private) according to whether they have low (DI value between 0 and 1/3), medium (between 1/3 or 2/3), or high (between 2/3 and 1) diversity and repeat this exercise every five years, tied to the cycle of plan allocations by the government.

The idea is to transform this system into action across all institutions in the country, both public and private, by linking the DI of an institution with financial rewards/penalties, such that the exercise of measuring diversity becomes a part of the social ethos. With this aim, the expert group proposed the creation of a *Diversity Commission* at the national level, an autonomous body answerable to the executive. This body (and its corresponding lower level institutions) would have the basic task of evaluating, ranking, and publicizing the status of institutions annually in a *Diversity Report*. In addition to financial incentives/penalties, publicizing the status of institutions via this report would provide yet another source of rewards/disincentives, to the extent that institutions value their public reputation.

The proposed DI system has several advantages: it is transparent, includes the major social groups, allows institutions flexibility in choosing weights to be applied to the social groups, is applicable across the board, and makes the target institutions stakeholders in the system by creating a system of financial rewards. It is not rigid and mechanical. However, when this proposal will be operationalized, if at all, is best known to the powers that be.

* * *

As with AA programmes the world over, the Indian programme is bitterly opposed by the non-beneficiaries both on meritocratic arguments as well as on grounds of non/inadequate performance, elitism, promoting casteism, and so forth. Each of these issues has been discussed in the chapter and it has been suggested that, first, labour markets in the real world do not function on the basis of first-best, perfectly competitive principles, but are in fact discriminatory to the detriment of the marginalized groups. Second, the Indian programme is only partially successful and perhaps flawed in several ways (for example, too mechanical, no monitoring, no penalties for non-implementation, no provisions for self-liquidating features), but in the absence of an alternative, comprehensive, and clearly articulated alternative (such as arguably the DI), it should be continued. Third, there is no evidence in support of the claim that AA lowers productivity or efficiency. As for the charge that AA programmes promote casteism (or racism in other contexts) that they are designed to counter, it is a highly insidious and fallacious argument, also not unique to the Indian context. The completely erroneous assumption this argument makes is that there is no casteism in the absence of AA programmes. If this were true, the material reality of the low castes would be the complete opposite of what it is at present and AA would be redundant. Of course, to move towards the ideal of a caste-blind society, AA needs to be restructured, strengthened in a combination of self-liquidating and self-perpetuating measures. This needs to be done with the clear understanding that AA is only one part of the solution. The other parts (land reforms, generation of rural non-farm productive employment, a strong anti-discriminatory framework, free and compulsory good quality universal primary education, arresting drop-outs at middle and high school levels, and so forth) are equally important and they have to be tackled in order to traverse the rocky road towards caste equality.

Table 7.A.1 Ministry/Department-wise Number of Vacancies Reserved for Scheduled Caste/Scheduled Tribe Officers and Officers Recommended for Appointment against Reserved/Unreserved Vacancies by Departmental Promotion Committees in India (2008–9)

Ministry/Department	No. of vacancies reserved			No. of officers recommended against reserved vacancies			No. of officers recommended against unreserved vacancies		
	SC	ST	Total	SC	ST	Total	SC	ST	Total
Agriculture & Cooperation	3	1	4	3	1	4	1	1	2
Telecommunications	2	1	3	2	1	3	2	–	2
Posts	–	–	–	–	–	–	1	3	4
Civil Aviation	–	–	–	–	–	–	4	–	4
Commerce	–	–	–	–	–	–	3	–	3
Micro, Small, & Medium Enterprises	–	–	–	–	–	–	1	–	1
Defence	205	108	313	123	22	145	16	5	21
External Affairs	10	10	20	5	4	9	–	–	–
Finance (CAG)	9	11	20	9	4	13	3	1	4
Finance (Revenue)	35	27	62	31	23	54	59	15	74
Expenditure	–	–	–	–	–	–	1	–	1
Economic Affairs	–	–	–	–	–	–	11	4	15

(contd...)

Table 7.A.1 (contd...)

Ministry/Department	No. of vacancies reserved			No. of officers recommended against reserved vacancies			No. of officers recommended against unreserved vacancies		
	SC	ST	Total	SC	ST	Total	SC	ST	Total
Culture	–	–	–	–	–	–	2	–	2
Home Affairs (Directorate of Forensic Science)	1	–	1	1	–	1	1	–	1
Health & Family Welfare	–	–	–	–	–	–	1	–	1
Central Bureau of Investigation	–	–	–	–	–	–	4	1	5
Central Industrial Security Force, MHA	6	3	9	–	–	–	6	2	8
Home Affairs	9	–	9	4	–	4	–	–	–
Home Affairs (RGI)	–	1	1	1	1	2	3	–	3
Home Affairs (CRPF)	–	1	1	–	1	1	–	–	–
Intelligence Bureau (Home Affairs)	47	22	69	41	17	58	1	2	3
Home Affairs (Official Language)	–	–	–	–	–	–	2	–	2
Information & Broadcasting	3	2	5	6	3	9	3	2	5
Labour & Empowerment	2	–	2	4	–	4	11	3	14
Railways	151	61	212	175	73	248	34	17	51

(contd...)

Table 7.A.1 (contd...)

Ministry/Department	No. of vacancies reserved			No. of officers recommended against reserved vacancies			No. of officers recommended against unreserved vacancies		
	SC	ST	Total	SC	ST	Total	SC	ST	Total
Shipping, Road Transport, & Highways	2	–	2	6	–	6	4	–	4
Election Commission of India	2	1	3	–	–	–	–	–	–
Statistics & Programme Implementation	1	1	2	1	1	2	4	4	8
Textiles	2	2	4	2	2	4	2	–	2
Tourism	–	–	–	–	–	–	2	1	3
Urban Development & Poverty Alleviation	2	–	2	2	–	2	6	–	6
Mines	73	37	110	26	9	35	4	3	7
Water Resources	2	3	5	1	–	1	5	1	6
Municipal Coorporation of Delhi	9	5	14	1	–	1	–	–	–
NCT of Delhi	112	83	195	102	14	116	87	–	87
Delhi Jal Board	3	2	5	3	1	4	–	–	–
ESIC	1	4	5	1	4	5	22	9	31
Power	3	2	5	3	2	5	–	–	–
Science & Technology	–	–	–	–	–	–	1	–	1

(contd...)

Table 7.A.1 (contd...)

Ministry/Department	No. of vacancies reserved			No. of officers recommended against reserved vacancies			No. of officers recommended against unreserved vacancies		
	SC	ST	Total	SC	ST	Total	SC	ST	Total
Environment & Forests	–	1	1	1	2	3	1	1	2
Chandigarh Administration	2	–	2	2	–	2	–	–	–
DOP&T	28	1	29	1	–	1	2	–	2
Chemical & Petrochemicals	–	–	–	–	–	–	1	–	1
Central Vigilance Commission	–	–	–	–	–	–	1	–	1
Industrial Policy & Promotion	–	–	–	–	–	–	1	–	1
Total	725	390	1115	557	185	742	313	75	388

Source: www.indiastat.com.

Table 7.A.2 Number of Posts Reserved for Scheduled Castes/Scheduled Tribes/Other Backward Classes and Candidates Recommended against Unreserved Posts by Union Public Service Commission (UPSC) in India (2007–8 and 2008–9)

Item	Reserved posts	SC/ST/OBC candidates recommended against reserved posts	Shortfall	SC/ST/OBC candidates recommended against unreserved posts	SC/ST/OBC candidates recommended	Reserved posts	SC/ST/OBC candidates recommended against reserved posts	Shortfall	SC/ST/OBC candidates recommended against unreserved posts	SC/ST/OBC candidates recommended
Direct recruitment by interview	249	198	51	19	217*	460	354	106	85	439
Percentage		79.5	20.5		87.1*		77	23		95.4

(contd...)

Table 7.A.2 (contd...)

(2005–6 and 2006–7)

Item	2006–7					2005–6				
	Reserved posts	SC/ST/OBC candidates recommended against reserved posts	Shortfall	SC/ST/OBC candidates recommended against unreserved posts	SC/ST/OBC candidates recommended	Reserved posts	SC/ST/OBC candidates recommended against reserved posts	Shortfall	SC/ST/OBC candidates recommended against unreserved posts	SC/ST/OBC candidates recommended
Direct recruitment by interview	545	448	97	71	519*	356	304	52	57	361
Percentage		82.2	17.8		95.2*		85.4	14.6		101

Source: Compiled from the statistics released by Union Public Service Commission.

Note: *Includes SC/ST/OBC candidates recommended against unreserved post.

Table 7.A.3 Other Backward Classes in Central Public Sector Enterprises in India
(as on 01.01. 2007)

Group	Total number of employees	No. of SC	% SC	No. of ST	% ST	No. of OBC	% OBC
Executive level*	191299	25058	13.0989	8835	4.61842	13098	6.84687
Supervisory level	169191	22860	13.5114	10739	6.34726	14526	8.58556
Workmen clerical level	665996	128352	19.2722	63809	9.58099	108653	16.3144
Semi-skilled/Unskilled (excluding *safai karamcharis*)	231640	50142	21.6465	37012	15.9782	49960	21.568
Total	1258126	226412	17.996	120395	9.56939	186237	14.8027
Semi-skilled/Unskilled (including *safai karamcharis*)	14553	11509	79.0834	439	3.01656	476	3.2708
Total	2530805	464333	18.3472	241229	9.53171	372950	14.7364

Source: Compiled from the statistics released by Ministry of Heavy Industries and Public Enterprises.
Note: * 01.01.2007 (Based on information furnished by 210 enterprises).

Table 7.A.4 Representation of Scheduled Castes/Scheduled Tribes/Other Backward Classes in Direct Recruitment for Indian Administrative Service (IAS), Indian Police Service (IPS), and Indian Foreign Service (IFS) in India

Particulars	IAS (Information as on 01.08.2006)	IPS (Information as on 01.01.2006)	IFS (Information as on 10.08.2006)
Total number of persons in position	4,804	3,209	608
Total number of direct recruits	3,464	2,297	–
Number of persons belonging to SCs, along with their percentage	476@ −13.74%	311@ −13.53%	84 −13.80%
Number of persons belonging to STs, along with their percentage	246@ −7.10%	162@ −7.05%	45 −7.40%
Number of persons belonging to OBCs, along with their percentage	246@ −7.10%	162@ −7.05%	48 −7.90%

Source: Compiled from the statistics released by Rajya Sabha Unstarred Question No. 2176, dated 17.08.2006.

Note: @Indicates the number and percentage out of the total number of direct recruits in the service.

Table 7.A.5 Number of Employees (Scheduled Castes/Tribes) in Department of Post in India (as on 31.3.2003 and 31.3.2004)

Group	As on 31.3.2003				As on 31.3.2004			
	Scheduled Castes	Percentage to total no. of employees	Scheduled Tribes	Percentage to total no. of employees	Scheduled Castes	Percentage to total no. of employees	Scheduled Tribes	Percentage to total no. of employees
Group 'A'	113	14	36	4.46	97	12.92	46	6.1
Group 'B' (Gazetted)	350	18.54	156	8.26	218	10.8	76	3.71
Group 'C'	38038	17.94	14297	5.72	35846	18.18	13573	6.81
Group 'D' (Excl. Sweeper)	9137	19.4	3395	7.21	8885	19.47	3240	7.1

Source: Department of Posts, Govt of India.

Note: Period of fiscal year in India is April to March, e.g., year shown as 1990–1 relates to April 1990 to March 1991.

APPENDIX 7.B: NCBC GUIDELINES FOR INCLUSION INTO THE CENTRAL LIST OF OBCS

The commission, after studying the criteria/indicators framed by the Mandal Commission and the commissions set up in the past by different state governments and other relevant materials, formulated the following guidelines for considering requests for inclusion in the list of Other Backward Classes.

A. Social

1. Castes and communities, generally considered as socially backward.

2. (a) Castes and communities, which mainly depend on agricultural and/or other manual labour for their livelihood and are lacking any significant resource base.

(b) Castes and communities, which, for their livelihood, mainly depend on agricultural and/or other manual labour for wage and are lacking any significant base.

(c) Castes and communities, the women of which, as a general practice, are for their family's livelihood, engaged in agricultural and/or other manual labour, for wage.

(d) Castes and communities, the children of which, as a general practice, are, for family's livelihood or for supplementing family's low income, mainly engaged in agricultural and/or manual labour.

(e) Castes and communities, which in terms of caste system, are identified with traditional crafts or traditional or hereditary occupations considered to be lowly or undignified.

(f) Castes and communities, which in terms of the caste system, are identified with traditional or hereditary occupations considered to be 'unclean' or stigmatised.

(g) Nomadic and semi-nomadic castes and communities.

(h) Denotified or Vimukta Jati castes and communities.

Explanation: The term refers to castes/communities which had been categorised as Criminal Tribes under the Criminal Tribes Act, 1924, Act No. VI of 1924, passed by the Indian Legislature and repealed by the Criminal Tribes (Repeal) Act, 1952, Act No. XXIV of 1952 and subsequently referred to as Denotified or Vimukta Jatis.

3. Castes and communities, having no representation or poor representation in the State Legislative Assembly and/or district-level

Panchayati Raj institutions during the ten years preceding the date of the application

Explanation: This is only intended to measure, as an indicator, the presence of a caste or community in these bodies.

The term 'poor representation' may be taken to refer to a caste or community whose presence in the body is less than 25% of its proportion in the population.

B. Educational

1. Castes and communities, whose literacy rate is at least 8% less than the State or district average.

2. Castes and communities of which the proportion of matriculates is at least 20% less than the State or district average.

3. Castes and communities, of which the proportion of graduates is at least 20% less than the State or district average.

C. Economic

1. Castes and communities, a significant proportion of whose members reside only in kachha houses.

2. Castes and communities, the share of whose members in number of cases and in extent of agricultural lands surrendered under the Agricultural Land Ceiling Act of the State, is nil or significantly low.

3. Castes and communities, the share of whose members in State Government posts and services of Groups A & B/Classes I & II, is not equal to the population-equivalent proportion of the caste/community.

D. Illustration

Population-equivalent proportion	
Population of a State	10,00,0000
Population of the caste/community under consideration in the State	1,00,000
Proportion of the population of the caste/community under consideration to the total population of the State	10%
Number of posts in Class-I in the State	1,000
Therefore, population-equivalent proportion of Class-I posts in the State in respect of the caste/community under consideration	100

Explanation 1: In the case illustrated above, if members belonging to the caste/community under consideration hold 100 Class-1 posts or more, its share is equal to or more than its population-equivalent proportion.

In that case that caste/community will not be considered to have fulfilled this indicator of backwardness.

In the case illustrated above, if the members of the caste/community under consideration have 99 Classes-1 posts or less, its share is less than its population-equivalent proportion and will, therefore, be considered to have fulfilled this criterion of backwardness.

Explanation 2: This guideline is only an indicator to assess backwardness or its absence and has no relation to the condition of inadequacy under Article 16(4).

Explanation 3: The population-equivalent proportion of posts may be composed of posts secured through merit only or through reservation only or through both—figures need to be furnished separately for posts secured through merit/posts secured through both—figures need to be furnished separately for posts secured through merit/posts secured through reservation.

In addition to the above, arising from Article 16(4) the following conditions have also to be fulfilled:

Castes and communities, which are not/are inadequately represented in the Central Government posts & services of Group A & B (Each Group/Class) should be taken separately.

Procedural Clarification on Guideline

1. The above social, educational and economic guidelines for consideration of requests for inclusion in the list of Other Backward Classes are intended to aid the Bench/Commission to identify castes and communities which deserve to be included in the list of OBC in terms of the National Commission for Backward Classes Act and not to fetter due exercise of discretion by it.

2. The term 'local', wherever used, is intended to mean State level or intra-State regional level or district level, as appropriate, in the light of the demographic distribution of the caste/community concerned.

However, wherever the Bench/Commission has adequate reasons, the sub-district level positions may be taken into account.

In some guidelines, State or local, or State or district have been given as alternatives. In such instances the appropriate alternative may be chosen depending on the circumstances such as demographic distribution, ready availability of data etc.

3. Some of the guidelines are capable of quantification but data are not available in every State. In respect of States, where such data are readily available (for example, specific percentage figures), the bench/Commission may examine the cases before it in terms of such quantifiable data and their own observations as well and other relevant materials that may be available to it. In respect of States where such quantifiable data are not available, the bench/Commission may consider castes/communities on the basis of their own observations and other relevant materials that may be available to it.

4. Under each of the categories A, B & C, of guidelines, there are 3 or 4 guidelines. They are not necessarily cumulative. Cumulative data would no doubt be advantageous. But where data-base does not readily permit, each caste or community may be considered in terms of such of the guidelines under each of the categories A, B & C as are practicable.

5. Regarding the condition at D, till information regarding the position of each caste in the Government of India's services becomes readily available, it may be presumed that this factor is fulfilled by a caste/community/sub-caste/synonym/sub-entry, in case it is found that it fulfills the guideline in C 3.

6. Wherever a caste or community fulfills the guidelines 2 (e) or (f) or (g) or (h), the Bench/Commission may take it as adequate evidence of backwardness. In such cases, the Bench shall take into account such other data/information that may be made available to it or comes to its notice, and it may make such further inquiry as it deems proper and necessary. Having done so and being satisfied that there are no sufficient grounds to take a contrary view regarding the backwardness of the caste or community making the request, the Bench may, after examining the matter inadequacy of representation as indicated in D, proceed to formulate its findings.

7. Occupations mentioned at guidelines 2(e) and 2(f) may include

traditional artisanal crafts; fishing, hunting, bird-snaring; agricultura[
labour on the lands of others; earth work, stone-breaking, salt manufacturing, lime-burning; toddy-tapping; animal rearing; butchery; hair-
cutting; washing of clothes; ferrying by boat; safai (that is, 'scavenging');
knife grinding, grain roasting; entertaining through song and dance,
acrobatics jugglery, snake-charming, acting; begging or mendicancy.

Explanation: This refers only to castes or communities which
traditionally depended on begging or mendicancy in the past, that is,
until it was prohibited by law.

The Bench/Commission may take into account any other occupation
which may be similar to these occupations.

8. In respect of any case of request, found to be one of apparent
'clerical' error, or factual mistakes at the stage of preparation of the
common lists and if there is no contrary view expressed and data
furnished before or otherwise available to/in the notice of the bench/
Commission such castes/communities may be included and findings/
advice formulated to that effect.

9. In case of synonyms/sub-castes/different names of the same caste
or community/local variants of the same caste or community, if and
after it is established that, they are, in fact, such synonyms/sub-castes/
different names of the same caste/local variants, etc. and if there are
no contrary views expressed and data furnished before or otherwise
available to/in the notice of the Bench/Commission and the Bench/
Commission does not find any ground to take a contrary view, such
synonyms/sub-castes/different names of the same caste/local variants
of the same caste, such cases may be included, and findings/advice
formulated to that effect.

10. In all cases, publicity regarding the date and venue of the sitting
of the Commission's bench and the castes/communities etc. to which
the sitting pertains may be made through mass media and all those
who have any views to express or data to furnish to the bench may be
invited to do so, in addition to addressing the State Governments and
applicants to furnish all material and data in their possession.

11. These guidelines of identification and procedure will be
applicable to all categories of States/UTs and all categories of castes/
communities whether included in the State list but not in the Mandal
list or included in the Mandal list but not in the State list, or included
in neither.

APPENDIX 7.C: THE CREAMY LAYER

Persons/Sections Excluded from Reservation which Constitute Creamy
Layer of the Society

Creamy Layer

Description of category	To whom rule of exclusion will apply
I. Constitutional Posts	Son(s) and daughter(s) of— (a) President of India; (b) Vice-President of India; (c) Judges of the Supreme Court and of the High Courts; (d) Chairman and Members of UPSC and of the State Public Service Commission; Chief Election Commissioner; Comptroller and Auditor-General of India; (e) Persons holding constitutional positions of like nature.
II. Service Category A. Group 'A'/Class I Officers of the All India Central and State Services (Direct Recruits)	Son(s) and daughter(s) of— (a) parents, both of whom are Class I officers; (b) parents, either of whom is a Class I officer; (c) parents, both of whom are Class I officers, but one of them dies or suffers permanent incapacitation; (d) parents, either of whom is a Class I officer and such parents dies or suffers permanent incapacitation and before such death or such incapacitation has had the benefit of employment in any International Organisation like UN, IMF, World bank, etc., for a period of not less than 5 years; (e) parents, both of whom are Class I officers die or suffer permanent incapacitation and before such death or such incapacitation of the both either of them has had the benefit of employment in any International Organization like UN, IMF, World Bank, etc., for a period of not less than 5 years before their death or permanent incapacitation; Provided that the rule of exclusion shall not apply in the following cases: (a) Sons and daughters of parents either of whom or both of whom are Class I officers and such parent(s) dies/die or suffer permanent incapacitation; (b) A lady belonging to OBC category has got married to a Class I officer, and may herself like to apply for job.
B. Group 'B'/Class II Officers of the Central and State Services (Direct Recruitment)	Son(s) and daughter(s) of— (a) parents, both of whom are Class II officers; (b) parents of whom only the husband is a Class II officer and he gets into Class I at the age of 40 or earlier;

Creamy Layer	
Description of category	To whom rule of exclusion will apply
	(c) parents, both of whom are Class II officers and one of them dies or suffers permanent incapacitation and either one of them has had the benefit of employment in any International Organisation UN, IMF, World Bank, etc., for a period of not less than 5 years before such death or permanent incapacitation;
	(d) parents of whom the husband is a Class I officer (direct recruitment or pre-forty promoted) and the wife is a Class II officer and the wife dies; or suffers permanent incapacitation; and
	(e) Parents, of whom the wife is a Class I officer (Direct Recruit or pre-forty promoted) and the husband is a Class II officer and the husband dies or suffers permanent incapacitation;
	Provided that the rule of exclusion shall not apply in the following cases:
	Sons and daughters of—
	(a) Parents both of whom are Class II officers and one of them dies or suffers permanent incapacitation.
	(b) Parents, both of whom are Class II officers and both of them die or suffer permanent incapacitation, even though either of them has had the benefit of employment in any International Organisation like UN, IMF, World Bank, etc, for a period of not less than 5 years before their death or permanent incapacitation.
C. Employees in Public Sector Undertakings, etc.	The criteria enumerated in A and B above in this category will apply mutatis mutandis to officers holding equivalent or comparable posts in PSUs, Banks, Insurance Organisations, Universities, etc., and also to equivalent or comparable posts and positions under private employment, pending the evaluation of the posts on equivalent or comparable basis in these institutions, the criteria specified in Category VI below will apply to the officers in these Institutions.
III. Armed Forces including Paramilitary Forces (Persons holding civil posts are not included)	Son(s) and daughter(s) of parents either or both of whom is or are in the rank of Colonel and above in the Army and to equivalent posts in the Navy and the Air Force and the Paramilitary Forces;
	Provided that—
	(i) If the wife of an armed forces officer is herself in the armed forces (i.e., the category under consideration) the rule of exclusion will apply only when she herself has reached the rank of Colonel;

Creamy Layer	
Description of category	To whom rule of exclusion will apply

	(ii) the service ranks below Colonel of husband and wife shall not be clubbed together; (iii) if the wife of an officer in the armed forces is in civil employment, this will not be taken into account for applying the rule of exclusion unless she falls in the service category under item No. II in which case the criteria and conditions enumerated therein will apply to her independently.
IV. Professional Class and Those Engaged in Trade and Industry	Criteria specified against Category VI will apply.
(i) Persons engaged in profession as a doctor, lawyer, chartered accountant, income tax consultant, financial or management consultant, dental surgeon, engineer, architect, computer specialist, film artists and other film professional, author, playwright, sports person, sports professional, media professional or any other vocations of like status.	
(ii) Persons engaged in trade, business and industry.	Criteria specified against Category VI will apply. EXPLANATION— (i) Where the husband is in some profession and the wife is in a Class II or lower grade employment, the income/wealth test will apply only on the basis of the husband's income. (ii) If the wife is in any profession and the husband is in employment in a Class II or lower rank post, then the income/wealth criterion will apply only on the basis of the wife's income and the husband's income will not be clubbed with it.
V. Property Owners A. Agricultural Holding	Son(s) and daughter(s) of persons belonging to a family (father, mother and minor children) which owns— (a) only irrigated land which is equal to or more than 85% of the statutory ceiling area, or (b) both irrigated and unirrigated land, as follows:

Creamy Layer

Description of category	To whom rule of exclusion will apply
	(i) The rule of exclusion will apply where the pre-condition exists that the irrigated area (having been brought to a single type under a common denominator) 40% or more of the statutory ceiling limit for irrigated land (this being calculated by excluding the unirrigated portion). If this pre-condition of not less than 40% exists, then only the area of unirrigated land will be taken into account. This will be done by converting the unirrigated land, on the basis of the conversion formula existing, into the irrigated type. The irrigated area so computed from unirrigated land shall be added to the actual area of irrigated land and if after such clubbing together the total area in terms of irrigated land is 85% or more of the statutory ceiling limit for irrigated land, then the rule of exclusion will apply and disentitlement will occur) (ii) The rule of exclusion will not apply if the land holding of a family is exclusively unirrigated.
B. Plantations (i) Coffee, tea, rubber, etc. (ii) Mango, citrus, apple plantations, etc.	Criteria of income/wealth specified in Category VI below will apply. Deemed as agricultural holding and hence criteria at A above under this category will apply. Criteria specified in Category VI below will apply.
C. Vacant land and/or buildings in urban agglomerations	EXPLANATION: Building may be used for residential, industrial or commercial purpose and the like two or more such purposes.
VI. Income/Wealth Test	Son(s) daughter(s)— (a) Persons having gross annual income of Rs 1 lakh or above or possessing wealth above the exemption limit as prescribed in the Wealth Act for a period of three consecutive years. (b) Persons in Categories I, II, III and V-A who are not disentitled to the benefit of reservation but have income from other sources of wealth which will bring them within the income/wealth criteria mentioned in (a) above. EXPLANATION— (i) Income from salaries or agricultural land shall not be clubbed; (ii) The income criteria in terms of rupee will be modified taking into account the change in its value every three years. If the situation, however, so demands, the interregnum may be less.

Creamy Layer	
Description of category	To whom rule of exclusion will apply
	EXPLANATION—Wherever the expression 'permanent incapacitation' occur in this schedule, it shall mean incapacitation which results in putting an officer out of service.

APPENDIX 7.D: A SHORT NOTE ON WOMEN'S RESERVATION

The normal process of economic development, on its own, may not increase women's participation in the political sphere. The continued low presence of women in the political spheres of the industrialized developed countries is testimony to that. India's actual record is impressive compared to most developed countries: a woman prime minister for 19 years, several women chief ministers, ministers of state, and other important political functionaries at both the central and state government levels. However, as elsewhere in the world, women are under-represented in key decision-making bodies, a feature that prompted the move to introduce affirmative action in elected decision-making bodies.

While the bulk of the affirmative action programme is caste-based, the demand for affirmative action for women, which was first raised in 1974, has been reiterated several times over the decades. A full analysis of the movement for women's reservation would require a separate essay. However, a few remarks are in order. In 1991, the government of India introduced a proposal to reserve 33 per cent of electoral constituencies for women in local self-governments (the municipality and metropolitan council levels). After much debate, the measure was passed in 1993 via the 73rd and 74th amendments. In 1996, 1998, and 1999, bills for extending such reservation to the parliamentary and state legislative councils were introduced, but these lapsed with the dissolution of the respective Lok Sabhas. The Constitution (108th amendment) Bill, 2008, was introduced in the Rajya Sabha and was passed in March 2070. The bill seeks to reserve one-third seats in Lok Sabha and stae legislative assemblies. It also recommends that one-third of seats reserved for SCs and STs would be reserved for women belonging to these groups. Further, reserved seats may be alloted by rotation within states or union territories.

While the novelty of the move lies in a version of affirmative action for half of the country's population, the implementation is complicated by the mechanics of working out the overlap with the caste-based reservation. The debate over the passage of the bill has seen a vitriolic upsurge of anti-affirmative action sentiment, in addition to intense anti-women tirades.

Just as major political parties have often revealed an ugly side during this whole debate, a consensus has emerged in the women's movement about the justification for affirmative action in the political arena for women. There is a belief that a greater representation of women in Parliament would ensure a gender shift in social and economic policies or at least modify the male-dominated and male-biased realm of policy-making. However, there are concerns that some women may be put up as puppets while the real control would lie with their husbands or other male family members. The counter-argument is that even if this happened initially, over time the presence of women in decision-making bodies would help alter both their self-perception and their actual position in society. Indeed, the evidence from reservations at the village council level, cited earlier in the volume, reveals that gender-based quotas have led to small but significant shifts in policies.

A key issue that has complicated the debate over women's reservation is that of 'quotas-within-quotas'. A section of the political class believes that reserved seats are likely to be dominated by women from relatively upper class/caste backgrounds and, thus, to ensure representation of the truly disadvantaged, there should be SC–ST–OBC quotas *within* the women's quota. The other argument used to argue for a quota-within-quota is that if caste-based quotas can be used for parliamentary representations in general (that is, for seats that are dominated by men), why should the same principle not be used for seats reserved for women? While the Bill has legislated for quotas-within-quotas, this issue remains contentious among the supporters of women's reservations.

Another issue that comes up in the theoretical literature is the appropriate level at which seats should be reserved for women: should political parties reserve seats for women, that is, field more women candidates, or should more constituencies be reserved for women? The question that the literature examines is which of these is more likely to increase representation of women in elected bodies. In India, at the practical level, the quota-within-quotas is currently the real debate.

Bibliography

Agarwal, Bina (1997), '"Bargaining" and Gender Relations: Within and Beyond the Household', *Feminist Economics*, 3(1), pp. 1–51.

Akerlof, George (1984), 'The Economics of Caste and of the Rat Race and Other Woeful Tales', *An Economic Theorist's Book of Tales*, pp. 23–44. Cambridge: Cambridge University Press.

Akerlof, George and Rachel Kranton (2000), 'Economics and Identity', *Quarterly Journal of Economics*, 115(3), pp. 715–53.

Ambedkar, B.R. (2002), 'Caste and Class', in Valerian Rodrigues (ed.), *The Essential Writings of B.R. Ambedkar*, pp. 99–105. New Delhi: Oxford University Press.

———— 'Castes in India', in Valerian Rodrigues (ed.), *The Essential Writings of B.R. Ambedkar*, pp. 241–62. New Delhi: Oxford University Press.

———— 'Annihilation of Caste', in Valerian Rodrigues (ed.), *The Essential Writings of B.R. Ambedkar*, pp. 263–305. New Delhi: Oxford University Press.

Arrow, Kenneth J. (1971), 'The Theory of Discrimination', Working Paper 403, Princeton University, Department of Economics, Industrial Relations Section.

———— (1998), 'What Has Economics to Say about Discrimination?', *Journal of Economic Perspectives*, 12(2), pp. 91–100.

Artecona, Raquel and Wendy Cunningham (2002), *Effects of Trade Liberalisation on the Gender Wage Gap in Mexico*. Washington, DC: The World Bank, Development Research Group/Poverty Reduction and Economic Management Network.

Ashenfelter, Orley (1970), 'Changes in Labour Market Discrimination over Time', *Journal of Human Resources*, 5(4), Autumn, pp. 403–30.

Ayers, Ian (2001), *Pervasive Prejudice? Unconventional Evidence of Race and Gender Discrimination*. Chicago: The University of Chicago Press.

Bajpai, Nirupam and Sangeeta Goyal (2004), 'India: Towards the Millennium Development Goals', Center on Globalization and Sustainable Development Working Paper No.3, The Earth Institute, Columbia University.

Baldwin, Marjore and William G. Johnson (1992), 'Estimating the Employment Effects of Wage Discrimination', *Review of Economics and Statistics*, 74(3), August, pp. 446–55.

Banerjee, Biswajit and Gabriella A. Bucci (1994), 'On-the-Job Search after Entering Urban Employment: An Analysis Based on Indian Migrants', *Oxford Bulletin of Economics and Statistics*, 56(1), pp. 33–47.

Banerjee, Biswajit and J.B. Knight (1985), 'Caste Discrimination in the Indian Urban Labour Market', *Journal of Development Economics*, 17, pp. 277–307.

Banerjee, Lopamudra, Ashwini Deshpande, Yan Ming, Sanjay Ruparelia, Vamsicharan Vakulabharanam, and Wei Zhong (2010), 'Growth, Reforms and Inequality: Comparing India and China', India China Institute Working Paper, New School, New York.

Becker, Gary S. (1957), *The Economics of Discrimination*. Chicago: The University of Chicago Press.

Bennet, Lynn (2005), 'Gender, Caste and Social Exclusion in Nepal: Following the Policy Process from Analysis to Action', Working Paper for the World Bank Conference on 'New Frontiers of Social Policy: Development in a Globalising World', 12–15 December. Available at http://siteresources.worldbank.org/INTRANETSOCIALDEVELOPMENT/Resources/Bennett.rev.pdf, accessed on 10 February 2010.

Berreman, Gerald D. (1971), 'Self, Situation and Escape from Stigmatised Ethnic Identity', paper presented at the 70th Annual Meeting of the American Anthropological Association Meeting, New York.

Bertrand, Marianne, Rema Hanna, and Sendhil Mullainathan (2008), 'Affirmative Action in Education: Evidence from Engineering College Admissions in India', National Bureau of Economic Research (NBER) Working Paper No. 13926.

Bertrand, Marianne and Sendhil Mullainathan (2003), 'Are Emily and Greg More Employable than Lakisha and Jamal? A Field Experiment on Labour Market Discrimination', NBER Working Paper No. 9873.

Besley, Timothy, Rohini Pande, Lupin Rahman, and Vijayendra Rao (2004), 'The Politics of Public Good Provision: Evidence from Indian Local Governments', *Journal of the European Economic Association*, 2(2–3), pp. 416–26.

Béteille, André (1971), 'Race, Caste and Ethnic Identity', *International Social Science Journal*, 23(4), pp. 519–35.

———— (1996), *Caste, Class and Power: Changing Patterns of Stratification in Tanjore Village*. New Delhi: Oxford University Press.

———— (1997), 'Caste and Political Group Formation in Tamilnad', in Sudipta Kaviraj (ed.), *Politics in India*, pp. 71–93. New Delhi: Oxford University Press.

Bhattacharjee, Debashish (1985), 'A Note on Caste Discrimination in a Bombay Automobile Firm', *Industrial Relations*, 24(1), pp. 155–9.

Black, Sandra and Elizabeth Brainerd (2004), 'Importing Equality? The Impact of Globalisation on Gender Discrimination', *Industrial and Labour Relations Review*, 57 (4), July, pp. 540–59.

Blinder, Alan S. (1973), 'Wage Discrimination: Reduced Form and Structural Estimates', *Journal of Human Resources*, 8(4), pp. 436–55.

Borjas, George and Stephen Bronars (1989), 'Consumer Discrimination and Self-Employment', *Journal of Political Economy*, 97 (3), pp. 581–605.

Bowen, William G. and Derek Bok (1998), *The Shape of the River: Long Term Consequences of Considering Race in College and University Admissions*. Princeton, NJ: Princeton University Press.

Burns, Justine (2006), 'Racial Stereotypes, Stigma and Trust in Post-Apartheid South Africa', *Economic Modelling*, 23, pp. 805–21.

Butler, Richard J. (1982), 'Estimating Wage Discrimination in the Labour Market', *Journal of Human Resources*, 17(4), pp. 606–21.

Cashin, Paul and Ratna Sahay (1996), 'Regional Economic Growth and Convergence in India', *Finance and Development*, 33(1), pp. 49–52.

Centeno, Miguel Angel and Katherine S. Newman (eds) (2010), *Discrimination in an Unequal World*. New York: Oxford University Press.

Center for Human Rights and Global Justice (CHRGJ) (2005), 'The Missing Piece of the Puzzle: Caste Discrimination and the Conflict in Nepal', Report by CHRGJ, NYU School of Law.

Chakravarty, Sujoy and E. Somanathan (2008), 'Discrimination in an Elite Labour Market? Job Placements at the Indian Institute of Management, Ahmedabad', *Economic and Political Weekly*, 43(44), pp. 45–50.

Chambers, Robert (1992), 'Poverty in India: Concepts, Research and Reality', in Barbara Hariss, S. Guhan, and R.H. Cassen (eds), *Poverty In India: Research and Policy*, pp. 301–32. Bombay: Oxford University Press.

Chandra, Vibha P. (1997), 'Remigration: Return of the Prodigals—An Analysis of the Impact of the Cycles of Migration and Remigration on Caste Mobility', *International Migration Review*, 31(1), pp. 162–70.

Chatterjee, Partha (1997), 'The Nation and Its Outcasts', in Sudipta Kaviraj (ed.), *Politics in India*, pp. 94–118. New Delhi: Oxford University Press.

Chattopadhyay, Debiprasad (1959), *Lokayata: A Study in Ancient Indian Materialism*. New Delhi: People's Publishing House.

Chattopadhyay, Raghabendra and Esther Duflo (2004), 'Women as Policy Makers: Evidence from a Randomised Policy Experiment in India', *Econometrica*, 72(5), pp. 1409–43.

Chaubisa, M.L. (1988), *Caste, Tribe and Exploitation: Exploration of Inequality at the Village Level*. Udaipur: Himanshu Publications.

Clark, K., and S. Drinkwater (2000), 'Pushed Out or Pulled In? Self-employment among Ethnic Minorities in England and Wales', *Labour Economics*, 7(5), pp. 603–28.

Coate, Stephen and Glenn Loury (1993), 'Will Affirmative Action Policies Eliminate Negative Stereotypes', *American Economic Review*, 83(5), pp. 1220–40.

Conceição, Pedro and James K. Galbraith (2000), 'Constructing Long and Dense Time-Series of Inequality Using the Theil Index', *Eastern Economic Journal*, 26(1), pp. 61–74.

Conley, Dalton (1999), *Being Black, Living in the Red: Race, Wealth, and Social Policy in America*. Berkeley, CA: University of California Press.

Cotton, Jeremiah (1988), 'On the Decomposition of Wage Differentials', *Review of Economics and Statistics*, 70(2), pp. 236–43.

Damodaran, Harish (2008), *India's New Capitalists: Caste, Business and Industry in a Modern Nation*. Basingstoke, Hampshire and New York: Palgrave Macmillan.

Darity, William A. Jr. and Ashwini Deshpande (2000), 'Tracing the Divide: Intergroup Disparity Across Countries', *Eastern Economic Journal*, 26(1), pp. 75–85.

———— (eds) (2003), *Boundaries of Clan and Color: Transnational Comparisons of Inter-Group Disparity*. London: Routledge.

Darity, William A. Jr. and Samuel L. Myers, Jr. (1998), *Persistent Disparity: Race and Economic Inequality in the United States since 1945*. Cheltenham, UK: Edward Elgar.

Das, Maitreyi Bordia (2010), 'Minority Status and Labour Market Outcomes: Does India Have Minority Enclaves?', in Sukhadeo Thorat and Katherine S. Newman (eds), *Blocked by Caste: Economic Discrimination in Modern India*, pp. 328–53. New Delhi: Oxford University Press.

Datta, Nonica (2002), 'On the Anti-Muslim Ethos of Hindu Women in Gujarat', *Muslim India*, No. 237, September.

Deaton, Angus (1997), *The Analysis of Household Surveys: A Microeconometric Approach to Development Policy*, published for the World Bank. Baltimore and London: Johns Hopkins University Press.

Deliege, Robert (1996), 'At the Threshold of Untouchability: Pallars and Valaiyars in a Tamil Village', in C.J. Fuller (ed.), *Caste Today*, pp. 65–92. New Delhi: Oxford University Press.

Desai, I.P. (1984), 'Should "Caste" be the Basis for Recognising Backwardness', *Economic and Political Weekly*, 19(28), pp. 1106–16.

Desai, Neera (1996), 'Women's Employment and Their Familial Role in India', in A.M. Shah, B.S. Baviskar, and E.A. Ramaswamy (eds), *Social Structure and Change, Volume 2: Women in Indian Society*, pp. 98–112. New Delhi: Sage Publications.

Desai, Sonalde, Amaresh Dubey, B.L. Joshi, Mitali Sen, Abusaleh Shariff, and Reeve Vanneman (2010), *Human Development in India: Challenges for a Society in Transition*, p. 234. New Delhi: Oxford University Press.

Deshpande, Ashwini (2000a), 'Does Caste Still Define Disparity: A Look at Inequality in Kerala, India', *American Economic Review, Papers and Proceedings*, 90(2), pp. 322–5.

_____ (2000b), 'Recasting Economic Inequality', *Review of Social Economy*, 58(3), pp. 381–99.

_____ (2001a), 'Caste at Birth? Redefining Disparity in India', *Review of Development Economics*, 5(1), pp. 130–44.

_____ (2001b), 'Casting off Servitude: Caste and Gender Disparity in India', in Kathleen Blee and France Winddance Twine (eds), *Feminism and Anti Racism: International Struggles for Justice*, pp. 328–48. New York: New York University Press.

_____ (2002), 'Assets versus Autonomy: Changing Face of the Gender Caste Overlap in India', *Feminist Economics*, 8(2), pp. 19–35.

_____ (2003), 'Gender Discrimination at the Workplace: India, Bangladesh and China', in Bill Kosanovich (ed.), *Improving Labour Market Opportunities and Security for Workers in Developing Countries*, pp. 223–66, ILAB Symposium Papers, Vol. 1. Washington, DC: United States Department of Labor, Bureau of International Affairs.

_____ (2004), 'Decomposing Inequality: Significance of Caste', in Bibek Debroy and D. Shyam Babu (eds), *The Dalit Question: Reforms and Social Justice*, pp. 33–52. New Delhi: Rajiv Gandhi Institute for Contemporary Studies, Globus Books.

_____ (2007), 'Overlapping Identities under Liberalization: Gender and Caste in India', *Economic Development and Cultural Change*, 55(4), July, pp. 735–60.

_____ (2013), Affirmative Action in India, Oxford India Short Introductions. New Delhi: Oxford University Press.

_____ (2016), 'Double Jeopardy? Caste, Affirmative Action and Stigma', 2016/71. Helsinki: UNU-WIDER.

_____ (forthcoming), 'Foreign Direct Investment and Intergroup disparities in India', in Ashok Kotwal, Moshe Hirsh, and Bharat Ramaswami (eds), The Right to Development: Making It Work in India. University of British Columbia Press.

Deshpande, Ashwini and Dean Spears (2016), 'Who Is the Identifiable Victim? Caste and Charitable Giving in Modern India', *Economic Development and Cultural Change*, 64(2), January, pp. 299–321.

Deshpande, Ashwini and Katherine S. Newman (2007), 'Where the Path Leads: The Role of Caste in Post University Employment Expectations', *Economic and Political Weekly*, 42(41), pp. 4133–40.

Deshpande, Ashwini and Rajesh Ramachandran (2016), 'Does Affirmative Action Work? The Political Economy of the Demand for Quotas', Centre for Development Economics Working Paper No. 267.

Deshpande, Ashwini and Smriti Sharma (2013), 'Entrepreneurship or Survival? Caste and Gender of Small Business in India', *Economic and Political Weekly*, 48(28), 13 July, pp. 38–49.

_____ (2016), 'Disadvantage and Discrimination in Self-Employment: Caste Gaps in Earnings in Indian Small Businesses', *Small Business Economics: An Entrepreneurship Journal*, 46(2), February, pp. 325–46.

Deshpande, Ashwini and Thomas E. Weisskopf (2010), 'Do Reservation Policies Affect Productivity in the Indian Railways', Centre for Development Economics Working Paper No. 185, May.

Deshpande, G.P. (ed.) (2002), *Selected Writings of Jotirao Phule*. New Delhi: LeftWord Books.

———— (2009), *The World of Ideas in Modern Marathi: Phule, Vinoba, Savarkar*. New Delhi: Tulika Books.

Deshpande, Rajeshwari and Suhas Palshikar (2008), 'Patterns of Occupational Mobility: How Much Does Caste Matter', *Economic and Political Weekly*, 43(34), 23 August, pp. 61–70.

Deshpande, Satish (2003), *Contemporary India: A Sociological View*. Delhi: Penguin Books.

Deshpande, Sudha and Lalit Deshpande (1999), 'Gender-based Discrimination in the Urban Labour Market', in T.S. Papola and Alakh N. Sharma (eds), *Gender and Employment in India*, pp. 223–48. New Delhi: Vikas Publishing House.

Dhesi, Autar S. (1996), 'Unequal Opportunities in Education and Labour Market in India', *International Policy Review*, 6(1), pp. 61–9.

Dhesi, Autar S. and Harbhajan Singh (1988), 'Education, Labour Market Distortions and Relative Earnings of Different Religion–Caste Categories in India (A Case Study of Delhi)', *Canadian Journal of Development Studies*, X(1), pp. 75–89.

Dirks, Nicholas (2003), *Castes of Mind: Colonialism and the Making of Modern India*. New Delhi: Permanent Black.

Dréze, Jean and Amartya Sen (1995), *Economic Development and Social Opportunity*. New Delhi: Oxford University Press.

Dréze, Jean and Mamta Murthi (2001), 'Fertility, Education, and Development: Evidence from India', *Population and Development Review*, 27(1), p. 33.

Dube, Leela (1996), 'Caste and Women', in M.N. Srinivas (ed.), *Caste: Its Twentieth Century Avatar*, pp. 1–27. Delhi: Viking Press, Penguin Books.

Dumont, Louis (1980), *Homo Hierarchicus: The Caste System and Its Implications*. Chicago: The University of Chicago Press.

Duraisamy, Malathy and P. Duraisamy (1999), 'Women in the Professional and Technical Labour Market in India: Gender Discrimination in Education, Employment and Earnings', *The Indian Journal of Labour Economics*, 42(4), pp. 599–612.

Durlauf, Stephen (2006), 'Racial Profiling as a Public Policy Question: Efficiency, Equity and Ambiguity', *American Economic Review*, 92(2), pp. 132–6.

Elson, Diane (1999), 'Labour Markets as Gendered Institutions: Equality, Efficiency and Empowerment Issues', *World Development*, 27(3), pp. 611–26.

Epstein, T. Scarlett (1996), 'Culture, Women and India's Development', in A.M. Shah, B.S. Baviskar, and E.A. Ramaswamy (eds), *Social Structure and Change, Volume 2: Women in Indian Society*, pp. 33–55. New Delhi: Sage Publications.

Fairlie, R. (2006), 'Entrepreneurship among Disadvantaged Groups: An Analysis of the Dynamics of Self-Employment by Gender, Race and Education', in

Simon C. Parker, Zoltan J. Acs, and David R. Audretsch (eds), *International Handbook Series on Entrepreneurship*, Vol. 2. New York: Springer.

Fiske, S.T., A.J. Cuddy, P. Glick, and J. Xu (2002), 'A Model of (Often Mixed) Stereotype Content: Competence and Warmth Respectively Follow from Perceived Status and Competition', *Journal of Personality and Social Psychology*, 82(6), pp. 878–902.

Gaiha, Raghav (1992), 'Estimates of Rural Poverty in India: An Assessment', in Barbara Hariss, S. Guhan, and R.H. Cassen (eds), *Poverty In India: Research and Policy*, pp. 171–84. Bombay: Oxford University Press.

Galanter, Marc (1991), *Competing Equalities: Law and the Backward Classes in India*. New Delhi: Oxford University Press.

——— (1997), 'Pursuing Equality: An Assessment of India's Policy of Compensatory Discrimination for Disadvantaged Groups', in Sudipta Kaviraj (ed.), *Politics in India*, pp. 187–99. New Delhi: Oxford University Press.

Gangopadhyay, Shubhashis and S. Subramanian (1992), 'Optimal Budgetary Interventions in Poverty-Alleviation Schemes', in S. Subramanian (ed.), *Themes in Development Economics*. New Delhi: Oxford University Press.

Ghurye, G.S. (1932), *Caste and Race in India*. Mumbai: Popular Prakashan, published in 2000.

——— (1963), *The Scheduled Tribes*. Bombay: Popular Prakashan.

Goffman, Erving (1961), *The Presentation of Self in Everyday Life*. New York: Doubleday.

Granovetter, Mark (2005), 'The Impact of Social Structures on Economic Outcomes', *Journal of Economic Perspectives*, 19(1), pp. 33–50.

Guhan, S. (1992), 'Social Security Initiatives in Tamilnadu 1989', in S. Subramanian (ed.), *Themes in Development Economics*. New Delhi: Oxford University Press.

——— (2001), 'Comprehending Equalities', in S. Subramanian (ed.), *India's Development Experience*. New Delhi: Oxford University Press.

Gupta, Dipankar (1984), 'Continuous Hierarchies and Discrete Castes', *Economic and Political Weekly*, XIX(46), pp. 1955–2053.

——— (ed.) (2004), *Caste in Question: Identity or Hierarchy?* Contributions to Indian Sociology: Occasional Studies, Vol. 12. New Delhi and Thousand Oaks, London: Sage Publications.

Hanna, R., and L. Linden (2012), 'Discrimination in Grading', *American Economic Journal: Economic Policy*, 4(4), pp. 146–68.

Heckman, James J. (1979), 'Sample Selection Bias as a Specification Error', *Econometrica*, 47(1), pp. 153–62.

——— (1998), 'Detecting Discrimination', *Journal of Economic Perspectives*, 12(2), pp. 101–16.

Heckman, James J. and Peter Siegelman (1993), 'The Urban Institute Audit Studies: Their Methods and Findings', in Michael Fix and Raymond J. Stuyk (eds), *Clear and Convincing Evidence: Measurement of Discrimination in America*, pp. 165–203. Washington, DC: Urban Institute Press.

Hnatkovska, Viktoria, Amartya Lahiri, and Sourabh Paul (2012), 'Castes and Labor Mobility', *American Economic Journal: Applied Economics*, 4(2), pp. 274–307.

Hoff, Karla, Avishay Braverman, and Joseph E. Stiglitz (eds) (1993), *Economics of Rural Organization: Theory, Practice and Policy*. New York: Oxford University Press for the World Bank.

Hoff, Karla and Priyanka Pandey (2004), 'Belief Systems and Durable Inequalities: An Experimental Investigation of Indian Caste', World Bank Policy Research Working Paper 3351, June.

Human Rights Watch (1999), *Broken People: Caste Violence against India's Untouchables*. New York, Washington, DC, London, and Brussels: Human Rights Watch.

Jaffrelot, Christophe (2003), *India's Silent Revolution: The Rise of the Lower Castes in North India*. New Delhi: Orient Blackswan.

Jenni, K. E., and G. F. Loewenstein. 1997. 'Explaining the "Identifiable Victim Effect"', *Journal of Risk and Uncertainty*, 14(3), pp. 235–57.

Jain, M.K. (1997), 'A Study of Socio-demographic Characteristics of Scheduled Castes of Uttar Pradesh', in Kamala Gupta and Arvind Pandey (eds), *Population and Development in Uttar Pradesh*, pp. 61–81. Delhi: B.R. Publishing Corporation.

Jayaraj, D. and S. Subramanian (1994), 'Caste Discrimination in the Distribution of Consumption Expenditure in India: Theory and Evidence', Centre for Development Economics Working Paper No. 18.

Jayaraman, Raji and Peter Lanjouw (1998), 'The Evolution of Poverty and Inequality in Indian Villages', Policy Research Working Paper No. 1870, World Bank.

Jha, Raghabendra (2002), 'Reducing Poverty and Inequality in India: Has Liberalization Helped'. Available at http://eprints.anu.edu.au/archive/00001812/01/wp-econ-2002–04.pdf, accessed on 15 September 2009.

Jodhka, Surinder (2009), 'The Ravi Dasis of Punjab: Global Contours of Caste and Religious Strife', *Economic and Political Weekly*, XLIV(24), 13 June, pp. 79–85.

———— (2010), 'Dalits in Business: Self-Employed Scheduled Castes in North-West India', *Economic and Political Weekly*, 45(11), 13–19 March, pp. 41–8.

Jodhka, Surinder and Katherine S. Newman (2007), 'In the Name of Globalisation', *Economic and Political Weekly*, 42(41), pp. 4125–32.

Kanungo, Sukla Deb (1993), 'Dalit Women's Search for Identity', *Social Action*, 43, pp. 481–94.

Kapadia, Karin (1995), *Siva and Her Sisters: Gender, Caste and Class in Rural South India*. Boulder, Colorado: Westview Press.

Kapur, Devesh, Chandra Bhan Prasad, Lant Pritchett, and D. Shyam Babu (2010), 'Rethinking Inequality: Dalits in Uttar Pradesh in the Market Reform Era', *Economic and Political Weekly*, XLV(35), pp. 39–49.

Karunakaran, Naren (2009), 'Bite the Caste Bullet', *Outlook Business*, 2 May.

Ketkar, S.V. (1909/2002), *History of Caste in India: Evidence to the Laws of Manu*. Delhi: Low Price Publications.

Kingdon, Geeta Gandhi (1997), 'Labour Force Participation, Returns to Education and Sex-Discrimination in India', *The Indian Journal of Labour Economics*, 40(3), pp. 507–23.

——— (2002), 'The Gender Gap in Educational Attainment in India: How Much Can Be Explained', *Journal of Development Studies*, 39(2), pp. 25–53.

Kirshenmann, Joleen and Kathryn Neckerman (1991), 'We'd Love to Hire Them, But ... The Meaning of Race for Employers', in Christopher Jencks and Paul Peterson (eds), *The Urban Underclass*, pp. 203–34. Washington, DC: The Brookings Institution.

Klass, Morton (1980), *Caste: The Emergence of the South Asian Social System*. Philadelphia: Institute for the Study of Human Issues.

Knowles, John, Nicola Persico, and Petra Todd (2001), 'Racial Bias in Motor Vehicle Searches: Theory and Evidence', *Journal of Political Economy*, 109(1), pp. 203–32.

Kosambi, Damodar Dharmanand (1985), *An Introduction to the Study of Indian History*. Bombay: Popular Prakashan.

Kothari, Rajni (1997), 'Caste and Modern Politics', in Sudipta Kaviraj (ed.), *Politics in India*, pp. 57–70. New Delhi: Oxford University Press.

Kreuger, Anne O. (1963), 'The Economics of Discrimination', *Journal of Political Economy*, 71(5), October, pp. 481–6.

Krishnan, P.S. (1993), 'Untouchability and Atrocities', *Social Action*, 43(4), pp. 412–26.

Kumar, Dharma (1965), *Land and Caste in South India*. Cambridge: Cambridge University Press.

——— (1990), 'The Affirmative Action Debate in India', *Asian Survey*, Vol. 32, pp. 290–302.

Kumar, Radha (1993), *The History of Doing: An Illustrated Account of Movements for Women's Rights and Feminism in India 1800–1990*. London and New York: Verso Books.

Kuran, Timur (1987), 'Preference Falsification, Policy Continuity and Collective Conservatism', *The Economic Journal*, 97, pp. 642–65.

Lamba, S., and D. Spears (2013), 'Caste, "Cleanliness," and Cash: Effects of Caste-Based Political Reservations in Rajasthan on a Sanitation Prize', *Journal of Development Studies*, 49(11), pp. 1592–606.

Lakshmanasamy, T. and S. Madheswaran (1995), 'Discrimination by Community: Evidence from Indian Scientific and Technical Labour Market', *Indian Journal of Social Sciences*, 8(1), pp. 59–77.

Lal, Deepak (1988), *Hindu Equilibrium; Vol. 1: Cultural Stability and Economic Stagnation: India, c. 1500 BC–AD 1980*. Oxford: Clarendon Press; New York: Oxford University Press.

Lanjouw, Peter and Nicholas Stern (1998), *Economic Development in Palanpur over Five Decades*. Oxford: Clarendon Press.

The Laws of Manu, translated by G. Buehler, Sacred Books of the East, Vol. XXV (edited by F. Max Mueller), 1964. Delhi: Motilal Banarsidass.

Liddle, Joanna and Rama Joshi (1986), *Daughters of Independence: Gender, Caste, and Class in India*. New Delhi: Kali for Women; London: Zed Books; Totowa, NJ: US distributor, Biblio Distribution Center.

Loury, Glenn C. (2002), *The Anatomy of Racial Inequality*. Cambridge, MA: Harvard University Press.

Lovell, Peggy A. (1994), 'Race, Gender, and Development in Brazil', *Latin American Research Review*, 29(3), pp. 1–36.

———— (2003), 'Race, Gender and Regional Labor Market Inequalities in Brazil', in William A. Darity Jr. and Ashwini Deshpande (eds), *Boundaries of Clan and Color: Transnational Comparisons of Inter-Group Disparity*, pp. 14–26. London: Routledge.

Loewenstein, G., and D. A. Small (2007), 'The Scarecrow and the Tin Man: The Vicissitudes of Human Sympathy and Caring', *Review of General Psychology*, 11, pp. 112–26.

Lukes, R., and J. Bangs (2014). 'A Critical Analysis of Anti-discrimination Law and Microaggressions in Academia', *Research in Higher Education Journal*, 24(August), pp. 1–15.

Madheswaran, S. and Paul Attewell (2007), 'Caste Discrimination in the Indian Urban Labour Market: Evidence from National Sample Survey', *Economic and Political Weekly*, 42(41), pp. 4146–53.

Mascarenhas-Keyes, Stella (1990), 'Migration, "Progressive Motherhood" and Female Autonomy: Catholic Women in Goa', in Leela Dube and Rajni Palriwala (eds), *Structures and Strategies: Women, Work and Family*, pp. 103–28. New Delhi: Sage Publications.

Massey, Douglas S., Camille Z. Charles, Garvey F. Lundy, and Mary J. Fischer (2003), *The Source of the River: The Social Origins of Freshmen at America's Selective Colleges and Universities*. Princeton: Princeton University Press.

Massey, Douglas S. and Garvey Lundi (1998), 'Use of Black English and Discrimination in Urban Housing Markets: New Methods and Findings', Population Studies Centre, University of Pennsylvania Working Paper, June.

Mayer, Adrian (1996), 'Caste in an Indian Village: Change and Continuity 1954–1992', in C.J. Fuller (ed.), *Caste Today*, pp. 32–64. New Delhi: Oxford University Press.

Mayoux, Linda (1993), 'A Development Success Story? Low Caste Entrepreneurship and Inequality: An Indian Case Study', *Development and Change*, 24(3), pp. 541–68.

McCaffery, Edward J. (1993), 'Slouching Toward Equality: Gender Discrimination, Market Efficiency, and Social Change', *The Yale Law Journal*, 103(3), December, pp. 595–675.

Meenakshi, J.V., Ranjan Ray, and Souvik Gupta (2000), 'Estimates of Poverty for SC, ST and Female-headed Households', *Economic and Political Weekly*, 35(31), pp. 2748–54.

Meera, V. (1979), 'Prisoners of Inequality: Sexual Abuse of Dalit Women', *Race and Class*, 20(4), pp. 417–21.

Mencher, Joan P. (1974), 'The Caste System Upside Down or the Not-so-Mysterious East', *Current Anthropology*, 15(4), December, pp. 469–93.

—— (1996), 'South Indian Female Cultivators: Who Are They and What They Do?', in A.M. Shah, B.S. Baviskar, and E.A. Ramaswamy (eds), *Social Structure and Change, Volume 2: Women in Indian Society*, pp. 56–78. New Delhi: Sage Publications.

Milanovich, Branko (2004), 'Half the World: Regional Inequality in Five Federations'. Available at http://www-wds.worldbank.org/servlet/WDSContentServer/WDSP/IB/2005/08/30/000016406_20050830161631/Rendered/PDF/wps3699.pdf, accessed on 16 July 2010.

Ministry of Minority Affairs (2008), *Report of the Expert Group on Diversity Index*. New Delhi: Government of India.

Ministry of Railways (2007), *Indian Railways Yearbook 2005–06*. New Delhi: Government of India.

Ministry of Women and Child Development (2015), 'Handbook on Sexual Harassment of Women at the Workplace'. Available at http://www.wcd.nic.in/sites/default/files/Handbook%20on%20Sexual%20Harassment%20of%20Women%20at%20Workplace.pdf, accessed on 13 November 2016.

Mishra, G.P. (1979), 'Bondage of Poverty: A Case Study of Scheduled Caste Households in Three Villages of Karnataka', *Economic Affairs*, 24(1–4), pp. 9–15.

Mohan, Rakesh and Pushpa Thottan (1992), 'The Regional Spread of Urbanisation, Industrialisation and Urban Poverty', in Barbara Hariss, S. Guhan, and R.H. Cassen (eds), *Poverty In India: Research and Policy*, pp. 76–141. Bombay: Oxford University Press.

Mookherjee, D. and A.F. Shorrocks (1982), 'A Decomposition Analysis of the Trend in UK Income Inequality', *Economic Journal*, Vol. 92, pp. 886–902.

Munshi, Kaivan and Mark Rosenzweig (2006), 'Traditional Institutions Meet the Modern World: Caste, Gender and Schooling Choice in a Globalizing Economy', *American Economic Review*, 96(4), pp. 1225–52.

—— (2009), 'Why is Mobility in India so Low? Social Insurance, Inequality and Growth', NBER Working Paper 14850. Available at http://www.nber.org/papers/w14850.

Myers, Samuel L., Jr. (2002), 'Analysis of Racial Profiling as Policy Analysis. Curriculum and Case Notes', *Journal of Policy Analysis and Management*, 21(2), pp. 287–300.

Nafziger, E.W. (1975), 'Class, Caste and Community of South Indian Industrialists: An Examination of the Horatio Alger Model', *Journal of Development Studies*, 11(2), pp. 131–48.

Nambissan, Geetha B. (2010), 'Exclusion and Discrimination in Schools: Experiences of Dalit Children', in Sukhadeo Thorat and Katherine S. Newman (eds), *Blocked by Caste: Economic Discrimination in Modern India*, pp. 253–86. New Delhi: Oxford University Press.

National Commission for Enterprises in the Unorganized Sector (NCEUS) (2008), 'The Challenge of Employment in India: An Informal Economy Perspective', Report published by NCEUS, Government of India.

National Family and Health Survey (NFHS-I), India (1992–3), International Institute for Population Studies, Mumbai.

—————— (NFHS-II), India (1998–9), International Institute for Population Studies, Mumbai.

—————— (NFHS-III), India (2005–6), International Institute for Population Studies, Mumbai.

Navsarjan Trust (2010), 'Understanding Untouchability: A Comprehensive Study of Practices and Conditions in 1589 Villages'. Available at http://navsarjan. org/Documents/Untouchability_Report_FINAL_Complete.pdf, accessed on 13 November 2016.

Nayak, Vijay and Shailaja Prasad (1984), 'On Levels of Living of Scheduled Castes and Scheduled Tribes', *Economic and Political Weekly*, 19(30), pp. 1205–13.

Nesiah, Devanasan (1997), *Discrimination with Reason? The Policy of Reservations in the United States, India and Malaysia*. New Delhi: Oxford University Press.

Newman, Katherine S. and Ashwini Deshpande (2010), 'Roadblocks at the High End: The Role of Caste in Postuniversity Employment', in Miguel A. Centeno and Katherine S. Newman (eds), *Discrimination in an Unequal World*, pp. 187–213. New York: Oxford University Press.

Oaxaca, Ronald (1973), 'Male Female Wage Differentials in Urban Labour Markets', *International Economic Review*, 14(3), pp. 693–709.

O'Hanlon, Rosalind (1985), *Caste, Conflict, and Ideology: Mahatma Jyotiba Phule and Low Caste Protest in Nineteenth-Century Western India*. Cambridge, UK: Orient Longman and Cambridge University Press.

Oliver, Melvin and Thomas Shapiro (2006), *Black Wealth/White Wealth: A New Perspective on Inequality*, 2nd edition. New York: Routledge.

Omvedt, Gail (2005), 'Capitalism and Globalisation: Dalits and Adivasis', *Economic and Political Weekly*, 40(47), 19 November, pp. 4881–5.

—————— (2012), 'Will Globalisation Emancipate Dalits?' Available at https://seekingbegumpura.wordpress.com/2012/09/13/will-globalization-emancipate-dalits/, accessed on 13 December 2014.

Page, Scott (2007), *The Difference: How the Power of Diversity Creates Better Groups, Firms, Schools, and Societies*. Princeton: Princeton University Press.

Pager, Devah and Bruce Western (2005), *Race at Work: Realities of Race and Criminal Record in the NYC Job Market*. New York: Shomburg Centre for Research in Black Culture.

Pager, Devah and Lincoln Quillian (2005), 'Walking the Talk? What Employers Say versus What They Do', *American Sociological Review*, 70(3), pp. 355–80.

Palriwala, Rajni (1996), 'Negotiating Patriliny: Intra-household Consumption and Authority in Northwest India', in Rajni Palriwala and Carla Risseeuw (eds),

Shifting Circles of Support: Contextualising Kinship and Gender in South Asia and Sub Saharan Africa, pp. 190–220. Walnut Creek, CA: Alta Mira.

Pande, Rohini (2003), 'Can Mandated Political Representation Provide Disadvantaged Minorities Policy Influence? Theory and Evidence from India', *American Economic Review*, 93(4), September, pp. 1132–51.

Pandian, M.S.S. (2007), *Brahmin and Non-Brahmin: Geneaologies of the Tamil Political Present*. New Delhi: Permanent Black.

Panini, M.N. (1996), 'The Political Economy of Caste', in M.N. Srinivas (ed.), *Caste: Its Twentieth Century Avatar*, pp. 28–68. New Delhi: Viking Press, India.

Paul, Satya (1999), 'The Population Sub-group Income Effects on Inequality: Analytical Framework and an Empirical Illustration', *The Economic Record*, 75(229), pp. 149–55.

Persico, Nicola (2002), 'Racial Profiling, Fairness, and Effectiveness of Policing', *American Economic Review*, 92(5), pp. 1472–97.

Phelps, E.S. (1972), 'The Statistical Theory of Racism and Sexism', *American Economic Review*, 62, September, pp. 659–71.

Pinto, Ambrose (1999), 'Saffronisation of Affirmative Action', *Economic and Political Weekly*, 34(52), 25–31 December, pp. 3642–5.

Platteau, J-Ph. (1992), 'Aristocratic Patronage as an Ingredient of the Caste System: Formal Analysis and Dynamic Considerations', STICERD Discussion Paper No. 36, London School of Economics.

Prasad, Chandra Bhan and Milind Kamble (2013), 'Manifesto to End Caste: Push Capitalism and Industrialization to Eradicate this Pernicious System', *Times of India*, 23 January. Available at http://articles.timesofindia.indiatimes.com/2013-01-23/edit-page/36485155_1_dalit-youth-upper-castes-caste-system, accessed on 27 October 2016.

The PROBE Team (1999), *Public Report on Basic Education in India*. New Delhi: Oxford Univeristy Press.

Radhakrishnan, S. (2004), 'The Dhammapada' (Chapter XXVI, 'Brahmanavaggo'), *The Buddhism Omnibus*. New Delhi: Oxford University Press.

Rao, Nitya, Arjan Verschoor, Ashwini Deshpande, and Amaresh Dubey (2010), 'Gender Caste and Growth Assessment—India, Report to Department for International Development', DEV Reports and Policy Paper Series, The School of International Development, University of East Anglia, UK.

Rodrigues, Valerian (ed.) (2002), *The Essential Writings of B.R. Ambedkar*. New Delhi: Oxford University Press.

Royster, Deirdre (2003), *Race and the Invisible Hand: How White Networks Exclude Black Men from Blue-Collar Jobs*. Berkeley, CA: University of California Press.

Saggar, Mridul and Indranil Pan (1994), 'SCs and STs in Eastern India: Inequality and Poverty Estimates', *Economic and Political Weekly*, 29(10), pp. 567–74.

Scoville, James (1991), 'Towards a Formal Model of a Caste Economy', in J. Scoville (ed.), *Status Influences in Third World Labour Markets: Caste, Gender and Custom*, pp. 49–59, de Gruyter Studies in Organisation, No. 32. Berlin and NY: Walter de Gruyter.

288   BIBLIOGRAPHY

———— (1996), 'Labour Market Underpinnings of a Caste Economy: Foiling the Coase Theorem', *The American Journal of Economics and Sociology*, 55(4), pp. 385–94.

Sen, Abhijit and Utsa Patnaik (1997), 'Poverty in India', mimeo.

Sen, Amartya (1997), *On Economic Inequality*. Oxford: Clarendon Press.

Shah, Ghanshyam (1985), 'Caste, Class and Reservation', *Economic and Political Weekly*, 20(3), pp. 132–6.

Shah, Ghanshyam, Harsh Mandar, Sukhadeo Thorat, Satish Deshpande, and Amita Baviskar (2006), *Untouchability in Rural India*. New Delhi: Sage Publications.

Sharma, S.S. (1986), 'Untouchability, a Myth or a Reality: A Study of Interaction between Scheduled Castes and Brahmins in a Western U.P. Village', *Sociological Bulletin*, 35(1), pp. 68–79.

Shyam Babu, D. (2004), 'India's Liberalization and the Dalits', *Royal Institute for International Affairs*, Asia Programme Working Paper.

Shyam Babu, D. and Chandra Bhan Prasad (2009), 'Six Dalit Paradoxes', *Economic and Political Weekly*, XLIV(23), pp. 22–5.

Siddique, Zahra (2009), 'Caste Based Discrimination: Evidence and Policy', Institute for the Study of Labour (IZA) Discussion Papers No. 3737. Available on SSRN at http://ssrn.com/abstract=1550883.

Singh, K.S. (1994), 'The Scheduled Tribes', *People of India National Series, Vol. III*. New Delhi: Oxford University Press.

Singh, Manjari and Debashish Bhattacharjee (1998), 'Pay Discrimination by Gender in the Corporate Sector: A Case Study', *The Indian Journal of Labour Economics*, 41(1), pp. 97–103.

Singh, Nirvikar, Laveesh Bhandari, Aayou Chen, and Aarti Khare (2003), 'Regional Inequality in India: A Fresh Look'. Available at http://129.3.20.41/eps/dev/papers/0412/0412006.pdf, accessed on 3 March 2010.

Slovic, P. 2007. '"If I Look at the Mass I Will Never Act": Psychic Numbing and Genocide', *Judgment and Decision Making*, 2(2), pp. 79–95.

Small, D. A., and G. Loewenstein (2003), 'Helping a Victim or Helping the Victim: Altruism and Identifiability', *Journal of Risk and Uncertainty*, 26, pp. 5–16.

Sokoloff, Natalie J. (1992), *Black Women and White Women in the Professions: Occupational Segregation by Race and Gender, 1960–1980*. London: Routledge.

Somanathan, Rohini (2006), 'Assumptions and Arithmetic of Caste Based Reservations', *Economic and Political Weekly*, XLI(24), pp. 2436–8.

Sowell, Thomas (2004), *Affirmative Action Around the World: An Empirical Study*. New Haven, Conn: Yale University Press.

Srikanth, H. (2000), 'No Shortcuts to Dalit Liberation', *Economic and Political Weekly*, 35(13), 25–31 March, pp. 1121–3.

Srinivas, M.N. (1962), *Caste in Modern India and Other Essays*. New York: Asia Publishing House.

———— (1976), 'The Changing Position of Indian Women', *Man (N.S.)*, Vol. 12, pp. 221–38.

_____ (1989), *The Cohesive Role of Ssanskritisation*. New Delhi: Oxford University Press.

_____ (1996), 'Introduction', in M.N. Srinvas (ed.), *Caste: Its Twentieth Century Avatar*, pp. ix–xxxviii. New Delhi: Viking Press, India.

_____ (2003), 'An Obituary on Caste as a System', *Economic and Political Weekly*, 38(5), pp. 455–60.

Srinivasan, T.N. and P.K. Bardhan (eds) (1974), *Poverty and Income Distribution in India*. Calcutta: Statistical Publishing Society.

_____ (eds) (1988), *Rural Poverty in South Asia*. New York: Columbia University Press.

Standing, Guy (1989), 'Global Feminization through Flexible Labour', *World Development*, 17(7), pp. 1077–95.

Sundaram, K. (2007), 'Fair Access to Higher Education Re-visited—Some Results for Social and Religious Groups from NSS 61st Round Employment–Unemployment Survey, 2004–05', Centre for Development Economics Working Paper No. 163.

Sundaram, K. and Suresh Tendulkar (1988), 'Toward an Explanation of Interregional Variations in Poverty and Unemployment in Rural India', in T.N. Srinivasan and P.K. Bardhan (eds), *Rural Poverty in South Asia*, pp. 316–62. New York: Columbia University Press.

Tendulkar, Suresh (1983), 'Economic Inequality in an Indian Perspective', in André Béteille (ed.), *Equality and Inequality: Theory and Practice*. New Delhi· Oxford University Press.

_____ (1992), 'Economic Growth and Poverty', in Barbara Hariss, S. Guhan, and R.H. Cassen (eds), *Poverty In India: Research and Policy*, pp. 27–57. Bombay: Oxford University Press.

Tilak, J.B.G. (1980), 'Education and Labour Market Discrimination', *Indian Journal of Industrial Relations*, 16(2), pp. 95–114.

Tharu, Susie and K. Lalita (1991), *Women Writing in India: 600 BC to the Present, Volume 1: 600 BC to the Early Twentieth Century*. New York: The Feminist Press at the City University of New York.

Thorat, Sukhadeo (1979), 'Passage to Adulthood: Perceptions from Below', in Sudhir Kakkar (ed.), *Identity and Adulthood*, pp. 65–81. New Delhi: Oxford University Press.

_____ (1997), 'Caste System and Economic Inequality: Some Unexplained Disparities', unpublished manuscript.

Thorat, Sukhadeo and Paul Attewell (2007), 'Legacy of Social Exclusion', *Economic and Political Weekly*, 42(41), pp. 4141–5.

Thorat, Sukhadeo and Katherine S. Newman (eds) (2010), *Blocked by Caste: Economic Discrimination in Modern India*. New Delhi: Oxford University Press.

Trautmann, Thomas (1997), *Aryans and British India*. Berkeley, CA: University of California Press.

Turner, M.A., F. Freiberg, E. Godfrey, C. Herbig, D.K. Levy, and R.R. Smith (2002), *All Other Things Being Equal: A Paired Testing Study of Mortgage Lending Institutions*. Washington, DC: The Urban Institute.

United Nations Development Programme (1990), *Human Development Report*. New York and Oxford: Oxford University Press.

Vaidyanathan, A. (1992), 'Poverty and Economy: The Regional Dimension', in Barbara Hariss, S. Guhan, and R.H. Cassen (eds), *Poverty In India: Research and Policy*, pp. 58–75. Bombay: Oxford University Press.

Verma, Vidhu (2016), 'Law and Justice in the Post-Liberalisation Era', mimeo.

Weisskopf, Thomas E. (2004), *Affirmative Action in the United States and India: A Comparative Perspective*. London: Routledge.

Wilfred, Felix (2007), *Dalit Empowerment*. New Delhi: Cambridge University Press.

World Bank (1998), *Reducing Poverty in India: Options for More Effective Public Service*. World Bank Country Study, World Bank, Washington, DC.

Xaxa, Virginius (2002), 'Ethnography of Reservation in Delhi University', *Economic and Political Weekly*, 37(28), 13 July, pp. 2849–54.

Yadava, R.C. and S.N. Chauhan (1997), 'A Study of Occupational Mobility in Eastern Uttar Pradesh', in Kamala Gupta and Arvind Pandey (eds), *Population and Development in Uttar Pradesh*, pp. 61–81. Delhi: B.R. Publishing Corporation.

Yinger, John (1998), 'Evidence on Discrimination in Consumer Markets', *Journal of Economic Perspectives*, 12(2), pp. 23–40.

Zacharias, A. and V. Vakulabharanam (2009), 'Caste and Wealth Inequality in India', The Levy Economics Institute Working Paper No. 566, The Levy Economics Institute.

Index

Adivasis 20. *See also* Scheduled Tribes
affirmative action (AA) 3, 10, 13, 15–18,
    21, 37, 39–41, 56, 58, 68, 185–6,
    212–17, 219–38, 249–51, 253–4,
    273–4; in higher education 236–8;
    policies 21, 39, 41, 186, 195, 197;
    in private sector 228–9
agricultural: caste 125; labour 72–4,
    83, 268
agriculture, division of labour in 122
Akerlof, George 38, 41, 45–8
Ambedkar, B.R. 5–7, 24, 27–8, 32,
    35–8, 40, 215, 225, 239, 241, 252;
    'Annihilation of Caste' 24, 36, 252;
    for casteless society 252; 'Castes in
    India' 24; and his education 239; on
    racial differences 28
Arrow, Kenneth J. 38, 147, 168, 174
Aryans 20, 25–8, 34, 141
Ashenfelter, Orley 150
Atishudras 19, 30–1, 33, 35, 108
Attewell, Paul 15, 154, 185, 187–8

Backward Classes Commission 218
Bahujan Samaj Party (BSP) 223, 251
Banerjee, Biswajit 153–4, 158, 184–5
Becker, Gary S. 14, 38, 41–3, 148, 150,
    152, 158–9, 165, 168, 174, 176,
    180; model of 41–3; theory of 14
Bertrand, Marianne 161, 237
Béteille, André 37
Bhakti movement 142–3
Blinder, Alan S. 152–3, 158
Blinder–Oaxaca decomposition method
    152–3
bonded labour 139–40. *See also* slavery
Brahmanism 22n4, 30–1
Brahmins 6, 19–20, 22–3, 26–8, 30–5,
    37, 53, 58, 75, 83, 108–9, 124, 141,
    143, 218, 226
Bucci, Gabriella A. 185
Buddhism 22–3; Buddhist poetry 141;
    Buddhist students 196
Burns, Justine 178–9
Butler, Richard J. 157